E–Novation for Competitive Advantage in Collaborative Globalization:

Technologies for Emerging E–Business Strategies

Hugh Pattinson
University of Western Sydney, Australia

David Low
University of Western Sydney, Australia

A volume in the Advances in E–Business Research (AEBR) Book Series

Senior Editorial Director:	Kristin Klinger
Director of Book Publications:	Julia Mosemann
Editorial Director:	Lindsay Johnston
Acquisitions Editor:	Erika Carter
Development Editor:	Christine Bufton
Production Editor:	Sean Woznicki
Typesetters:	Mike Brehm, Jennifer Romanchak, Natalie Pronio, Deanna Zombro
Print Coordinator:	Jamie Snavely
Cover Design:	Nick Newcomer

Published in the United States of America by
Business Science Reference (an imprint of IGI Global)
701 E. Chocolate Avenue
Hershey PA 17033
Tel: 717-533-8845
Fax: 717-533-8661
E-mail: cust@igi-global.com
Web site: http://www.igi-global.com

Library of Congress Cataloging-in-Publication Data

E-novation for competitive advantage in collaborative globalization :
technologies for emerging e-business strategies / Hugh M. Pattinson and David R. Low, editors.
     p. cm.
  Includes bibliographical references and index.
  Summary: "This book highlights new business products, services, strategies, and philosophies drawn from an emerging collaborative information platform and explores connections between the development of new e-business technologies with consumers, businesses, and links to social and political visions and strategies"--Provided by publisher.
  ISBN 978-1-60566-394-4 -- ISBN 978-1-60566-395-1 (ebook) 1. Electronic commerce. 2. Technological innovations. I. Pattinson, Hugh. II. Low, David R., 1962-
  HF5548.32.E18725 2010
  658'.046--dc22
                                        2010030572

This book is published in the IGI Global book series Advances in E-Business Research (AEBR) Book Series (ISSN: 1935-2700; eISSN: 1935-2719)

British Cataloguing in Publication Data
A Cataloguing in Publication record for this book is available from the British Library.

All work contributed to this book is new, previously-unpublished material. The views expressed in this book are those of the authors, but not necessarily of the publisher.

Advances in E–Business Research (AEBR) Book Series

In Lee (Western Illinois University, USA)

ISSN: 1935-2700
EISSN: 1935-2719

MISSION

Technology has played a vital role in the emergence of e-business and its applications incorporate strategies. These processes have aided in the use of electronic transactions via telecommunications networks for collaborating with business partners, buying and selling of goods and services, and customer service. Research in this field continues to develop into a wide range of topics, including marketing, psychology, information systems, accounting, economics, and computer science.

The **Advances in E-Business Research (AEBR)** series provides multidisciplinary references for researchers and practitioners in this area. Instructors, researchers, and professionals interested in the most up-to-date research on the concepts, issues, applications, and trends in the e-business field will find this collection, or individual books, extremely useful. This collection contains the highest quality academic books that advance understanding of e-business and addresses the challenges faced by researchers and practitioners.

COVERAGE

- E-Business Management
- E-Business Models and Architectures
- E-Business Systems Integration
- E-Business Technology Investment Strategies
- E-CRM
- E-Marketing
- Global E-Business
- Outsourcing and E-Business Technologies
- Semantic Web
- Sustainable E-Business
- Virtual Organization

IGI Global is currently accepting manuscripts for publication within this series. To submit a proposal for a volume in this series, please contact our Acquisition Editors at Acquisitions@igi-global.com or visit: http://www.igi-global.com/publish/.

Titles in this Series

For a list of additional titles in this series, please visit: www.igi-global.com

Strategy, Adoption, and Competitive Advantage of Mobile Services in the Global Economy
In Lee (Western Illinois University, USA)
Information Science Reference • copyright 2013 • 333pp • H/C (ISBN: 9781466619395) • US $190.00 (our price)

Mobile Services Industries, Technologies, and Applications in the Global Economy
In Lee (Western Illinois University, USA)
Information Science Reference • copyright 2013 • 366pp • H/C (ISBN: 9781466619814) • US $190.00 (our price)

Strategic and Pragmatic E-Business Implications for Future Business Practices
Karim Mohammed Rezaul (Glyndwr University, UK)
Business Science Reference • copyright 2012 • 327pp • H/C (ISBN: 9781466616196) • US $185.00 (our price)

Electronic Commerce Management for Business Activities and Global Enterprises Competitive Advantages
In Lee (Western Illinois University)
Business Science Reference • copyright 2012 • 514pp • H/C (ISBN: 9781466618008) • US $185.00 (our price)

Electronic Business Interoperability Concepts, Opportunities and Challenges
Ejub Kajan (State University of Novi Pazar, Serbia)
Business Science Reference • copyright 2011 • 776pp • H/C (ISBN: 9781609604851) • US $180.00 (our price)

E-Novation for Competitive Advantage in Collaborative Globalization Technologies for Emerging E-Business Strategies
Hugh M. Pattinson (University of Western Sydney, Australia) David R. Low (University of Western Sydney, Australia)
Business Science Reference • copyright 2011 • 330pp • H/C (ISBN: 9781605663944) • US $180.00 (our price)

Handbook of Research on Mobile Marketing Management
Key Pousttchi (University of Augsburg, Germany) Dietmar G. Wiedemann (University of Augsburg, Germany)
Business Science Reference • copyright 2010 • 582pp • H/C (ISBN: 9781605660745) • US $295.00 (our price)

Emergent Strategies for E-Business Processes, Services and Implications Advancing Corporate Frameworks
In Lee (Western Illinois University, USA)
Information Science Reference • copyright 2009 • 424pp • H/C (ISBN: 9781605661544) • US $195.00 (our price)

Handbook of Research on Telecommunications Planning and Management for Business
In Lee (Western Illinois University, USA)
Information Science Reference • copyright 2009 • 1212pp • H/C (ISBN: 9781605661940) • US $495.00 (our price)

www.igi-global.com

701 E. Chocolate Ave., Hershey, PA 17033
Order online at www.igi-global.com or call 717-533-8845 x100
To place a standing order for titles released in this series, contact: cust@igi-global.com
Mon-Fri 8:00 am - 5:00 pm (est) or fax 24 hours a day 717-533-8661

Editorial Advisory Board

Table of Contents

Section 1
E-Marketing and the New Collaborative Information Platform

Section 2
What is E-Novation?

Detailed Table of Contents

Section 1
E-Marketing and the New Collaborative Information Platform

    Stephen L. Vargo, University of Hawaii at Manoa, USA
    Robert F. Lusch, University of Arizona, USA

A major change is taking place in most national economies, and even the world economy. It has been variously described under rubrics of globalization, global flattening, and global outsourcing, and has resulted in debate over how firms and nations gain and retain competitive advantage. Innovation has become perhaps the most often used term to capture the process of achieving this competitive advantage.

    Kayvan Miri Lavassani, Carleton University, Canada
    Bahar Movahedi, Carleton University, Canada
    Vinod Kumar, Carleton University, Canada

This chapter provides a review of the historical evolution and development in the field of Electronic Marketplaces (EMs) and explores the classifications of EMs. The researchers employ a systematic approach to propose a comprehensive definition of EMs and their application with reference to recent advances in the study of EMs. Based on the review of the most cited definitions of EM in the literature of the past three decades, this chapter proposes a comprehensive definition of EM. It also identifies several classifications of EMs. There is a gap in the literature for a multi-dimensional classification system of EMs. Therefore, for the purpose of further exploration of the notion of EMs, this chapter provides an explicit review of the different classification models of EMs and presents a nine-dimensional taxonomy of EMs. The chapter concludes with a discussion of the future trends in the field of EMs and a chapter summary.

Chapter 3

Alessia D'Andrea, National Research Council, Italy
Fernando Ferri, National Research Council, Italy
Patrizia Grifoni, National Research Council, Italy

This chapter provides a framework to analyse the marketing and promotion advantages of Virtual Communities. Virtual Communities offer companies the possibility to carry out a new products and services promotion and to develop trustful relationships with customers. The key element in the use of Virtual Communities for these purposes is the wide amount of customers that can be reached. Virtual Communities present the aptitude to generate social influence and knowledge sharing among customers. As a consequence, it brings out the increasing number of skills, competencies and "knowledge profiles" of each customer involved in the virtual environment. The framework is consequently applied to Second Life in order to analyse three different business strategies that companies usually implement by using this platform. The first strategy allows companies to perform the placement of their products/services in a dynamic form. The second strategy provides companies the possibility to have a better knowledge of customers' needs in order to develop products and services that satisfy customer's expectations. Finally, the third strategy allows companies to develop high brand awareness.

Section 2
What is E-Novation?

Chapter 4

David R. Low, University of Western Sydney, Australia
Hugh M. Pattinson, University of Western Sydney, Australia

"E-novation" is defined as a combination of innovation and e-marketing enabled by new collaborative platforms that are being developed and released using Web 2.0 methodologies, allowing for a different level of connectivity around the world. This chapter explores innovation and its contribution to firm performance, links to market orientation – and development of a new collaborative information platform to support innovation. E-marketing is also defined in terms of marketing in computer-mediated environments with emphasis on service-dominant logic (SDL) and collaborative value creation approaches. Aspects of the evolving new collaborative information platform such as the Semantic Web and Web 2.0 applications are discussed from e-marketing and innovation perspectives. Will "e-novation" challenge businesses to rethink how their employees will create or participate in collaborative groups with others where future revenue prospects appear to mainly from service development? This question is also explored through subsequent chapters in the book.

Chapter 5

Ehsan Ehsani, Accenture Management Consulting, USA

Managing product development in an efficient manner is considered a crucial element for a company's survival in today's world. Current markets usually consist of highly fragmented segments of customers looking for customized and differentiated products at lower costs. Intense competition has also pressured companies to launch the products faster to the market in order to reap the planned benefits. Usage of collaborative Web-enabled models for innovation and product development, what we refer to as E-Novation, has become more popular as a result of responding to the aforementioned challenges. From technological point of view, the E-Novation models are particularly enabled through collaborative Web solutions, Web 2.0 tools, and Web-based virtual worlds. This chapter deals with the application of such collaborative Internet-based technologies in the product development and discusses their use in various stages of product development process; from idea management to prototyping. Based on existing literature in the area, the analysis of four cases (Dell, InnoCentive, Ponoko, and Implenia), participant observation and experience with such applications and semi-structured interviews with both managers of such projects and the projects' stakeholders, this chapter demonstrates that new organizational models and skills are required to manage interdependencies internally and externally in collaboration through E-Novation. It also provides some insights about the future trends and opportunities in this era and guidelines for successful implementation of these technologies in reality.

Section 3
E-Novation Marketing Issues

Chapter 6

Robert F. Lusch, University of Arizona, USA
Stephen L. Vargo, University of Hawai'i at Manoa, USA
Melissa Archpru Akaka, University of Hawai'i at Manoa, USA

Organizations and people within organizations cling to traditions, industry practices, and managerial frameworks well beyond their usefulness. Perhaps this is just another way of stating the obvious that habits die slowly. One habit or tradition that is experiencing a slow death is the traditional marketing paradigm, referred to as the goods-dominant (G-D) logic paradigm. Essentially, traditional marketing practice is focused on the creation of units of output and their distribution to customers. Applying this framework, the firm attempts to study these exogenous customers and then uses its resources to shape a market offering, conceptualized as product, price, place, and promotion (what is known as the marketing mix or four Ps) in order to effectively position the offering for a targeted segment, thus capturing the customer to create a sale (economic exchange). Although this paradigm has been under assault for decades, it continues to survive and has changed only modestly over the last fifty years. Importantly, it is a paradigm (and practice) that continues to be presented in the leading marketing and marketing management textbooks used on college campuses and in executive education throughout the world.

Open source taught us that communities are a powerful tool for harnessing collaboration. That power has been reconfirmed by the pioneering efforts of a few early adopters who have sponsored new communities within their industry ecosystems. This chapter profiles a number of interesting examples of e-novation through collaborative communities. The strategic use of collaborative communities is now crossing the chasm into the early majority category of adopters. Research and analysis has revealed the issues, controversies, and problems related to collaborative communities and the role they play in e-novation. It has also revealed useful insight about, and solutions to, many of these challenges. Business leaders can benefit by learning from the insights offered by these pioneers. This chapter offers a process by which business leaders can leverage to add a community of their industry ecosystem. Harnessing e-novation through collaborative communities is now a strategic opportunity for any organisation.

Chapter 8

This chapter contributes to the active debate about the significance of branding in the online channel, by exploring the opportunities and challenges associated with online branding. A discussion of online branding objectives and how they might be achieved is complemented by an exploration of the unique facets of online branding. Case studies of successful brands with interesting approaches to branding in the online channel provide interesting illustration. Finally, some thoughts on the future of online branding conclude the chapter.

Chapter 9

Marketing techniques need to reflect the era that they operate in, match customer needs, environmental dynamics such as social media, and evolve through educative processes to enhance ethical and expert practice. The future will reflect a scenario where customers become sparser than capital (Rogers, 2007), and if dissatisfaction levels in surveys can register highs of 70%, marketing approaches need to change (Jaffe 2007). Marketers are still fixated on labelling and attributing general characteristics to different generations and groups of people so that marketing can be targeted "appropriately." For example the exposure of Generation Y to technology is unequivocal but the descriptions of people in this generation elevate this to levels where somehow these consumers have become genetically modified human beings, without the same frailties, emotional responses, and foibles because of their exposure to technology. Images from YouTube could be collected everyday to provide us with ready examples of Generation Y consumer frailties. Generic labelling of consumers does not demonstrate sophisticated marketing and does not reflect the level of analysis that can be done to target appropriate or one to one marketing. On an ethical level, marketers need to focus on permission based marketing and apply co-creation models which have the potential to address the bottom line and shareholder returns without compromising the interests and wellbeing of consumers. Emotion rather than reason remains the key brand response from consumers, but the new online research environment offers opportunities for analytical diversity and the use of creative and lateral thinking (Cooke & Buckley, 2007), rather than just intrusive marketing practices enhanced by technological capabilities. Improved practice, together with ethics, should be represented in marketing and business training and in the profession. All of this is influenced by technology and its flawed or decent application reflects human intervention as always. How much protection or care then should marketers exercise towards consumers in their environments especially since consumers are deemed to be more sophisticated? Educative systems should also ensure that sustainability practices are a promise of future marketing.

Chapter 10

In the early 1990's, marketing theory experienced a paradigm shift from a transactional approach focusing on sales to a relationship one. This shift was due to several limits of traditional mix marketing based on the "four P's" and to the change in the market business models. In fact, the growing role of branding in mass markets, the development of services marketing, and the importance of network and human interactions in business are some of the main reasons behind relationship marketing emergence. Relationship marketing is then aimed at developing and maintaining mutually profitable relationships with customers and even stakeholders. In the era of technology evolution and Internet, customer relationship management (CRM) is moving forward to better manage, drive, and keep value-added relationships. However, CRM is, first of all, a company strategy and a shared vision that involves organization, people, and processes in satisfying and retaining customers. This chapter deals with the concept of customer centricity and its development, customer lifecycle with acquisition and retention, and finally the issue of CRM implementation.

Chapter 11

Space is the final frontier for e-marketing. Advances in storage space, digital data transmission, and infrastructure development have created a near limitless marketspace that exists over the contemporary physical marketplaces, and as an independent market of ideas, data, experience, and content. This chapter overviews a series of key issues in the use of the new "space" for e-novation with attention given to the rise of user generated content, prosumer activity. This chapter is based on exploring how companies and individuals are currently co-creating value in the dynamic marketplace of the new collaborative platforms, and how these new concepts such as the home shipping channel, digital rights management, and user generated distribution channels can factor in the future success on and offline for marketing.

Author experiences from working jointly and within startups inform this chapter. Emphasizing the importance of employees achieving unprecedented productivity through working collaboratively and supported by flexible roles and social technologies cannot be understated. Startup employees led by the entrepreneur are masters of embracing complexity. This means the startup team understands cause and effect follow a non-linear relationship with the subtlest of changes potentially resultant in producing chaotic behavior and surprise. For the startup, especially in recessionary times, this means counterintuitive thinking wins the day. In light of this, small expenditures can have a greater impact on developing new business compared with the large budgets available to incumbent players. The startup employee prefers not to be constrained by the old broadcast model of email instead exploiting social technologies. This includes the use of wikis as an enabler of both interactive communications and repository of company knowledge. A founding myth helps drive new hires and can underpin a service centric focus creating unique customer experiences based on the vision of the entrepreneur and storytelling. A startup is a learning organization improving processes and results on an ongoing basis mirroring entrepreneurship as a learning process. Within a startup, limited processes exist, and core employees embrace next practice to help drive a major source of competitive advantage. Startup employees realize success goes beyond consideration of product functionality or a track record of existing customers. Each business development opportunity for the startup is driven by experience co-created with the customer. By 2010 the potential to launch a "startup-in-a-box" with an E-Novation framework (Pattinson and Low 2008) supported by social technologies to foster intense collaboration among core employees will become both a reality and essential. Only through a combination of framework and social technologies can startups and founding employees keep pace with the changing business landscape and generate a rapid amount of knowledge to sustain sufficient advantage in the market.

This chapter explores the lessons learned by large corporations that have been pioneers of e-novation. These pioneers have much to teach us about the opportunities for competitive impact and business value. These are explored within the framework of Porter's Five Forces model. The impact of e-novation on employees and, especially on the employee-employer relationship is explored to reveal possible insights. Although a significant portion of these pioneers are in the high tech sector, many of the insights are broadly applicable to all sectors of the economy. A case is made that e-novation is well on its way to broad adoption in the business community. Recommendations are offered for those wishing to take up the challenge of e-novation.

This chapter introduces a new organizational entity for government organisations, the E-Novation Program Office (EPO). The basis for this structure is researcher experiences of the divide between organizational decision-making capability and the actual delivery of innovation using new technology initiatives within Australian organizations. Key EPO decision-making mechanisms include cognitive mapping, road maps, scenario planning, and complexity thinking. The proposed model of the EPO is informed through author experiences within a variety of Australian organisations and government enterprises focusing on technological innovation rather than other forms of innovation. The EPO serves to guide innovative actions, prioritization of effort, and better execution by acting as a counterbalance between technology, strategy, and delivery to ensure the successful introduction of innovation. The robustness, flexibility, and adaptability of the EPO arises from modeling processes arising from research in the governance of enterprise wide service orientated architectures for information systems. The EPO explicitly supports the central tenant of government organisations, the provision of service to citizens. Most importantly, service is taken to be the provision of knowledge and skills (Vargo & Lusch, 2004) for the benefit of citizens.

Section 5
Emerging E-Novation, Platforms and Marketing

Current new and next generation e-novation collaborative platforms are explored through a "Day-In-The-Life-Of" scenario in 2020 based on key semantic concepts drawn from chapters within the E-Novation book. Key themes for an emerging e-novation collaborative platform include: triple convergence (before and after), Web 3.0/4.0 – the Web is a brain, redefined collaborative communication, virtual/augmented reality, service-dominant logic (SDL), marketing and innovation, open-source creation, development and distribution, digital branding, CRM redefined, complexity and SMEs, e-novation office, e-novation curriculum, social graphing e-novation, and sustainability platforms and innovation. These themes are discussed both in relation to the current new collaborative platform and how they may develop from 2010-2020. E-novation will be the innovation and marketing social and business service.

Foreword

Editors David Low and Hugh Pattinson define "e-novation" as a combination of innovation and e-marketing, enabled by new collaborative platforms that are being developed and released using Web 2.0 methods, allowing for a different level of connectivity around the world. Acquiring a deep understanding of e-novation is necessary now because firms and educational and governmental organizations are transitioning beyond digital branding to online social media marketing using multiple media touchpoints.

The pace of successful new product-service developments via e-novation platforms is equivalent to compressing the acceleration phase of the Industrial Revolution to a decade rather than a century after its worldwide startup. The decade 2010-2020 is the e-novation acceleration phase. All the chapters in this book include strong evidence supporting this assertion.

Dwell for a moment on the title: *E-Novation for Competitive Advantage in Collaborative Globalization: Technologies for Emerging E-Business Strategies*. The book delivers this promise by describing and explaining what is here now and the reality-virtual infusion of business models in operating scenarios that are most likely to dominant during 2015-2020. Broadly, the book focuses on vision and the will to succeed in electronic-enabled workplaces and relationships. It is an invaluable focus as Tellis and Golder (2006) confirm—after spending the last 10 years studying the history of 66 industries, Tellis and Golder (2001, iii) conclude that "the real causes of enduring market leadership are vision and will. Enduring market leaders have a revolutionary and inspiring vision of the mass market and they exhibit an indomitable will to realize that vision."

Where can executives acquire the necessary facts-of-life for nurturing brands in achieving successful e-novation? Answer: Here. The thick descriptions of firm and organizational level e-novations in Pattinson and Low's book bring to life the vision-and-will focus of their treatise. The many citations, websites, and references appearing in all the chapters inform the reader on where-to-go-next for developing e-novation operational skills. Thus, the book is a wellhead for knowledge and skills necessary for designing and implementing e-novations in the acceleration phase of this latest post Industrial Revolution. Concisely put: the book delivers on the title's promise. Good reading!

Arch G. Woodside
Boston College, USA

Arch G. Woodside *is Professor of Marketing, Boston College. He is a Fellow and member of the American Psychological Association, Association of Psychological Science, Royal Society of Canada, Society for Marketing Advances, and the International Academy for the Study of Tourism. His 2010 books include Case Study Research: Theory, Methods and Practice (Elsevier Publishing) and edited volumes in the Advances in Business Marketing & Purchasing and Advances in Culture, Tourism and*

Hospitality Research book series. He is the Editor-in-Chief of the Journal of Business Research. His research reports in publications of more than 200 articles appearing in 34 different marketing, management, psychology, and tourism journals. He is the founder of the International Academy of Culture, Tourism, and Hospitality Research.

REFERENCE

Tellis, G. J., & Golder, P. (2001). *Will and vision: How latecomers grow to dominate markets*. New York, NY: McGraw-Hill.

Preface

The aim of this book is to highlight new products, services, strategies, and philosophies drawn from an emerging collaborative information platform. The World-Wide Web has metamorphosed into a powerful multimedia, multipurpose, multipoint, and creative vehicle for development and delivery of new, emergent products and services.

This book explores symbiotic connections between the development of new e-business technologies with new users and consumers, existing and new businesses, and links to social and political visions and strategies.

Friedman's (2006) conceptualization and discussion of a "Flat World" with an advanced collaborative platform expressed through "Globalization 3.0" provides a strong underpinning description of the new platform. This book explores and discusses the new platform that is relevant—indeed critical—to existing and new small and medium businesses, who may in turn become new industry leaders in the coming decade.

E-Novation starts with businesses using the new platform to research, develop, and market new things within and out from that platform. *E-Novation* is important for businesses that already have basic or more advanced e-business features, but should move on take advantage of more features within the new platform.

E-Novation explores a new composition of marketing elements relevant to competing in a new collaborative business world. e-novation Marketing Elements incorporating Web 2.0 concepts include collaboration, pricing, online presence & branding, curriculum, and deployment.

The book recognizes a revolutionary change in e-business to a new advanced collaborative information platform that supersedes previous e-business Information Systems, perspectives, and business and marketing philosophies. The book introduces relevant advancing new information thinking for new agendas of marketing and business research and practice – and indeed for new research and practice with and from the new information platform.

The book will be useful to academics, teachers and researchers, professionals in the field of e-learning, and to people that belong to the broader field of education. The book builds on new conceptualisations of a new collaborative platform—but encapsulates philosophies, strategies, and actions under an e-novation umbrella expressed in useful terms for business researchers and managers. These approaches may also be of significant importance to researchers in the area of the Semantic Web, especially when the semantic augmentation of the data concerns those interested in using online communities for business processes.

SECTION ONE: E-MARKETING AND THE NEW COLLABORATIVE INFORMATION PLATFORM

The book commences by recognising that a major change is taking place in most national economies. It has been variously described under rubrics of globalization, global flattening, and global outsourcing and has resulted in debate over how firms and nations gain and retain competitive advantage. *Innovation* has become perhaps the most often used term to capture the process of achieving this competitive advantage.

Frequently, along with noting this change in globalization, time-series statistics on employment in different sectors of the economy are offered as evidence of the direction firms and nations need to move. The data suggest that relatively fewer people are working in agriculture and other extractive industries, such as logging, mining, and fishing, and fewer also are working in manufacturing sectors. They also indicate that there has been a corresponding ascendance in what is characterized as "services" industries. That is, developed countries, if not the global economy in general, are going through a service revolution, and the world is moving toward a service economy. Thus, not surprisingly, the mantra has become: to be globally competitive, firms need to learn to innovate in services.

The book then provides a review of the historical evolution and development in the field of Electronic Marketplaces (EMs) and dedicates a chapter to classifications of EMs. A comprehensive definition of EMs and their application with reference to recent advances in the study of EMs is provided. Based on the review of the most cited definitions of EM in the literature of the past three decades, we propose a comprehensive definition of EM in this chapter. This chapter also identifies several classifications of EMs. There is a gap in the literature for a multi-dimensional classification system of EMs. Therefore, for the purpose of further exploration of the notion of EMs, this chapter provides an explicit review of the different classification models of EMs and presents a nine-dimensional taxonomy of EMs. The chapter concludes with a discussion of the future trends in the field of EMs and a chapter summary

A framework to analyse the marketing and promotion advantages of Virtual Communities is then presented. Virtual Communities offer companies the possibility to carry out a new products and services promotion and to develop trustful relationships with customers. The key element in the use of Virtual Communities for these purposes is the wide amount of customers that can be reached. Virtual Communities present the aptitude to generate social influence and knowledge sharing among customers. As a consequence, an increasing number of skills, competencies, and "knowledge profiles" of each customer involved into the virtual environment emerge. The framework is consequently applied to Second Life in order to analyse three different business strategies that companies usually implement by using this platform. The first strategy allows companies to perform the placement of their products/services in a dynamic form. The second strategy provides companies the possibility to have a better knowledge of customers' needs in order to develop products and services that satisfy customer's expectations. Finally, the third strategy allows companies to develop high brand awareness.

SECTION TWO: WHAT IS E-NOVATION?

Further to the definition of e-novation as how to manage the product development in an efficient manner is considered. Current markets usually consist of highly fragmented segments of customers looking for customized and differentiated products at lower costs. The intense competition has also pressured companies to launch the products faster to the market in order to reap the planned benefits. Usage of collaborative Web-enabled models for innovation and product development, what we refer to as e-novation, has become more popular as a result to respond to the above mentioned challenges. From technological point of view, the e-novation models are particularly enabled through collaborative Web solutions, Web 2.0 tools, and Web-based virtual worlds. This chapter deals with the application of such collaborative Internet-based technologies in the product development and discusses their use in various stages of product development process; from idea management to prototyping. Based on existing literature in the area, the analysis of four cases (Dell, InnoCentive, Ponoko, and Implenia), participant observation and experience with such applications and semi-structured interviews with both managers of such projects and the projects' stakeholders, the chapter here demonstrates that new organizational models and skills are required to manage interdependencies internally and externally in collaboration through e-novation. It also provides some insights about the future trends and opportunities in this era and guidelines for successful implementation of these technologies in reality.

SECTION 3: E-NOVATION MARKETING ISSUES

The marketing issues section commences with a discussion on how organizations and people within organizations cling to traditions, industry practices, and managerial frameworks well beyond their usefulness. Perhaps this is just another way of stating the obvious that habits die slowly. One habit or tradition that is experiencing a slow death is the traditional marketing paradigm or what was referred to in the first chapter as the goods-dominant (G-D) logic paradigm. Essentially, traditional marketing practice is focused on the creation of units of output and their distribution to customers. Applying this framework, the firm attempts to study these exogenous customers and then uses its resources to shape a market offering, conceptualized as product, price, place, and promotion (what is known as the marketing mix or four Ps) in order to effectively position the offering for a targeted segment, thus capturing the customer to create a sale (economic exchange). Although this paradigm has been under assault for decades, it continues to survive and has changed only modestly over the last fifty years. Importantly, it is a paradigm (and practice) that continues to be presented in the leading marketing and marketing management textbooks used on college campuses and in executive education throughout the world.

The weaknesses in the dominant practice and teaching of marketing began to be noted as scholars, especially in Northern Europe, began to identify relationship and services as central elements of a new marketing paradigm (e.g., Gronroos 1994; Gummesson 1995). Marketing slowly began to be viewed as less and less in terms of the transactions involving goods and more in terms of the exchange relationships and service(s). Subsequently, organizations began to be viewed less in terms of the products they produce and more in terms of the competences and capabilities they develop (e.g., Prahalad and Hamel 1990; Day 1994). The customer began to be viewed as a potential collaborator and co-creator of value (Lusch, Brown and Brunswick 1992; Prahalad and Ramaswamy 2000), rather than just a receiver of value. Vargo and Lusch (2004), developed what became known as the service-dominant (S-D) logic of marketing to capture and extend these and other converging trends, as well as the often-heard mantra for both firms and countries to develop better competitive strategies for a global economy that was increasingly being characterized in terms of service provision rather than goods production. In this chapter we show that S-D logic can be translated into a new framework for marketing management and, importantly, as a source of insight for developing e-novative market offerings.

A discussion on what open source taught us follows and suggests that communities are a powerful tool for harnessing collaboration. That power has been reconfirmed by the pioneering efforts of a few early adopters who have sponsored new communities within their industry ecosystems. This chapter profiles a number of interesting examples of e-novation through collaborative communities. The strategic use of collaborative communities is now crossing the chasm into the early majority category of adopters.

Research and analysis has revealed the issues, controversies, and problems related to collaborative communities and the role they play in e-novation. It has also revealed useful insight about, and solutions to, many of these challenges. Business leaders can benefit by learning from the insights offered by these pioneers. The chapter on collaborative communities offers a process by which business leaders can leverage to add a community of their industry ecosystem. Harnessing e-novation through collaborative communities is now a strategic opportunity for any organisation.

The book then focuses on how brands communicate with customers bringing them in context with E-novation and a Web 2.0 environment. Brands are a means of making an immediate impact on new customers and reminding returning customers. Strong brands have high brand equity and make a significant contribution to business performance and organizational success. In an increasingly networked economy and environment, messages about what an organization or its products and services mean, and the value that they offer increasingly needs to be communicated remotely, through the organization's website. The website is not just another channel designed to increase visibility and access. It is a shop window, through which the organization delivers marketing communication, purchase opportunities, information, advice, customer care, service, and experiences. The website has the potential to deliver the company's identity, products, and service in the space of a few screens and within seconds; the whole experience comes together for the user, or, if not managed properly, it falls apart. The website experience defines the brand experience of the online brand

A discussion of marketing techniques needing to reflect the era that they operate in then follows. As scarce as capital may be in the future, new customers may be even harder to find. and if dissatisfaction levels in surveys can register highs of 70% marketing approaches need to change (Jaffe 2007). Marketers are still fixated on labelling and attributing general characteristics to different generations and groups of people so that marketing can be targeted "appropriately." For example, the exposure of Generation Y to technology is unequivocal, but the descriptions of people in this generation elevate this to levels where somehow these consumers have become genetically modified human beings, without the same frailties, emotional responses, and foibles because of their exposure to technology. Images from YouTube could be collected everyday to provide us with ready examples of Generation Y consumer frailties.

Generic labelling of consumers does not demonstrate sophisticated marketing and does not reflect the level of analysis that can be done to target appropriate or one to one marketing. On an ethical level, marketers need to focus on permission based marketing and apply co-creation models which have the potential to address the bottom line and shareholder returns without compromising the interests and wellbeing of consumers. Emotion rather than reason remains the key brand response from consumers, but the new online research environment offers opportunities for analytical diversity and the use of creative and lateral thinking (Cooke & Buckley, 2007) rather than just intrusive marketing practices enhanced by technological capabilities. Improved practice, together with ethics, should be represented in marketing and business training and in the profession. All of this is influenced by technology, and its flawed or decent application reflects as always human intervention. How much protection or care, then, should marketers exercise towards consumers in their environments, especially since consumers are deemed to be more sophisticated? Educative systems should also ensure that sustainability practices are a promise of future marketing.

The focus of the marketing issue section then turns to Customer Relationship Management (CRM). Stating that the aim of CRM strategy is the development of customer-centric business culture comes with the hope of achieving two results – improving the customer's experience and lowering sales and marketing costs. Relationship marketing consists of acquiring and maintaining customers by creating and providing better value than competitors do. Relationship marketing is at the heart of a successful CRM implementation. The process begins with the development of a clear relationship marketing strategy. This requires the definition of roles for customer facing functions like sales, marketing, and customer service. Once the roles are defined within the relationship marketing strategy, the processes have to be reengineered to operationalize the relationship marketing strategy. Finally, the appropriate level of technology needs to be acquired to support the customer centric approach now in place. In globalized markets and while products and services offers become standardized, customer knowledge represents the imperative key to gain a competitive advantage. From a marketing point of view, the customer should be the center of marketing decisions. In other words, customer centricity is the result of the evolution of marketing from a transactional approach to relational paradigm supported with knowledge of the customer and their preferences and behavior. Marketing has moved from being a company's function dedicated to simply promote products to shift inventory to playing a major role in customer satisfaction and retention.

This section ends with the assertion that space is the final frontier for e-marketing. Advances in storage space, digital data transmission, and infrastructure development have created a near limitless marketspace that exists over the contemporary physical marketplaces, and as an independent market of ideas, data, experience, and content. This chapter overviews a series of key issues in the use of the new "space" for e-novation with attention given to the rise of user generated content, prosumer activity. The chapter is based on exploring how companies and individuals are currently co-creating value in the dynamic marketplace of the new collaborative platforms, and how these new concepts such as the home shipping channel, digital rights management, and user generated distribution channels can factor in the future success on and offline for marketing.

SECTION 4: E-NOVATION BUSINESS DEVELOPMENT

The Business Development section commences by emphasizing the importance of employees achieving unprecedented productivity through working collaboratively and supported by flexible roles, and social technologies cannot be understated. Startup employees led by the entrepreneur are masters of embracing complexity. This means the startup team understands cause and effect follow a non-linear relationship with the subtlest of changes potentially resultant in producing chaotic behavior and surprise. For the startup, especially in recessionary times, this means counterintuitive thinking wins the day. In light of this, small expenditures can have a greater impact on developing new business compared with the large budgets available to incumbent players.

The startup employee prefers not to be constrained by the old broadcast model of email, instead exploiting social technologies. This includes the use of wikis as an enabler of both interactive communications and repository of company knowledge. A founding myth helps drive new hires and can underpin a service centric focus creating unique customer experiences based on the vision of the entrepreneur and storytelling. A startup is a learning organization improving processes and results on an ongoing basis mirroring entrepreneurship as a learning process. Within a startup, limited processes exist, and core employees embrace next practice to help drive a major source of competitive advantage. Startup employees realize success goes beyond consideration of product functionality or a track record of existing customers. Each business development opportunity for the startup is driven by experience co-created with the customer.

By 2010 the potential to launch a "startup-in-a-box" with an e-novation framework (Pattinson and Low 2008) supported by social technologies to foster intense collaboration among core employees will become both a reality and essential. Only through a combination of framework and social technologies can startups and founding employees keep pace with the changing business landscape and generate a rapid amount of knowledge to sustain sufficient advantage in the market

The section ends with a more reflective chapter that begins by exploring the lessons learned by large corporations that have been pioneers of e-novation. These pioneers have much to teach us about the opportunities for competitive impact and business value. These are explored within the framework of Porter's Five Forces model. The impact of e-novation on employees and, especially on the employee-employer relationship is explored to reveal possible insights. Although a significant portion of these pioneers are in the high tech sector, many of the insights are broadly applicable to all sectors of the economy. A case is made that e-novation is well on its way to broad adoption in the business community. Recommendations are offered for those wishing to take up the challenge of e-novation.

SECTION 5: EMERGING E-NOVATION, PLATFORMS AND MARKETING

This section brings together key themes addressed in the book into discussion on current new and emerging E-Novation Collaborative Information Platforms. A "Day-I-The-Life-Of" Scenario in 2020 is presented highlighting and extending key themes into an emerging next generation e-novation Platform. The scenario is discussed, followed by a discussion of key themes of an emerging e-novation collaborative platform, including: triple convergence (before and after), Web 3.0/4.0 – the Web is a brain, redefined collaborative communication, virtual/augmented reality, service-dominant logic (SDL), marketing and innovation, open-source creation, development and distribution, digital branding, CRM redefined, complexity and SMEs, e-novation office, e-novation curriculum, social graphing e-novation, and sustainability platforms and innovation. The Section ends on the note that e-novation will be *the* Innovation and Marketing Social and Business Service.

Hugh M. Pattinson
University of Western Sydney, Australia

David R. Low
University of Western Sydney, Australia

REFERENCES

Cooke, M., & Buckley, N. (2008). Web 2.0, social networks and the future of market research. *International Journal of Market Research, 50*(2), 267–292.

Friedman, T. L. (2006). Chapter three: The triple convergence . In Friedman, T. L. (Ed.), *The world is flat (updated and abridged)*. London, UK: Penguin.

Gronroos, C. (1994). From marketing mix to relationship marketing: Towards a paradigm shift in marketing. *Asia-Australia Marketing Journal, 2*(August), 9-29. Day, G. (1994). The capabilities of market-driven organization. *Journal of Marketing, 58*(October), 37–52.

Gummesson, E. (1995). Relationship marketing: Its role in the service economy . In Glynn, W. J., & Barnes, J. G. (Eds.), *Understanding service management*. New York, NY: John Wiley and Sons.

Jaffe, D. (2007). *Do not disturb* [Electronic Version]. The Advertiser.

Lusch, R. F., Brown, S. W., & Brunswick, G. J. (1992). A general framework for explaining internal vs. external exchange. *Journal of the Academy of Marketing Science, 20*(Spring), 119–134. doi:10.1007/BF02723452

Prahalad, C. K., & Hamel, G. (1990). The core competence of the corporation. *Harvard Business Review, 68*(May-June), 79–91.

Prahalad, C. K., & Ramaswamy, V. (2000). Co-opting customer competence. *Harvard Business Review, 78*(January-February), 79–87.

Vargo, S. L., & Lusch, R. F. (2004). Evolving to a new dominant logic for marketing. *Journal of Marketing, 68*(January), 1–17. doi:10.1509/jmkg.68.1.1.24036

Section 1
E–Marketing and the New Collaborative Information Platform

Chapter 1
Service–Dominant Logic Foundations of E–Novation

Stephen L. Vargo
University of Hawaii at Manoa, USA

Robert F. Lusch
University of Arizona, USA

ABSTRACT

A major change is taking place in most national economies, and even the world economy. It has been variously described under rubrics of globalization, global flattening, and global outsourcing, and has resulted in debate over how firms and nations gain and retain competitive advantage. Innovation has become perhaps the most often used term to capture the process of achieving this competitive advantage.

INTRODUCTION

Frequently, along with noting the change in globalization, time-series statistics on employment in different sectors of the economy are offered as evidence of the direction firms and nations need to move. The data suggest that relatively fewer people are working in agriculture and other extractive industries, such as logging, mining, and fishing and fewer also are working in manufacturing sectors. They also indicate that there has been a corresponding ascendance in what is characterized as "services" industries. That is, the

developed countries, if not the global economy in general, is going through a service revolution and the world is moving toward a service economy. Thus, not surprisingly, the mantra has become: to be globally competitive, firms need to learn to innovate in services.

We disagree. Rather, though it might appear paradoxical (if not incoherent), we argue that, whereas the world economy is going through a significant shift and the national and global economies are service based, there is *no services revolution* there is just a *service revelation*. That is, what appears to be a services revolution is an artifact of wrong thinking about economic exchange. We argue that *economic activity has always been*

DOI: 10.4018/978-1-60566-394-4.ch001

primarily about the exchange of service – one party using its knowledge and skills to do something for another party, under conditions of reciprocity. We call this orientation *service-dominant (S-D) logic* and contrast it with *goods-dominant (G-D) logic*, the traditional orientation, in which services are seen either as add-ons to goods (e.g., after-sale service) or a special (often inferior) class of (intangible) goods.

On the other hand, we suggest that there is an economic (and social) revolution taking place, one that is having a profound impact on our view of economic activity. It is a revolution dealing with the manner in which we can detangilbalize, store, and transmit information, which, together with the natural progression in development of specialized knowledge and skills, is making the real nature of exchange more apparent and compelling. In short, there is an *information technology* (IT) *revolution* and an *information communication technology (ICT) revolution*, which, together, are *revealing* that economic activity is actually all service based, rather than goods based.

This distinction is important as we wrestle with issues of innovation, because the locus and process of value creation, and thus of innovation, are strikingly different in a goods-centered and a service-centered model, regardless of whether innovation is being discussed in relation to an organization traditionally characterized as "manufacturing" or "services," local or global, or profit or non-profit. The advances in IT and ICT, along with increasing specialization, reveal a service logic that points toward a model of innovation in which electronic, digital information and communication are at the heart of developing new interactive and collaborative, networked approaches to value creation, such as "open innovation," "customer-initiated innovation;" and the "democratization of innovation" (e.g., von Hippel, 2005). It points toward E-Novation, innovation reframed in terms of collaboration in resource integration through collaborative platforms for value creation.

In the following sections we will: (1) contrast goods-dominant with service-dominant logic and show why Adam Smith, and thus economic science and business, relied on what has become known as G-D logic as the key to wealth creation, based on conditions of world trade and purposes of scholarship which do not apply today; (2) elaborate the foundations of S-D logic; (3) explore the concept of service ecosystems as value creation platforms and (4) explain how S-D logic and a service ecosystems conceptualization can provide a foundation for E-Novation.[1]

CONTRASTING GOODS-DOMINANT WITH SERVICE-DOMINANT LOGIC

The easiest way to conceptualize S-D logic is by contrasting it with G-D logic. In its most rudimentary form, goods-dominant logic postulates the following (see Vargo and Lusch 2004):

1. The purpose of economic activity is to make and distribute products, ideally tangible goods, at a profit.
2. These products are embedded with value (utility) by the firm(s) during the production and distribution processes.
3. To maximize profits, production efficiency should be maximized; thus the (ideally tangible) good should be standardized, produced away from the market, and inventoried until demanded.

In short, the purpose of the firm is to make value-laden, (ideally) tangible goods efficiently and sell them at a profit. In this logic, "services" are seen either as add-ons to goods (i.e., value added, such as after-sale service) or a particular type of good, characterized by their intangibility, inability to be standardized (heterogeneity), inability to be produced away from the market (inseparability) and inability to be inventoried (perishability) (Zeithaml, Parasuraman & Berry,

1985) – what have become known as the IHIP characteristics. It is a logic that is so pervasive that it is paradigmatic in every sense of the word. Also in this G-D logic, economic activity is characterized relative to its tangible output, as in extracted and manufactured, with "services" being a residual category.

Paradigms are powerful. They are worldviews that are foundational in providing a framework for understanding how the world works. But these worldviews are formulated in the context of a particular time and to address particular issues and this context and these issues change. Thus, paradigms need to be reexamined and occasionally reformulated. A short digression into the context and development of G-D logic suggests why this might be particularly appropriate in the case of G-D logic.

Historical Roots of G-D Logic

Much of G-D logic can be traced to Adam Smith, the author of *An Inquiry into the Nature and Causes of the Wealth of Nations* (1776). It is important to note that although Smith later became known as the "father of economics," this was not his purpose. Rather, as the title of this work suggests, his intention was to explain how nations could become wealthy. The context of this inquiry was the beginning of the Industrial Revolution and a time when national wealth was largely defined in terms of the accumulation of globally abundant, but often dispersed and difficult to obtain, natural resources.

Initially, Smith laid out what might be considered a general foundation for understanding economic exchange based on a value-creation concept grounded in specialized knowledge and skills ("labor") and he distinguished between *value-in-use* ("real value," the value to the beneficiary) and *value-in-exchange* ("nominal value," market value, as represented by price). However, he then partially abandoned that model to discuss the specific, contextual national-wealth issue.

Smith's context was one characterized by limitation in the ability to share and exchange information, such as specialized knowledge, which was at the center of his discussion of the purpose of the market. Information could not be digitized, stored, except in text form (e.g., books, pamphlets, etc.) and telecommunications, such as telephone and the Internet, had of course not been invented. Thus, if a firm or nation desired to exchange with other distant firms and nations, it was necessary to either send an expert or embed the specialized information in tangible, transportable matter – that is to make and export a good.

In that context, Smith (1776) identified *"production"* as the key to wealth. Production for Smith meant the creation (i.e., manufacturing) of surplus *tangible goods that could be exported*. He acknowledged that many other activities (e.g., those of kings, scholars, military, personal service providers, etc.) that were involved in exchange were necessary and useful for human survival and wellbeing; they just were not productive in the sense of contributing to national wealth, as defined at the time. Many of the economic scholars who followed Smith objected to this narrow view of productivity but it prevailed nonetheless and the concept of a "product" became a tangible good, embedded with exchange value ("value-in-exchange," utility).

Although it developed from Smith's (1776) normative work on how to create national wealth, throughout the next two centuries this goods-dominant logic, which views units of output (goods) as the central components of exchange, guided not only economics but also, increasingly, the metrics, policies, and actions of firms and governments. This goods-centered perspective was also developed from the economic philosophers' desire to make economics a true science at a time when *Newtonian Mechanics* served as the model for the scientific mastery of nature (Vargo and Morgan 2005). The idea of stuff embedded with utility fit this model well and economics largely succeeded at this goal; but to do so required some powerful but restrictive, if not incorrect, assumptions – the ideas that objects (matter or goods) have innate properties (utility) and relationships to other objects, which can be measured in terms of price mechanisms and value-in-exchange. Importantly, as economic theory became formalized in the mathematics of calculus and differential equations it became the overriding framework for financially engineering and optimizing the economy and the firm (Vargo and Lusch 2004).

Therefore, economic, political and management thought developed on a foundational notion of tangible goods embedded with value and exchanged for other goods, which were also so embedded. In the context of this paradigm, the exchange of intangible resources became conceptually identified as "services" and was aligned with what Smith had identified as "non-productive" activities and, perhaps worse, was largely ignored.

Reconsidering Resources

Before discussing how a service mindset has begun to overtake this goods mindset it is instructive to briefly review the concept of resources. Malthus (1798), in the first comprehensive analysis of world resources, concluded that, with a projected geometric growth in human population, society would soon run out of resources. Resources, in a Malthusian world, meant natural resources that humans draw upon for support. This was the stuff that nations went to war over and that was viewed as the key ingredient in the production of goods for exchange, export, and hence, national wealth. It was the concept of resources with which Smith (1776) had defined national wealth.

Zimmerman (1951), who also examined world resources, however, conceptualized resources quite differently. For Zimmerman everything is neutral (or perhaps even a resistance) until humankind learns what to do with it. As Constantin and Lusch (1994), drawing upon Zimmerman (1951), later suggested: resources are not; they become.

Constantin and Lusch (1994) also made the distinction between operand and operant resources. An *operand resource* is one upon which an operation or act must be performed to create benefit. Usually, these are static and tangible resources or what are often referred to as natural resources. For most of economic history, firms were largely viewed as acting upon the resources of nature to produce tangible goods with exchange value. Operand resources are also generally viewed as finite and thus, as noted, tribes, clans and nations that possessed them were viewed as wealthy.

On the other hand, *operant resources* are those which act on other resources (both operand and operant) to produce effects (Constantin and Lusch, 1994). Operant resources are seldom tangible but mostly intangible and invisible. They are likely to be dynamic and can enable humans to multiply operand resources through innovation and allow them to multiply the productive capacity and usefulness of operand resources. As will be shown, *S-D logic views operant resources as primary*, because they are necessary facilitators of effects. Importantly, the fundamental shift from focusing on operant, rather than operand, resources has implications for how to conduct the affairs of businesses and nations. It also has implications for understanding innovation.

The Liquefaction of Operant Resources

In economic exchange, the central operant resources are knowledge and skills. As noted, this notion of exchange as sharing competences goes back at least as far as Smith (1776), before shifting his focus from exchange to national wealth creation. What Smith captured in the "division of labor" was not so much about physical work but rather the specialized knowledge and skills behind the work—the *division of competences*. These competences are what Mokyr (2002) calls "useful knowledge,' a form of information. This model of economic exchange being about the application of specialized information is strikingly different from the classical and neoclassical economic model, a model centered on the exchange of matter (goods), which was derived from Smith's normative concern with national wealth creation. It is a model that has an importance that is amplified, if not necessitated by recent advances in the way information can be exchanged and applied.

As discussed, in Smith's day, for useful knowledge to be exchanged, especially across large distances, it had to be carried by a person or embedded in some object. That is, it could be used as a basis for personal service, which was often impractical, or transformed into a good. Given this inseparability limitation, thinking about exchange in terms of a good was, arguably, sufficient, even though the good was a surrogate, the carrier. Over the last century or so however, we have made enormous strides in information technology, which allows us to store large amounts of information and to send it digitally and instantly across large distances. Normann (2001) calls this ability to separate, and thus exchange, information apart from goods "*liquification.*"

Liquification refers to the separation of information from people and things, Historically information was embedded into tangible things. For example, in the past, listening to music required the proximity of musician and listener. More recently, technological advances first allowed music to be recorded on various physical media, allowing near-precise replication at great distances and then through advancements in various combined information technologies allowed digitization and transportation of the associated information through distances without having to be embed it in people (musicians) or goods (e.g., records, CDs). When the information can be separated from physical substance it becomes liquefied (Normann, 2001).[2] It is the advances in IT and ICT, rather than a shift in economic exchange to a service economy that makes the shift from goods logic to service logic compelling.

Service-Dominant Logic

S-D logic superordinates service (the *process* of using resources to provide benefit) in relation to products (*units of output* that are sometimes used in the process). In turn, it points to the superordination of operant resources to operand resources. That is, it is a dynamic view of business and marketing in which social and economic processes are largely focused on operant resources (vs. operand resources) and understands the organization as constantly striving to make better value propositions (rather than products) than competitors. Furthermore, S-D logic argues that in a relatively free-market economy, the firm primarily (but not exclusively) knows whether it is offering better value propositions from the feedback it receives from the market in terms of financial performance. Consequently, S-D logic views marketing, and business in general, as a continuous learning process (directed at improving operant resources). The normative view (Vargo and Lusch 2004) of S-D logic can be summarized as follows:

1. Identify or develop competences, the fundamental knowledge and skills of an economic actor that represent potential competitive advantage.
2. Identify other actors (potential customers) that could benefit from these competences.
3. Cultivate relationships that involve the customers in developing customized, competitively compelling value propositions to meet specific needs.
4. Gauge marketplace feedback by analyzing financial performance and other relevant non-financial metrics, from exchange to learn how to improve the firm's offering to customers and improve firm performance.

Rather than a revolution from goods (manufacturing) to service economies, we are evolving from a goods-based to a service-based logic. Some of this evolution in thinking about economic activity is analogous to the recent evolution in thinking about activity in information and connectivity, especially as captured in the World Wide Web, as we move from Web 1.0 to Web 2.0 and beyond. Given the E-Novation focus of this book, the analogy is instructive.

When formal marketing thought developed in the early 1900's, marketing was concerned with taking goods and services *"to market."* In fact, the American Marketing Association initially (mid 1930's) defined marketing as the set of business activities that direct the flow of goods and services from producer to consumer. Perhaps this was not too surprising since there was a general lack of market offerings that fulfilled basic needs of humans for food, lodging, and clothing. If a firm could get things to market it generally could do well. Similarly in the early days of the internet there was a need for basic information technology infrastructure, much of it consisting of tangible cables, routers, modems and servers and other internet plumbing.

After World War II, marketing thought in the U.S. moved to a *"marketing to"* orientation in which the market and customer was researched and analyzed and then products were produced to meet customer or marketplace needs. However, under this "marketing concept," the customer is exogenous to the firm and viewed as an *operand resource*—a resource to be acted on. The customer was treated as a relatively passive recipient of firm offerings. Similarly once the internet was plumbed it moved to being a distribution vehicle for documents that users would retrieve and read. This became known as Web 1.0, in which the user was relatively passive recipient of document offerings.

In contrast, S-D logic advocates viewing the customer as an operant resource—a resource that is capable of acting on other resources, a collaborative partner who *co-creates value with* the firm (Vargo & Lusch, 2004)--and promotes a *"market with"* philosophy. In S-D logic, *collaboration* between the firm (and relevant partners) and the customer allows for market offerings to

be co-produced. In the internet world this has become known as Web 2.0 and the semantic web. The intersection of S-D logic and Web 2.0 can be characterized as the frontier of E-Novation.

It is not sufficient to have the Internet serve as a distribution mechanism for documents but, rather, it becomes a platform, through which social and economic actors (firms, customers, citizens, etc.) can exchange service and co-create value. That is, it is a platform in which customers are endogenous to value creation. Some of this value occurs because of network effects. Recent IT innovations such as wikis, social bookmarking (tags), mashups, blogs and social networks reflect the "market with" movement that is central to S-D logic. Figure-1 represents a marketing frame of reference for S-D logic.

Briefly the key processes include:

1. Seeing all customers and other exchange partners at the center of the firm's thinking. The centrality of customers and partners is further amplified by viewing them as active collaborators with the firm.

2. Recognizing that the firm needs to draw upon resources that are both internal and external to it and often to do this, resistances need to be overcome.

3. Including customers and partners as helping to co-create the service offering, co-create the firm's value proposition, co-create conversation & dialogue, and co-create the value network and processes, all as part of co-creating value with exchange partners.

A fuller understanding of this marketing framework can be obtained by reviewing the ten foundational premises upon which S-D logic is built.

Figure 1. The s-d logic marketing framework

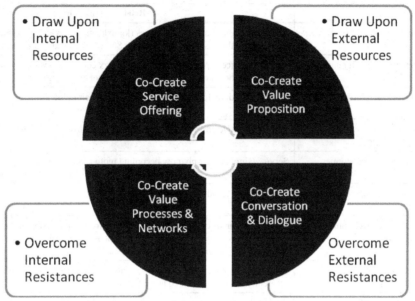

FOUNDATIONS OF S-D LOGIC

Not only does a review of the foundational premises of S-D logic enhance the usefulness of the marketing framework just presented but also it can help one gain creative insights into how to E-Novate by reframing the traditional conceptualization of organizations and businesses. Service-dominant logic is grounded in ten foundational premises; eight of which were initially elaborated in Vargo and Lusch (2004) and the ninth in Vargo and Lusch (2006), and then Vargo and Lusch (2008) added a tenth and updated the initial premises. These are reproduced in Table 1.

Foundational Premise 1

S-D logic defines service as the application of specialized competences (knowledge and skills) for the benefit of another entity or the entity itself (Vargo & Lusch, 2004). Stated more simply, service is the use of one actor's resources for the benefit of another actor. Foundational premise one (FP1), states that *service is the fundamental basis of exchange*. It is thus compatible with the insight

of Frederic Bastiat (1848/1964) that services are exchanged for services and that this is the foundation upon which all economics should be built.

Essentially, as societies advance there is increased specialization of competences and it is these competences or resources in the form of service that are exchanged. Think of a primitive economy in which one family or tribe exchanges wheat for fish that another family or tribe has caught. Is fish being exchanged for wheat as a goods-dominant logic would suggest or is carbohydrate producing competencies being exchanged for protein gathering competencies as S-D logic would suggest? Many E-Novation opportunities deal with developing and exchanging competences directly or embedded in tangible products. One area of particular growth is where individual become part of a internet based community and share their expertise or insights on market offerings, problems they confront such as depression or weight gain, or lifestyle, social, economic or political issues of common interest. It is certainly possible that E-Novation could develop around people directly exchanging service could develop such as an accountant exchanging skills and exper-

Table 1. The ten foundational premises of s-d logic

Foundational Premise	Brief Explanation
FP1. Service is the fundamental basis of exchange.	The application of operant resources (knowledge and skills), "service," as defined in S-D logic, is the basis for all exchange. Service is exchanged for service.
FP2. Indirect exchange masks the fundamental basis of exchange.	Because service is provided through complex combinations of goods, money, and institutions, the service basis of exchange is not always apparent.
FP3. Goods are a distribution mechanism for service provision.	Goods (both durable and non-durable) derive their value through use – the service they provide.
FP4. Operant resources are the fundamental source of competitive advantage.	The comparative ability to cause desired change drives competition.
FP5. All economies are service economies.	Service (singular) is only now becoming more apparent with increased specialization and outsourcing.
FP6. The customer is always a co-creator of value.	Implies value creation is interactional.
FP7. The enterprise cannot deliver value, but only offer value propositions.	Enterprises can offer their applied resources for value creation and collaboratively (interactively) create value following acceptance of value propositions, but can not create and/or deliver value independently.
FP8. A service-centered view is inherently customer oriented and relational.	Because service is defined in terms of customer-determined benefit and co-created it is inherently customer oriented and relational.
FP9. All social and economic actors are resource integrators.	Implies the context of value creation is networks of networks (resource integration).
FP10. Value is always uniquely and phenomenologically determined by the beneficiary.	Value is idiosyncratic, experiential, contextual, and meaning laden.

Source: Based on Stephen L. Vargo and Robert F. Lusch, "Service-Dominant Logic: Continuing the Evolution," *Journal of the Academy of Marketing Sciences* 46(Spring 2008), p.7.

tise with a piano teacher who provides instruction for the accountant's child.

Foundational Premise 2

As economies grow and as societies advance it is relatively infrequent that service is directly exchanged one-to-one (i.e., is bartered) between two actors. Therefore, foundational premise two states that *indirect exchange masks the fundamental basis of exchange*. That is, as economies grow and become more complex, organizations, networks of organizations, tangible products, and money increase in ascendance and these mask the fundamental basis of exchange. Firms find that by having a high division of labor within the firm overall output can be increased and thus efficiency rises. Often these specialized activities are performed on operand tangible matter and, thus, as suggested by Vargo and Lusch (2004),

the matter becomes frozen or embedded with the resources of the worker or creator. As this occurs increasingly in society there are more and more micro-specialized workers that seldom interface with the ultimate customer and thus do not understand the needs and wants of the customer. Because the workers do not get direct feedback they find they can ignore the customer which ends up ultimately hurting the organization. Many E-Novation opportunities enable firms and their partners and customers to deal more directly. Consider for example that, in the past, one had to employ someone to clip newspaper and other articles that mentioned an organization and then analyze these documents for trends. Today one can use Google to feed directly the information that is being published about an organization. Other tools are being developed that automatically analyze this information for positive and negative segments about the organization.

Foundational Premise 3

Foundational premise three states that goods *are distribution mechanisms for service provision.* Knowledge and skills can be transferred (1) directly, (2) through education and training, or (3) indirectly by embedding them in objects. Therefore service is the common denominator and is not separate from tangible goods. When tangible goods are involved, they serve as appliances. It is in the use of the appliance where service becomes evident. An automobile that is driven provides transportation service. A computer including hardware and software that is used provides service. An air conditioner in its use provides cooling service but also a shady tree could do something similar. Goods therefore are not an end but a means to providing a performance that fulfills a need that an actor may have.

E-Novation opportunities can be based around selling the service flow that comes from goods vs. selling the goods per se. A manufacturer of heating and cooling equipment could thus provide temperature control service and charge the beneficiary a fee to maintain the temperature of a building within a established comfort range. To accomplish this the manufacturer would assemble and integrate all of the resources to make the building energy efficient.

Foundational Premise 4

The notion that *operant resources are the fundamental source of competitive advantage* is the fourth foundational premise. The firm that can serve other actors, better then competitors, by using its knowledge, skills, and competencies will gain relative competitive advantage. Operant resources are dynamic and thus knowledge renewal becomes very important. Learning, rather than knowing ascends. A large E-Novation market revolves around assisting firms, customers and other actors in learning or developing operant resources and human resources and specifically

employees and customers are at the fountainhead of a firm's operant resources. It is possible for firms to develop virtual worlds such as in Second Life, in which employees and customers can learn how to interact for positive results. Virtual training and development may become a very large growth opportunity.

Foundational Premise 5

All economies are service economies is the fifth foundational premise. Conventional wisdom is that economies begin as hunter-gatherer, move to agricultural, then to industrial, and then to services and information economies. However, this classification is largely a result of how we have defined services. As noted, services are traditionally defined as the residual of what extractive industries and manufacturing are not. Thus if a firm does not farm, fish, mine or gather and process timber or manufacture goods it is classified as providing an intangible output or services.

An S-D logic definition of service (i.e., the application of resources to benefit another) helps one to see that all economies are service based and that perhaps the traditional classification at best focused on macrospecializations. Agriculture focused on the refinement and application of foraging and hunting knowledge and skills; the industrial economy focused on the refinement of competences for large-scale mass production and organizational management; and the services and information economies focused on the development of competencies about information and the exchange of pure, unembedded knowledge. This foundational premise suggests that E-Novation opportunities exist globally and not just in countries that have low extractive, agriculture and manufacturing employment. Perhaps the biggest opportunity is for countries in their early stages of economic development that are heavily focused on the production of agricultural commodities and to a lesser extent on manufactured goods to become IT and ICT intensive and then develop within their population the skills and knowledge to perform jobs (activities and tasks) that are not reliant on physical labor (such as the processing of medical records or insurance claims or warranty claims). With the decline in the price of computers and cell phones it is certainly possible that in the near future virtually everyone on the planet will be more closely linked in a network of service providers and beneficiaries.

Foundational Premise 6

Foundational premise six states that *the customer is always a cocreator of value*. G-D logic views the firm as a producer of value or utility and the customer through the use of the product as a destroyer (consumer) of value. However, it is only in the use of a product to perform service and the combination of service(s) with other resources that the customer obtains value. Consequently the firm provides the product and the customer the uses of the product and together in this interface value is created. E-Novation opportunities are enhanced when the firm can use information technologies to help the customer co-create value.

Foundational Premise 7

A seventh foundational premise follows from the prior one and states that *the enterprise cannot deliver value, but only offer value propositions*. The intent here is to reinforce that the enterprise cannot unilaterally create and/or deliver value. A value proposition can be thought of as the promised or expected benefits in comparison to expected efforts or costs. Both the offeror and the beneficiary of service collaboratively create value. For a firm to succeed at making a competitively compelling value proposition it should engage potential beneficiaries in dialog and conversation.

E-Novation can be focused on engaging the customer and the firm in co-creating value propositions. Value propositions are another way of stating that the firm needs to balance the

benefits in relation to the total costs (price and cost of acquisition and ownership) of a market offering. The costs of acquisition and ownership are not only influenced by the firm but also by the customer. E-Novation can thus find ways, in which the customer can customize the value proposition to their context – a situation in which a purchaser of a car can decide upon a payment that not only includes the financing of the auto but also bundled together insurance, mobile phone service, fuel and maintenance. Potentially, what the beneficiary might find ideal is paying a fee per mile of usage rather than a fee per month.

Foundational Premise 8

A service-centered view is inherently customer oriented and relational is the eighth foundational premise. Importantly, this is not intended to be a normative statement related to the desirability of repeat patronage, but rather a positive statement of how value is created interactively, exogenously and usually among and in the context created by large numbers of actors, rather than within the firm. That is, with an S-D orientation, value creation is an interactive process and thus the firm and the customer *must be considered in a relational context*. Also, no customer orientation is needed with S-D logic because value is always determined by the beneficiary of service in the unique experience of that benefit and thus it is inherently customer oriented. If the customer and partners of the firm are considered endogenous to the firm then E-Novation can use information technology and especially collaboration technologies to strengthen relationships. A key possibility is digital design studios where customers can assist the firm's design staff in developing new prototypes. Another possibility is where the customers can design or create promotion or advertising content such as in videos or photography to be used by the firm. More extensive possibilities emerge when offerings are seen as relatively discrete "crossing points" in complex, relationally based service ecosystems (see below).

Foundational Premise 9

Foundational premise nine states that *all social and economic actors are resource integrators*. It is tempting to view the customer as only receiving service from a firm's market offering; either directly or with the aid of a good. However, S-D logic places a heavy focus on value-in-use and when an actor uses a resource it almost always uses it in conjunction with other resources. The use of a resource in conjunction with other resources is a process of integration: (1) market and non-market facing resources and (2) resources directly under the control of the actor and indirectly accessible and (3) integrating both tangible and intangible or operand and operant resources.

Consider an actor using the service offering of an internet provider. The actor is integrating this with a home or office computer, home or office space and related equipment, heating and cooling to create a comfortable environment and, payment mechanisms, such as credit or debit cards, to transact economic exchanges, along with norms of appropriate internet protocol and behavior. Resource integration is one of the largest frontiers for E-Novation. In fact, education innovation may be largely about resource integration. For instance being able to lecture to a class but embed your lecture with video clips and current news from the internet. Or consider students taking the same class in a different culture where the students can form discussion groups on the internet. Textbook publishers could reframe their business and provide learning platforms that become the foundation for integration of learning resources.

Foundational Premise 10

Finally the tenth foundational premise is that value is always uniquely and phenomenologically determined by the beneficiary. First this suggests that value is idiosyncratic and unique to each actor; the firm may make the same offering to all but what each beneficiary experiences will be quite different. Second, value is experiential or is obtained via use of the offering as it is integrated with other resources. Third, value is contextual. An actor receiving the offering in one context realizes different value from that in another context. For this reason we have recently been using the term *"value-in-context,"* (see Vargo, 2008) in lieu of the somewhat more G-D logic oriented "value-in-use. Finally, value is meaning laden. The meaning is not only controlled by the beneficiary but is also socially constructed. E-Novation can allow customization to the unique needs of the beneficiary and, thus, represents a major growth opportunity for most businesses. Increasingly the value that actors are experiencing in the use of a firm's market offering is the topic of conversation on the internet. This often occurs through brand communities. E-novation could develop around a service that automatically extracts and analyzes this conversation for key insights into how to better serve the customer.

SERVICE ECOSTSTEMS, DENSITY, AND VALUE-CREATION PLATFORMS

As implied by FP1, FP6, FP 9, and FP10, S-D logic recognizes that value is derived from applied operant resources (competencies) – service – and thus innovation is related to finding new ways to create, combine, and share resources in the context of the customer's other accessible resource (e.g., market-facing, public, and private) to collaboratively create value.

This increase in the ability to exchange relatively pure operant resources, and thus for collaboration in value creation, requires not only a shift in mental model, from G-D logic to S-D logic; it also requires that we zoom out from the a firm-customer dyadic focus to a broader perspective of value creation in which the actors are all

Figure 2. The contextual nature of network-to-network exchange

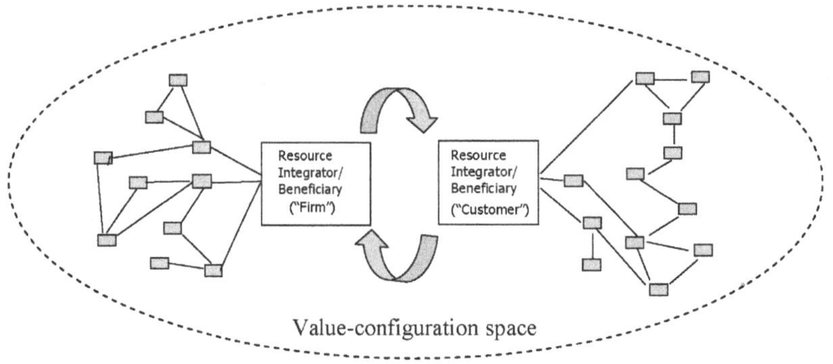

Value-configuration space

Source: Adapted from Vargo, Stephen L. (2008), Customer Integration and Value Creation: Paradigmatic Traps and Perspectives, *Journal of Service Research*, 11, 211-215.

integrating and exchanging applied resources (see FPs 1 and 9). This broader perspective is depicted in Figure 2 (Vargo 2008) and suggests the need for reconceptualizing the venue for and process of value cocreation (FP6).

In the traditional G-D logic model, in which, exchange is conceptualized in terms of units of output, the model of value creation is fairly linear. One firm buys components from supplying firms and then assembles these components to create value. This value is then sold and delivered to customers who consume (destroy) the value and the process starts over.

However, S-D logic focuses instead on *value-creation processes*, rather than *production of units of output*, in which "suppliers," customers, and competitors are all active co-creators of value. This requires thinking in terms of a value network, value constellation (e.g., Normann & Ramierez, 1993) or ecosystem (e.g., Iansiti & Levien, 2004). Increasingly, we are referring to this value-creation space as a *service ecosystem*. A service ecosystem[3] is defined as a loosely coupled, dynamic, spatial-temporal structure formed by the trinity of resources (e.g., information), social and economic actors (i.e., competence creators), and service-relationships that cocreate (i.e., collaboratively and reciprocally) value.

This service ecosystem should be thought of as a living system and living systems constantly regenerate themselves by sensing and responding (Haeckel, 1999) across space and time to be of service to others. To be spontaneously sensing and responding, the firm needs to be agile and adaptable.

Density Creation and Platforms

The networked, service-ecosystem conceptualization of the market requires reconceptualizations regarding the (usually joint) output (tangible or intangible) of the actors. In an S-D logic world, "goods" and "services" don't capture what is provided. Value propositions are promises and service and value cocreation are the (anticipated) outcome but not the output. Clearly, it relates to configurations of resources (operant and operand). Thus, one possible conceptualization of these configurations is in terms of *density*.

Normann (2001, p.27) refers to maximum density as the best (necessary) combination of resources "mobilized for a particular situation— e.g., for a customer at a given time in a given place—independent of location, to create the optimum value/cost result." Think of it as follows: At a given time and place, can the focal firm bring and integrate all of the resources necessary to co-create the best possible value? When it can, there is maximum density.

Arguably, the business model that currently approaches maximum density is the internet search models, such as Google. An individual anywhere in the world, with a PC appliance connected to the WWW, can get access to the resources to answer to virtually any question on demand. Consider asking the same question and seeking an answer twenty five years ago or one-hundred or a thousand years ago. Not surprisingly, the potential for density creation increases as the ability to liquefy information resources rises.

In a service-ecosystem conceptualization, the offering of the firm (product in G-D logic terms) becomes a "platform," a *density-potential foundation* upon which customizable, actor-specific densities can be created as directed by the beneficiary. Again, Google's provides a good example; its search engine is a platform for customized density creation through resource access and resource integration.

S-D LOGIC, SERVICE ECOSTSTEMS, AND E-NOVATION

The traditional goods-centered, firm-focused model of value creation points toward concepts of innovation in which the firm finds novel methods of design and manufacturing, with an emphasis on efficient production for maximum profits. By contrast, in a service-centered and ecosystems-focused model of value cocreation, innovation involves finding new ways of collaboratively creating and facilitating customized, densities.

We have already indicated how Google is a good example of creating a platform for firm-supplied, customer-defined, resource integration (FP9). A more advanced example is the Google Mashup Editor, which not only allows finding and using diverse resources but also integrating them in novel, user-defined ways to create new

densities. Other good examples of platforms are eBay auctions and Apple's iPod. Each represents a prime example of how firms can create value for themselves by focusing on the process of facilitating the resource-integrative, value co-creative activities of other parties, rather than on the internal creation of value for other parties.

As the "sense and respond" (Haeckel, 1999) mantra implies, collaborative innovation does not have to be firm initiated. Rather, it often is initiated by and requires assisting in (potential) customers' own auto-innovation process. For example, much of the innovation in kitesurfing has been taken place through the interaction of lead-users in online communities, what von Hippel (2006) identifies as the democratization of innovation. Similar examples can be found in the social networking of brand and fan (e.g., sport) communities.

Since value creation is mostly operant resource driven, innovation is also information centered. Thus, IT and ICT play central, rather than supportive roles and much of innovation becomes E-Novation. The importance of E-Novation is amplified as the scope of ecosystems increases, which can also be thought of as an outcome of E-Novation.

There are eight primary reasons why IT growth allows for the expansion of service eco-systems and E-Novation and thus reinforcing the benefits of adopting S-D logic[4].

1. As information technology increases, the service potential of tangible things become liquefied (e.g. digital manufacturing, start/smart parts that embed intelligence, collaborative design through virtual modeling, idea generation through virtual conference rooms, product lifecycle management (PLM) to support liquefication).

2. As information technology increases goods become embedded with microprocessors and intelligence and become improved platforms for service provision.

3. As information technology increases the ability to self-serve rises.

4. As information technology increases the ability to serve others rises.

5. As the ability to communicate increases the need to transport decreases.

6. As the ability to communicate increases the ability to know customers and suppliers rises.

7. As the ability to communicate increases, opportunities for collaboration increase.

8. As the ability to communicate increases, at lower and lower costs, coordination between firms becomes more efficient and responsive.

Individually and collectively, these eight drivers of improved IT suggest an increased opportunity for and growth of E-Novation. This is because improved IT lowers the cost of actors collaborating and integrating resources and at the same time increases the number of actors around the world that can participate in developing and implementing innovations.

CONCLUDING COMMENTS

As information became dislodgeable, transportable, and exchangeable, apart from people and physical matter, the stage became set for rethinking our understanding of markets in terms of the application of specialized information and service ecosystems, rather than in terms of goods and supply chains. Likewise, it sets the stage for new forms of service ecosystems and value propositions to emerge and proliferate, especially in terms of resource-integration platforms that facilitate value creation through the creation of additional resource-integration platforms.

None of this is purely new. Rather, although economic and social networks have existed since humans began to specialize and the division of labor led to markets, it has become more obvious, if not more salient, in the last quarter century as a function of the explosive growth of IT

and ICT, which some argue together represent a meta-force altering business and society (Benkler, 2006; Brown & Duguid, 2000). Thus, so has the understanding of value as being something that is created collaboratively and emergent, rather than something created unalterably and embedded. This collaborative nature of value creation, as reflected in finding new ways of co-conceptualizing, co-creating, and uniquely and phenomenologically determining value, is reflected in the growth of E-Novation. We offer S-D logic as a more robust foundation for understanding and advancing E-Novation, than traditional models based on the exchange of goods.

REFERENCES

Bastiat, F. (1964). Selected essays on political economy. In de Huszar, G. B. (Ed.), *Seymour Cain reprint*. Princeton, NJ: D. Van Nordstrand.

Benkler, Y. (2006). *The wealth of networks: How social production transforms markets and freedom*. New Haven, CT: Yale University Press.

Brown, J. S. a., & Duguid, P. (2000). Balancing act: How to capture knowledge without killing it. *Harvard Business Review*, *78*(3), 73–80.

Constantin, J. A., & Lusch, R. F. (1994). *Understanding resource management*. Oxford, OH: The Planning Forum.

Haeckel, S. (1999). *Adaptive enterprise: Creating and leading sense-and-respond organizations*. Boston, MA: Harvard School of Business.

Iansiti, M., & Levien, R. (2004). Strategy as ecology. *Harvard Business Review*, *82*(3), 68–78.

Malthus, T. (1798). *An essay on the principle of population*. London, UK: J. Johnson, St. Paul's Church-Yard.

Mokyr, J. (2002). *The gifts of Athena: Historical origins of the knowledge economy*. Princeton, NJ: Princeton University Press.

Normann, R. (2001). *Reframing business: When the map changes the landscape*. New York, NY: John Wiley & Sons.

Normann, R., & Ramirez, R. (1993). From value chain to value constellation: Designing interactive strategy. *Harvard Business Review*, (Jul/Aug): 65–77.

Smith, A. (2000). *The nature and causes of the wealth of nations*. New York, NY: The Modern Library.

Vargo, S. L. (2008). Customer integration and value creation: Paradigmatic traps and perspectives. *Journal of Service Research, 11*, 211–215. doi:10.1177/1094670508324260

Vargo, S. L., & Lusch, R. F. (2004). Evolving to a new dominant logic for marketing. *Journal of Marketing, 68*, 1–17. doi:10.1509/jmkg.68.1.1.24036

Vargo, S. L., & Lusch, R. F. (2008). Service-dominant logic: Continuing the evolution. *Journal of the Academy of Marketing Science, 36*(1), 1–10. doi:10.1007/s11747-007-0069-6

Vargo, S. L., & Lusche, R. F. (2006). Service-dominant logic: What it is, what it is not, what it might be. In Lusch, R. F., & Vargo, S. L. (Eds.), *The service-dominant logic of marketing: Dialog, debate and directions* (pp. 43–56). Armonk, NY: M.E. Sharpe, Inc.

Vargo, S. L., & Morgan, F. W. (2005). Services in society and academic thought: A historical analysis. *Journal of Macromarketing, 25*(1), 42–53. doi:10.1177/0276146705275294

Von Hippel, E. (2005). *Democratizing innovation*. Cambridge, MA: MIT Press.

Zeithaml, V. A., Parasuraman, A., & Berry, L. L. (1985). Problems and strategies in services marketing. *Journal of Marketing, 49*(Spring), 33–46. doi:10.2307/1251563

Zimmerman, E. (1951). *World resources and industries*. New York, NY: Harper and Row.

ENDNOTES

[1] Considerable portions of this chapter draw upon: Stephen L. Vargo and Robert F. Lusch, "Evolving to a New Dominant Logic for Marketing," *Journal of Marketing* 68(January 2004), pp. 1-17; Robert F. Lusch, Stephen Vargo and Alan J. Malter, "Taking a Leadership Role in Global Marketing Management," *Organizational Dynamics* 35 (3, 2006), pp. 264-278; Robert F. Lusch, Stephen Vargo, and Matthew O'Brien, "Competing Through Service: Insights from Service-Dominant Logic," *Journal of Retailing* 83(2007, 1), pp. 5-18; Stephen L. Vargo and Robert F. Lusch, "Service-Dominant Logic: Continuing the Evolution," *Journal of the Academy of Marketing Science* 36(Spring 2008), pp.1-10; Robert F. Lusch, Stephen L. Vargo and Mohan Tanniru, "Converging on a Service-Dominant Logic: Organizational Survival and Growth in a Value Network," *Journal of the Academy of Marketing Science* (forthcoming).

[2] Resources other then information can also be potentially liquefied. For example when energy from coal is liquefied it can be more easily transported.

[3] We have little problem if rather then service eco-system one labels this as a value constellation or value network; however, the systems nature is important to retain.

[4] Roland Rust, in a variety of public presentations, has identified some of these factors and this has encouraged us to identify others.

Chapter 2
E–Marketplaces:
Taxonomy of the New Collaborative Information Platform

Kayvan Miri Lavassani
Carleton University, Canada

Bahar Movahedi
Carleton University, Canada

Vinod Kumar
Carleton University, Canada

ABSTRACT

This chapter provides a review of the historical evolution and development in the field of Electronic Marketplaces (EMs) and explores the classifications of EMs. The authors employ a systematic approach to propose a comprehensive definition of EMs and their application with reference to recent advances in the study of EMs. Based on the review of the most cited definitions of EM in the literature of the past three decades, we propose a comprehensive definition of EM in this chapter. This chapter also identifies several classifications of EMs. There is a gap in the literature for a multi-dimensional classification system of EMs. Therefore, for the purpose of further exploration of the notion of EMs, this chapter provides an explicit review of the different classification models of EMs and presents a nine-dimensional taxonomy of EMs. The chapter concludes with a discussion of the future trends in the field of EMs and a chapter summary.

INTRODUCTION

The development of Electronic Marketplaces (EMs) is tightly linked with the advancements in telecommunication technologies and collaboration platforms. The roots of EM can be traced to the mid-1940s when an EM known as Selevision was founded for Florida citrus fruit (Cassidy, 1967). From the very beginning, the EM assisted in the purchasing functions as a communication platform for vendors. However, the EMs did not receive much attention until the development of a tele-

DOI: 10.4018/978-1-60566-394-4.ch002

phone auction for butcher hogs in Ontario, Canada, during the early 1960s. This auction operated manually and the market used as a clearinghouse. During the 1960s, thanks to the development of Electronic Data Interchange (EDI) systems, Schrader et al. (1968) proposed a computerized egg exchange market, which received much attention in 1978 when the U.S. Department of Agriculture financed a pilot project for the first computerized EM (Peer, 1976; Henderson, 1984). During this time, agricultural economists such as Bailey and White (1974) proposed the application of such a technology in other markets (Berglund, 1977). For example, Felton (1970, 1974) proposed the use of this technology in car market using teletype (Berglund, 1977).

In recent decades, with the advancements in communication technologies, EMs have been implemented in a more advanced communication platform and with more integration. Figure 1 shows the historical evolution of the developments in organizational electronic networks. EDI systems of the 1960s were the first electronic information platforms widely used in organizations. With advancements in the computation, communication, and data storage technologies, Enterprise Resource Planning (ERP) systems were widely employed during the 1990s. It is important to mention that the new technologies in this evolution process do not replace the previous information platforms, rather the new technologies use the previous platforms to advance the organizational electronic networks. During the 1990s, the organizational electronic networks expanded beyond organizational boundaries, and web-based trading exchanges started to be employed for promoting inter-organizational integration. During this time, internet-based collaborative systems – including EMs – attracted the attention of many businesses and scholars.

The growth of the Internet as an e-business platform has highlighted the use of EMs. The application of EMs has been expanded from "baseline interaction and directory services to specialty market services, such as dynamic trading, [and] cooperative supply-chain integration and management" (Ghenniwa, Huhns, and Shen, 2005). In recent years, the notion of EM has evolved through the exploitation of intelligent agents. Several authors have considered Kasbah as one of the first agent base EMs. The MIT media lab first introduced Kasbah in October 1996 (Chavez and Maes, 1996; Maes et al., 1999; Lau, 2007). Many researchers have highlighted the role of software agents on the effectiveness of EM (Lau et.al, 2008). These agents can identify the need for transaction, conduct negotiations, and finalize the transactions without human intervention (Louta et. al., 2008).

During the late 1990s, the number of new EMs grew rapidly, and by late 2001, the operation of 2,233 EMs was reported worldwide (Laseter et al., 2001). However, the EMs faced significant challenges in regards to adoption of the new technology, "plugging in suppliers and customers," and "compliance and performance" (Willcocks et al., 2002). Consequently, many of these EMs faced significant challenges in the first few years of the twenty-first century. White et al. (2007) reported that by mid-2006 only 750 active EMs were registered in the directory of the eMarket Services trade organization. This number declined to 630

Figure 1. Development of organizational electronic networks

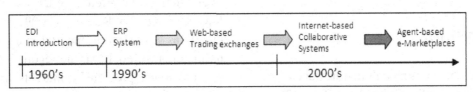

Adapted from McNichols and Brennan (2006), and modified by the authors of this chapter

by February 2008 (Muylle, and Basu, 2008), to 616 by May 2008, and to 604 by February 2009.

While the number of EMs has decreased in the past few years, some mature EMs have expanded and developed to become prominent and strong e-commerce platforms. One example is the Canadian-based Mediagrif Interactive Technologies Inc., which manages 13 networks serving about 50,000 businesses worldwide. Broker-Forum and Globalwinespirits are two of the EMs that this company established. Broker-Forum, established in 1996, provides one of the largest EMs for electronic components. Since 2000, Globalwinespirits has helped to connect many wine producers and global markets globally. Another example is Covisint, which was established by a consortium of automakers. Established in 1999, Covisint connected the supply-chain of General Motors, Ford Motor Company, DaimlerChrysler[1], Nissan, and Renault. With advancement of communication technologies, the key to the success of EMs remains the ability of the EM operators to expand the network of buyers and sellers. This challenge is more apparent for EMs that have not been founded or supported by major market players.

This chapter presents a multi-dimensional classification system for EMs. In the quest to do so, the following section employs a systematic approach to propose a comprehensive definition of EM that can best describe the applications of EMs concerning the recent advancements in this area. The second section of this chapter provides a precise review of the different classification models of EMs and presents a nine-dimensional classification model. The final sections of the chapter contain a discussion of future trends in the field of EMs and the concluding remarks.

BACKGROUND

EMs are new business models that are developing and changing rapidly (Dai and Kauffman, 2003; Singh and Waddell, 2003). The terms Electronic Hub (e-Hub), Electronic Intermediary (EIM), and Internet-based electronic-markets have also been used to refer to this concept (Muylle and Basu, 2008; Kaplan and Sawhney, 2000; Rosson, 2000). Traditionally, markets have three roles: facilitating the transaction, matching buyers and sellers, and providing institutional infrastructure (Bakos, 1998). As a result, some scholars consider the EMs as a form of the business-to-business type of e-commerce (e.g. see Lau et al., 2008).

EM as a business model is based on the notion that it can help organizations to (Eng, 2004):

- Streamline complex business processes,
- Gain efficiencies,
- Aggregate buyers and sellers in a single contact point,
- Allow participant organizations to enjoy greater economies of scale and liquidity,
- Buy or sell anything easily, quickly and cost effectively, [and]
- Eliminate geographical barriers, and expand globally to reap profits in new markets."

The literature presents a number of definitions for EMs, which reflects how academia has viewed the concept. Table 1 displays the most cited EM definitions in the literature and their main themes.

A review of the available literature on the "types" of EMs shows that the existing definitions lack the required level of generalizability. For example, McCoy and Sarhan (1988) view EM as an open system, and Petersen et al. (2007) consider EM as a neutral marketplace, while our study of the types of EMs shows that many EMs are closed-EMs and not necessarily neutral. Alternatively, definitions offered by Bakos (1998) and Kwon, Yang and Rowley (2009) view EMs merely as a transaction facilitator and overlook the important role of EM in the negotiation process. As mentioned previously, markets have three roles: facilitating the transaction, matching buyers

Table 1. Definition of EM

Author	Definition	Main theme(s)
McCoy and Sarhan (1988)	An EM separates the negotiating function from the physical transfer of the product or commodity in which the market trades. It can manage buyers and sellers' offers and bids, as well as moving products directly from sellers to buyers. The system is open to all buyers and sellers, regardless of their location, and can provide instant market information to all traders.	Open system, separation of negotiation function from physical transfer
Bakos (1998)	An EM facilitates the exchange of information, goods, services, and payments. In this exchange process, EMs create economic value for buyers, sellers, market intermediaries, and society at large.	Exchange facilitator
Bakos (1991)	EM is an inter-organizational information system that allows the participating buyers and sellers to exchange information about prices and product offerings.	Inter-organizational information system
Bradley and Peters (1997)	EM is a public listing of products and their attributes from all suppliers in an industry segment that is available to all potential buyers.	Public listing
Schmid and Lindemann (1998)	EM is a media that fosters market-based exchanges between agents in all transaction phases.	Agent-based transaction
Segev *et al.* (1999)	Compared to many other electronic procurement solutions, EMs represent a relatively neutral position between buyer and seller, providing services to both sides of a transaction. An EM represents a virtual place where buyers and sellers meet to exchange goods and services.	A neutral e-procurement solution
Dai and Kauffman (2000)	EMs function as digital intermediaries that focus on industry verticals or specific business functions. They set up marketplaces where firms participate in buying and selling activities after they obtain membership.	Digital intermediaries
Mueller (2000)	EMs allow buyers and sellers to exchange information about product offerings and prices bid and asked.	Exchange information about products
Kaplan and Sawhney (2000)	EM is a meeting-point where suppliers and buyers can interact online.	Meeting point
Lipis *et al.* (2000)	EM is an Internet-based solution that links businesses that are interested in buying and selling related goods or services from one another. EMs can be distinguished from a procurement or distribution system insofar as it must be neutral, considering the interests of both buyers and sellers in its governance.	Neutral, Internet-based solution
IBM, i2, and Ariba (2000)	A many-to-many, web-based trading and collaboration solution that enables companies to more efficiently buy, sell, and collaborate on a global scale.	Web-based efficient global Collaboration solution
Archer and Gebauer (2000)	EM is a virtual marketplace where buyers and suppliers meet to exchange information about product and service offerings, and to negotiate and implement business transactions.	Virtual place for negotiation and transaction
Fortino, Garro, and Russo (2004)	EM is an e-commerce environment that offers new channels and business models for buyers and sellers to effectively and efficiently trade goods and services over the internet.	Effective and efficient channel and business model
Hadaya (2004)	EM is an intermediary that allows buyers and sellers to meet on an electronic platform that rests on the Internet infrastructure in order to exchange information about products/services, conduct transactions online, and adhere to other value-added services offered by the intermediary.	An intermediary based on electronic platform
Petersen et al. (2007)	EM is a neutral, web-based location where businesses can conduct buying and selling transactions for goods or services.	Neutral, web-based location
Kwon et al. (2009)	EM is virtual marketplace on the Internet where organizations can conduct economic transactions.	Virtual marketplace for economic transactions

and sellers, and providing institutional infrastructure (Bakos, 1998). A comprehensive definition of EM needs to specifically address these three functions. We propose the following definition for the EMs. Our proposed definition uses the main points of the previously mentioned definitions and focuses on the application of EM as a collaborative medium (we will present more discussion of the different types and applications of EMs later in this chapter):

E-Marketplaces are effective and efficient collaborative, Internet-based[2] institutional infrastructures for inter-organizational and intra-organizational negotiation and transaction.

This defines the role of EMs as a collaborative and enabler medium. The effectiveness of an EM is defined by the ability of the EM to facilitate the transaction, match buyers and sellers, and provide institutional infrastructure (Bakos, 1998). In this definition, efficiency is defined in relation to the timeliness and cost of EMs.

It is important to mention that the early studies in this area (for example see Henderson, 1984) referred to the concept of EMs, as "electronic marketing." However, in this chapter we differentiate the concept of electronic marketing from EMs. Electronic marketing in recent literature (Peterson, 1997; Strauss et al, 2003; Reedy and Schullo, 2004; Zappala, and Gray, 2006, p.139) is specifically concerned with the process of marketing planning, situation analysis, and marketing implementation accomplished or facilitated through the application of "electronic devices, appliances, tools, techniques, technologies and or systems" (Peterson, 1997). While the studies of electronic marketing concerns the wide variety of activities associated with these three processes in/or associated with an electronic environment, EMs are one of the electronic environments where different interrelated activities occur; these include, but are not limited to, marketing, procurement, information sharing, negotiation, and transaction. In other words, while electronic marketing is a form of *marketing*, the EM is a *business environment*.

The following section provides a clear review of the different classification models of EMs and presents a nine-dimensional classification model.

TAXONOMY ELECTRONIC MARKETPLACES

One of the fundamental themes in studying EMs is exploring the various types of EMs. A number of researchers have proposed different classification of EMs. However, considering that EMs can be classified from various dimensions, there is a need for a multi-dimensional classification model of EMs. It seems that this area of study lacks a comprehensive classification of EMs. This section provides an explicit discussion of our proposed taxonomy of EMs.

EMs can be differentiated by using different perspectives. Based on a comprehensive literature review, nine criteria for classifying EMs were identified. Figure 2 displays the nine dimensions for determining the different types of EMs. In this section, we introduce and describe each dimension for a taxonomy of EMs.

Type of Parties: Business, Customer, and Government

Perhaps one of the most common classifications of EMs is the taxonomy of the EM based on the types of parties involved in the transactions. Generally, three types of parties can be assumed for any transaction: business, customer (final consumer of the finished product/service), and government (Coppel, 2000). There are nine possible combinations of these groups, and each identifies one type of EM (Table 2). In some of the recent literature, various authors have also used the term peer-to-peer (P2P) in order to emphasise the neutrality of the marketplace (i.e., Ragone, Straccia, Noia, Sciascio and Donini, 2009)

It is important to mention that while some scholars consider the EMs as a form of B2B type of e-commerce (Lau et al., 2008), others (Standing et al., 2006; Kwon et al., 2009) believe that EMs can assume not only B2B but also other forms such as B2C or C2B. The focus of this

Figure 2. Criterions for classifying EMs

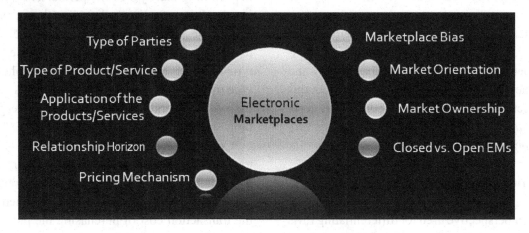

Table 2. Types of parties involved in electronic commerce

	Government	*Business*	*Consumer*
Government	G2G	G2B	G2C
Business	B2G	B2B	B2C
Consumer	C2G	C2B	C2C

chapter is on the B2B type of EM as one of the most popular types of EMs.

Type of Product/Service: Vertical vs. Horizontal

A classification of EMs can also be based on the types of products/services that are traded in the EM. From this perspective, EMs can be categorized into horizontal and vertical EMs (Dai and Kauffman, 2000; Kaplan and Sawhney, 2000; Madanmohan et al., 2005; Kwon et al., 2009). Vertical EMs, also known as *industry-specific* or *sector-specific* EMs, focus on aggregating the supply and demand of products/services in a specific industry. The primary goal of these marketplaces is optimizing the buyer-seller relationship (Martina and Kia, 2007; Yu and Tao, 2007). In horizontal EMs, also known as *functional* EMs, the primary goal of the marketplace is optimizing specific function in organizations through

facilitating cross-industry transactions (Grieger, 2003). The horizontal type of EM is used for products/services that are common among several industries. One example of the horizontal type of EMs is the previously mentioned Broker Forum (www.brokerforum.com), which is dedicated to the trade of electronic components across a wide range of industries.

Application of the Products/Services

Another way to differentiate EMs is based on the application of products/services offered in the vertical or horizontal EMs. From this perspective, EMs can be classified into two categories: a) EMs that provide direct goods; and b) EMs that provide in-direct goods. Direct goods (Murtaza, et al., 2004), also known as *manufacturing inputs*, are products/services that are used in production and are usually, obtained from vertical EMs (Kaplan and Sawhney, 2000). Input raw material is an example of direct goods. In contrast, indirect goods, also known as *repair and operating inputs* (Kaplan and Sawhney, 2000; Kwon et al. 2009) are used for support of production process and are usually bought in from horizontal EMs (Murtaza, et al., 2004). Examples of this type of EM include computer network maintenance, and operations repair and maintenance.

Relationship Horizon

Another criteria used to identify different types of EMs, is the structure and horizon of relationship between the firms and EMs (Kaplan and Sawhney, 2000; Murtaza, et al., 2004). From this perspective, an EM can be viewed as a *long-term systematic sourcing* solution, or a *short-term spot sourcing* solution.

Pricing Mechanism

Another perspective used for differentiating EMs is the pricing mechanism employed in EMs. Based on the pricing mechanism, EMs can be categorized into two groups: EMs with fixed pricing mechanisms (EMFP) and EMs with variable pricing mechanisms (EMVP) (Kaplan and Sawhney, 2000; Schmid, 1999; Kambil and Heck, 2002; Grieger, 2003; Grieger, 2004; Shen and Su, 2007; Muylle and Basu, 2008).

In EMFP, the price of products and services is fixed, although the prices may have pre-set and defined variations based on the quantities traded. Electronic Catalogues (e-Catalogues) are the most common forms of EMs with fixed price strategies. This type of EM is popular in markets where supply and/or demand are fragmented and the marketplace aggregates the supply and/or demand (Skjøtt-Larsen et al., 2003; Kwon et al., 2009). In contrast, in the EMVP, the buyer or seller offers no pre-set price. Many of the EMVP work like a clearinghouse similar to stock market. Electronic auctions (e-auction) are the most popular forms of EMVP. We describe different types of e-auctions in this section. However, it is noteworthy to mention that in some EMVPs that have no pre-set prices the buyers and/or sellers can provide their upper and/or lower-limit price range. In this case, when the EM recognizes a match between the quoted price offered by the seller and the requested price by the buyer for an item, the EM informs the parties of the match. In some EMVPs, while the upper and lower price limits of buyers and sellers are kept confidential by the EM operators, the parties involved can negotiate online directly via email, instant messaging, or through a software agent to reach an agreement. One example of the latter type of EM is www.brokerforum.com. The last type of EMs is not categorized as EMFPs, since the sellers/buyers offered/requested a pre-set price range instead of a pre-set absolute value.

Comparison of EMFP and EMVP has been a topic of interest to some researchers in this area. Vakrat and Seidmann (1999) explored the transaction cost of EMFP vs. EMVP and concluded that the transaction cost of purchasing the products/services from e-auctions (as one of the popular forms of EMVP) may be relatively higher than e-catalogues (as a popular form of EMFP). This is because there are four additional costs that are usually associated with the e-auction transactions: auction membership cost, monitoring costs, delay costs, and search costs. Auction membership cost includes the costs associated with learning the auction rules and the sign-up cost. Monitoring cost refers to the cost of monitoring the price changes and deciding on the maximum biding price. Delay cost refers to the fact that "not all items in the catalogue are being auctioned off continuously" and, therefore, "consumers incur... a consumption delay cost when they have to wait for the right auction to conclude" (Dans, 2002). Search cost includes the opportunity cost of the time that customers spend in finding a particular EM (Dans, 2002). It is important to note that the cost factors of auctions are most applicable to B2C transactions with less frequency and little to no integration between the EM participants. Another important difference between EMVP and EMFP pricing mechanisms is that in EMs with a variable price mechanism, buyers and sellers can incorporate price-discrimination into the marketplace. In addition, it is important to note that bargaining opportunity (bargaining on price) by definition can only be incorporated into EMs with a variable price mechanism. The following paragraphs provide a more detailed description of the concepts of EMFP and EMVP.

Fixed pricing mechanism: The EMs that employ a fixed pricing mechanism are not equipped with a self-price adjustment mechanism for achieving specific goals (e.g., market clearance, profit maximization, and cost minimization). A fixed pricing mechanism is best for the markets where vendors and buyers are highly fragmented. The application of this pricing mechanism is most common in electronic catalogues (Grieger, 2003). Since "a price list is often obsolete by the time it gets printed" (McNealy, 2001), EMs that use the fixed pricing mechanism are more effective as a means of information sharing and collaboration, rather than a transactional medium (Grieger, 2003). According to McNealy, the CEO of Sun Microsystems, "the Internet is rendering fixed prices obsolete." The increase in the use and application of the Internet is shaping the EMs more and more toward a free market, in which the fixed-pricing mechanism is "an endangered species" (McNealy, 2001).

Variable pricing mechanism (Auction): The EMs using the variable pricing mechanism – also known as an auction or market-driven exchange in EM literature – have self-price adjustment mechanisms that determine the market value of the product/services based on supply and/or demand. This pricing mechanism is appropriate for EMs that aim for collaboration and defined financial goals – such as market clearance, profit maximization, and cost minimization. B2B auctions, specifically, have increased the competitiveness of businesses through more transparency and high efficiency (Kinney, 2000). B2B EMs have enabled many companies that heretofore could not compete on price and quality not only to survive but also to stand out among their competitors. For better understanding of the variable pricing mechanism, the following section describes different types of auctions.

Auctions are stylized markets with predefined and transparent rules (Rasmusen, 2001, 2007). The word auction comes from the Latin word *auctus,* which means an increase. The roots of auctions can be traced back to 500 BC in Babylon (Smeltzer and Carr, 2003). Since then, new forms of auction have developed and with the advancement of communications technology and, consequently, the development of e-commerce things changed even more. The auctions used in EMs – whether the marketplace is a B2B, B2C, or C2C – are known as electronic auctions or e-auctions. Our review of literature showed that the term e-auctions was first observed in the work of Berglund (1977), where she described the proposal of Felton (1974) for using a master teletype (teletype auction) in car market.

Selection of the appropriate auction design is one of the most important factors affecting the success of any EM. A survey of more than 350 EMs showed that bad auction design – in addition to excessive squeeze of market participants' profit – is the major cause of EM failure (Shen and Su, 2007). For better understanding of the functioning of auctions in markets, this section describes different types of auctions. Numerous types of auctions are being used in traditional markets and, interestingly, many of them have been employed in EMs. E-auctions can be differentiated based on the pricing and bargaining schemas (Morali et al., 2005). In an empirical study of 301 business models for auctions, Dans (2002) identified 11 types of auctions and their distribution in the online world. Table 3 and Figure 3, respectively, represent detail description and the use of different types of auctions.

The English, Yankee, Reverse, and Online-Dutch are among the most popular e-Auctions (Dans, 2002). Figure 4 illustrates the use of e-auctions across different categories of e-commerce (B2B, B2C and C2C).

Three common auction mechanisms are buyer-biding auctions, seller-biding auctions, and neutral auctions. These three auction mechanisms are described in the following paragraphs.

Table 3. Types of auctions

Auction	Description
Double Auction (continuous and sealed)	Similar to NASDAQ, buyers and sellers make real-time offers, which clear at market price. Using this format, both sellers and buyers submit bids, which are then ranked from highest to lowest, to generate demand and supply profiles. From these profiles, the maximum quantity exchanged can be determined by matching sell offers (starting with the lowest price and moving up) with demand bids (starting with the highest price and moving down).
Double Dutch (online)	Double Dutch auction is a special type of auction designed to handle situations where a seller has a number of identical items to sell. The seller should specify the minimum price (or starting bid) and the exact number of items that are available at that price. The bidders bid at or above that minimum price for the number of items that they are interested in buying. That is, bidders submit both the number of units they wish to buy, and the price they are willing to bid per unit.
Dutch (traditional)/ AutoMarkDown/ Descending Auction	In this type of auction, the bidding starts at a high price that is progressively lowered until a buyer claims the item by shouting "mine!" The equivalent, in modern times, has been to press a button that stops an automatic clock at an acceptable price.
English	The seller announces an initial low bid, which is progressively increased until demand fails to match the fixed amount at auction.
Japanese	The price rises at set increments and participants drop out until only the winning bidder remains. Japanese auction can be considered equivalent to the English auction. The main advantage in this type of auction is that the system is more "automatic" – since the increments are set – so it is usually faster.
Name Your own Price	Customers make an offer to a seller or group of sellers for goods based on their estimate of the sellers' lowest acceptable bid.
Quick Win	A seller can enter his/her product into a quick win auction by specifying a minimum price that he/she will accept. When a buyer agrees to pay that amount the item is sold immediately, which is considered a quick win.
Reverse Auction	Reverse Auction is a buyer-driven auction where sellers, rather than buyers, compete to offer the lowest price for goods.
First Price Sealed bid	This type of auction is normally a sealed bid auction rather than an open bid auction. Bidders submit written bids in ignorance of all others, bids are opened simultaneously, and the highest bid is declared the winner.
Second Price Sealed bid	This type of auction is also a sealed bid auction. Bidders submit written bids in ignorance of all others. When a single item is auctioned, the highest bidder is awarded the item at a price equal to the highest unsuccessful bid. Hence, this type of auction is called the second price auction.
Yankee	A Yankee Auction is a variation of the Dutch Auction (Online Version) where successful bidders pay what they bid as opposed to paying the price determined by the lowest qualified bidder.

Adapted from: Dans (2002)

Figure 3. Use of auction mechanisms

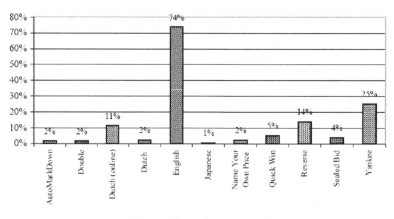

Adapted from: Dans (2002)

Figure 4. Use of auction mechanisms

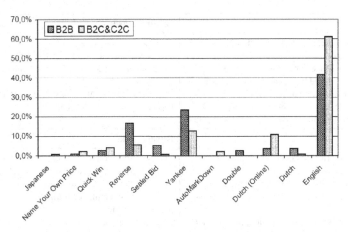

Adapted from: Dans (2002)

Buyer-bidding auctions, also known as forward auctions (Smeltzer and Carr, 2003) and English progressive auction (Vickrey, 1961; Smeltzer and Carr, 2003), are traditionally the most common types of auctions. They count for more than 40 percent of the total B2B EMs (Figure 4). Buyer-bidding auctions operate on the basis of many-to-one relationships, where there is one seller of the product/service and there are a number of potential buyers who bid on the product(s)/service(s). It is important to note that, depending on the EM regulations, the bids can be in the form of an absolute dollar value or of a price range. The buyer-bidding auctions can be open auctions or closed auctions. Closed auctions are also known as sealed auctions (Vickrey, 1961). In open auctions the bidders (or in some cases any third party) have access to the absolute value of almost all of the bids on a product/service in EMs. EBay auctions are one example of open auctions where all of the bids are open. However, the absolute value of the highest bidder is not open. In closed auctions, the bids of potential buyers are not available to any third party or even to other buyers. However, in some auctions the bids become accessible after the auction is closed.

Seller-biding auctions, also known as reverse auctions, are one-to-many relations that have become more popular in the past several years (Smeltzer and Carr, 2003). This type of auction is most popular where there is a one-sided market structure – oligopoly – in which there is only one buyer and several sellers (Kinney, 2000). Smeltzer and Carr (2003) studied the risks and conditions of the success of using reverse auctions from both the buyers' and the sellers' perspectives. Reasons for using reverse auctions and the risks involved have been displayed in Table 4.

Neutral auctions are also known as classical bid-ask neutral marketplaces (Kinney, 2000). In these auctions, a many-to-many relationship exists between buyers and sellers in the sense that more than one seller can offer a product/service and more than one buyer can bid on the product/service, just like the stock exchange markets. This pricing mechanism is suitable for EMs where a many-to-many relationship exists on highly standardized products/services. Supply and demand determine the price through the "invisible hand" (Adam Smith, 1776). One example of these types of EMs is the Canadian based Broker Forum, which is specialized for electronic components (Kinney, 2000). In these EMs, the EM operator can easily maintain the anonymity of the buyers and sellers, especially in closed EMs. In most cases, the identity of buyer and seller is not im-

Table 4. Reasons for using reverse auctions and the risks involved

Suppliers' reasons	Buyers' reasons
- New business: promises of increased business and improved communication about the market - Market penetration: Easier when seller can see market prices - Cycle time reduction: time reduced between bidding and winning the business, less paper work, and buyer and seller - Inventory management: seller can better plan inventory level through product scheduling – less time lost between bid and sale	- Reduced purchase prices: 5% to 12% price reductions common - Administrative costs: reduced the time to process the RFQ by 25% to 35% - Inventory levels: allowed inventory to be quickly replenished, thus less safety stock was needed
Suppliers' risks	**Buyers' risks**
- Buyer focused on the lowest price: results in no chance of a long-term relationship with the buyer - Negotiation ploy: buyer may be trying to get an existing supplier to lower its price and not award business to the suppliers participating in the bid process - In the excitement of the electronic reverse auction, the supplier may offer an unrealistic price to the buyer and lose business by trying to back out of the agreement	- Lack of trust could develop between the buyer and the supplier and destroy a previously established relationship - Lack of buyers' commitment could result in supplier not investing in the tooling, employee training, or capital investment to make products for the buyer - Too few suppliers could result in a noncompetitive electronic reverse auction environment: at least four or five suppliers are needed to begin the bid process

Adapted from: Smeltzer and Carr (2003)

portant for the seller and buyers, as the products are highly homogenous and the transaction regulations are highly standardized by the EM operators. It is important to note that, depending on the EM regulations, the bids and/or asking prices can be in the form of an absolute dollar value or of a price range.

Marketplace Bias

An EM may be structured to provide more value to certain group of stakeholders based on the design of roles and regulations. The importance of understanding the market bias stems from the evidence that indicates that the EM proposes different value sets to buyers and sellers (Barratt and Rosdahl, 2002; Wilson and Abel, 2002; Buyukozkan, 2004). The market players compete in the EM to gain the highest value from the marketplace. Table 5 presents the different and competing value proposition of EMs for buyers and sellers.

Based on the EM bias, EMs can be categorized into hierarchical (biased) and market-driven (third party). Hierarchical and market-driven markets are both buyer and seller markets. In hierarchical markets, a market sponsor or a market maker

carries out transactions in the marketplace as either buyer or seller. Since market sponsors or market makers in these EMs have more power through EM to collect more value, these EMs may become biased toward the market makers and the market sponsors. On the contrary, the market-driven EMs are expected to be unbiased, since the market makers and market sponsors are the third parties that do not carry out transactions in EMs (Malone et al., 1994; Eng, 2004). The latter type of EMs may have a better chance to dominate fragmented industries and provide a basis for integration of a collaboration of the fragmented suppliers and buyers (Krantz, 1999; Eng, 2004).

Table 5. EM value proposition

Buyers' Value Proposition	Sellers' Value Proposition
-Lower transaction costs -Better prices -Increased IT effectiveness	-Lower transaction costs -Improved marketing and customer relationship -Back-office facilitation -Access to new revenue potentials -Increased IT effectiveness

Adapted from: Buyukozkan, 2004

Market Orientation

From a stakeholders' perspective, EMs can be categorized into three types: buyer-oriented, seller-oriented, and neutral EMs. A buyer-oriented EM is operated by one or a number of suppliers that come together to aggregate the defragmented demand. The buyer-oriented EMs, if owned and/or operated by the suppliers, are expected to be biased toward the interest of seller(s). In contrast, in seller-oriented EMs the marketplace is operated by one or a number of buyers that come together to aggregate the defragmented supply. Seller-oriented EMs may be biased toward the interest of buyer(s). In a neutral (two-sided) EM, the marketplace is usually operated by a third party that acts as an intermediary (Gebauer, 1996; Weller, 2000). The intermediary is expected to be unbiased toward the interest of either buyers or sellers. Neutral EMs bring together the fragmented buyers and sellers. ChemConnect is an example of a marketplace that is formed by a third party. The buyers and sellers in the chemical industry are very fragmented and ChemConnect provides a platform that benefits both buyers and sellers (Fairchild et al., 2004).

Market Ownership

From an ownership perspective, EMs can be categorized into three types: 1- Buyer-side or Seller-side in which a major market player – the buyer or seller – owns and operates the EM; 2- Neutral (third party) in which an independent third party sets up and operates the EM; and 3- Consortia in which several major market players (buyers and/or sellers and/or intermediaries) join together to set up and operate the EM (Murtaza, et al., 2004; Turban *et al.*, 2002).

Some correlation exists between the ownership and orientation of EMs. However, there are also dissimilarities between EM ownership and EM orientation. For example, we cannot assume that an EM that one or two buyers own is necessarily seller-oriented, and only the EM that a third party operates is neutral. For example, www.amazon.com is a major supplier and yet it provides a neutral platform for other sellers to sell their products on the www.amazon.com website. In classifying EMs based on their ownership, there exists an assumption that market owners have a major role in the operation of the EM and that the EM may be biased toward the interests of EM owners. As a result, it is expected that an EM owned by a third party acts as a relatively neutral intermediary. In other words, this type of EM is expected to be somewhat less biased towards the interest of a specific party (i.e. buyers or sellers). However, it can be expected that an EM, which is owned by a third party, would be biased toward the interest of some market participants (e.g., those who have relatively great market power).

Closed vs. Open EMs

EMs can also be classified based on access to the market. From this perspective, EMs can be categorized into open and closed EMs. Open EMs are those marketplaces whose market transactions are open to any buyer and/or seller. In contrast, transactions in closed markets require membership, as in a club. EBay is an example of an open EM, while Brokerforum is considered a closed EM. There are six major differences between open and closed EMs (Grieger, 2003):

- Open EMs can be in the form of B2C, B2B, and C2C, but closed EMs are most popular among businesses (B2B). However, there exist evidence of applications for open EMs in B2B trading (e.g. Li et al., 2002).
- While closed EMs are more industry-specific than open EMs, open EMs are more globally oriented.
- The number of participants in closed EMs is limited, while the number of participants in open EMs is unlimited.

- The participants in closed EMs can be known, but in open EMs, the participants are usually unknown.
- The security of closed EMs is mostly concerned with the securing their network, while the security of open EMs is mostly concerned with effective identification of participants.
- In closed EMs there is a high degree of information sharing and collaboration, while the degree of information sharing and collaboration in open EMs is low.

FUTURE TRENDS

The recent studies in the area of EMs seem to focus on two main venues: software and algorithm development, and EM implementation and integration.

In the software and algorithm development side, the recent studies tend to focus on the development of automated agents that are more effective and at the same time can increase the EMs' technical compatibilities. The attention of scholars and researchers in this domain is mostly on development of powerful software using more effective algorithms that can offer more value to marketplace participants. For example, Ragone et al. (2009), in a recent study, explore the use of utility theories and data logs to facilitate transactions.

In regards to EM implementation and integration, recent studies seem be concerned with the process-model and success factors of EM implementation and strategic planning. There are some strengths and weaknesses associated with each type of EM. Identifying and exploring the properties of different types of EMs are vital for selecting the right strategy and successful implementation of EMs. For example, Driedonks, Gregor, & Wassenaar (2005) studied the implementation of EM in Australian beef industries. In another study, Gengatharen and Standing (2005) explored the regional EMs. Integration of EM into the organizational processes, and specifi-

cally into the organizational supply-chain as part of EM implementation, has received significant attention during the past few years. Coi, Li, and Houmin (2004), Eng (2004), Wei et al. (2007), Lavassani, Movahedi and Kumar (2008), White and Mohdzain (2009), are some examples of the recent studies on the integration of EM into organizational supply chain.

While there have been empirical studies on the implementation and integration of EMs in organizations, most of the studies rely on conceptual models and case studies. Empirical studies with large sample sizes in specific industries can provide valuable insights. The findings from empirical studies can lend themselves more readily to generalization. Practitioners can also use them as benchmarks for EM implementation and integration.

CONCLUSION

In this chapter, we have discussed the historical evolution and different types of EMs. We have found the development of EM to be parallel to the development of telecommunication technologies. This chapter documented the development of EMs from ones based on telephone and teletype to the ones implemented over the Internet. We employed a systematic approach to propose a comprehensive definition of EMs and their application with reference to recent advances. Based on the review of the most cited definitions of EM in the literature of the past three decades, we proposed a comprehensive definition of EM in this chapter. We defined EM in this chapter as effective and efficient collaborative Internet-based institutional infrastructures for inter-organizational and intra-organizational negotiation and transaction.

There exists a gap in the available literature for multi-dimensional classification of EMs. For the purpose of further exploration of the notion of EMs, this chapter provides an explicit review of different classification models of EMs and presents a nine-dimensional taxonomy of EMs. The nine dimensions of EM taxonomy are: 1. Type of Parties, 2. Type of Product/Service, 3. Application of the Products/Services, 4. Relationship Horizon, 5. Pricing Mechanism, 6. Marketplace Bias, 7. Market Orientation, 8. Market Ownership, and 9. Closed vs. Open EMs. We explicitly described each dimension of EM taxonomy. This model assists the researchers in understanding and exploring the applications of EMs. Finally, we discussed the recent trends in the studies of EMs. Specifically, we mentioned two areas of research as promising venues for further studies: Software and Algorithm Development, and EM Implementation and Integration. Furthermore, we discussed some examples of recent studies in these areas.

REFERENCES

Archer, N., & Gebauer, J. (2000). Managing in the context of the new electronic marketplace. *Proceedings 1st World Congress on the Management of Electronic Commerce,* Hamilton, Ontario, Canada, January 19 – 21, 2000.

Bailey, E. E., & White, L. J. (1974). Reversals in peak and offpeak prices. *The Bell Journal of Economics and Management Science, 5,* 75–92. doi:10.2307/3003093

Bakos, J. Y. (1991). A strategic analysis of electronic marketplaces. *Management Information Systems Quarterly, 15*(3), 295–310. doi:10.2307/249641

Bakos, Y. (1998). The emerging role of electronic marketplaces on the Internet. *Communications of the ACM, 41*(8), 35–42. doi:10.1145/280324.280330

Barratt, M., & Rosdahl, K. (2002). Exploring business-to-business market sites. *European Journal of Purchasing & Supply Chain Management, 8,* 111–122. doi:10.1016/S0969-7012(01)00010-7

Berglund, M. F. (1977). Institutional impediments to efficiency: The case of rail freight car supply. *Source: Land Economics, 53*(2), 157–171. doi:10.2307/3145921

Bradley, D. B., & Peters, D. (1997). *Electronic marketplaces: Collaborate if you want to compete.* 42nd World Conference International Council for Small Business, San Francisco, June.

Büyüközkan, G. (2004). Multi-criteria decision making for e-marketplace selection. *Internet Research, 14*(2), 139–154. doi:10.1108/10662240410530853

Cassidy, R. J. (1967). *Auctions and auctioneering.* Berkeley & Los Angeles, CA: University of California Press.

Chavez, A., & Maes, P. (1996). Kasbah: An agent marketplace for buying and selling goods. In *Proceedings of the First International Conference on the Practical Application of Intelligent Agents and Multi-Agent Technology,* (pp. 75-90).

Choi, T. M., Li, D., & Yan, H. (2004). Optimal returns policy for supply chain with e-marketplace. *International Journal of Production Economics, 88*(2), 205–227. doi:10.1016/S0925-5273(03)00188-9

Coppel, J. (2000). *E-commerce: Impacts and policy challenges.* OECD Economics Department Working Paper: 252.

Dai, Q., & Kauffman, R. J. (2003). *Understanding B2B e-market alliance strategies.* MISRC Working Papers 03-03. Carlson School of Management, The University of Minnesota. Minneapolis, MN.

Dai, Q., & Kauffman, R. J. (2000). *To be or not to B2B? An evaluative model for e-procurement channel adoption.* Working Paper, Carlson School of Management, University of Minnesota, Minneapolis, MN.

Dai, Q., & Kauffman, R. J. (2002). Business models for Internet-based B2B electronic models. *International Journal of Electronic Commerce, 6*(4), 41–72.

Dans, E. (2002). Existing business models for auctions and their adaption to electronic markets. *Journal of Electronic Commerce Research, 3*(2).

Driedonks, C., Gregor, S., & Wassenaar, A. (2005). Economic and social analysis of the adoption of B2B electronic marketplaces: A case study in the Australian beef industry. *International Journal of Electronic Commerce, 9*, 49–72.

Eng, T. Y. (2004). The role of e-marketplaces in supply chain management. *Industrial Marketing Management, 33*, 97–105. doi:10.1016/S0019-8501(03)00032-4

Fairchild, A. M., Ribbers, P. M. A., & Nooteboom, A. O. (2004). A success factor model for electronic markets: Defining outcomes based on stakeholder context and business process. *Business Process Management Journal, 10*(1), 63–79. doi:10.1108/14637150410518338

Felton, J. R. (1970). *The problem of freight car supply.* Lincoln, NE: The Agricultural Experiment Station, University of Nebraska-Lincoln.

Felton, J. R. (1974). *The economics of freight car supply.* Report to the Association of American Railroads. Lincoln, Nebraska, Feb.

Fortino, G., & Russo, W. (2004). A statecharts-based software development process for mobile agents. *Information and Software Technology, 46*(13), 907–921. doi:10.1016/j.infsof.2004.04.005

Gebauer, J. (1996). *Electronic market from an economic perspective.* 2nd International Workshop on Electronic Markets, University of St. Gallen, Ermatingen, Switzerland.

Gengatharen, D. E., & Standing, G. (2005). A framework to assess the factors affecting success or failure of the implementation of government-supported regional e-marketplaces for SMEs. *European Journal of Information Systems, 14,* 417–433. doi:10.1057/palgrave.ejis.3000551

Ghenniwa, H., Huhns, M., & Shen, W. (2005). E-marketplaces for enterprise and cross enterprise integration. *Data & Knowledge Engineering, 52*(1), 33–59. doi:10.1016/j.datak.2004.06.005

Grieger, M. (2003). Electronic marketplaces: A literature review and a call for supply chain management research. *European Journal of Operational Research, 144*(2), 280–294. doi:10.1016/S0377-2217(02)00394-6

Grieger, M. (2004). An empirical study of business processes across Internet-based electronic marketplaces. A supply chain management perspective. *Business Process Management Journal, 10*(1), 80–100. doi:10.1108/14637150410518347

Hadaya, P. (2004). Determinants of the future level of use of electronic marketplaces among Canadian firms. *Proceedings of the 37th Hawaii International Conference on System Sciences, 2004.*

Henderson, D. R. (1984). Electronic marketing in principle and practice. *American Journal of Agricultural Economics, 66*(5). doi:10.2307/1241012

IBM. i2, & Ariba, A. M. (2000). *E-marketplaces changing the way we do business.* Ariba whitepaper. Retrieved from www.ibm-i2-ariba.com

Kambil, A., & Heck, E. V. (2002). *Making markets: How firms can design and profit from online auctions and exchanges.* Boston, MA: Harvard Business School Press.

Kaplan, R. S., & Sawhney, M. (2000). B-to-B e-commerce hubs: Towards a taxonomy of business models. *Harvard Business Review, 79*(1), 97–100.

Kinney, S. (2000, April). R.I.P. fixed pricing: The Internet is on its way to "marketizing" everything. *Business Economics (Cleveland, Ohio)*, 39–44.

Krantz, M. (1999, July 12). The next e-volution. *Time, 47*, 1999.

Kwon, S. D., Yang, H. D., & Rowley, C. (2009). The purchasing performance of organizations using e-marketplaces. *British Journal of Management, 20*(1), 106–124. doi:10.1111/j.1467-8551.2007.00555.x

Laseter, T., Long, B., & Caper, C. (2001). B2B benchmark: The state of electronic exchanges. *Strategy+Business, 25*, 33–42.

Lau, R. Y. K. (2007). Towards a Web services and intelligent agents-based negotiation system for B2B e-commerce. *Electronic Commerce Research and Applications, 6*(3), 260–273. doi:10.1016/j.elerap.2006.06.007

Lau, R. Y. K., Li, Y., Song, D., & Kwok, R. C. W. (2008). Knowledge discovery for adaptive negotiation agents in e-marketplaces. *Decision Support Systems, 42*(2), 310–323. doi:10.1016/j.dss.2007.12.018

Lavassani, K., Movahedi, B., & Kumar, V. (2008). Transition to B2B e-marketplace enabled supply chain: Readiness assessment and success factors. *Proceedings of 2008 International Conference on Information Resources Management (Conf-IRM 2008)*, Ontario, Canada.

Li, H., Cao, J., Castro-Lacouture, D., & Skibniewski, M. (2002). A framework for developing a unified B2B e-trading construction marketplace. *Automation in Construction, 12*, 201–211. doi:10.1016/S0926-5805(02)00076-6

Lipis, L. J., Villars, R., Byron, D., & Turner, V. (2000). *Putting markets into place: An e-marketplace definition and forecast*. Retrieved from http://www.idc.com

Louta, M., Roussaki, I., & Pechlivanos, L. (2008). An intelligent agent negotiation strategy in the electronic marketplace environment. *European Journal of Operational Research, 187*(3), 1327–1345. doi:10.1016/j.ejor.2006.09.016

Madanmohan, T. R., Kumar, V., & Kumar, U. (2005). Success or failure of e-marketplaces. *Proceedings of Administrative Sciences Association of Canada*. Technology and Innovation Management Division. Toronto, Canada, May 2005.

Maes, P., Guttman, R., & Moukas, A. (1999). Agents that buy and sell. *Communications of the ACM, 42*(3), 81–91. doi:10.1145/295685.295716

Malone, T., Yates, J., & Benjamin, R. (1994). Electronic markets and electronic hierarchies. In Malone, T., & Morton, M. S. (Eds.), *Information Technology and the corporation of the 1990s* (pp. 61–83). New York, NY: Oxford University Press.

Martina, G., & Kia, J. (2007). E-business standardization in the automotive sector: Role and situation of SEMs. In MacGregor, R. C., & Hodgkinson, A. (Eds.), *Small business clustering technologies*. Hershey, PA: Idea Group Inc.

McCoy, J. H., & Sarhan, M. E. (1988). *Livestock and meat marketing*. New York, NY: Van Nostrand Reinhold.

McNealy, S. (2001). Welcome to the bazaar. *Harvard Business Review, 79*(3), 18–19.

McNichols, T. J., & Brennan, L. (2006). Evaluating partner suitability for collaborative supply networks. *International Journal of Networking and Virtual Organizations, 3*(2), 220–237.

Morali, A., Varela, L., & Varela, C. (2005). *An electronic marketplace: Agent-based coordination models for online auctions*. In XXXI Conferencia Latinoamericana de Informática, Cali, Colombia, October 2005.

Mueller, R. A. E. (2000). Emergent e-commerce in agriculture. Agriculture Issues Center. *AIC Issues Brief, 14*, December.

Murtaza, M. B., Gupta, V., & Carroll, R. C. (2004). E-marketplaces and the future of supply chain management: Opportunities and challenges. *Business Process Management Journal, 10*(3), 325–335. doi:10.1108/14637150410539722

Muylle, S., & Basu, A. (2008). Online support for business processes by electronic intermediaries. *Decision Support Systems, 45*(4)..doi:10.1016/j.dss.2008.02.005

Peer, D. (1976). *Pricing systems for hogs in Ontario.* Lecture, Agr. Econ. and Extens. Educ., University of Guelph, 22 Oct. 1976.

Petersen, K. J., Ogden, J. A., & Carter, P. L. (2007). B2B e-marketplaces: A typology by functionality. *International Journal of Physical Distribution & Logistics Management, 37*(1), 4–18. doi:10.1108/09600030710723291

Peterson, R. A. (Ed.). (1997). *Electronic marketing and the consumer.* Thousand Oaks, CA: Sage.

Ragone, A., Straccia, U., Noia, T. D., Sciascio, E. D., & Donini, F. M. (2009). Fuzzy match making in e-marketplaces of peer entities using Datalog. *Fuzzy Sets and Systems, 160*, 251–268. doi:10.1016/j.fss.2008.07.002

Rasmusen, E. (2001). *Games and information: An introduction to game theory.* London, UK: Blackwell Publishing.

Rasmusen, E. (2001). *Strategic implications of uncertainty over one's own private value in auctions.* Working Papers-2001, Indiana University, Kelley School of Business, Department of Business Economics and Public Policy.

Rasmusen, E. (2007). *Getting carried away in auctions as imperfect value discovery.* Working Papers 2007-05, Indiana University, Kelley School of Business, Department of Business Economics and Public Policy.

Reedy, J., & Schullo, S. (2004). *Electronic marketing.* Mason, OH: Mason Publishing.

Rosson, P. (2000). Electronic trading hubs: Review and research questions. *Proceedings, 16th. IMP Conference,* Bath, UK.

Schmid, B. F. (1999). Elektronische Maerkte - Merkmale, Organisation und Potentiale. In Sauter, M., & Hermanns, A. (Eds.), *Handbuch Electronic Commerce* (pp. 29–48). Munich.

Schmid, B. F., & Lindemann, M. A. (1998). *Elements of a reference model for electronic markets.* 31st Hawaii International Conference on System Sciences, IEEE Computer Society Press, (pp. 193-201) Los Alamitos, CA.

Schrader, L. F., Heifner, R. G., & Larzelere, H. E. (1968). *The electronic egg exchange, an alternative system for trading shell eggs.* Michigan State University. Agr. Econ. Rep. No. 119, Dec. 1968.

Segev, A., Gebauer, J., & Farver, F. (1999). Internet based electronic markets. *Electronic Markets, 9*(3), 138–146. doi:10.1080/101967899359021

Shen, Z., & Su, X. (2007). Customer behavior modeling in revenue management and auctions-A review and new research opportunities. *Production and Operations Management, 16*(6), 713–728. doi:10.1111/j.1937-5956.2007.tb00291.x

Singh, M., & Waddell, D. (2003). *E-business innovation and change management.* Hershey, PA: IGI Global.

Skjøtt-Larsen, T., Kotzab, H., & Grieger, M. (2003). Electronic marketplaces and supply chain relationships. *Industrial Marketing Management, 32*, 199–210. doi:10.1016/S0019-8501(02)00263-8

Smeltzer, L., & Carr, A. (2003). Electronic reverse auctions: Promises, risks, and conditions for success. *Industrial Marketing Management, 32*(6), 481–488. doi:10.1016/S0019-8501(02)00257-2

Smith, A. (1904). *An inquiry into the nature and causes of the wealth of nations* (5th ed. by Edwin Cannan). London, UK: Methuen and Co., Ltd.

Standing, C., Love, P. E. D., Stockdale, R., & Gengatharen, D. (2006). Examining the relationship between electronic marketplace strategy and structure. *IEEE Transactions on Engineering Management, 53*(2), 297–311. doi:10.1109/TEM.2005.861801

Strauss, J., El-Ansary, A., & Frost, R. (2003). *E-marketing*. Upper Saddle River, NJ: Prentice Hall.

Turban, E., King, D., Lee, J., Warkentin, M., & Chung, H. M. (2002). *Electronic commerce*. Upper Saddle River, NJ: Prentice-Hall.

Vakrat, Y., & Seidmann, A. (1999). *Optimal design of online auction*. William E. Simon Graduate School of Business Administration, University of Rochester, Rochester, NY. Working Paper, November, 1999.

Vickrey, W. (1961). Counterspeculation, auctions, and competitive sealed tenders. *The Journal of Finance*, 16.

Wei, T., Kan, J., & Zi-Gang, Z. (2007). *Supply chain coordination study based on retailers' inventory transshipment via e-marketplace*. International Conference on Management Science and Engineering, China, (pp. 1019-1024).

Weller, T. C. (2000). *B2B e-commerce: The rise of e-marketplaces. Research report*. Reston, VA: Legg Mason Wood Walker, Inc.

White, A., Daniel, E., Ward, J., & Wilson, H. (2007). The adoption of consortium B2B e-marketplaces: An exploratory study. *The Journal of Strategic Information Systems, 16*, 71–103. doi:10.1016/j.jsis.2007.01.004

White, A. D., & Mohdzain, M. B. (2009). An innovative model of supply chain management: A single case study in the electronic sector. *International Journal of Information Technology and Management, 8*(1), 69–84. doi:10.1504/IJITM.2009.022271

Willcocks, L., Petherbridge, P., & Olson, N. (2002). *Making IT count: Strategy, delivery, infrastructure*. Butterworth-Heinemann.

Wilson, S., & Abel, I. (2002). So you want to get involved in e-commerce. *Industrial Marketing Management, 31*(2), 85–94. doi:10.1016/S0019-8501(01)00188-2

Yu, C. S., & Tao, Y. H. (2007). Enterprise e-marketplace adoption: From the perspectives of technology acceptance model, network externalities, and transition costs. *Journal of International Management, 14*(4), 231–265.

Zappala, S., & Gray, C. (2006). *Impact of e-commerce on consumers and small firms*. Surrey, UK: Ashgate Publishing, Ltd.

ENDNOTES

[1] Daimler bough Chrysler in 1998; in 2007 the two companies (Daimler AG and Chrysler) separated.

[2] Internet-based solutions refers to e-commerce solutions that are based on the use of IP (internet protocol)

Chapter 3
A Business Model Framework for Second Life

Alessia D'Andrea
National Research Council, Italy

Fernando Ferri
National Research Council, Italy

Patrizia Grifoni
National Research Council, Italy

ABSTRACT

This chapter provides a framework to analyse the marketing and promotion advantages of Virtual Communities. Virtual Communities offer companies the possibility to carry out a new products and services promotion and to develop trustful relationships with customers. The key element in the use of Virtual Communities for these purposes is the wide amount of customers that can be reached. Virtual Communities present the aptitude to generate social influence and knowledge sharing among customers. As a consequence, it brings out the increasing number of skills, competencies and "knowledge profiles" of each customer involved in the virtual environment. The framework is consequently applied to Second Life in order to analyse three different business strategies that companies usually implement by using this platform. The first strategy allows companies to perform the placement of their products/services in a dynamic form. The second strategy provides companies the possibility to have a better knowledge of customers' needs in order to develop products and services that satisfy customer's expectations. Finally, the third strategy allows companies to develop high brand awareness.

1. INTRODUCTION

The advent of digital economy has given rise to the design and implementation of new business models. In this scenario a deep innovation has been produced by Virtual Communities (VCs). The history of the term virtual community can be traced back to a time long before the rise of the Internet. The term indicates a web-based services that allow individuals to (i) construct a public or semi-public profile, (ii) articulate a list of other users with whom they share a connection, and

DOI: 10.4018/978-1-60566-394-4.ch003

(iii) view and traverse their list of connections and those made by others within the community (Ellison, 2007). There are many descriptions of the VCs that depend upon the perspective from which they are defined which may be multidisciplinary: sociology, technology and business. From the sociology perspective VCs are defined based on its physical features or the strength and type of relationship. Etzioni & Etzioni (1999) view VCs from the perspective of bonding and culture and define it as having two attributes namely, a web of affect-laden relationships encompassing group of individuals (bonding) and commitment to a set of shared values, mores, meanings and a shared historical identity (culture). Romm et al. (1997) define VCs as group of people who communicate with each other via electronic media, such as the Internet and share common interests unconstrained by their geographical location, physical interaction or ethnic origin. Ridings et al. (2002) define VCs as groups of people with common interests and practices that communicate regularly and for some duration in an organized way over the Internet through a common location or mechanism. The technology perspective refers to VCs based on the software supporting them like list server, newsgroup, bulletin board and Internet Relay Chat (IRC). These software technologies support the communication within the network, and help in creating the boundaries (Lazar, 1999). Hagel & Armstrong (1997) take a business perspective and define VCs as groups of people drawn together by an opportunity to share a sense of community with like-minded strangers having common interest. The business potential of VCs is mainly given in terms of added value they provide, resulting from a new combinations of information, products and services and an innovative integrations of resources, roles and relationships between companies and customers. VCs present significant business opportunities because they offer excellent marketing and promotion advantages. First of all, they provide customers the possibility to establish an easy interaction/communication with others customers and/or with the company without spatial and temporal constraints and with reduced search costs. VCs also have the advantage to be delivered and accessible 24 hours a day and 7 day a week. This allows customers to access every time to all the necessary information about products and services offered by companies. There are many virtual communities, of which Second Life (SL) is one of the most prominent. SL is having an evolution similar to that the Internet had in the mid nineties and it is deeply impacting the way to do business. Created in 2003 by Linden Research Inc, this 3-D virtual community is driving new forms of Internet-based communication, networking and collaboration by customers and companies. Many companies such as American Apparel, Toyota, IBM, Nissan etc. are promoting their products and services by using SL platform. On combining different communications channels in SL, companies can enable customers to live an immersive experience. By creating their "Avatars" customers can walk through virtual shopping locations, examine and use virtual products and services and talk with sales people (Subramaniam et al., 2000). The immersive nature of SL allows companies both to develop an interactive business, by involving customers in the products and services development and to enhance the brand awareness, by creating unique branded events to which customers can participate. This chapter provides a framework to analyse the marketing and promotion advantages of VCs. The framework takes into account Internal factors (companies, customers, products/services promotion and financial aspect) and External factors (competitors and technological aspects). The framework is consequently applied to SL in order to analyse the different business strategies that companies usually implement by using SL platform.

The chapter is organised as follow. Firstly we provide a brief literature review on business models categorizations (section two). Section three introduces the framework for analysing the business model of VCs. The framework, applied to SL, is described and discussed in section four. The chapter concludes with section five.

2. BACKGROUND

The term business model is defined as "the commercial relationship between a business enterprise and the products and/or services it provides in the market" (Hawkins, 2001). More specifically, it is a way of structuring various cost and revenue streams such that a business becomes viable, usually in the sense of being able to sustain itself on the basis of the income it generates. In its basic sense, a business model is the method of doing business by which a company can generate revenue. Slywotzky (1996) describes business model as "the totality of how a company selects its customers defines and differentiates its offerings, defines the tasks it will perform itself and those it will outsource, configures its resource, goes to market, creates utility for customers, and captures profits". Timmers (1998) defines business model as "an architecture for the product, service and information flows, a description of the various business actors and of their roles, as well as a description of the potential benefits of these actors and finally a description of the sources of revenue". Hamel (2000) defines a business model as "a short statement that will capture the unique strengths with the new way of doing business". The author also make an all-inclusive definition of a business model that includes 1) customer interface, 2) core strategy, 3) strategic resources, and 4) value network. Sweet (2001) underlines intricate connections between value creation and business models. The author argues that "the management of fundamental strategic value configuration logics such as relationships to suppliers, access to technologies, insight into the users' needs etc., are far more relevant than inventing new revolutionary business models", an opinion accentuated by Stabell & Fjeldstad (1998). It is in these connections and interrelations

that value creation can be found. Value creation can e.g. be related to "solving a problem, improving performance, or reducing risk and cost" (Sandberg, 2002) which might require specific value configurations including relationships to suppliers, access to technologies, insight in the users needs etc. Chaharbaghi et al. (2003) identify three interrelated strands, which form a business model: "characteristics of the company's way of thinking, its operational system, and capacity for value generation". Although their generality, the three above cited elements can be concretely identified. For instance, the features of the company's way of thinking essentially pertain to a strategic dimension, while capacity for value generation can be considered in the resource-based perspective. Kaplan & Norton (2004) have provided a useful framework for analysing businesses, such as profit models. The framework is based on a long tradition of classifying firms into "internally consistent sets of firms" referred to as strategic groups or configurations. These groups are then often used to explore the determinants of performance.

Regarding the VCs many are the companies that use them to fulfill their business goals. VCs are seen as the preserve of technical support or service groups within a company. However, used effectively they can be an excellent way of building dialogue with customers from a marketing and promotion point of view. There is a growing body of literature that underline the benefits of VCs to support new marketing efforts (Moon & Sproull, 2001). In particular VCs seems to have the potential to be the new infrastructure providers for customer-to-customer (C2C) marketing because they are exceptionally effective at putting individuals who are geographically dispersed into virtual contact with each other. That, in turn, has the potential to support the growth of virtual worlds, by bringing in users interested in trade who would not otherwise join them, in a closed feedback loop process (Kock, 2008). Moreover participation in a virtual community could motivate consumers to cooperate with a marketer in such efforts.

Nambisan (2002) puts forth several typologies of customer roles and interactions in virtual communities that are focused on developing new products. The key aspect is the critical mass of members that can be reached that could facilitate stronger relationships between firms and their customers (Hagel & Armstrong (1997), Brown et al. (2002)). The enjoyment gained from participation enhances a member's desire to participate in virtual communities (Bagozzi & Dholakia (2002), Dholakia at al. (2004)). A customer's desire to participate could stimulate his or her intention to revisit the community and, en masse, this behaviour among customers could lead to increased site 'stickiness.' Indeed, virtual community members can become loyal customers (Mathwick, 2002). These processes allow marketers to collect information about consumers in order to know them better by removing some barriers present in traditional channels. For example, through the VCs, the marketer provides to the consumer, easier access to product information, aggregation of services, convenient ordering procedures and delivery of some category of products.

3. A BUSINESS MODEL FRAMEWORK FOR VIRTUAL COMMUNITIES

In literature several authors have proposed business model frameworks (Bell et al. (1997), Hedman & Kalling (2001), Chesbrough & Rosenbloom (2002), Morris et al. (2005)). These frameworks have been described by considering several factors able to give different point of views. In this chapter we propose a classification of these factors, extensively analysed in the above studies, into the following two categories:

Internal factors:
- *companies;*
- *products/services promotion;*
- *customers;*
- *financial aspect.*

External factors:
- *competitors;*
- *technological aspects.*

As said before, the framework is based on marketing and promotion aspect of VCs. The key element in the use of VCs for this purpose is the wide amount of customers that can be reached.

Figure 1. A business model framework for VCs

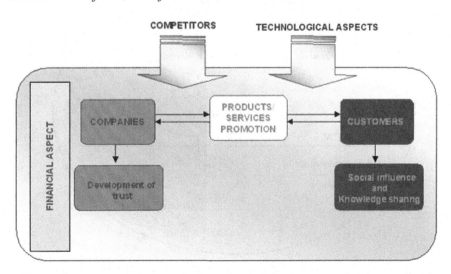

Companies usually start from building a loyal community of customers through advertisement on discussion forums, providing links to experts in specific areas for free consultation. Companies may also open discussion forums to specifically attract new members according to their profiles of interest. These discussion forums are rich sources of information about companies and their products and services and, at the same time, should be closely monitoring by the company to identify the customer's needs. VCs present also the aptitude to generate interaction among customers. Many companies have recently started to capture data on the social interaction among customers in VCs, with the objective of understanding and leveraging how this interaction can generate social influence. Social influence is the process by which the individual opinion can be changed by other individual(s) (Bales, 1950). It is characterized by three main features:

- *conformity*, that occurs when an individual expresses a particular opinion in order to meet the expectations of a given other,

even if he/she does not necessarily believe that the opinion is appropriate.

- *power*, that is the ability to force someone to behave in a particular way by controlling his/her outcomes.

- *authority*, that is the power perceived to be legitimate by those who are subjected to it.

Customers can really modify their opinions about products and/or services according to the social influence process (Friedkin, 1998) (as showed in Figure 2).

In the social influence process a customer "A" has her/his initial opinion about products and/or services. This opinion evolves according to the interaction with other customers that, in turn, evolve their opinion as a result of the interaction with the complex network of social influences. VCs also have the aptitude to generate knowledge sharing among customers. They facilitate the collaboration and exchange of ideas among customers, and preserve explicit as well as implicit (or tacit) knowledge created by the customers' relations. Community's explicit knowledge is stored in the community repository and includes

Figure 2. The social influence process

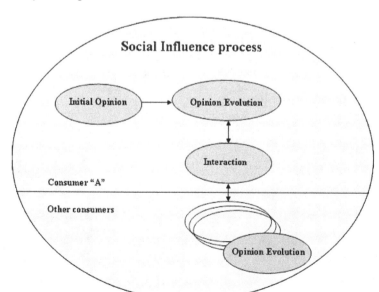

any kind of information readily available to community's members, while tacit knowledge resides in minds of the community's members. Both these kinds of knowledge have to be managed in order to preserve and organize information and to improve the business power of VCs. Knowledge management involves a set of practices aimed at creating, organizing, sharing and disseminating knowledge, at making this knowledge more productive and at producing significant benefits. Knowledge management technologies enable companies to facilitate collaboration and exchanging of ideas among community's members, and to preserve explicit as well as implicit knowledge that is created through VCs among customers. VCs provide a more dynamic environment, oriented to innovation and knowledge sharing, than traditional communities. As a consequence, it emerges the increasing number of skills, competencies and "knowledge profiles" of each customer involved into the virtual environment. Even if advantages related to the use of VCs in business process often seem obvious, however the widespread deployment of these technologies does not come without its potential disadvantages. The most important concerns the lack of (face-to-face) social contact between customers and companies. VCs offer company the opportunity to establish a contact with a wide amount of customers, but they must never replace the interpersonal contacts that are the basis of companies-customers relationship. Actually, the idea of "virtual interaction with companies" disturbs a lot of customers. These customers believe only in interpersonal contacts with companies and they assign a relevant role to a face-to-face communication. This is due to the absence of a very important element: the trust. Rousseau et al. (1998) define trust as "a psychological state comprising the intention to accept vulnerability based upon positive expectations of the intentions or behaviour of another". Similarly, Lewicki et al. (1998) describe trust as "an individual's belief in, and willingness to act on the basis of, the words, actions, and decisions of

another". The need for trust arises from our interdependence with others. We often depend on other people to help us obtain, or at least not to frustrate, the outcomes we value. Many studies provide evidence of the importance of trust for VCs business models. Customers who trust the company are more likely to visit its "virtual location" again and to recommend its products and services to other peoples. This means that companies are increasingly encouraged to build trustful relationship with customers. Through the interaction with the members of a VC, companies will learn more about the needs of their customers, they will strengthen their relationships and they will be able to customise their products and services. After analysing the advantages of VCs and considering the importance of trustful relationships between companies and customers, the further step companies have to perform is to focus attention on financial aspect and on External factors (competitors and technological aspects) that could have an impact on the design and development of the business model. The evaluation of the financial aspects is relevant in order to establish costs and expected revenues. The steps that help companies to look at where they financially are and where they want to be positioned are three:

- collection of financial data - such as details on company income and expenses, debt level, commitments, etc.;
- identification of financial company goals;
- identification of any financial problems.

Starting from these aspects companies can define a business strategy that involves the:

- definition pricing policies;
- identification of market needs;
- adaptation of the existing services and products;
- promotion of new services and products.

To evaluate the feasibility of business strategy, companies have to consider External factors too. Firstly companies must analyse how they can cope with competitors in particular on considering:

- how often competitors improve or replace their products/services;
- what is their market share;
- how they promote their products/services;
- how widely do they advertise their products/services;
- what is their reputation among customers.

Finally, it is important for companies to consider technological aspects in order to underline both, how the evolution of Information and Communication Technologies contribute to improve the virtual communities access and the benefits that this evolution has on business processes. The advent of Web 2.0 technologies represents the milestone of the virtual communities achievement. They give people the possibility to access virtual communities and to have a connection with other members everytime. The communication is both one-to-many and many-to-many. Since the explosion of Web 2.0 technologies over the last few years, some one have been discussing how guarantee virtual communities access also by using mobile devices. This discussion has produced the explosion of Mobile 2.0. In Mobile 2.0 the value of connectivity "is determined by the mobile setting, shared locale, shared context, shared history, and so on. Rather than connecting with anyone on the Net, it can be more useful to find someone who is in the same place right now, or who was here two hours ago, or who is in a similar place somewhere else in the world" (Holmquist, 2007). The popularity of virtual communities, combined with the widespread diffusion of mobile technologies, such as Personal Digital Assistant (PDA), pocket PC (Personal Computer) and cell phone, has given rise to the phenomenon of mobile virtual communities. Mobile virtual communities are considered to be the natural evo-lution of virtual communities. They can be seen as virtual communities to which mobile services are added. Using mobile technologies, users have an anytime-anywhere connection to their community. Many companies are still missing out on the huge potential benefits of using mobiles business as a part of their marketing process. According to Askarzay & Unelkar (2008) the mobile business presents al lot of advantages:

1. has a non-physical structure: this allows business to operate from any where to any time
2. supports production processs because it allows to manage the staff any where at any time
3. provides collboration between different elements of a business
4. suits a globall business that can be defined as all the economics activities that are global scope and operation

The VCs evolution in the mobile business perspective has being involving SL too. This aspect is detailed below.

4. APPLYING THE FRAMEWORK TO SECOND LIFE VIRTUAL COMMUNITY

The introduced framework is applied to SL (see Figure 3). On considering Internal factors (companies, products/services promotion; customers; financial aspect) and External factors (competitors and technological aspects), the framework presents a classification of tree different business strategies that companies usually implement by using SL. The first strategy allows companies to perform the placement of their products/services; the second strategy provides companies the possibility to have a better knowledge of the customer's needs and finally the last strategy allows companies to develop a high brand awareness.

Figure 3. A business model framework for Second Life platform

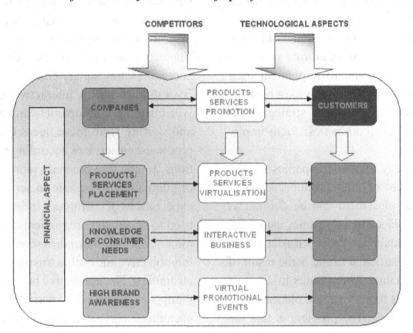

A lot of companies consider SL as an important component of their business strategies. Never before they had an opportunity such as this to promote their products and services. A pool developed by the Global Market Institute asserted that SL holds potential for real-life products/ services promotion. Their study underlines that: "56% of SL users say the virtual world is a good promotional vehicle, and only 16 percent say they would not be more likely to buy or use a brand that is represented there. Of the more than 9,500 or so respondents to the poll, only 5% (roughly 475) said they have a SL account. A third said they don't know what SL is; three of ten said they have been planning to open an account but just haven't gotten around to it. Nearly all SL users - 97% - said they tend to access SL from home". With respect to products promotion SL supports companies in the different phases of products diffusion, testing and redesign. SL carries out the diffusion of the product in a way that has been traditionally reserved to manufacturers and large-scale distributors. In the product testing it allows companies to receive a feedback by customers

around the world. Finally, in the product redesign it enables customers to share their ideas and to post continuously their suggestions to the company. With respect to services promotion, SL allows companies to furnish new type of services. A K Zero case study "Metamoney" explores and explains the opportunities for Financial Services companies in SL. According to this study, "SL has seen a number of financial services companies enter recently, with several more on the way. Due to the economic backbone of SL, it's a no-brainer for companies offering financial services to set-up in virtual worlds. After all, in a way, it's just another `country' (albeit virtual) with residents, currency and transaction". First Meta was the first virtual bank to provide credit cards and corporate financial services in SL, where current banks are mostly small and offer only deposit services. Also Germany's Wirecard Bank entered the virtual SL world, joining existing resident ABN Amro. There is also a stock market in SL, called World Stock Exchange, which enables virtual companies to raise capital and allows investors to buy stock using the fictional Linden

Dollar and World Internet Currency that can then be sold for real US Dollars. According to the Second Life Business Communicators Wiki many companies today use the SL platform to promote their products/services and to implement their business strategies. Below we provide a description of three different business strategies (as showed in Figure 3) that companies usually implement by using SL.

The first strategy allows companies to perform the placement of their products/services. Products/services placement can be defined as promotional ads placed by companies using real commercial products and services in media, where the presence of a particular brand is the result of an economic exchange. Many times it is not so easy for companies to perform the placement of their products/services. The problem is that the product/service placement frequently is done in a static form. SL allows overcoming this issue by enabling the placement of products/services in a dynamic form. In fact by using SL platform companies can offer their virtual products and services in an interactive way (Brendel, 2008). Customers by creating their avatars have the possibility to examine, use and create virtual products and services. American Apparel was the first "real world" to perform the placement of their products on SL. Its ultra-modern clothing store is located on a beach resort and has quickly become a hot spot within SL. IBM used SL platform to involve customers in the creation of "a virtual version of a kitchen, complete with exact dimensions and layout". Similarly, Adidas involved customers in designing their own sneaker, helping them to design more remarkable *first life* sneakers. Starwood Aloft used their SL location as "an inexpensive prototyping solution to get customer feedback on design for future hotel layouts".

The second strategy provides companies the possibility to have a better knowledge of customers' needs in order to develop products and services that satisfy their expectations. Customers have a limited knowledge and experience with new products/services and in many cases this aspect can lead to unrealistic expectations, which may generate product/service dissatisfaction. Therefore, an important research question is how companies may satisfy customer's expectations. By establishing an interactive communication with customers, companies can know their needs and starting from these needs they can develop products and services according to their expectations. Interactive business represents the dream of companies to be able to serve the needs and expectations of customers; indeed they have long tried to establish communication links with customers. The use of SL allows companies to achieve this objective and build a trustful relationship with customers. The interactive nature of SL provides the opportunity to build a personal environment for customers, each one considered as an individual in addressing promotional messages, providing a wide range of products and services, and making the virtual community a truly worthwhile place for the customer to visit. The possibility to individually and interactively address customers, allows companies to better understand their target and to provide new products and services promotion in fulfilling the customer's needs.

Let us consider finally the third strategy, which allows companies to develop a high brand awareness. Among customers, strong brands influence buying decisions and inspire loyalty. Many customers only buy from a select group of brands, or a single brand, in each product range. Ideally companies need to develop a "buzz" around their products and services, generating a level of excitement in the marketplace. SL platform provides companies the opportunity to increase their brand awareness as everyone may be recognised in a smaller, yet more specific, group of people. For example by creating unique branded events companies have the possibility to engage target customer audience. A recent white paper released by Kaplow & Pelaez (2002) states that "moving events to the virtual world can reduce spending and boost attendance, lead generation and attendee interest". There are several types of events in SL:

- *Live:* companies can create real-time event and manage customers (avatars) live. These events are used most frequently for presentations to a group or audience,
- *Streamed:* companies can record and stream an event with a short delay. This is often used for some real-world events,
- *Mixed Reality:* a registered event can be streamed in real time by companies and may include feedback via text or audio from the SL audience.

Aside from convenience, events in SL have proven so successful because they can mimic nearly every aspect of real world. This characteristic allows customers to be more receptive to promotional messages and to enhance their brand awareness. Before choosing any implementation strategy it is important to consider the financial aspect. SL definitely is a great for brand building and advertising real-world products and services. However, on considering the financial aspect, according to Daniel Terdiman, author of *The Entrepreneur's Guide to Second Life: Making Money in the Metaverse* (Terdiman, 2007) "in SL companies are not necessarily going to make a lot of money - at least not right now. It's worth the minimal cost for a presence in SL (they must pay for real estate (about $20) and a monthly maintenance fee (from $5 to $15 a month) but companies have to think clearly about what they're trying to achieve and how you go about it - the community is extremely sensitive to companies that come in and try to exploit them". Many companies have set up a virtual shop in SL, which customers (residents) can visit and purchase products. However, as just discussed, the companies main motivation for staying on SL is not the profit but the opportunity they have to promote their brand awareness to a wider number of people respect to traditional business processes. While SL is one of the largest virtual world populations, other 3-D VCs (such as HiPihi, Multiverse, Twinty, Smallwords etc.) are progressively improving their importance in the virtual world economy. The worlds listed above present the same attributes of SL such as: RMT economy, persistent world and 3-level user-generated content (avatar, objects, environment). At first glance they could be consider competitors to SL, but just because they have the same attributes doesn't mean that they are competitors. On considering different studies that K Zero developed to assess total registered accounts across virtual worlds, it's pretty clear that actually SL doesn't have much competition. This does not imply that new virtual words could surpass SL in the future. However, in discussing the advent of "new entrants", what we're talking about primarily are barriers that they have to consider to sate their presence in the virtual world economy. The first barrier is represented by the low availability of programmers and hardware required to create virtual worlds. Another important barrier is represented by the government policies and in particular the way in which they can influence the virtual world category. For example, it is possible that that government in certain countries could prevent their citizens from accessing particular worlds. It is also important to consider costs associated with the initial investment in creating a virtual word. The necessary capital implies a small number of new entrants will enter the market. On considering the technological aspects as discessed in section (3) the evolution of Information and Communication Technologies has involved Second Life too, that can now be accessed from mobile devices. The company Vollee has made avalaible the technology that makes it possible to run Second Life on mobile devices. Second Life is difficult to use, is very graphics intensive, and requires a huge amount of streaming data, the Vollee technology is able to adapt applications for screen size and key layout according to the used device.

5. CONCLUSION

The chapter has analysed how companies use the SL platform to improve their business over the Internet discussing how this virtual community can affect the business process. In the first part of the chapter a framework has been developed to consider the VCs' business model from a broad perspective. In the beginning the framework takes into account Internal factors (companies, customers, products/services promotion and financial aspect) and successively, External factors (competitors and technological aspects) are incorporated into the framework too. On considering all these components the chapter has analysed business opportunities of VCs. They give companies the possibility to carry out new products and services promotions. The key element in the use of VCs for this purpose is the wide amount of customers that can be reached (mainly if they are mobile virtual communities). VCs present the aptitude to generate social influence and knowledge sharing among customers too. As a consequence, it emerges the increasing number of skills, competencies and "knowledge profiles" of each customer involved into the virtual environment. In the second part of the chapter the proposed framework is applied to SL in order to discuss benefits that this platform can represent for companies. The real benefits of SL can be exploited when companies: 1) use the interactive and cooperative capabilities of the new medium and build a personal community environment for each customers, 2) consider each customer as an individual that can be a potential receiver of promotional messages, 3) provide all related services at a unique point, and 4) make the virtual community a truly engaging and attractive place for the customer. Furthermore the chapter has presented a classification of tree different business strategies that companies can implement by using the SL platform. The first strategy allows companies to perform the placement of their products/services in a dynamic form. Companies offer their virtual products and services

in an interactive way. By creating their avatars customers have the possibility to examine and use products and services, walk through virtual shopping aisles and talk with sales people. The second strategy provides companies the possibility to have a better knowledge of customers' needs in order to in order to develop products and services that satisfy customer's expectations. The use of SL allows companies to achieve this objective and build a trustful relationship with customers. The interactive capabilities of SL provide the opportunity to build a personal environment for customers, each one considered as an individual in addressing promotional messages, providing a wide range of products and services, and making the virtual community a truly worthwhile place for the customer to visit. The possibility to individually and interactively address customers, allows companies to better understand their target and to provide new products and services promotion in fulfilling the customer's needs. Finally, the third strategy allows companies to develop a high brand awareness. SL platform provides companies "the opportunity to increase their brand awareness and everyone may be recognised in a smaller, yet more specific, group of people" (Franz & Wolkinger, 2003). By creating unique branded events companies have the possibility to engage target customer audience. Events in SL have proven so successful is because they can mimic nearly every aspect of live events. This characteristic allows customers to be more receptive to promotional messages and to enhance their brand awareness.

REFERENCES

Askarzay, W., & Unelkar, B. (2008). Strategic approach to globalization with mobile business. In Unelkar, B. (Ed.), *Handbook of research on mobile business: Technical, methodological and social perspectives*. Hershey, PA: IGI Global.

Bagozzi, R. P., & Dholakia, U. M. (2002). Intentional social action in virtual communities. *Journal of Interactive Marketing, 16*(2), 2–21. doi:10.1002/dir.10006

Bales, R. F. (1950). *Interaction process analysis.* Reading, MA: Addison Wesley.

Bell, T., Marrs, F., Solomon, I., & Thomas, H. (1997). *Auditing organizations through a strategic-systems lens: The KPMG business measurement process.* KPMG LLP.

Brendel, J. (2008). *Information Technology the impact of virtual communities on marketing practices* [White paper].

Brown, S. L., Tilton, A., & Woodside, D. M. (2002). The case for on-line communities. [from http://www.mckinseyquarterly.com]. *The McKinsey Quarterly, 1*, Retrieved 1 October, 2004.

Chaharbaghi, K., Fendt, C., & Willis, R. (2003). Meaning, legitimacy and impact of business models in fast-moving environments. *Management Decision, 41*(4), 372–382. doi:10.1108/00251740310468013

Chesbrough, H., & Rosenbloom, R. S. (2002). The role of the business model in capturing value from innovation: Evidence from Xerox Corporation's technology spin-off companies. *Industrial and Corporate Change, 11*(3). doi:10.1093/icc/11.3.529

Dholakia, U. M., Bagozzi, R., & Pearo, L. K. (2004). A social influence model of consumer participation in network- and small-group-based virtual communities. *International Journal of Research in Marketing, 21*(3), 241–263. doi:10.1016/j.ijresmar.2003.12.004

Ellison, N. B. (2007). Social network sites: Definition, history, and scholarship. *Journal of Computer-Mediated Communication, 13*(1).

Etzioni, A., & Etzioni, O. (1999). Face-to-face and computer-mediated communities: A comparative analysis. *The Information Society, 15*(4), 241–248. doi:10.1080/019722499128402

Franz, R., & Wolkinger, T. (2003). Customer integration with virtual communities. Case study: The online community of the largest regional newspaper in Austria. In *Proceedings of the 36th Annual Hawaii International Conference on System Sciences,* (pp. 6-9).

Friedkin, N. (1998). *A structural theory of social influence.* Cambridge, UK: Cambridge University Press. doi:10.1017/CBO9780511527524

Hagel, J., & Armstrong, A. (1997). *Net gain: Expanding markets through virtual communities.* Boston, MA: Harvard Business School Press.

Hamel, G. (2000). *Leading the revolution.* Boston, MA: Harvard Business School Press.

Hawkins, R. (2001). *The business model as a research problem in electronic commerce. STAR (Socio-economic Trends Assessment for the digital Revolution) IST Project, Issue Report, 4, July 2001.* Brighton, UK: SPRU – Science and Technology Policy Research.

Hedman, J., & Kalling, T. (2001). *The business model: A mean to understand the business context of information and communication technology.* Working paper 2001/9, Institute of Economic Research, School of Economics and Management, Lund Universitet, Lund Sweden.

Holmquist, L. E. (2007). *2.0. Interaction.* Mobile: March-April.

InvestorWords.com. (2006). *Business model definition.* Retrieved 21 April, 2006, from http://www.investorwords.com/629/business_model.html

Kaplan, R. S., & Norton, D. P. (2004). *Strategy maps: Converting intangible assets in to tangible outcomes.* Boston, MA: Harvard Business School Press.

Kaplow, D., & Pelaez, J. (2002). *Understanding the economic value and business impact of B2B portals.* FactPoint Group White Paper.

Kock, N. (2008). E-collaboration and e-commerce in virtual worlds: The potential of Second Life and World of Warcraft. *International Journal of e-Collaboration, 4*(3), 1–13. doi:10.4018/jec.2008070101

Latane, B. (1981). The psychology of social impact. *The American Psychologist, 36*, 343–356. doi:10.1037/0003-066X.36.4.343

Lazar, J. R., Tsao, R., & Preece, J. (1999). One foot in cyberspace and the other on the ground: A case study of analysis and design issues in a hybrid virtual and physical community. *Web Net Journal: Internet Technologies. Applications and Issues, 1*(3), 49–57.

Lewicki, R. J., McAllister, D. J., & Bies, R. J. (1998). Trust and distrust: New relationships and realities. *Academy of Management Review, 23*, 438–458.

Mathwick, C. (2002). Understanding the online consumer: A typology of online relational norms and behavior. *Journal of Interactive Marketing, 16*(1), 40–55. doi:10.1002/dir.10003

Moon, J. Y., & Sproull, L. (2001). *Turning love into money: How some firms may profit from voluntary electronic customer communities.* Unpublished manuscript

Morris, M., Schindehutte, M., & Allen, J. (2005). The entrepreneur's business model: Toward a unified perspective. *Journal of Business Research, 58*(6), 726–735. doi:10.1016/j.jbusres.2003.11.001

Nambisan, S. (2002). Designing virtual customer environments for new product development: Toward a theory. *Academy of Management Review, 27*(3), 392–413.

Ridings, C. M., Gefen, D., & Arinze, B. (2002). Some antecedents and effects of trust in virtual communities. *The Journal of Strategic Information Systems, 11*, 271–295. doi:10.1016/S0963-8687(02)00021-5

Romm, C., Pliskin, N., & Clarke, R. (1997). Virtual communities and society: Toward an integrative three phase model. *International Journal of Information Management, 17*(4), 261–270. doi:10.1016/S0268-4012(97)00004-2

Rousseau, D. M., Sitkin, S. B., Burt, R. S., & Camerer, C. (1998). Not so different after all: A cross-discipline view of trust. *Academy of Management Review, 23*, 393–404. doi:10.5465/AMR.1998.926617

Sandberg, K. D. (2002). Is it time to trade in your business model? *Harvard Management Update,* (January), 3-5.

Slywotzky, A. J. (1996). *Value migration: How to think several moves ahead of the competition.* Boston, MA: Harvard Business School Press.

Stabell, C. B., & Fjeldstad, D. (1998). Configuring value for competitive advantage: On chains, shops and networks. *Strategic Management Journal, 19*, 413–437. doi:10.1002/(SICI)1097-0266(199805)19:5<413::AID-SMJ946>3.0.CO;2-C

Subramaniam, C., Shaw, M. J., & Gardner, D. M. (2000). Product marketing and channel management in electronic commerce. *Information Systems Frontiers, 1*(4), 363–378. doi:10.1023/A:1010061924822

Sweet, P. (2001). Strategic value configuration logics and the "new" economy: A service economy revolution? *International Journal of Service Industry Management, 12*(1), 70–83. doi:10.1108/09564230110382781

Terdiman, D. (2007). *The entrepreneur's guide to Second Life: Making money in the metaverse.* Indianapolis, IN: Sybex.

Timmers, P. (1998). Business model for electronic markets. *Electronic Markets, 8,* 3–8. doi:10.1080/10196789800000016

Section 2
What is E-Novation?

Chapter 4
Defining E–Novation

David R. Low
University of Western Sydney, Australia

Hugh M. Pattinson
University of Western Sydney, Australia

ABSTRACT

"E-Novation" is defined as a combination of innovation and e-marketing enabled by new collaborative platforms that are being developed and released using Web 2.0 methodologies, allowing for a different level of connectivity around the world. This chapter explores innovation and its contribution to firm performance, links to market orientation – and development of a new collaborative information platform to support innovation. E-marketing is also defined in terms of marketing in computer-mediated environments with emphasis on service-dominant logic (SDL) and collaborative value creation approaches. Aspects of the evolving new collaborative information platform such as the Semantic Web and Web 2.0 applications are discussed from e-marketing and innovation perspectives. Will "e-novation" challenge businesses to rethink how their employees will create or participate in collaborative groups with others where future revenue prospects appear to mainly from service development? This question is also explored through subsequent chapters in the book.

INTRODUCTION

We define E-Novation as an approach which is more powerful than traditional forms of innovation processes, through the incorporation of a diverse range of views and ideas directly into development of service-dominant knowledge-based goods and services. E-Novation is a combination of Innovation and E-Marketing enabled by New Collaborative Platforms that are being developed and released using Web 2.0 methodologies and allow for a different level of connectivity around the world.

This chapter outlines an approach to innovation that incorporates more diverse views and ideas, to foster creativity and to co-produce goods and services. Where expression of a diverse range of ideas and views is achieved within a group

DOI: 10.4018/978-1-60566-394-4.ch004

setting, the result being that outputs are more creative and ultimately more innovative for the co-users of those outputs (Woodman et al 1993). Supporting this drive to increase creativity and innovation is a reframing of "group production" and underlying information technology into an enabling "platform".

This chapter discusses developments in an emerging information environment into a collaborative information platform and its contribution toward reframing innovation and e-marketing, to produce new products, services, strategies and philosophies.

INNOVATION AND NEW COLLABORATIVE PLATFORMS

Innovation within a firm is seen as having a positive impact on the economy (Teece 2002) as well as being a key element in the entrepreneurial process (Schaper and Volery 2003). Many definitions of innovation can be found in the literature; Zaltman, Duncan and Holbeck (1973), Damanpour and Fariborz (1984), Damanpour (1991) and Boer and During (2001) all provide definitions of innovation. Each of these has a common theme that the item being innovated must be new to the target audience. It has also been suggested that when viewed as a process, innovation may be culture specific (Sawy, Eriksonnen, Raven and Carlsson 2001).

Innovation, or at least the firm's capacity to innovate, is a characteristic that has been shown as having a relationship to firm performance. Studies have found, for instance, that successful product and process innovation has a positive link to firm performance (Caves and Ghemawat 1992). New product development can lead to increased market share (Zahra and Covin 1983) and product innovation has been linked to increasing market share (Banbury and Mitchell 1995). Yamin, Gunasekaran and Mavondo (1999) studied innovation and firm performance on Australian manufactur-

ing companies and found a link between financial performance and innovation performance.

The literature indicates therefore that there is a positive relationship between firm innovativeness and firm performance, with many authors suggesting innovation as a firm strategy to achieve superior performance. However, one can conjecture that there may be both internal (to the firm) and external influences on firm innovation performance and the motivation to innovate.

One such internal influence identified within the literature is the concept of market orientation, which has also been shown to have a positive relationship to firm performance. Market orientation refers to the organization-wide generation, dissemination, and responsiveness to market intelligence (Kohli & Jaworski 1990). Shapiro (1988) suggests that a number of areas of the business other than marketing participate in all three functions; hence, the function is wider than the marketing department. By this they mean that "market orientation entails (1) one or more departments engaging in activities geared toward developing an understanding of customer's current and future needs and the factors affecting them, (2) sharing of this understanding across departments, and (3) the various departments engaging in activities designed to meet select customers' needs."

One study that linked a high level of market orientation with the innovation performance of the firm was Atuahene-Gima (1996: 94) which, in a cross-sectional study of 600 firms in Australia, found that there was a significant negative correlation between market orientation and the product newness to customers, suggesting "market orientation helps to reduce the chances of the firm producing innovations that require major behavioural changes on the part of potential customers for adoption". Han, Kim and Srivastava (1998: 41) found "some support that innovations facilitate the conversion of market-oriented business philosophy into superior corporate performance". Erdil, Erdil and Keskin (2004) investigated this link in a study of 55 European firms and found that the undertaking of market orientation activities by firms, as defined in previous literature, was correlated with firm innovativeness.

Developments in collaborative innovation processes, that is collaboration with parties outside the firm conducting the innovation, have gained momentum in recent years with some methodologies as we will see later depending on a level of market orientation on firms part to successfully pursue these innovation methods.

Collaborative innovation is where product/service development is undertaken with participation from external organizations (Krishnan & Ulrich 2001). Ideas and views are shared by people and groups across organizations to produce a creative outcome greater than if the product or service is created largely within one organization. Recent business and marketing literature on emerging business models highlight a shift toward collaborative goods and services development, to the point where buyers and sellers merge into a converged community both developing and using goods and services (examples include Prahalad & Ramaswamy 2004, Vargo & Lusch, 2004).

Concepts such as co-creation and co-production related to software application development have been established for over 15 years, but have recently gained prominence outside the software arena to encompass information-based goods and services. "open-source" software development highlights development processes and a collaborative form of innovation, which now stretches way beyond software, into a wide range of goods and services development (for discussion on open-source development see Raymond 2001; Chesborough 2003; Pattinson & Woodside 2007).

The open-source development of the Linux operating system focused on initially using Internet News Group to share operating system code in text files, and then using the World-Wide as the main vehicle for thousands of software programmers to share, update and return their contributions to the overall application to a coordinating who integrated the updates into a revised operating that

was available for end-use – and further updating through the Internet (see Torvalds & Diamond 2001; Pattinson & Woodside 2007, in the Red Hat Case Study). Linux development provides a blueprint for collaborative information goods and services innovation and development because information goods and services are essentially digitized software files that can be collaboratively updated using the Internet. Furthermore, it illustrates how this type of innovation process can ensure that customer (or end user) needs are fulfilled in a process that has definite elements of Market Orientation surrounding it.

The Internet revolutionized software development and distribution system from mid-1990's, but is now challenging us to think again about how groups can collaborate to produce new and creative goods and services.

Today the Internet is now part of a collaborative information "platform". Thomas Friedman (2007) defines a "platform" as "the basic underlying operating systems for innovation and production" with "combinations of hardware, software technology and applications, and related systems". Freidman identified a set of information technology "flatteners" that built cumulatively to produce a powerful platform including:

- Microsoft Windows Operating System (1989)
- Netscape Navigator Web Browser (1994-5)
- Workflow Software (Mid-1990's)
- Outsourcing to address Y2K challenges (mid-late 1990's)
- Offshoring full product development/manufacturing activities (early 2000s);
- Supply-Chaining (early-mid 2000s)
- Uploading of user-generated content (mid-2000s)
- Insourcing activities into other organizations supply-chains and information flows (mid-2000s)

- In-forming through search-engine optimisation and information flows through managed portals (mid-2000s)
- Offering information through Digital Mobile, Personal, and Virtual enhancement (late-2000s). *(From Friedman, 2007)*

The ten flatteners are then activated at a new collaborative platform level through a "triple convergence" based on technological convergence of all 10 flatteners, followed by enhanced goods and services developed by businesses using the new platform, and then further by individuals and small groups working together with the platform. (Friedman 2007).

Friedman's platform view sets up a new collaborative information platform which he sees as contributing to a new form of globalization based on individuals and small groups collaborating across a "flat world" to produce new benefits and services.

There is a view now that new internet technologies available under Web 2.0 can have large commercial impacts when those participating in such media do so in a way that relates to commercial interests (Riegner, 2007).

E-MARKETING AND NEW COLLABORATIVE PLATFORMS

E-Marketing refers to marketing in Computer-Mediated Environments (CME's). Hoffmann & Novak (1996, 2009) highlighted the World-Wide Web as an exemplary CME with its multimedia, interactive capabilities. Early E-Marketing strategy focused on utilising the World-Web to deliver new forms of customer value through distribution of goods and services online and to express marketing communication through effective online presence.

The World-Wide Web has grown into a powerful multimedia, multipurpose, multipoint, and creative environment vehicle for innovative development and delivery of new, emergent goods and services. The current stage of World-Wide Web evolution is often referred to as Web 2.0 where the Internet is viewed as a "platform" and business and marketing opportunities are produced associated with that platform (O'Reilly 2006; Low et. al. 2007). The Web 2.0 notion of "platform" can be seen as being embedded within Friedman's platform and it echoes emphasis on collaboration to develop new content, new goods and new services. Web 2.0 also challenges us think differently about marketing.

In recent years there has been a growth of portable smart devices that are semantic web enabled (Terziyan, 2005) and must be considered in any definition of Computer-Mediated Environments. These devices enable us to interact with the web in various ways and *"The increasing use of wireless networks enables more devices and infrastructure to be added piecemeal and less disruptively into the physical environment"* (Poslad, 2009, pg1). These portable devices have aided our mobility in the current physical world *"users can move in between Internet nodes, to log on and to access Web-based content and email, anywhere, anytime. Users can carry personalised mobile networked devices with them to access services filtered according to their personal preferences..."* (Poslad, 2009, pg 115) and enable us to interact with our digital networks in a variety of ways and locations.

Collaboration is an emerging and key theme in new generation Service-Dominant Logic (SDL) Marketing. A Service-Driven logic views Services as benefits of specialized skills or competencies. "Goods" are transmitters of embedded knowledge (or codified knowledge) that are transformed by people into these benefits (Vargo & Lusch, 2004). Service-Driven innovation is research development, delivery and exchange of benefits collaboratively across individuals, groups, and Organizations – or co-production. We also believe that service-driven innovation can be translated from business services into a platform through Service-Oriented-Architecture (SOA).

Collaboration, or at least platforms from which to collaborate, is one of the "new" applications often associated with the development of Web 2.0. The most publicised of these are applications, and used worldwide by marketers, are applications such as Facebook and Twitter. The increasing popularity of Collaborative Innovative Networks (COINs) facilitated by the new web architecture has brought about ever increasing levels and sophistication of collaboration (Gloor, 2006) and supports the proposition of Service-Dominant Logic.

The idea of "products as a medium containing codified knowledge" was highlighted back in the late-1990s in relation to software applications (Pattinson & Woodside, 2007; and Armour 2000), with distinct development processes promoting flexibility, and multiple collaborative updating processes (see Iansiti 1998). Service-Dominant Logic highlights co-creation and co-discussion themes we have already discussed as innovation. We go further to highlight that SDL marketing is about exchange based on co-creation and co-production. A Web 2.0 perspective highlights a range of platform technologies that encourage SDL Marketing – or E-Marketing 2.0.

An Open-source marketing concept was proposed by Sood and Pattinson (2006) (also Pattinson and Woodside 2007) where the "Community" collectively develops and uses products and services. Applications such as Netscape Navigator and Linux have used customers (or users) to assist in the development of their products and set the direction of future developments.

One use of collective intelligence is to develop new goods and services. Examples such as Wikipedia representing the collaborative development of an online encyclopedia; Ideas, Concepts and New Frameworks can be developed using Wikis (See Marketing Ontology Wiki Project in Sood & Pattinson 2006); books are now created using Wiki's (See Libert. Spector, Et. Al. 2008)

Creation as well as communication can occur through social media where ideas can be roughly and quickly thrown into an online social network for conversation, discussion, debate and generation into changed content that may become new communication content and possibly new goods and services. Social media is currently an antithesis to mainstream media characterised by highly structured and professional set marketing messages.

The Semantic Web further supports SDL marketing where the "platform" has the intelligence to understand the meaning of descriptions and services requested by other machines – and humans – and to collect and deliver part of most of those services (Berners-Lee, Hendler & Lassila 2005, Sood & Pattinson 2005). The Semantic Web will be a key enabler for E-Marketing 2.0 – and may become a virtual E-Marketer

Thus the new collaborative information platform, provided by Web 2.0 technology, supports E-Marketing 2.0 based on Service-Dominant Logic focused in collaboration and co-production principles; a Semantic Web supporting new virtual marketing capabilities and applications as well as Social Media redefining developer-user communication, creation and service innovation and development.

E-NOVATION

So far this chapter has discussed separately the emergence of a powerful collaborative information platform and distinct impacts on innovation and E-Marketing. We have combined these three elements into one new E-Novation concept. We define "E-Novation" as a distinct form of innovation coupled with a new approach to E-Marketing supported by an emerging Collaborative Information Platform.

E-Novation recognizes that the collaborative information platform continues to develop and has an underlying effect on innovation and E-Marketing. At this point the platform offers technologies and applications to foster creative innovation processes that work with an E-Marketing logic of co-production. E-Novation is Innovation and E-Marketing enabled by New Collaborative Platforms.

One example of how information is being used in new ways is Google Flu-Trends (Google Inc 2010). Google has found a link between the number of searches related to flu topics and how many people actually have flu-like symptoms; this can then be used to track the spread of flu within a region and is real-time compared with traditional doctor reported methods. Using this methodology we can determine the number of online searches for various products by country, for example the search term "Apple I-Phone" shows us the top searches (by country) are Nigeria, Singapore, India, Pakistan, Hong Kong and Australia, at the time of writing. With an ability to break this down by region within a country it provides a powerful marketing tool to understand the level of interest in a product. Google has extended and developed this service to now cover a wide-range of trends on various popular topics and issues.

The congruence of three elements of our definition of E-Novation highlights that it is the interaction of these elements that in fact facilitates the outcomes being seen from the E-Novation process. The elements of our definition are the (a) New Collaborative Platforms, (b) Innovation and (c) E-Marketing (see Figure 1)

New Collaborative Platforms are set at the Friedman (2007) standard (i.e. making the world a level playing field) with focus on developments associated with the triple convergence – with flatteners amplifying and reinforcing each other's impact and new economies being opened up by the technology. However, we also consider additional developments that may enhance or change the platform, developments such as technologies considered under Web 2.0 but also future technologies that analysts may perhaps regard as "Web 3.0 or 4.0" such as Semantic Web and 3D Web. These platform developments have symbiotic link to innovators, marketers and people collaborating using the platform.

Innovation, in our definition, is based on an open-source collaborative input of diverse range of ideas with a view toward more creative co-production of benefits within the community. This does mean that there is more than one entity or per-

Figure 1. E-novation elements

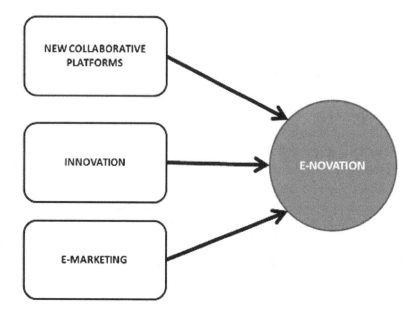

son collaborating within the innovation process, enabled by new collaborative platforms, which in a pre-Web 2.0 world would not have otherwise collaborated. This does not mean that there is not aggressive screening and scrutiny of ideas – there is ample evidence of high quality development, screening and commitment to creative solutions in the open-source software community.

E-Marketing is built around an E-Marketing 2.0 perspective of Service-Dominant Logic Marketing not just with a computer mediated environment but a full collaborative information platform. Symbiotic links between marketers and the platform should lead to co-production (i.e. "new marketing") of a large range of new innovative goods and services.

Manipulating these elements will unearth new insights and knowledge for industry transformation – and for E-Novators who will need skills and resources across these three elements.

CONCLUSION

The E-Novation framework presented in this chapter, challenges marketers in particular to rethink just what "marketing" really is – and to recast just who are "marketers". We believe the conventional definition of marketing and marketers will expand to include those activities we have described as being part of the E-Novation process. Progressive marketers are aware that that the new collaborative information platform demands further investigation and understanding, especially where increasing numbers of "users" are busy in conversing with their social networks through social media – and not seeing or listening to conventional marketing communication. Just how far they may to immerse themselves and pass or share their "vocation" in a "co-production" paradigm in these environments, is yet to be seen.

E-Novation also questions the traditional separation between buyers and sellers to highlight a different view where innovation is a collaborative

set of activities between a developer and user – and that may be interchangeable within a social network, or in cross-organizational communities. E-Novation is based on assumptions that higher creativity and more innovative output is achieved where much greater collection and discussion of a diverse range of views and ideas can be shared using the collaborative information platform.

We would like to leave the reader with a question, will E-Novation challenge businesses to rethink how their employees will create or participate in collaborative groups with others where future revenue prospects appear to mainly from service development? These issues are explored in the chapters that surround this definitional chapter.

REFERENCES

Armour, P. G. (2000). The case for a new business model – Is software a product or a medium? *Communications of the ACM, 43*(8), 19–22. doi:10.1145/345124.345131

Atuahene-Gima, K. (1996). Market orientation and innovation. *Journal of Business Research, 35*, 93–103. doi:10.1016/0148-2963(95)00051-8

Banbury, C., & Mitchell, W. (1995). The effect of introducing important incremental innovations on market share and business survival. *Strategic Management Journal, 16*, 161–182. doi:10.1002/smj.4250160922

Berners-Lee, T., Hendler, J., & Lassila, O. (2001). The Semantic Web. *Scientific American, 284*(5), 34. doi:10.1038/scientificamerican0501-34

Boer, H., & During, W. (2001). Innovation, what innovation? A comparison between product, process and organisational innovation. *International Journal of Technology Management, 22*(1), 83–107. doi:10.1504/IJTM.2001.002956

Caves, R., & Ghemawat, P. (1992). Identifying mobility barriers. *Strategic Management Journal*, *13*, 1–12. doi:10.1002/smj.4250130102

Chesbrough, H. W. (2003). *Open innovation: The new imperative for creating and profiting from technology*. Boston, MA: Harvard Business School Press.

Damanpiur, F. (1991). Organisational innovation: A meta-analysis of effects of determinants and moderators. *Academy of Management Journal*, *34*(3), 555–590. doi:10.2307/256406

Damanpour, F., & Fariborz, W. M. (1984). Organisational innovation and performance: The problem of organisational lag. *Administrative Science Quarterly*, *29*(3), 392–411. doi:10.2307/2393031

Erdil, S., Erdil, O., & Keskin, H. (2004). The relationships between market orientation, firm innovativeness and innovation performance. *Journal of Global Business and Technology*, *1*(1).

Friedman, T. L. (2007). *The world is flat: The globalized world in the twenty-first century – Expanded and updated edition*. London, UK: Penguin Books.

Gloor, P. (2006). *Swarm creativity: Competitive advantage through collaborative innovation networks*. New York, NY: Oxford University Press.

Google, Inc. (2010). *Google flu trends*. Retrieved 1 June, 2010, from http://www.google.org/flutrends/

Han, J. K., Kim, N., & Srivastava, R. K. (1998). Market orientation and organisational performance: Is innovation a missing link? *Journal of Marketing*, *62*(October), 30–45. doi:10.2307/1252285

Hoffman, D. L., & Novak, T. P. (2009). Flow online: Lessons learned and future prospects. *Journal of Interactive Marketing*, *23*, 23–34. doi:10.1016/j.intmar.2008.10.003

Hoffmann, D. L., & Novak, T. P. (1996). Marketing hypermedia computer mediated environments: Conceptual foundations. *Journal of Marketing*, *60*, 50–68. doi:10.2307/1251841

Iansiti, M. (1998). *Technology integration: Making critical choices in a dynamic world*. Boston, MA: Harvard Business School Press.

Kohli, A. K., & Jaworski, B. J. (1990). Market orientation: The construct, research propositions, and managerial implications. *Journal of Marketing*, *54*(2), 1–18. doi:10.2307/1251866

Krishnan, V., & Ulrich, K. T. (2001). Product development decisions: A review of the literature. *Management Science*, *47*(1), 1–21. doi:10.1287/mnsc.47.1.1.10668

Libert, B., & Spector, J. (2008). *We are smarter than me*. Upper Saddle River, NJ: Wharton School Publishing.

Low, D. R., Lee, G., Pattinson, H. M., & Adam, S. (2007). *Web 2.0 effects on marketing management in the 21st century*. Special Session, ANZMAC 2007, Dunedin, New Zealand, December 3-5.

O'Reilly. (2006). *Web 2.0 compact definition: Trying again*. Retrieved July 6, 2008, from http://radar.oreilly.com/archives/2006/12/web_20_compact.html Pattinson, H. M., & Woodside, A. G. (2007). *Innovation and diffusion of software technology: Mapping strategies*. Oxford, UK: Elsevier.

Poslad, R. (2009). *Ubiquitous computing: Smart devices, environment and interactions*. Chichester, UK: Wiley.

Prahalad, C. K., & Ramaswamy, V. (2004). Co-creation experiences: The next practice in value creation. *Journal of Interactive Marketing*, *18*(3), 5–14. doi:10.1002/dir.20015

Raymond, E. S. (2001). *The cathedral & the bazaar: Musings on Linux and open source by an accidental revolutionary* (revised edition). Sebastopol, CA.

Riegner, C. (2007). Word of mouth on the Web: The impact of Web 2.0 on consumer purchase decisions. *Journal of Advertising Research, 47*(4), 436–447. doi:10.2501/S0021849907070456

Sawy, O., Eriksonnon, I., Raven, A., & Carlsson, S. (2001). Understanding shared knowledge creation spaces around business processes: Precursors to process innovation implementation. *International Journal of Technology Management, 22*(1), 149–173. doi:10.1504/IJTM.2001.002959

Schaper, M., & Colery, T. (2003). *Entrepreneurship and small business: A Pacific Rim perspective.* Brisbane, Australia: John Wiley.

Shapiro, B. P. (1988). What the hell is market orientated? *Harvard Business Review, 66,* 119–125.

Sood, S. C., & Pattinson, H. M. (2005). *Semantics in marketspace: Emerging semantic marketing computer-mediated environments.* Presented at The Annual Meeting Of The Society For Marketing Advances, San Antonio, Texas – November 2-5, 2005.

Sood, S. C., & Pattinson, H. M. (2006). The open source marketing experiment: Using Wikis to revolutionize marketing practice on the Web. In *Proceedings of the 22nd Industrial and Purchasing Group (IMP) Conference "Opening the Network: New Perspectives in Industrial Marketing and Purchasing,"* IMP Group, Milan, Italy, 7-9 September 2006.

Teece, D. J. (2002). *Managing intellectual capital.* Oxford, UK: Oxford University Press. doi:10.1093/0198295421.001.0001

Terziyan, V. (2005). Semantic Web services for smart devices based on mobile agents. *International Journal of Intelligent Information Technologies, 1*(2), 43–55. doi:10.4018/jiit.2005040104

Torvalds, L., & Diamond, D. (2001). *Just for fun: The story of an accidental revolutionary.* New York, NY: Texere.

Vargo, S. L., & Lusch, R. F. (2004). Evolving a new dominant logic for marketing. *Journal of Marketing, 68,* 1–17. doi:10.1509/jmkg.68.1.1.24036

Woodman, R. W., Sawyer, J. E., & Griffin, R. W. (1993). Toward a theory of organizational creativity. *Academy of Management Review, 18*(2), 293–321.

Yamin, S., Gunasekaran, A., & Mavondo, F. (1999). Innovation index and its implications on organisational performance: A study of Australian manufacturing companies. *International Journal of Technology Management, 17,* 495–503. doi:10.1504/IJTM.1999.002733

Zahra, S. A., & Covin, J. G. (1993). Business strategy, technology policy and firm performance. *Strategic Management Journal, 14,* 451–478. doi:10.1002/smj.4250140605

Zaltman, G., Duncan, R., & Holbek, J. (1973). *Innovations and organisations.* New York, NY: Wiley.

Chapter 5
Defining E-Novation in Action

Ehsan Ehsani
Accenture Management Consulting, USA

ABSTRACT

Managing product development in an efficient manner is considered a crucial element for a company's survival in today's world. Current markets usually consist of highly fragmented segments of customers looking for customized and differentiated products at lower costs. Intense competition has also pressured companies to launch the products faster to the market in order to reap the planned benefits. Usage of collaborative Web-enabled models for innovation and product development, what we refer to as E-Novation, has become more popular as a result of responding to the aforementioned challenges. From technological point of view, the E-Novation models are particularly enabled through collaborative Web solutions, Web 2.0 tools, and Web-based virtual worlds. This chapter deals with the application of such collaborative Internet-based technologies in the product development and discusses their use in various stages of product development process; from idea management to prototyping. Based on existing literature in the area, the analysis of four cases (Dell, InnoCentive, Ponoko, and Implenia), participant observation and experience with such applications and semi-structured interviews with both managers of such projects and the projects' stakeholders, this chapter demonstrates that new organizational models and skills are required to manage interdependencies internally and externally in collaboration through E-Novation. It also provides some insights about the future trends and opportunities in this era and guidelines for successful implementation of these technologies in reality.

DOI: 10.4018/978-1-60566-394-4.ch005

INTRODUCTION

Managing the product development in an efficient manner is considered a crucial element for a company's survival in today's world. Current markets usually consist of highly fragmented segments of customers which are looking for customized and differentiated products at lower costs. The intense competition has also pressured companies to launch the products faster to the market in order to reap the planned benefits. Usage of collaborative web-enabled models for innovation and product development, what we refer to as E-Novation, has become more popular as a result to respond to the above mentioned challenges. From technological point of view, the E-Novation models are particularly enabled through collaborative web solutions, Web 2.0 tools and web-based virtual worlds.

In this chapter, our aim is to explain the current application of collaborative internet-based technologies in the product development and discusses their use and limits in various stages of product development process; from idea management to prototyping. Based on existing literature in the area, the analysis of four cases (Dell, InnoCentive, Ponoko and Implenia), participant observation and experience with such applications and semi-structured interviews with both managers of such projects and the projects' stakeholders, this chapter demonstrates that new organizational models and skills are required to manage interdependencies internally and externally in collaboration through E-Novation. We also provide some insights about the future trends and opportunities in this era and guidelines for successful implementation of these technologies in reality.

BACKGROUND

Two of the major trends shaping the business landscape today include the increasing consumer expectations and the growing role of the internet in structuring economic transactions (Oliver Young, 2008). Maturity of traditional markets and the global competition have lead to erosion of the margins for established products. This has put increasing pressure on companies to diversify and to innovate for specific needs of the customers to meet their expectations and maintain profitability. Innovation and new product development, thus, have become the corner stones of competitive advantage across diverse industries.

The last decade has also witnessed the rise of the internet to the center of economic activity. In today's business environment, many business processes, information flows, and economic transactions in product development are moved over to the internet, reducing costs, increasing speed, and multiplying the available options for offering and receiving the products or services to both firms and consumers (Buyukozkan, Baykasoglu & Dereli, 2007). The adoption of internet based technologies has been a response to one of the challenges companies face today, especially in the area of innovation management and capability creation, which is to capture, use and effectively manage the fragmented sources of knowledge which exist inside and outside their value chain (Grant, 1997).

The two major trends of innovation and use of internet are at last converging to fuel the rise of web-enabled innovation. This new phenomena is enabling companies to significantly sharpen their innovative capabilities by having more direct, cheap, and universal access to consumers, innovators, and innovative ideas. Web 2.0, the amalgam of technologies that has significantly increased the interactive capabilities of the internet, is reinforcing what we here refer to as E-Novation significantly. Increasingly companies are using the internet to innovate more efficiently through virtual concept testing, "listening in" to customer discussions on web forums, online focus groups, online feedback methods, and online markets for designs and solutions, among others (Buyukozkan, Baykasoglu & Dereli, 2007).

The new aspect in this phenomenon is the use of internet and its use is very recent. Pioneers of web-enabled innovation entered this area largely in the past five years. Therefore very little rigorous research result or practical insight is available on the types of technologies used, successful initiatives, potential pitfalls, and implementation challenges. Yet the idea of using web 2.0 to enable innovation is taking hold in many firms (Prandelli, Verona & Raccagni, 2006). A global forecast by Forrester research (2008) finds that over half of the North American and European companies see web 2.0 as one of their investment priority areas for the coming years. Benefiting from E-Novation requires a firm to know the available technologies and their application, their strengths and weaknesses, the process and organizational changes required and the implementation challenges, in order to select the most appropriate combination for the purpose at hand. This chapter reviews current practices in collaboration through the internet to streamline innovation and new product development, namely E-Novation, and provides some insights for the future trends.

E-NOVATION AND PRODUCT SERVICE RESEARCH AND DEVELOPMENT

E-Novation has emerged as a new paradigm to respond to the necessities of the companies in respect to the effective innovation management in 21st century. In principle, E-Novation is trying to leverage the opportunities World Wide Web provides and also existing collaborative technologies to effectively manage the company's innovation and product development processes and also the relationships with external parties in a distributed innovation network.

Companies have been using Web-based technologies and other collaborative systems for quite some time. Online questionnaires, for example, have been used to gather customers' comments or complaints regarding companies' products and services; or searching for market data in the websites has now become a mainstream. What is new in E-Novation is to take these processes to the next level and change the "conventional knowledge management" to "conversational knowledge management" (Lee & Lan, 2007). So the fundamental new thing in E-Novation compared to conventional web-based tools is high level of interactivity based on a collaboration platform.

Figure 1. Knowledge and collaboration in e-novation era (Adapted from Lee & Lan, 2007)

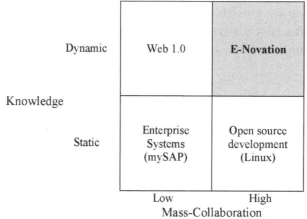

Our view, then, is that E-Novation encompasses a range of concepts and technologies such as web 2.0, Virtual Prototyping, virtual communities and collaborative product lifecycle management (PLM). Another new aspect of E-Novation which makes it a different phenomenon compared to conventional ways of knowledge management is a dynamic structure which permits a group of people to modify, related or create new pieces of knowledge based on existing information. Figure 1 shows the position of E-Novation compared to movements such as open source development or Web 1.0 is represented.

In the upcoming parts, first we are going to review the activities in the formal process of product development and then will explain how E-Novation can and is applied in each stage of the development process.

Even though our definition of the term E-Novation is broad and incorporates all types of web-based collaboration, an increasingly movement in the new applications such as Wikis or blogs is the tendency to create shared property or common ground in which it is in everyone's interest to create a positive outcome (Lee & Lan, 2007). Rather than having millions of separate webpages which have limited sources of knowledge creation, one million, the idea is to collect them in one place and open them up to the users to read, edit and make comments. This way, everyone's best pieces of knowledge can combine, and by tracking the changes, the whole process is kept open and self-governing. The best example of this phenomenon is seen in Wikipedia® but companies such as Nokia® and Angel.com® are also taking advantage of this by creating wiki websites.

FORMAL PROCESS OF NPD AND DEVELOPMENT FUNNEL

The formal process of product development typically is in the form of a structured set of activities which is designed to transform a product idea to a new product in the market (Wheelwright & Clark, 1992, Cooper, 2001, Ulrich & Eppinger, 2003). There is a continuum of product/service in respect to what companies offer in the market and many companies use such structured approach for developing and launching not only new products but also services (Johnston & Clark, 2005). Different researchers have defined different phases to capture these set of activities in a model; but in terms of nature of the activities, the differences are marginal. Typically, the processes in the existing literature require a mechanism to get the ideas and select the promising ones, develop a product/services concept, do a feasibility study, engage in actual design activities and testing and at last prepare for launch. Thus, we consider the following phases for the purpose of our study:

- Idea Management
- Concept Development
- Feasibility study
- Product design
- Testing and Refinement

The brief description of each of these phases is according to the following (Wheelwright & Clark, 1992, Urban & Hauser, 1993, Cooper, 2001, Ulrich & Eppinger, 2004):

- *Idea Management phase:* This is the first phase in the NPD process. Through this phase usually organizations are trying to get the ideas for new products from inside and outside the organization, evaluate them and select the most promising ones. Given the low percentage of the initial ideas which are finally turned into products, organizations should try to get as much ideas as possible from various sources and make sure that these ideas have a minimum certain level of quality.
- *Concept development phase:* In this phase the selected ideas are developed further

and more marketing and engineering details are incorporated with the idea. Some of the issues which are determined in this phase are: The type of the features which the final product should include the benefits which the product might provide, the possible reaction of the customers to the product and early technical feasibility for making the product.

- *Feasibility study phase:* Selected concepts should be evaluated based on profitability, alignment with manufacturing capabilities, resource availability, risk point of view and market research. These activities are done in the feasibility phase. This is a critical phase through the NPD, as it links research and development activities (Links R with D).
- *Product design phase:* This phase takes the approved product/service concepts in the feasibility phase to the next level and conducts the detail and system level design activities which are required to develop a sample product (prototype).
- *Testing and refinement:* In this stage, prototype or sample product developed within the design phase is tested in production or among the customers/suppliers to find out possible bugs, improvement areas before real launch.

In the following, a brief overview of the E-Novation applications in each stage of the development process will be offered; these stages can be used for development of a new service as well however, a short part has been dedicated at the end to specific characteristics of service development. The descriptions will be accompanied by four case studies which demonstrate application of E-Novation in new product/service development through different technologies.

E-NOVATION DEVELOPMENT FROM IDEA MANAGEMENT TO PRODUCT TESTING

Internet and web-based tools can help to increase the efficiency of product development process in many ways; They can speed up the connection between firm's employees and customers (Buyukozkan, G., Baykasoglu, A., & Dereli, T., 2007), they can get the voice of the customer from the users in such a way which is impossible to get with traditional ways (Prandelli, Verona & Raccagni, 2006), and they can also test their product and service prototypes with them via Internet (Dahan & Srinivasan, 2000).

The valuable information which can be received from customers, suppliers, and other stakeholders in the firm's value network can play an important role in company's innovation success. Enabled by collaborative technologies such as virtual world environments, online platforms (e.g. Indea brokers) and also web 2.0, E-Novation tries to leverage the above mentioned benefits to achieve high performance (Edery, 2006). In summary, considering the same representation of the product development process as a funnel (Wheelwright & Clark, 1992), E-Novation helps the NPD process in the following ways:

1. Idea Management Phase

Use of the web-enabled tools to capture customers' ideas is one of the areas which has got significant popularity in the recent years (Prandelli, E., et. al, 2006). Companies are using a variety of ways from simple questionnaire in companies like Ben & Jerry®, the ice cream maker, to the blogs and discussion forums as in the case of Sturbucks®.

One of the ways which has been increasingly used to generate new product ideas is the use of virtual communities. These communities are usually consist of the users, suppliers, and other interested parties which are sharing the same interest related to the product/service and are willing to express and discuss their opinions with other members. These communities which were initially used mostly in the software industry have found their way to other sectors and products such as consumer goods (P&G), automobiles (Toyota), motorcycles (Harley Davidson) and videogames (World of Warcraft).

Motivated members of such communities if encouraged to communicate with others, will reveal type of the information about the consumption patterns, their expectation and the ideas to improve or create new products which are literally impossible to get through traditional methods of interacting with the customers.

Two main types of incentive are typically provided for the members in such communities in order to raise their level of participation: Financial rewards and intangible incentives. Open source communities for Linux are example of the communities in which non-financial incentives such as the status in the technical communities have motivated the participants to contribute. InnoCentive on the other hand, rewards the members with financial compesation and companies like threadless.com use a combination of both financial and non-financial motives. While financial incentives are more common in business owned communities, other virtual groups, usually the ones created by the product fans and users themselves are relying on a social ranking mechanism for increase user participation.

In the existing literature, however, even though many authors have provided examples of the idea management using online communities (Prandelli, E. et. al, 2006, Dodgson, M., et al, 2006, Huston & Sakkab, 2006), there are few examples of the companies which have realized expected benefits.

CASE STUDY 1: DELL COMPUTER'S® APPROACH TO E-NOVATION: DELLIDEASTORM.COM

Dell Computer is one of the pioneering companies which are using the power of E-Novation to improve their products and services. Dellideastorm.com is the flagship of the company's movement: The name has been taken from the word "brainstorm"; the website is used by Dell to build an online community of customers and people interested in its products, allowing them to share ideas and collaborate with one another. The goal for the members is to tell the company what new products or services they'd like to see Dell develop.

There is no need to be a Dell customer to browse ideas and comments posted on IdeaStorm. After registration, users can post, promote, and comment on ideas. Dell employees are also joining the conversations, vote for the more promising ideas or ask for additional input regarding an idea.

Every time a user promotes an idea, the score on the idea is bumped up by 10 points. And when an idea is demoted, it loses 10 points. This score indicates how well-liked the idea is. The more well-liked the idea, the higher on the "Popular Ideas" page it goes. However, as the ideas get older, they move lower down on the page. The combination of these forces influences the final decision on perusing an idea or not.

There is no formal form of giving incentives for participation rather than the voting system. Users can also contact the moderator in the website's blog for improving the website itself.

The company has used the suggestions from the community to make improvements in some of its products and services. To mention a few, the decision for selling computer systems with Ubuntu 7.04 preinstalled in them or moving technical support telephone lines to be based in the USA and operated by people who speak and understand English well, as opposed to being based outside the USA or operated by foreigners who do not speak and understand English well, are among the new service and product improvements based on community ideas.

2. Concept and Market Research Phase

While there exist a possibilities of using E-Novation in three steps of concept phase, namely concept generation, concept evaluation and concept selection (Ulrich & Eppinger, 2004), the sub-activities related to evaluation of the concepts have been used more by the businesses.

Web-based platforms such as virtual worlds have been used increasingly to show the concept product visually to the outside world and get their feedback. Secondlife.com®, as an example, has been a place where several companies are using in order to evaluate their future products. Being in a virtual environment provides the users, potential customers and other groups to analyze the product and its complexity from different angles. Companies such as Philips®, Nike®, Mercedes Benz® and Starwood Hotels® are just some of the companies which are using Secondlife for testing the product concepts. The evaluation of the concepts through virtual tools is limited to visual representation, sound and video and the users can not use the products to see the functionality. So the use of this method makes more sense for the type of products which the physical appearance is of great importance to the customer. The result of such initiatives are mixed though; some companies such as Philips continue with their work and are satisfied but others such as Mercedes Benz and Satrwood Hotels left Second Life as they couldn't maintain external visitors to keep contributing to the new initiatives and compensate the associated costs.

Another way of evaluating product concepts is through the use of virtual labs (Paustian, 2001). Google® is using this strategy effectively through creation of its Google Labs: Customers can view and use the new concepts brought directly from Google R&D projects, evaluate them and make comments for improving them. This is a great way for Google to see which concepts would be more popular in the market and identify the potential bugs.

3. Feasibility Study Phase

During the feasibility study phase, the viability and possibility of the product launch in a profitable manner is analyzed. Techniques such as focus groups, interviews and panel assessments are used to get the required information related to marketing, production, engineering, manufacturing and sourcing from within the company, users and individual experts outside the firm boundaries. Interactive E-Novation based tools are helping companies to do some of the same activities faster and with lower transaction costs.

Blogs and discussion forums are used by some companies to get information regarding pricing, preferred way of distribution, and possible suppliers for the components and raw materials. The users and potential customers can talk about how much they are going to pay for the product, how do they like to receive it and why. The blog media has been successfully used by companies such as Goldcorp® to get such data. Goldcorp, a Canadian gold mining company, made 400 megabytes of geological data available to the public over the web. The company offered a $575,000 prize to anyone who could analyze the data and suggest places where gold could be found. The company claims that the effort resulted in identification of 110 targets, over 80% of which proved productive; yielding 8 million ounces of gold, worth more than $3 billion. The highest prize was won by a small consulting firm in Australia, called Fractal Graphics.

As the pioneers of community-based Q&A websites, members of Google Answers and UClue. com® paved a way for accessing the feasibility study required data by linking the individual experts with companies in an interactive way. The companies can ask their questions about the difficulties they have for market estimation, potential sources of supply, modes of distribution etc., in a fashion similar to the Delphi method, and use the opinions of the external experts who have registered in these websites.

Getting feasibility data can also be done through the use of some private network services. Innocentive®, the website launched originally by the pharmaceutical firm Eli Lilly® is a good example. Companies can post the description of their problems in a broad range of domains such as engineering, computer science, math, life sciences, physical sciences, chemistry and business to the InnoCentive website. The company then opens them up for its registered problem solvers to solve. Cash awards are given to solvers who meet the challenge criteria in the best way.

While financial reward is used as the main incentive mechanism for problem solvers, the company has found recently that many of its solvers also participate for the thrill of the challenge and the opportunity to use their knowledge and expertise to help others. This is often a key motivator over financial reasons for them.

CASE STUDY 2: INNOCENTIVE USE OF DISTRIBUTED PROBLEM SOLVING

InnoCentive is one of the most-known examples of applying E-Novation in reality. Being part of the pharmaceutical giant, Eli Lilly, this company started its services in 2000 and initially was focusing on Chemical and Life Sciences but then expanded to a broad range of domains such as Engineering, Computer Science, Math, Physical Sciences and Business. Basically, the company connects companies/entities with a problem to potential solvers using web. If the solvers can solve a problem, they will be rewarded by receiving a financial prize.

Apart from companies such as Eli Lilly and P&G® (Huston & Sakkab, 2006), a lot of Fortune 500 companies such as Dow®, Xerox®, Church & Dwight® and SCA® now use InnoCentive services. In December 2006 the company also signed an agreement with the Rockefeller Foundation to add a non-profit area dedicated to find solutions to pressing problems in the developing world. Since early 2007, the company's website features an award from "Prize 4 Life" foundation to give a $1 million prize for finding a biomarker that can measure amyotrophic lateral sclerosis (ALS) disease progression.

Seekers and solvers are kept anonymous to each other throughout the problem solving process. InnoCentive is also taking care of protecting the intellectual property (IP) rights of seekers and solvers. When a problem is broadcasted, solvers initially see an abstract of the problem definition. If they are interested in seeing full details and requirements about the problem they have to first agree to a solver agreement which outlines the general contract terms, confidentiality, and intellectual property transfer clauses for accepted solutions. Solvers that submit solutions give a temporary license to the seeker firm and InnoCentive to evaluate their solution. If the solution is deemed acceptable by the seeker firm, the solver then receives the pre-announced award prize and transfers all intellectual property rights (IP) to the seeker company.

In the case the solution is rejected by the seeker, it relinquishes any rights to use the information provided in the submission in any future work and any IP remains with the solver. This is enforced by contracts between solver and the seeker firm, and it is managed by InnoCentive. InnoCentive even has the right conduct audits on the output of the seeker's research laboratories.

Regarding the financial prize, InnoCentive also monitors its network to ensure that the prizes have been set in a reasonable range and has the right to reject the award amounts that are too low.

Apart from its problem solving service, Inno-Centive also provides consultancy services to its clients to make the most of its "solver" network. "science advisers" and "problem definers" help clients to identify a challenge appropriate for posting on its network. They then estimate an appropriate award fee by determining the complexity of the problem, the resources required find a solution, and the value transferred to the company. The company's another consulting service is called "science experts" which is designed for solvers and provide feedback to explain the terms of the challenges as well as why submitted solutions may be deficient. It also provides the solvers with the legal information required for maintaining their control over the intellectual property until its sale to the seeker company.

The company's clients such as Eli Lilly, SCA or BASF express overall satisfaction with their use of InnoCentive and the company have been to increase its problem solving capacity to the level that it distributed more than $3 million of prize money during only one month, April 2008.

As the company evolves and makes its presence stronger in the Crowd Sourcing for R&D area, it is adding new services to its portfolio and tries to benefit from the collaboration between the solvers as well. For example, Group Problem Solving is one of the new services the company is working on. The individuals can work and develop solutions in collaboration with each other and InnoCentive provides them with tools to facilitate award distribution. The members of the team can also use a wide variety of features such as group messaging, community managed wikis, online whiteboards, file sharing and so forth in order to communicate better.

The company's future plan is to extend the boundaries of its services even further and offer competitive market mechanisms such as auction style bidding, competitions for challenges and preemptive purchasing (e.g. features such "Buy me now" in InnoCentive website which provide

a short description of a solution or intellectual assets and can be purchased online).

4. Product Design Phase

Designing the products through a collaborative network of developers has long been in use in software industry (Feller, J., et al., 2005). Traditional models of collaborative software development through the Open Source movement have now led to new business models such as TopCoder®. In the traditional open source communities which pioneered development of applications such as Linux® and Apache®, development relies on one or a group of moderators and a set of developers who are participating because of their own needs or for the sake of social ranking.

In a more modern form, companies such as Top-Coder have basically shaped a for-profit twist on the open-source software approach with a process of collaboration through software programming competitions. Each week the company hosts online, single-match programming competitions in which developers from across the globe compete for ratings and bragging rights, and apply their skills for TopCoder's larger, multi-round tournaments, which are held biannually. Programmers write small software modules that are ultimately assembled into large programs for TopCoder's corporate clients.

However, in the other industries such as consumer goods, engineering products, motor cycles and automobiles, the interactive product design using external parties is still in an earlier stage. Hauser & Dahan (2002) developed and used two web-based methods of User Design (UD) and Web-based Conjoint Analysis (WCA) in order to interact with the customers at feature-based level in order to find out what are the combinations of different possible features in which customers consider in their ideal product. The method was successfully applied to a range of consumer goods products and automotive sector at the experimental level.

On the B2C level, a lighter version of the above-mentioned method is used today by companies which are offering mass-customized products even though many of such initiatives are not very successful (Berger & Piller, 2003). The German footwear company, Adidas, challenged by an increasing individualization of demand, launched a mass-customization program in mid-1990s which reached a wide scale in 2002. The mass-customization program which is called mi Adidas provides customers with the opportunity design unique footwear to their personal specifications in terms of fit, function and design in specialized retail stores through a web-based platform (Berger & Piller, 2003).

Beside more traditional forms of web-based interaction such as mass-customization, companies like Ponoko® are experimenting new business models of product design via mass collaboration. Even though the model is at an early stage, outsourcing product design to web is finding more solid ground.

CASE STUDY 3: PONOKO AND ONLINE PRODUCT DESIGN BROKERING

Started in New Zealand and now based in San Francisco, Ponoko is the world's biggest online broker of product designs. Creators and consumers use these designs to share, buy, sell and make individualized goods.

Visitors to Ponoko's website can either upload a digital design for a product or select another user's design, and ask the company to manufacture it for them (Gibson, 2007). They can also design products without building them, leaving them in the online "showroom" of Ponoko for others to use. Visitors can go through the catalogue of available designs, the pictures and prices of designs and products created by other users.

Designers create their design using one of the four software programs; Adobe Illustrator CS®,

CorelDraw X3®, Inkscape® or Macromedia Freehand MX®. They can also upload their hand-drawn sketches along with the design files.

During the process of uploading a design file, users can choose a "sell" option, which lets them sell the blueprints of their products on the website. Otherwise, then can ask Ponoko to give them a price quote for making the product and if the price is acceptable for them, order manufacturing it.

At the moment, the company's focus is on design brokering and manufacturing the products for its registered designers, a business which is growing around 30% due to the advantages such as reducing lead time and waste for the clients. The company, however, expects its revenue to come entirely from growing digital services in the future; buying and selling designs.

5. Product Test and Refinement Phase

Continuous feedback from the users before proceeding to the manufacturing and launching of the product to the market is an essential issue. Therefore, companies run a series of test cycles during and after product design phase (Cooper, 2001). The typical strategies involve making physical prototypes of the product, evaluate the prototype with the users, suppliers, and manufacturers to ensure the final product will meet customer expectation and is manufacturable.

Virtual prototyping however, has substituted the physical prototyping for the products which are complex or very expensive to build. Caterpillar® for example, in the mid 1990s teamed up with a company named Fakespace® to create virtual prototypes of the products which were too expensive to make by physical prototyping.

The emergence of virtual worlds, has taken this movement to the next level and has brought the cost and required time of making the prototypes much less. A Swiss company in the construction sector for example is working with SAP® and IBM® to put the prototypes of its construction projects such as skyscrapers or football stadiums in the Second Life. Clients can go inside the buildings, view the different parts of the building from inside and outside and make comments and recommendations for improvement. The use of avatars (Galanxhi & Nah, 2007), which is the graphic representation of the self in a 3D virtual environment, differentiates the experience of virtual worlds from traditional virtual reality environments and makes it more engaging and easier for communication as well as collaboration (Kohler & Matzler, 2008).

Even though there is some concern about putting the final product prototypes in Second Life from security point of view, companies might try to find a more secure virtual environment as an alternative, or perhaps add security elements within Second Life.

Using virtual worlds in order to test the new products and concepts in the pipeline is already popular among the companies in consumer goods.

CASE STUDY 4: IMPLENIA® GOES SECOND LIFE

Implenia, the largest construction company and building services provider in Switzerland, handles a variety of different projects on large scales: From big residential buildings to commercial towers, stadiums and undergrounds.

Often times, the company has to make a foam model of the buildings in the design phase, to get a better idea of how the final design. These models can also be used as an early prototype to show to the clients, get their inputs and build consensus. The company might spend up to $ 130,000 on such prototypes.

In 2007, in an attempt to cut the cost of its design process, the company teamed up with IBM and SAP, to move to Second Life. The idea is to create the 3D models of the company's projects in Second Life instead of using CAD software or foam models. The company believes that the use

of Second Life will lead to major cost savings by reducing the cost of building models.

By using Second Life, the client doesn't have to come to a physical location and walk through the foam models, but it can become engaged in a much more interactive experience, go inside the building, see the surroundings, and attach its comments to different parts of the building models.

The company is also experimenting the possibility of offering new services to the clients leveraging the power of Second Life. These services will be combined with traditional business of the company, namely construction and maintenance of the buildings, to offer more advance solutions.

The company has made a doll-house model in the physical world which has been hooked up with a similar model in the Second Life. Opening the doors of the model in the Second Life or turning the lights will show up in the dollhouse model, and a virtual thermostat also tells the real house what to do in terms of decreasing or increasing the temperature. Implenia already monitors 4,500 buildings in Switzerland using normal, physical presence and as it's proving to be inefficient to physically monitor all the buildings via traditional data centers, a virtual world based tool would be a source of reducing cost for the company. The company estimated the total savings for management costs at around 20%. The users of the new system were using avatars to move around, to go inside the buildings, communicate with each other and put comments. The integration of virtual 3D environments, avatars, voice and text communication was found by the company to be a value adding combination and more engaging for the users.

For about $2,000, the company is also looking to adapt 3-bedroom houses to help monitor elderly citizens, making it easier to continue to live alone. Some volunteers have already started testing the new technology.

THE USE OF E-NOVATION FOR SERVICE DEVELOPMENT

Even though similar in many aspects, comparing product-based companies with service organizations reveals that these two have some quite different requirements (Johnston & Clark, 2005): Service usually created and offered at the moment when the customers makes the request for it, it can't be stored and sometimes based on the nature of the business, can be different for each client (e.g. in medical services). Therefore, the application of the E-Novation in this sector sometimes is a bit different.

There is little research available in the existing literature regarding the application of the E-Novation in service development, however a number of observations according to a survey we conducted reveal that E-Novation based service development is typically practiced in the form of the following models:

Social Networking: Use of the professional social networking sites in the service sector is getting more momentum (Vascellaro, 2007). Individual professionals in sectors such as medical services, finance and telecom services are using these networks to discuss their views on the industry trend, get feedback about their company or consult with others. A social networking site called Sermo.com®, for example, is used by more than 25,000 doctors to consult with their colleagues and make a better diagnosis. The site is used in areas from dermatology to psychiatry. Inmobile. org® and AdGabber.com® are other examples of social networking site used by wireless operators and advertising companies respectively.

Self-publishing (Blogs): Similar to the product companies, blogs are used extensively by service companies to collaborate with outside world and get feedback on their services. DocMorris®, a Dutch mail-order pharmacy is using its blog (www.docmorri-blog.de) to discuss current trends in pharmaceutical industry, drug development and discuss its services with the customers.

Virtual Worlds: Some service organizations find it easier and even more compelling to take the whole service operations to the virtual worlds. The use of 3D characters in these environments, referred to as avatars, provide a form of interaction and interaction which is more attractive for some users. As an example, mental health therapists in Camden, N.J. are using a virtual world platform developed by Forterra Systems® in order to hold their therapy sessions. Mental patients and offenders in this center find it more engaging to attend the sessions through their avatars and talk about their experiences via a virtual world (Driver & Jackson, 2008). Virtual worlds have also been used by governmental organizations such as UK's National Health Service® to make an information center for the public use.

IMPLEMENTING E-NOVATION

It's crucial to understand that making a radical change from a conventional R&D structure to an E-Novation enabled R&D structure doesn't happen overnight (Dodgson, Gann & Salter, 2006). New skills should be adopted, organization is supposed to have a certain level of IT maturity and this also requires a significant amount of cultural change.

In order to make sure that a company is approaching E-Novation in a more structured manner and is utilizing more benefits from the opportunities provided by the technologies, companies need to define a coherent strategy and an operating model to accommodate and integrate E-Novation with traditional parts of their organization. Based on the observations in our case studies, an E-Novation initiative should consider four main components:

Strategy: This is a fundamental part in an E-Novation model which encompasses issues such as: Where in the product development chain of activities this change is supposed to happen? What are the product categories which are subjected to change? To whom should we collaborate? And how we can create incentive for these collaborators to interact with us? This element was also observable in the case studies previously provided, as the companies reviewed were selective about the type of the products and users in the scope of their E-Novation experience.

Processes: Implementation of E-Novation requires change in the existing processes; namely business process reengineering, and also creation of new processes for R&D collaboration (Chesbrough, 2003). The new required processes can range from the ones required for getting the ideas from pool of outside customers and Innovators to testing the prototypes in virtual worlds with the external parties. Establishment of Dell Idea Storm created new processes in Dell for connecting to the community of customers which in this case is used for receiving new product/service improvement ideas. The decision about the model of governance is also an important issue in this category as the E-Novation models can vary from hierarchical structures like InnoCentive to more flat ones like normal open source software communities.

Organization: New skills are required as a result of implementing E-Novation. E-Novation will also cause more complexity to the organization activities due to the increased number of interdependencies internally and externally (Dodgson, Gann & Salter, 2006). This requires a redefinition of roles and responsibilities in the organization. The companies should also make

some choices on issues such as: Whether we are going to conduct E-Novation activities through the traditional innovation units or through establishing a new unit in the company. The relation of Eli Lilly with InnoCentive demonstrates creating a new unit for managing E-Novation which finally lead to a spin-off. On the other hand, activities of Dell Idea Storm is performed by existing customer facing departments of Dell.

Systems and technologies: Technology is at the heart of E-Novation as it comes to life through the use of web-enabled technologies. Companies entering the E-Novation space, especially multinationals, should think about what type of technology best supports their aim of E-Novation initiatives, how they are going to use proper use of a knowledge management system to harness the outcomes of collaboration and should be clear about issues such as compatibility with other systems, data security risk and implementation effort required. Implenia, as an example, uses rich 3D environment of Second Life as this fits with its strategy of virtual prototyping and collaboration; on the other hand Sermo uses social networking technology based on web 2.0 to achieve its goals.

Apart from required organizational and system capabilities, implementation of E-Novation initiatives, like any other novel concept includes a number of challenges. Some of the challenges in E-Novation are discussed below:

Figure 2. The components of an e-novation program

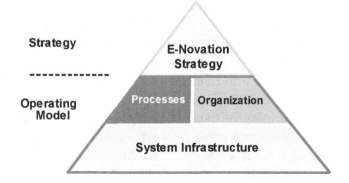

Intellectual Property: There is always the risk that the information shared by external parties or the concepts offered by them are subject to intellectual rights of another entity (Kuppler, et al., 2008). The Lawsuit of Viacom vs. Youtube.com is a famous example. In addition to negative effect on the company's brand, the intellectual property mishandlings have the extra cost of following the lawsuits and will seriously damage the financial performance. In order to mitigate this risk, early in the process, collaborating partners should be notified about the company's policies regarding intellectual properties.

Data Bias: It should be beard in mind that the customers who usually interact with the companies via E-Novation technologies are not a representative sample of the whole market. These are typically tech-savvy people (Driver & Jackson, 2008) who are spending significant amount of time navigating in the web or the ones who use such technologies on a regular basis. Thus combining the data derived from E-Novation with the results from traditional market research activities is crucial before data analysis and interpretation.

Incentive Mechanism: Having technical problems with a product or difficulty in using it usually isn't enough for motivating a great pool of customers to come to collaborate with companies or share their opinions. Depending on the type of the product or a customer segment, suitable incentive mechanisms should be in place. The incentive types can vary greatly: Classic incentives are typically in the form of the immediate reward using real/virtual currency or giving a share of product's success while newer from of incentives such as social status in the community or return on contribution are also getting momentum.

FUTURE TRENDS

The benefits of the E-Novation goes far from the boundaries of innovation process and encompasses the whole value chain; processes such as production, service after sales, and so on.

In despite of the benefits of E-Novation and the fact that many companies are increasingly moving toward utilizing E-Novation in product development, the movement is still in its early, pioneering days (Driver & Jackson, 2008). For example in the case of Web 2.0 technologies, the steady growth rate from 2004 to 2007 will continue with the same rate till 2010 but still the number of companies investing in Web 2.0 applications such as discussion boards, social networking and blogs remains around 3 percent and wide spread adoption takes place after 2011 (Oliver Young, 2008).

Prandelli, Verona & Raccagni (2006) did an analysis regarding diffusion of web-based innovation in five sample industries, namely, automobiles, motorcycle, consumer electronics, food and beverages and toiletries. They found out that only specific stages of product development value chain are supported by web-based interactive tools. Most of the companies conducting online development activities were large international firms with well-known brands and the companies had a tendency to use web-enabled tools in the initial and final stages of the development processes.

Even though the use of mass-customization configuration and virtual prototyping has become more mainstream, relationship building with knowledge brokers, product forums, social network and blogs has diffused relatively to a less degree. Most of the web-enabled applications in innovation has remain limited to doing the tasks which can be done offline through the web and the extended benefits such as interaction with an extended community and collaboration are being underused.

There are a number of reasons for low presence of E-Novation in the industry in despite of steady growth in adoption:

Using E-Novation in product development processes will increase the complexity of a firm's innovation network. As a result of the increasing number of interdependencies and sophisticated and competing demands in each communication channel, measuring costs of using E-Novation becomes uncertain (Dodgson, et. al, 2006). This acts as one of the reasons behind slow diffusion of E-Novation in the companies.

Another reason for low percentage of adoption is intellectual property issues. It's rather unclear how intellectual property will be managed in E-Novation, even though emergence of online knowledge brokers such as Innocentive and CrowdSpirit® has established a foundation for start in this respect.

And at last, the cost and benefits of using E-Novation are still uncertain to some extent (Dodgson, et. al, 2006). This adds to the fact that well-defined processes to integrate E-Novation with traditional Innovation activities in the companies haven't been fully developed either. Driver and Jackson (2008) report that many companies which have gone to the virtual world, for example, have been doing it as a "me-too" strategy rather than thinking about the value it can bring for them. Failure of many of such initiatives, therefore, has kept many companies reluctant in despite of the clear benefits to real business problems such as working with and sharing the D models.

However, even though the rate of adoption for E-Novation in research and development is quite low, the companies will continue to experiment with these technologies in the coming years (Driver & Jackson, 2008). An E-Novation enabled product development organization has the potential to leverage innovation performance by bring together external and internal sources of knowledge together in a relatively low cost way. Given the novelty of the concept, doing more research for identifying specific process and system requirements is necessary and will assist application in reality as well.

CONCLUSION

E-Novation technologies draw a quite promising picture about the enhancements in the product development process. The opportunities they provide for communication through web, along with a more engaging experience, makes them a potential alternative for receiving ideas, comments and feedbacks from extended community of suppliers, customers, partners and other individuals in a fast and less costly manner. However, new organizational models and skills are required to manage interdependencies internally and externally in collaboration through E-Novation as company should make choices about the type of the processes which should be created and also the roles and the governance models required to run the new model. Issues such as the governance model, choice of the technology and the type of the product/service for E-Novation initiatives are among the key decision points which should be answered. During the implementation phase, certain risks such as legal or technical exist which should be taken into account. Even though more companies are investing E-Novation, the adoption rate and awareness about these technologies are still relatively low. There are few successful examples but many companies are still experimenting with such technologies and many of them have abandoned their efforts after some failure. The reasons can be related to unclear cost and benefits, intellectual property issues and technology maturity levels. However as the learning is necessary for better understanding of the required organizational skills, we conclude that the companies should continue experimenting and exploring the opportunities provided by such technologies to be able to realize business value.

REFERENCES

Berger, C., & Piller, F. (2003). Customers as co-designers. *Manufacturing Engineering*, *82*(4), 42–45. doi:10.1049/me:20030407

Buyukozkan, G., Baykasoglu, A., & Dereli, T. (2007). Integration of Internet and Web-based tools in new product development process. *Production Planning and Control*, *18*(1), 44–53. doi:10.1080/09537280600940705

Chesbrough, H. (2003). The era of open innovation. *MIT Sloan Management Review*, *44*(4), 35–41.

Cooper, R. G. (2001). *Winning at new products: Accelerating the process from idea to launch*. New York, NY: Perseus Books.

Dahan, E., & Hauser, J. R. (2002). The virtual customer. *Journal of Product Innovation Management*, *19*(5), 332–353. doi:10.1016/S0737-6782(02)00151-0

Dahan, E., & Srinivasan, V. (2000). The predictive power of Internet-based product concept testing using visual depiction and animation. *Journal of Product Innovation Management*, *17*(2), 99–109. doi:10.1016/S0737-6782(99)00029-6

Dodgson, M., Gann, D., & Salter, A. (2006). The role of technology in the shift towards open innovation: The case of Procter & Gamble. *R & D Management*, *36*(3), 333–346. doi:10.1111/j.1467-9310.2006.00429.x

Driver, E., & Jackson, P. (2008). *Getting real work done in virtual worlds*. Cambridge, MA: Forrester Research.

Edery, D. (2006). Reverse product placement in virtual worlds. *Harvard Business Review*, December.

Feller, J., Fitzgerald, B., Hissam, S. A., & Lakhani, K. (2005). *Perspectives on free and open source software*. Cambridge, MA: MIT Press.

Grant, R. M. (1997). The knowledge-based view of the firm: Implications for management practice. *Long Range Planning*, *30*(3), 450–454. doi:10.1016/S0024-6301(97)00025-3

Huston, L., & Sakkab, N. (2006). Connect and develop: Inside Procter & Gamble's new model for innovation. *Harvard Business Review*, March.

Johnston, R., & Clark, G. (2005). *Service operations management: Improving service delivery*. Harlow, UK: Financial Times/ Prentice Hall.

Kohler, T., Matzler, K., & Füller, J. (2008). *Avatar-based innovation: Using virtual worlds for real world innovation*. In 15th International Product Development Management Conference. Hamburg: EIASM (European Institute for Advanced Studies in Management).

Koplowitz, R., & Driver, E. (2008). *Walking the fine line between chaos and control in the world of enterprise Web 2.0*. Cambridge, MA: Forrester Research.

Kuppler, F., Mertens, M., Skiba, A., & Linnow, J. (2008). *Customer@Company.net: Competitive advantage through Web-based interaction with customers in innovation and production*. Detecon International. Retrieved from http://www.detecon.com

Lee, M. R., & Lan, Y. (2007). From Web 2.0 to conversational knowledge management: Towards collaborative intelligence. *Journal of Entrepreneurship Research*, *2*(2), 47–62.

Oliver Young, G. (2008). *Top enterprise Web 2.0 predictions for 2008*. Cambridge, MA: Forrester Research.

Oliver Young, G., Brown, E. G., Keitt, T., Owyang, J. K., Koplowitz, R., & Lo, H. (2008). *Global enterprise Web 2.0 market forecast: 2007 to 2013*. Cambridge, MA: Forrester Research.

Paustian, C. (2001). Better products through virtual customers. *MIT Sloan Management Review*, Spring.

Prandelli, E., Verona, G., & Raccagni, D. (2006). Diffusion of Web-based product innovation. *California Management Review*, *48*(4), 109–135.

Ulrich, K., & Eppinger, S. (2004). *Product design and development*. New York, NY: McGraw-Hill/Irwin.

Urban, G. L., & Hauser, J. R. (1993). *Design and marketing of new product*. Englewood Cliffs, NJ: Prentice-Hall.

Vascellaro, J. E. (2007). Social networking goes professional. *Wall Street Journal*. Retrieved from http://online.wsj.com/article/SB118825239984310205.html

Wheelwright, S., & Clark, K. (1992). *Revolutionizing product development: Quantum leaps in speed, efficiency, and quality*. Florence, MA: Free Press.

Section 3
E-Novation Marketing Issues

Chapter 6
Service–Dominant Logic:
Toward Reframing Business for Enhanced E–Novation

Robert F. Lusch
University of Arizona, USA

Stephen L. Vargo
University of Hawai'i at Manoa, USA

Melissa Archpru Akaka
University of Hawai'i at Manoa, USA

ABSTRACT

Organizations and people within organizations cling to traditions, industry practices, and managerial frameworks well beyond their usefulness. Perhaps this is just another way of stating the obvious that habits die slowly. One habit or tradition that is experiencing a slow death is the traditional marketing paradigm, referred to as the goods-dominant (G-D) logic paradigm. Essentially, traditional marketing practice is focused on the creation of units of output and their distribution to customers. Applying this framework, the firm attempts to study these exogenous customers and then uses its resources to shape a market offering, conceptualized as product, price, place, and promotion (what is known as the marketing mix or four Ps) in order to effectively position the offering for a targeted segment, thus capturing the customer to create a sale (economic exchange). Although this paradigm has been under assault for decades, it continues to survive and has changed only modestly over the last fifty years. Importantly, it is a paradigm (and practice) that continues to be presented in the leading marketing and marketing management textbooks used on college campuses and in executive education throughout the world.

DOI: 10.4018/978-1-60566-394-4.ch006

INTRODUCTION

The weaknesses in the dominant practice and teaching of marketing began to be noted as scholars, especially in Northern Europe, began to identify relationship and services as central elements of a new marketing paradigm (e.g., Gronroos 1994; Gummesson 1995). Marketing slowly began to be viewed as less and less in terms of the transactions involving goods and more in terms of the exchange relationships and service(s). Subsequently, organizations began to be viewed less in terms of the products they produce and more in terms of the competences and capabilities they develop (e.g., Prahalad and Hamel 1990; Day 1994). The customer began to be viewed as a potential collaborator and co-creator of value (Lusch, Brown and Brunswick 1992; Prahalad and Ramaswamy 2000), rather than just a receiver of value. Vargo and Lusch (2004), developed what became known as the service-dominant (S-D) logic of marketing to capture and extend these and other converging trends, as well as the often-heard mantra for both firms and countries to develop better competitive strategies for a global economy that was increasingly being characterized in terms of service provision rather than goods production. In this chapter we show that S-D logic can be translated into a new framework for marketing management and, importantly, as a source of insight for developing E-Novative market offerings.

In what follows we will: (1) review S-D Logic basics, (2) discuss the role of the market as it relates to marketing and e-nnovation, (3) discuss the role of the firm as it relates to marketing and e-nnovation, (4) illustrate how to reframe traditional business and marketing functions, and (5) discuss marketing as integration and a source of E-Novation. Importantly, in all of these discussions we illustrate the central importance of E-Novation and especially how it is fostered with an S-D logic lens.

S-D LOGIC BASICS

A new lexicon is an important part of S-D logic. There are four concepts or sets of concepts that have a specialized meaning and these include: (1) service, (2) operant resources, (3) customers, suppliers and environments as endogenous, and (4) collaboration, co-production, and co-creation of value.

Service

The singular "service" has a connotation quite different from the more often used plural "services." *Service* is the act of using one's resources and competences for the benefit of another (or for oneself via self-service). The recipient of the service is the beneficiary. This service can either be provided directly to another actor through personal service or it can be provided to the beneficiary indirectly through tangible goods, which function as appliances for service delivery. Predictably, often both are used; that is, physical resources are mixed with human resources to provide service.

By contrast, the plural, services derives its meaning from a goods-dominant logic. That meaning suggests the firm is producing and delivering intangible "units of output" as, for example, in a "service-factory" conceptualization (Chase and Garvin 1989). In a service factory there is a high division of labor as workers specialize in performing standardized activities that comprise a service and then pass their work product along to other service workers in the service factory; similar to an assembly line in a production factory.

The services output provided to the customer or client may be such things as audits completed by an accounting firm, rooms booked in a hotel, meals served in a restaurant, surgical procedures completed in a hospital, or airplane seats filled on an airplane. Because of the focus on an output rather than the process of serving, the firm tries to engineer cost efficiency into the system. How to *efficiently* complete audits, book hotel rooms, provide meals, complete surgical procedures, or fill airline seats at the lowest cost becomes the overriding objective of the firm.

On the other hand, the concept of service (singular) has a focus more on the process benefiting another entity (e.g., customer). This focus on both the process and the beneficiary enables the firm to keep *effectiveness* as primary and, within this constraint, to perform the service efficiently.

Operant Resources

Resources have often been viewed as stockpiles of static things. For the firm, this has included stockpiles of raw materials, semi-finished goods and finished goods inventory, plant and equipment, cash, buildings, etc. or for a nation a stockpile of minerals, timber, water, and public infrastructure such as highways, airports, government buildings, military equipment, etc. These types of resources are only one type of resource – *operand resources*, resources that require some activity of operation on them for benefit to be realized. That is, they are the type that some other actor acts upon to create something else. Witness a firm acting upon its stock pile of raw materials inventory with the plant and equipment it has at its disposal to produce finished goods.

Another, arguably more important, type of resource, at least in S-D logic, is an *operant resource*. In contrast to resources acted upon, operant resources act upon or affect other resources. Consequently, these resources are often dynamic; they are also often intangible. For example the physical and mental abilities of a person can be used to act upon static operand resources to create something. Or, a firm can be viewed as a bundle of capabilities and competences (operant resources) that help the firm to gain competitive advantage. In fact, foundational premise four of S-D logic suggests that operant resources are the fundamental source of competitive advantage (Vargo and Lusch 2008). Among those operant

resources it can be persuasively argued that applied knowledge is the most fundamental (Vargo and Lusch 2004).

Customers, Suppliers and Environments as Endogenous

Customers and suppliers are often viewed as separate from the firm and thus exogenous to value creation. From this G-D logic perspective, the firm develops marketing strategies and tactics to target and capture customers. Essentially, customers are operand resources to be acted upon. The same logic applies to suppliers. In these efforts to treat both customers and suppliers as operand resources, the firm tries to extract as much economic value from them as possible by purchasing from suppliers on the best possible terms and selling to customers on the terms most favorable to the firm. Under this paradigm, the firm has been heavily focused on obtaining as much profit as possible through the careful management of how much it pays suppliers for resources and how much in turn it can charge customers (price) for the firm's output. Price, if a payment to suppliers or the receipt of payment from customers, is what is referred to as value-in-exchange. An item purchased or sold for X units of monetary currency has X amount of economic value or value-in-exchange.

Service-dominant logic, on the other hand, treats customers and suppliers as endogenous to value creation and as operant resources. Suppliers and customers are potential partners (operant resources) for co-creating mutually beneficial value. As such, the firm co-creates with customers and suppliers through mutually beneficial value propositions. A *value proposition* is the promised benefits vs. expected burdens that are offered to customers or the market. Both benefits and burdens are not necessarily restricted to monetary benefits and burdens.

Under the old logic, firms were also viewed as operating in a system in which a variety of external environments such as the legal/political, competitive, technological and ecological environment were separate and exogenous. However, with service-dominant logic, these environments and the institutions that they comprise are viewed as potential partners with which to collaborate in the co-creation of value. Consequently, S-D logic embraces a stakeholder perspective, in which the firm seeks exchange relationships with all stakeholders that provide mutual value.

Collaboration, Co-Production, and Co-Creation of Value

Being able to treat customers, suppliers, and external environments as endogenous enables the organization to begin to see how working together in partnership is critical to success. With a collaborative model, the firm and its various stakeholders are involved in dialogue to learn together how to create mutuality of benefit. Often, this involves including customers or suppliers in co-producing the firm's core offering such as when a supplier takes over part of a firm's manufacturing process or a customer performs part of the work of product assembly.

In addition, S-D logic goes beyond a focus on *value-in-exchange* – i.e., the price a person is willing to pay – which undoubtedly can not be ignored (Vargo and Lusch 2004, 2008; Ballantyne and Varey (2006). S-D logic recognizes that over time it is value-in-use – i.e., the value a customer derives through the use of a firm's offering – that is most critical to long-term success. If the firm obtains high value-in-exchange (price) from customers, for instance, and the customers fail to witness *value-in-use* (benefit) materialize there will be declining future patronage (value-in-exchange) or declining sales.

With a focus on value-in-use, it becomes clear that customers integrate the output of the firm with other resources to create value for themselves and for others. Essentially the output of the firm is an input into the customer's value-creating, resource-integrating process. Value is something that customers co-create by using the resources provided by the firm and other organizations to include publicly provided resources (via government) coupled with a user's own resources. Customers therefore are not destroyers of value, as viewed in a goods-dominant logic, but are co-creators of value. For instance, a customer using an automobile is not viewed as destroying or using up the value of the automobile but as co-creating transportation and/or other service(s). Since the automobile user is most interested in the transportation service it also becomes clear that legal possession of the automobile may not be the most important thing but rather the use of the automobile and other resources to create the transportation service. Under these conditions E-Novation that allows people to share an automobile may be advantageous to the firm and the customer and also more protective of the natural environment.

One of the methods for co-production and co-creation between actors is *collaboration*. Collaboration occurs when two or more actors decide to work together to solve a joint problem or pursue a joint opportunity for mutual advantage. One of the additional reasons for the need for collaboration is that the global environment that firms confront is increasingly dynamic. Trying to navigate and survive independently in this sea of change and uncertainty is simply not prudent and wise. The organization needs to be constantly adjusting their value proposition and part of this is a new or modified service offering that often is based in part on E-Novation. Many E-Novations enable the organization to more effectively collaborate with other organizations and the customer and thus allows them to be part of the firm's response to a rapidly changing marketplace. These innovations are dependent upon the firm continually renewing, creating, integrating, and transforming competences to better serve customers. To effectively do this requires agility and flexibility and collaborative partnerships with suppliers and customers.

Increasingly, firms across all industries and geographies are recognizing that the development of collaborative competence is vital if the firm wants to have sustained competitive advantage. *Collaborative competence* is a dynamic capability and deals with the ability to identify, develop and manage the collaboration process. It involves recognizing the best opportunities to collaborate, selecting the best partners for collaboration and knowing how to resolve the inevitable conflicts that arise during the collaboration process (Lusch, Vargo, O'Brien 2007).

Collaboration and Information Technology

Throughout the Industrial Revolution, humans made great strides in embedding operant resources (human knowledge and skills) in operand resources—that is, in making goods. Goods therefore are appliances or tools that allow individuals to serve them or others. A person, when using an appliance, is essentially collaborating with the producer of that good and using the knowledge of that producer and/or designer. The knowledge has been frozen in the product and, by use of the product, one is unleashing that knowledge as a service resource. Goods, thus, often play a central role in S-D logic. Increasingly, the knowledge embedded in products is software and when coupled with digital signal processors and wireless communication the products themselves become smart. For example, witness one recent E-Novation, the ability of your automobile to e-mail you about service needs or forthcoming parts failure. Today, we are witnessing what is often referred to as the "Information Revolution," which can also be viewed as the unembedding or the decoupling of information from physical matter. Consequently, the refinement of specialized operant resources can be exchanged relatively independently of operand resources--pure information (Normann and Ramirez 1993). Web 2.0 is increasingly becoming the platform

for this exchange and, consequently, considerable E-Novation will be around Web 2.0 (Shuen 2008).

Information technology also is rising in ascendance because many costs of doing business can be better managed and reduced with information technology. What we increasingly recognize is that virtually all of the costs of business are what we refer to as the 3-Cs. The 3-Cs is the cost of *coordination, computation and communication*. The 3-Cs is a vital part of most information technology solutions. As the 3's are explained below you should be able to begin to see E-Novation opportunities that were mostly invisible before.

Set aside for a moment the tangible or physical matter that a firm uses to function. Now think of what is occurring as activities are being performed. Three things occur: (a) coordination of activities and all of the related processes, (b) computation of what to do, when to do it, and how to do it, and (c) communication between the actors doing the coordination and computation. Forget for a moment the business enterprise but consider your individual activities over a day, week or month and how your cell phone has become the platform for E-Novation. The cell phone can now be used to schedule daily activities, remind you of appointments or activities to accomplish, route or map your travel, search the internet, track your household budget, and communicate with family and friends. Contrast this with a wire based phone in 1980 where the phone was merely a communication device and not a coordinating and computing device.

Returning to our example of the business enterprise, consider the physical or tangible matter and that the firm needs to: (a) coordinate the flow of this matter, (b) compute what physical matter is needed for production processes, (c) compute when that physical matter is needed and how to use it, and (d) communicate with suppliers of the physical matter. It is even possible that communication will occur with the physical matter which is made possible by smart products and parts embedded with information technology. Think of all the E-Novation opportunities. Furthermore, consider if the physical or tangible component of your business is reduced, it is easier to do a better job at managing coordination, computation and communication. For instance, if the enterprise outsources production and distribution as Nike and Apple do then the job of managing becomes not of the physical processes but of the abstract information processes and relationships that link together members of the service ecosystem.

Finally, consider what managers do at the operations, middle management, or senior level in the organization. They coordinate, compute, and communicate. This is true of marketing, production, financial, human resource and all other managers. Next, consider services workers regardless of whether they are cutting hair or grass or performing surgery or psychological counseling; they are mostly coordinating, computing and communicating. Couple with this fact that physical labor is being replaced by smart machines, even in surgery, banking and education, and it should be possible to envision even more E-Novation opportunities based on the 3-Cs.

Over the last fifty years the unit cost of computation and communication and information processing bhave declined to the point where they are approaching zero. Similar to the Cambrian explosion over 500 million years ago when oxygen spread around the earth and became free to all organisms, we now witness the spread of the World-Wide Web around the earth with a corresponding increasingly pervasive occurrence of free computation and communication. As this occurs over the next decade, more and more entities will be connected and collaboration will become increasingly feasible (Nambisan and Sawhney 2008). Not only will the increased connections and collaborations be with employees and suppliers but also with customers (Von Hippel 2005; Chesbrough 2006). Because of this increased collaboration, the E-Novation that is unleashed could be unprecedented and, as with the Cambrian explosion, we will witness a geometric and rapid growth in businesses that are IT embedded.

THE MACRO/SYSTEMS VIEW: THE ROLE OF THE MARKET

Firms are networks that are embedded in networks and those networks are embedded in larger networks. Thus, firms are a system and part of a larger system. Stated alternatively, firms are a set of actors in a network, which itself is embedded in markets and in relationships with other actors (firms and individuals) via networks. Service relationships connect actors in the firm and the firm to other networks and markets. We believe four factors are driving the trend to viewing firms and markets as networks. These are open standards, specialization, connectivity, and network ubiquity (Lusch, Vargo, O'Brien 2007).

Contemporary thought is that open standards are relatively new and best illustrated with the open source code of LINUX. However, more abstractly, open standards deal with co-production and collaboration. They also deal with the enabling of interfacing and interactivity among actors. Arguably, therefore, the first effort at open-standards was language, which allowed entities to develop and share rules that enabled more interfacing and interactivity. The consequence of open standards is that information is increasingly symmetric, rather than asymmetric, as more and more information and experiences are shared. As a result, collaboration becomes the norm and innovation is stimulated. From a macro-systems perspective, the relationship between actors in the network and market becomes a source of shared well-being.

Another key factor that is driving the trend to understanding markets as networks is specialization. As individuals, organizations, and nations become more specialized they need others for what they themselves cannot do or prefer not to do because others can do it more efficiently or effectively. Thus, more and more specialization leads to larger and larger markets. The consequence of intense specialization is increased interdependency among all entities, which stimulates more collaboration, which, in turn, stimulates innovation. Importantly, this trend is worldwide and with the growth of digital resources more and more work is being outsourced to specialists that can do the work less costly.

A third major trend is the rise in connectivity of all social and economic actors. For hundreds of years buyers have not had much knowledge of what sellers had and sellers had little knowledge of what buyers needed or wanted. When both had this knowledge, there were often substantial geographic gaps between entities that could only be overcome by heavy reliance on transporting tangible things at high costs and great time delays. Connectivity makes the market system much more timely and quick in responding to changes in demand and supply. The market, then, becomes highly flexible. No longer is the market seen as geographically static but rather as the abstract property of networks. By actors being connected, they create networks but also exchange with each other and thus markets emerge from the networks.

The final force that has contributed to the creation of an inflection point in the role of markets in the macro-system is network ubiquity. We all recognize that more and more of the human race is connected to the internet. However, not as well recognized are things being connected to the internet. Witness for example digital surveillance cameras or machinery in a factory being connected to the internet. This is what is meant by network ubiquity; the network is everywhere and connects everyone and everything on a 24/7 basis. Network ubiquity accelerates the consequences of open standards, specialization, and connectivity. The consequences are higher levels of collaboration and more innovation. The e-novation opportunity is in establishing technology-driven networks that humans can use to help them navigate other networks and markets.

The dominant firms of the future will be those that are able to best integrate resources by using the network as a market, rather than those that best produce and distribute goods. This opportunity emerges because, as network ubiquity emerges, humans become engulfed in too much information and connectivity and, thus, need network partners to help them navigate service exchange.

From a macro-systems perspective, we are witnessing not only the market as providing information on prices but increasingly the function of the market is seen as on-demand service provisioning. Markets work well not only when they provide competitive prices but because they are able to sense and respond across space and time to provide on-demand service to other actors. This notion beckons back to Bastiat (1848) and his insight that "services are exchanged for services" in society and in the economy. From this perspective, the market becomes a macro, on-demand, service-provisioning institution of society. As societies developed money as a medium of exchange the money essentially became service rights or the right to receive a service. Actors with service rights are service summoners who summon service on an as needed basis. When markets are pervasive then the service function of the market is to respond to service summoners both effectively and efficiently. Finally, when or if the market fails or is perceived to fail in providing service then society will experiment with different institutions to provide service, as has occurred with health care in many societies.

THE MICRO VIEW: THE ROLE OF THE FIRM

From a service-dominant perspective, the firm is viewed as a resistance remover and resource integrator. Organizations need energy to survive and function. The energy is found in the resources it draws upon for support. However, often there are resistances to obtaining these resources. Perhaps they are too expensive, perhaps they are not available at the time and place needed, or perhaps they are not of sufficient quality. Essentially, the firm, operating entrepreneurially, finds ways to overcome the resistances to get the resources it needs.

The firm also gains energy by integrating resources; synergy occurs by firms masterfully integrating resources (Madhavaram and Hunt 2008). When these resources are masterfully integrated they are often hard for competitors to duplicate and thus can provide a sustained competitive advantage for the firm. That is, when a firm is able to masterfully integrate the various functions of purchasing, production, finance and marketing, and all of the intricate interactions and tradeoffs in these functions, it has an internal competence that is hard for competitors to copy.

To be effective at removing resistances and integrating resources, organizations need to be flexible and responsive members of a larger service ecosystem. They need to know how to work with their customers and supply chain partners to help remove resistances and integrate resources. A G-D logic mindset views the organization as a machine; as an integrated set of individual parts that were assembled to produce output and, thus, the organization has traditionally been rigid, structured, and stable, as is characteristic of machines. However, S-D logic focuses on the service ecosystem, rather than the firm per se. This service ecosystem is not a machine; it is best thought of as a living system and living systems constantly regenerate themselves by sensing and responding (Haeckel 1999) across space and time to be of service to others. To be spontaneously sensing and responding, a firm needs to be agile and adaptable.

Social and economic actors that comprise the service ecosystem are not hierarchically arranged and controlled but are loosely coupled together in flexible arrangements. They are part of a network system and a network is fundamentally different then a supply chain, or marketing channel. A chain or channel implies a linear, highly structured assembly line with strong linkages and staged processes or flows. Models based on chains and channels appeared to function reasonably well when information flowed slowly and was largely embedded in goods or people as in the case of traveling salespeople, goods, and sales catalogs. However, with information being dislodged from physical matter and humans, often idiosyncratic investments in fixed assets and technology are too restrictive and hamper the flexibility and responsiveness that is required. Tightly coupled, vertically aligned, and hierarchical and bureaucratic organizations, operating through traditional marketing channels and supply chains, are less able to sense market shifts that are rampant in a global knowledge economy and act responsively.

Competences, relationships, and information hold the social and economic actors of a service ecosystem together. This constellation has structural integrity because each organization (economic and social actor) has competences (used to offer and provide service to others),, relationships (with customers and suppliers – output and input relationships and governance), and information that is shared through common standards and protocols. Value propositions are then used to connect the firm with its suppliers and customers. Consequently, the most valuable resources are those that center on competences and relationships (Normann and Ramirez 1993; Vargo and Lusch 2004) and information (Evans and Wurster 1997; Lusch, Vargo, O'Brien 2007).

REFRAMING BUSINESS AND MARKETING FUNCTIONS

Service-dominant logic provides a different perspective for understanding virtually every business and marketing function. S-D logic brings a process and dynamic perspective to virtually everything the firm does. Stated alternatively, S-D logic focuses on flows and not states or conditions. Although not comprehensive a large amount of what the firm does relates to products, employees, suppliers, customers, cash management, and the management of form, place, time and possession. When each of these are viewed not as things or activities but as processes and flows the door is open for more E-Novation.

Reframing the Product: Density

Firms should not be viewed as product producers but as creators of market offerings that represent high density. Norman (2001, p.27) refers to maximum density as a situation in which "the best combination of resources is mobilized for a particular situation—e.g., for a customer at a given time in a given place—independent of location, to create the optimum value/cost result." Think of it as follows: At a given time and place, can I access and integrate all of the resources necessary to co-create the best possible value? When I can, I have maximum density.

Most likely, the business model that currently approaches maximum density is an internet search engine such as Google. An individual anywhere in the world, with a cell phone or PDA connected to the WWW, can get the answer to virtually any question on demand. Consider asking the same question and seeking an answer twenty-five years ago or one-hundred or one-thousand years ago.

Not surprisingly, the potential for density creation increases as the ability to "liquefy" information resources rises. Historically, information was embedded into tangible things. This could have been symbols marked on a cave, words written or printed on paper, or information embedded in employees. Also the transmission of this information involved the physical movement of the material that the information was embedded in such as the transport of the salesman, or the shipping of books or promotional brochures or magazines with printed advertisements. When the informa-

tion can be separated from physical substance it becomes liquefied.[1]

Let's consider an example of an E-Novation directed at improving density. Retailers have primarily used land based stores to sell to their customers, however, there is a long history of non-store based retailing such as mail order catalogs, door-to-door or in-home selling such as with cosmetics, and selling on via the television for direct to home delivery. However, a traditional retailer could create higher density by creating a virtual store in Second Life or another virtual world which would mirror its traditional land based store. This would allow customers to shop 7/24 and be able to go easily between the virtual and land based store.

Reframing Employees as Operant Resources

Employees have often been viewed as operand resources -- resources that firms do things to make them more useful. This is often based upon the assumption that people do not like work, get little meaning from it, and thus have to be controlled and stimulated to produce. S-D logic takes a quite different perspective. It views workers as wanting to provide service if they are put into the type of setting or context that encourages the development of their competences and use of them to serve others. Service to others can be either within the firm and thus indirectly serving the final customer (e.g, payroll staff) or directly serving to customers (e.g., sales people). This philosophy encourages employee empowerment that allows employees to solve problems and pursue opportunities as they arise. Hence, an organization can become more of a sense and respond organization if the employees at all levels and especially those that interface with customers and supply chain partners can be empowered to serve the firms' partners. It should be noted that information technology can be a vital part of empowering employees. For instance, using

CRM software frontline employees can view an integrated information profiles about customers and thus have a better sense for how to serve them. This CRM software could be the platform for an E-Novation. For example, consider retail clerks in a department store that have a PDA vs. a fixed based checkout stand. These employees could handle customer inquiries, complaints, returns and payment with their PDA connected to the CRM software and database. In this situation both the employees become more empowered and thus more satisfied in their work and the customer is better served and thus more satisfied.

Reframing Suppliers as Operant Resources

Suppliers can be active partners of the firm but, for this to occur, they need to be treated as operant resources. If organizations take advantage and harshly negotiate with their suppliers by treating them as static resources, then, over time, suppliers will find more satisfying relationships. Firms that treat suppliers with open communication, flexibility, and mutuality (so that benefits are mutual) will find that they are able to unlock suppliers as operant resources. This can result in the supplier taking over more and more of the activities of the organization that are not central to its core competences. E-Novation can be an important stimulant to achieving this result For instance, consider an apparel firm that makes casual jeans and slacks. One E-Novation may be an informediary which is a firm that concentrates on collecting, processing and disseminating data and information from everyone in the service eco-system to everyone else in the service ecosystem. The system could be linked to retail sales and thus when a pair of jeans sells the members of the service ecosystem immediately know fine-grained information such as the color of the thread, the style of button, type of zipper, etc. This information helps everyone on a real-time with the information needed to run

their part of the service ecosystem. What about E-Novations of the nature discussed above but that deal with processed food products?

Reframing the Customer as a Co-Creator of Value

Customers have also often been viewed as operand resources -- objects of the firms marketing efforts and prey. However, in S-D logic, they are viewed as partners in the firms marketing program and co-creators of value – they are operant resources. In S-D logic, value is not embedded in the product but rather is obtained as the customer uses the product as an appliance. Organizations can begin to understand how to reframe customers into more active co-creators of value by studying the processes customers go through in obtaining, using and integrating the firm's offering. This process is often referred to as customer activity mapping. Consider, for example, the activities customers may go through in getting an automobile repaired. The customer may spend a lot of time scheduling the repair, taking the car in for repair, waiting to have the car repaired and perhaps taking it back to correct mistakes. When these steps are mapped out fully it is possible to see ways for how the firm and customer can rearrange activities to co-create value. Consider an E-Novation where you do not need to schedule up to a week prior an appointment to take your auto back to your dealership or other service facility and wait a few hours for it to be serviced. What if you could check on-line about excess capacity to serve on an on-demand basis? For instance, you are about to get away from the office or have some unexpected opening on your calendar and you need your car serviced. You go on-line and find that there is a slot opening in 20 minutes at your car dealership which is exactly the amount of time you need to drive to the dealership. Think of other E-Novations that involve the customer as an active participant in the firm's marketing efforts.

Reframing Cash Management: Learning from the Market

Although service-dominant logic places a strong emphasis on value-in-use and understanding how customers use the firm's output to integrate with other resources to co-create value, it does not ignore value-in-exchange. In fact, since an organization requires energy and energy renewal to function it becomes critical that the firm has a means of obtaining this energy or resources. In developed economies, the medium for obtaining energy is cash or credit, which provides access to service rights and, in the case of credit, a service obligation. For any organization to survive over the long term the service rights it earns must meet or exceed the service rights it uses. Stated alternatively, cash-in must meet or exceed cash-out. If the organization abides by the laws in society and its ethical norms and treats it customers and partners as service-dominant logic would advocate then cash flow is a major indicator of whether the organization is serving its customers and its partners well.

Since the organization does not operate in a static equilibrium market but in an out-of-equilibrium market, which is constantly in flux and changing, one of the ways the firm learns is via the flows of cash in and out of the organization. Over a sufficiently long period of time, when the firm is serving well, its cash flows are positive and when serving poorly cash flows are negative. Predictably there are other measures of doing well and in fact S-D logic encourages the development of process measures that capture how well the organization is doing on a continuous basis.

In summary, in S-D logic, organizations do not maximize profits, which is an elusive goal in an ever-changing world. Rather, they attempt to serve better and tend to do this one step at a time as they adjust service offerings and resource integration to enhance cash flow. Consequently, financial flows to the firm are not something to maximize but rather they are feedback loops that allow the firm to better learn and sense and respond to the marketplace.

This philosophy is made more complete by viewing positive cash flow as the building up of service rights and negative cash flow as the loss of future service rights. Cumulative service rights are then a form of capital that a firm creates by serving others well.

Virtually all enterprises develop accounting systems around accrual accounting which involve matching revenues and costs and thus allow for calculating net profit. However, net profit is not equivalent to cash flow. Since it is relatively easy for an enterprise to track cash payments to its various suppliers and cash receipts from customers an E-Novation could thus revolve around a software program that tracks and reports daily the various outflows of cash to employees, government, suppliers and inflows from customers, financial institutions, etc. This data could be refined by geography or other relevant business segment and it also could be displayed on a financial dashboard that individuals could access with a password. It is even possible to use this E-Novation as a way to be more transparent with the stakeholders of the enterprise.

Reframing Forms (Structure)

Forms, or structures, have purpose or function but the need for those purposes and functions change and need constant reexamination because the environment the firm operates in is continuously changing. A form can present both constraints, such as in the physical form of building, and increased service potential, such as when a building is formed to make it handicap accessible. Furthermore, a building that is embedded with digital signal processors and related equipment can have smart doors, windows and other appliances that are more responsive to the handicapped. Reconfiguring with form starts by examining how tangible and intangible forms become shaped and structured (informed) to better perform a function(s) (i.e. to become a more useful tool or service appliance). Evidence has shown that by challenging all functions and the forms that enable them, organizations can also become more innovative.

One aspect of reconfiguring with form involves creating standardized components, especially through the use of modular architecture (Baldwin and Clark 1997) such as in componentized software and web services. A key determinant becomes the ability of the standardized components to interface across service platforms with other components. This can actually increase customization because the customer is able to buy a unique service solution that involves the integration of many distinct components into a customized market offering with a compelling value proposition. It is similar to writers using a standardized language of thousands of words which they can then combine into an almost infinite number of narratives, as long as they use the interfacing roles that grammar provides.

E-Novations can revolve around providing customers the ability via a digital design platform to customize a product offering. This can be as simple as selecting a customized color to more sophisticated product modifications such as additional product attributes. In addition the package the product arrives in could be customized.

Time Reframing

Activities often do not need to be performed in the time sequence in which they are customarily performed. By mapping a set of activities that is involved in the sourcing of inputs for production, the production of the product, the distribution and sale of the product and the use by the customer of the product, one will immediately see that these activities are arranged along a time continuum that is not necessarily as rigid as it may appear. Either by custom or necessity, certain activities precedes others. For instance in full-time MBA programs throughout the world the time sequence

is recruiting students, educating students and placing students in careers with employers. However, what if we reverse the process? What if we recruit employers that have specific employment needs, we then recruit students that are interested in these employers and careers, and we then educate the students. In fact, perhaps we involve the employers, students and faculty in co-producing a customized learning experience. Stated alternatively, most full-time MBA programs are like speculative built houses; build it and you think the customer will come. However, perhaps full-time MBA programs should be like custom built architecturally designed houses.

E-Novation opportunities can allow customers to rearrange the time sequence of activities associated with a service. For instance the standard procedure when one is not feeling well is to make an appointment with the doctor and then visiting with the doctor which inevitably results in going to a medical lab for the drawing of blood and associated body chemistry tests and then returning to the doctor for more medical advice. This results in an unnecessary time lag and an unresponsive health care system. Alternatively an individual could either with a home medical test or one at a local lab have routine tests performed every six months and have this stored on a secure website where the doctoral could view the historical health status of the patient over a long period of time and thus before the appointment order additional tests or during the doctor visit be better prepared to provide health care advice.

Place Reframing

The place at which activities are performed is another possibility for reconfiguration. Digitization and ubiquitous networks have altered the concept of place; where a task is performed or where a product is delivered for receipt. In today's world when firms are networked across the globe with its customers and suppliers/partners, an order may originate in Australia and the parts ordered from manufacturing sites in Taiwan and Europe and assembled in Korea. Similarly, a call center service request can be placed anywhere in the world, processed initially at some location in India, escalated up to someone in New York, and responded to the customer in a few minutes. In fact, personalized web portals (e.g. myDell) can make the "place" a product is ordered and delivered to be a consumer's home or office, from which the customer can track the order from initial placement to final delivery.

Increasingly, collaborations throughout the value network are occurring through virtual collaborations where the participants meet via the internet to work on projects, such as through GoogleGroups.com. Not only can documents be shared within the organization but with any other relevant parties in the value network. Team members can work on these documents at their place of business or elsewhere and become part of a virtual team where place is independent of work. This is not only being done with simple, repetitive and explicit tasks but also in collaborations involving more complex projects such as new product development (Ganesan, Malter, and Rindfleisch 2005).

Many E-Novations are emerging that allow individuals to work remotely. In fact some of this is occurring with customer service and even order taking. For instance a person taking a fast food order could be 10,000 miles away or a physician could review medical tests from her home office.

Reframing Possession

Some have argued that to possess material things offers a sense of security and well-being. Although this may be so in some cases, S-D logic argues that it is always the use of things or the flow of service from things that provides utility. This simple idea is behind the software as service movement in which the value is in the service flow and its use and not in the software or hardware per se (Tormabene and Wiederhold 1998).

However, this reframing can also occur with hardware. Consider Chep[2], a container company, which is deeply ingrained in a commodity business, in which product differentiation is difficult. Despite this, Chep dominates its competitors. One of the biggest product lines Chep produces is wood pallets, one of the oldest products in existence; wood pallets have been used since antiquity. Although recent versions have been adapted to include radio frequency identification functionality, their basic design, features, and use have not changed. They are made of wood blocks and planks fastened together with nails or staples. Their only purpose is to stabilize stuff (i.e. keep it from breaking) during transportation. Therefore, they add to the pure cost of transportation when they work, and more so when they fail to work. A manufacturer must purchase a pallet, place goods on it, and absorb the cost, or transfer it as a shipping and handling fee. For large shippers or manufacturers the cost of these pallets can add up, hence there is constant pressure to reduce this cost.

Chep recognized that it was not in the ownership and possession of pallets that value was obtained but in their use. It also recognized that if the firm retained ownership of the pallets and could re-use them then it could manufacture a pallet with more materials, such as better and more bulky wood and stronger fasteners. As a result, Chep pallets don't break easily, and better, they don't pile up. Instead of selling pallets, Chep leases pallets to manufacturers, distributors and others within the value network, and picks up pallets when they are empty. Chep's value proposition therefore becomes: for the same cost of purchasing needed pallets, Chep will provide the service that pallet ownership offers, which is integrated with the customers' storage systems and requirements, and, in addition, will relieve the burden of pallets piling up in the loading dock.

E-Novations regarding possession are on the rise. Many of these address the common unused nature of tangible goods that people have purchased and then seldom use. This can be true of books, formal apparel, carpentry or mechanical tools, etc. A local network or even a network of people dispersed geographically could evolve where lending or sharing of these tangible goods can become feasible. The net result is not only economic savings but also less environmental degradation due to use of natural resources.

MARKETING AS INTEGRATION

Marketing has been often viewed as the processes that facilitate exchange between two actors in the marketplace. The exchange has been viewed as a means to increase the potency of the assortment that each actor has at its disposal. From a user perspective, however, one might at least consider that what actors are attempting to accomplish is not building assortments but a more potent configuration of resources. To accomplish this they exchange and thus create new assortments on both sides of the exchange. However, by adding to its existing assortment of resources the actor is in reality involved in the process of integration of resources. Virtually no resources are independent of other resources, but rather resources interface with other resources to either result in additional resistances or ideally enhance the resourcefulness of the integrated set of resources. Consider for example a household obtaining a new pet dog, a new car, a new house, or taking a two week family vacation. Each of these acquisitions results in the need for integration with other household resources. When the new resource can be masterfully integrated with other resources the household significantly enhances its well being.

Going a step further, the integration of resources has a purpose for the actor. That purpose, we suggest, is the creation of an enhanced integration of solutions and experiences and not the accumulation of tangible stuff. It is in these solutions and experiences that value is obtained for actors. Therefore, by viewing marketing as the integration of resources from the user perspective

we are able to better listen to the voice and meaning of the market and marketing.

CONCLUDING COMMENTS

A marketing and business logic that was centered on goods and their efficient production was never a very good logic and is even less so today. We think the time has come for a new logic of marketing and business; a logic that is service centered. Service is the process of using one's resources or competences for the benefit of another. It is not centered on the firm but on all of its partners as operant vs. operand resources. Of utmost importance is specialized applied knowledge and competences where firms and other actors can engage either directly or indirectly in service-for-service exchange. Working together, rather than independently, the firm, its suppliers, and its customers will co-produce more effective and appropriately efficient offerings. Consequently the beneficiary of these offerings will be able to better co-create value with them as they are used and integrated with other resources. Understanding these basic and associated ideas of S-D logic can unleash the organization to be more e-nnovative.

REFERENCES

Baldwin, C., & Clark, K. (1997). Managing in an age of modularity. *Harvard Business Review*, *75*(5), 84–93.

Ballantyne, D., & Varey, R. (2006). Creating value-in-use through marketing interaction: The exchange logic of relating, communicating and knowing. *Marketing Theory*, *6*(3), 335–348. doi:10.1177/1470593106066795

Bastiat, F. (1964). *Selected essays on political economy*, (S. Cain, trans. & G. B. de Huszar, Ed.). Princeton, NJ: D. Van Norstrand.

Chase, R., & Garvin, D. (1989). The service factory. *Harvard Business Review*, (July-August): 61–69.

Chesbrough, H. (2006). *Open business models: How to thrive in the new innovation landscape.* Boston, MA: Harvard Business School Press.

Day, G. (1994). The capabilities of market-driven organization. *Journal of Marketing*, *58*(October), 37–52. doi:10.2307/1251915

Evans, P. B., & Wurster, T. S. (1997). Strategy and the new economics of information. *Harvard Business Review*, *75*(September-October), 71–82.

Ganesan, S., Malter, A. J., & Rindfleisch, A. (2005). Does distance still matter? Geographic proximity and new product development. *Journal of Marketing*, *69*(October), 44–60. doi:10.1509/jmkg.2005.69.4.44

Gronroos, C. (1994). From marketing mix to relationship marketing: Towards a paradigm shift in marketing. *Asia-Australia Marketing Journal*, *2*(August), 9–29. doi:10.1016/S1320-1646(94)70275-6

Gummesson, E. (1995). Relationship marketing: Its role in the service economy. In Glynn, W. J., & Barnes, J. G. (Eds.), *Understanding service management.* New York, NY: John Wiley and Sons.

Haeckel, S. H. (1999). *Adaptive enterprise: Creating and leading sense-and-respond organizations.* Boston, MA: Harvard Business School Press.

Lusch, R. F., Brown, S. W., & Brunswick, G. J. (1992). A general framework for explaining internal vs. external exchange. *Journal of the Academy of Marketing Science*, *20*(Spring), 119–134. doi:10.1007/BF02723452

Lusch, R. F., Brown, S. W., & Malter, A. (2006). Marketing as service-exchange: Taking a leadership role in global marketing management. *Organizational Dynamics*, *35*(3), 264–278. doi:10.1016/j.orgdyn.2006.05.008

Lusch, R. F., Brown, S. W., & O'Brien, M. (2007). Competing through service: Insights from service-dominant logic. *Journal of Retailing*, *83*(1), 5–18. doi:10.1016/j.jretai.2006.10.002

Lusch, R. F., Brown, S. W., & Tanniru, M. (forthcoming). Service, value networks and learning. *Journal of the Academy of Marketing Science.*

Madhavaram, S., & Hunt, S. D. (2008). The service-dominant logic and a hierarchy of operant resources: Developing masterful operant resources and implications for marketing strategy. *Journal of the Academy of Marketing Science*, *36*(Spring), 67–82. doi:10.1007/s11747-007-0063-z

Nambisan, S., & Sawhney, M. (2008). *The global brain.* Upper Saddle River, NJ: Wharton School Publishing.

Normann, R. (2001). *Reframing business: When the map changes the landscape.* Chichester, UK: John Wiley & Sons, Ltd.

Normann, R., & Ramirez, R. (1993). From value chain to value constellation: Designing interactive strategy. *Harvard Business Review*, *71*(July-August), 65–77.

Prahalad, C. K., & Hamel, G. (1990). The core competence of the corporation. *Harvard Business Review*, *68*(May-June), 79–91.

Prahalad, C. K., & Ramaswamy, V. (2000). Co-opting customer competence. *Harvard Business Review*, *78*(January-February), 79–87.

Shuen, A. (2008). *Web 2.0: A strategy guide.* Sebastopol, CA: O'Reilly Media, Inc.

Tormabene, C. A., & Wiederhold, G. (1998). Software component licensing: A primer. *IEEE Software*, *15*(5), 47–53. doi:10.1109/52.714771

Vargo, S. L., & Lusch, R. F. (2004). Evolving to a new dominant logic for marketing. *Journal of Marketing*, *68*(January), 1–17. doi:10.1509/jmkg.68.1.1.24036

Vargo, S. L., & Lusch, R. F. (2008). Service-dominant logic: Continuing the evolution. *Journal of the Academy of Marketing Science, 36*(Spring), 1–10. doi:10.1007/s11747-007-0069-6

Von Hippel, E. (2005). *Democratizing innovation*. Cambridge, MA: MIT Press.

ENDNOTES

[1] Resources other then information can also be potentially liquefied. For example when energy from coal is liquefied it can be more easily transported.

[2] We thank Gunter Wessels for identifying and helping to develop this example. The example is further elaborated upon in Lusch, Vargo and Tanniru (forthcoming).

Chapter 7
E–Novation Collaboration

Michael Conlin
EDS Applications Services Asia Pacific, Australia

ABSTRACT

Open source taught us that communities are a powerful tool for harnessing collaboration. That power has been reconfirmed by the pioneering efforts of a few early adopters who have sponsored new communities within their industry ecosystems. This chapter profiles a number of interesting examples of e-novation through collaborative communities. The strategic use of collaborative communities is now crossing the chasm into the early majority category of adopters.

Research and analysis has revealed the issues, controversies, and problems related to collaborative communities and the role they play in e-novation. It has also revealed useful insight about, and solutions to, many of these challenges. Business leaders can benefit by learning from the insights offered by these pioneers. This chapter offers a process by which business leaders can leverage to add a community of their industry ecosystem. Harnessing e-novation through collaborative communities is now a strategic opportunity for any organisation.

INTRODUCTION

Collaborative communities will play a significant role for most corporations in the near future. This dynamic is fully emerged in the high-tech sector where collaborative communities play a strategic role for most corporations and individuals.

In order to explore the impact of collaborative communities in large, high-tech firms, a series of structured interviews[1] was conducted with executives from Microsoft, Sun, Cisco, Tibco, Borland, EMC, Fuji Xerox, Symantec, and EDS, an HP Company. These interviews were supported by the direct experience of using many of the community websites, as a registered community member where that was possible. The interview

DOI: 10.4018/978-1-60566-394-4.ch007

Table 1. E-novation collaboration communities in brief

E-Novation Collaboration Communities in Brief	
Community	**Theme**
ARC Research Project	- knowledge shared is knowledge grown
Australia.NET Community	- giving everyone a fair go
CodePlex	- helping developers help themselves
EDSource	- forging new approaches to Open Source Software
Microsoft MVP Program	- it takes an "A player" to spot an "A player"
Microsoft STEMD MVP Program	- developing tomorrow's technology leaders
NetBeans project	- anyone can do it.
Sun MySQL Community	- what's mine is yours.
Sun OpenSolaris Community	- we're all in this together.
Sun Solaris Community	- communities first, then customers
SymIQ	- peer pressure drives higher performance
Tibco User Groups	- we few, we proud few
TibCommunity	- strengthening the voice of the customer

results, and exercises in community participation, were analysed to reveal the underlying dynamics and trends. Table 1 lists the sample communities that are profiled in depth at the end of this chapter.

Both large and small organisations are forming, and avidly participating in, collaborative communities, and not just in the IT sector. Collaborative development of products (goods and services) will become the norm. Already, collaborative offering development is providing speed, productivity and quality improvements over traditional approaches. Many leading organisations are exploring the possibilities for collaborative communities.

The early examples of E-Novation – from the LINUX and Open Source communities to Cisco's breakthrough website – involved broad participation from the entire industry ecosystem.

By contrast, many of the new examples, from large high-tech organisations, have been purpose built to serve specific stakeholder communities which are functioning as a subset of the industry ecosystem.

As a rule these communities are not the social networking sites, like FaceBook, that garner so much attention from the press. Social networking sites offer the greatest business value to a narrow range of corporations. This reflects the fundamental business model of social networking sites. Content attracts consumers. Consumers represent an audience. An audience attracts advertisers. Advertisers contribute ad content and, more importantly, advertising dollars. Advertising dollars can be used to generate new content. The virtuous cycle of this business model supports content generators and aggregators, web hosting firms, advertising firms, and the telecommunications firms that carry the traffic. Consumer products companies can also leverage social networking community into opportunities to build brand equity. For the remainder of businesses, social networking sites are a secondary opportunity, not a primary opportunity.

BACKGROUND

Although this chapter does not focus on open source communities[2] per se, they still offer important insights on collaborative communities in general. The LINUX experiment is more than a decade old, and now surely past the experimental stage. Microsoft, Sun and IBM all offer a wide range of open source products. The power of open-source development is that it merges developers and users into one community. This provides for any extremely tight feed-back loop, bringing the most desirable new product features to the front of the queue. It also harnesses the enthusiasm and professional abilities of the participants.

Members are able to participate in and help drive the strategy and direction in each community. Communities typically include competitors, suppliers, standards bodies, regulators, business customers, end consumers, etc. There needs to be some degree of control exercised over any of these community efforts. The governing body usually co-ordinates performance-related issues like maintenance of an effective roadmap; quality assurance; achievement of timeframes from roadmap. Decision making and control is specific to the governance policies and practices of each community. Like all communities, control needs to be as democratic as possible without jeopardising the final aims. The governing body usually co-ordinates performance-related issues like maintenance of an effective roadmap; quality assurance; achievement of timeframes from roadmap. Sponsoring corporations try to guide the community and co-ordinate the efforts in a structured fashion. This has the potential to generate friction in some cases but leads to end-products, or other outcomes, that sponsoring enterprises want to leverage.

Tangible rewards, like cash bonuses tend not to be a motivation for most community members. However, some sponsoring corporations have started to experiment with awards to try to recognise the significance of the contributions from the community. Generally, award recipients are selected by the community. As one example, Sun instituted a $1 Million Open Source Community Innovation Awards Program (Oracle, 2008) to foster innovation and recognize the most interesting initiatives within open source communities worldwide.

Culture and behavioural norms are important to the performance of the community. There will occasionally be tensions as a result of the culture and opinions of some elements of the community. This is part of the cost of community diversity. One of the countervailing benefits of community diversity is the way it neutralises group-think, and leads to higher levels of innovation.

Sponsoring a collaborative community requires a willingness to supply collaboration tools,

for example Web 2.0 technologies and a strong web site. Strong participation from the sponsor's staff has, in many cases, made an equally important contribution to community success. Sponsors generally "seed" a community with a core of staff until the community reaches critical mass. The effort does not end there because, in general, the larger the community the better. The smartest people don't work for you and a collaborative community gives its sponsor access to more bright people than it could possibly employ.

Open source communities have much in common with the cadre of pioneer communities identified through the interviews. In-depth examples of a number of pioneering E-Novation communities are profiled at the end of the chapter. The variety of communities — from different collaborative approaches to different organizational models to different distribution models to different governance models — is instructive. Further, as many of the communities presented here are not simple variants of open source communities, indeed many do not produce software at all, these communities can serve as analogies for open communities across all industries.

Communities are powerful, but communities are not an end in themselves, at least for most corporations. Instead, corporations sponsor communities to create value for the corporation. The trick is to align the value created for the corporation with the value created for, and by, the community. The community organiser must have a value proposition for each group of community members.

Interpersonal-communication may be the ultimate value proposition. People are social by nature. They like to interact in all walks of life from play to work. When at work, they need to interact in order to collaborate, debate, solve problems, coordinate, and communicate. In any large organisation a significant plurality of work is performed in extended processes that involve cross-functional teams. Without interaction, the extended process is condemned to be non-functional. With interaction the extended process can function effectively and efficiently. Without interaction the entire team will be un-productive. With interaction the entire team can be productive. Enabling effective interaction and collaboration is a key to operational excellence.

E-Novation communities are exercises in social productivity, where an idea introduced by a community member is nurtured by the contributions of a wide spectrum of people who bring their own valuable perspectives, making this initial idea much stronger. Ultimately, the community is the foundation for collaboration, the catalyst which can bring an idea to reality or turn a concept into a product. The trick is providing the environment to create tangible assets. Not just any assets, but assets which solve a real issue, a need which hasn't been solved yet. Since projects live and die according to their utility for the community. Activity and energy gravitate to solutions spaces that address a widely acknowledged need.

Is your organisation struggling with the challenge of how to transform ideas into practical innovation? E-Novation collaboration is the catalyst which can bring an idea to reality or turn concepts into tangible assets. Not just any assets, but assets which solve a real issue, a need which hasn't been solved yet. The question is this, how does one create and harness collaborative communities like these in order to foster E-Novation in new settings?

To provide some perspective, Figure 1 positions each of these example communities based on architecture of community and architecture of product. [The author is grateful to Dr. Charles Fine, as well as to Don Tapscott, David Ticoll and Alex Lowey, for permission to adapt from their seminal work.] Earlier analyses (Fine (1998) and Tapscott, Loewy and Ticoll (2000)) indicated that Open Source communities were best understood as aligned with modular product architectures and modular ecosystem architecture. Time has marched on. The analysis of early-adopters shows that collaborative communities can be harnessed to support any blend of product and ecosystem architectures. In other words, the advances of

Figure 1. Collaborative communities in action [Adapted from (Fine. 1998), (Tapscott, Ticoll & Lowey. 2000)]

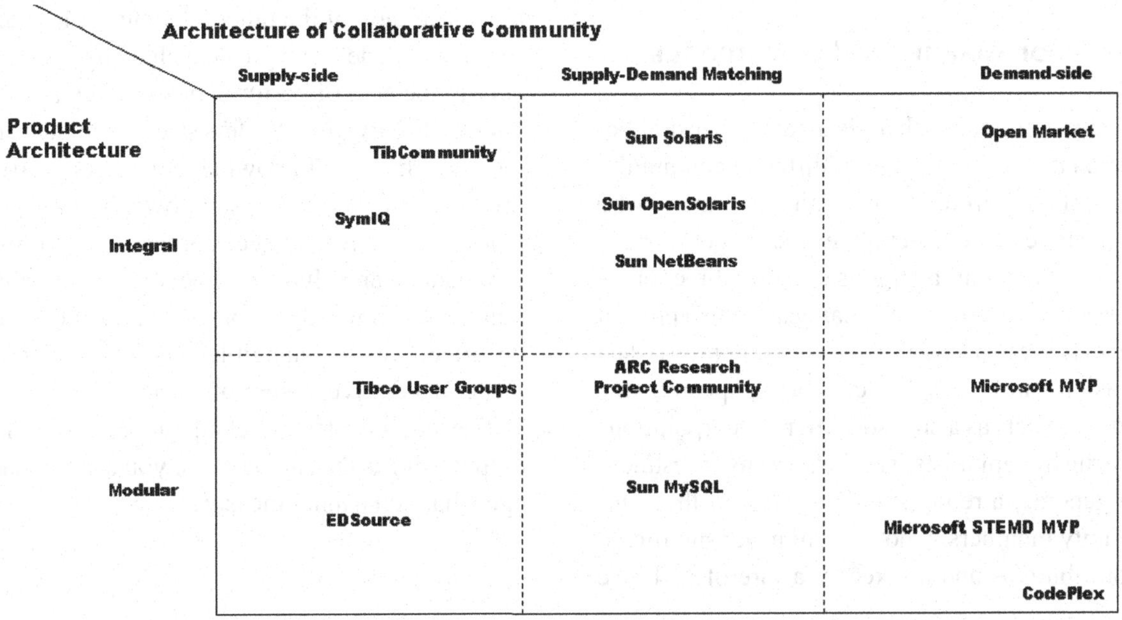

Architecture of Collaborative Community			
Product Architecture	**Supply-side**	**Supply-Demand Matching**	**Demand-side**
Integral	**TibCommunity** **SymIQ**	**Sun Solaris** **Sun OpenSolaris** **Sun NetBeans**	**Open Market**
Modular	**Tibco User Groups** **EDSource**	**ARC Research Project Community** **Sun MySQL**	**Microsoft MVP** **Microsoft STEMD MVP** **CodePlex**

E-Novation have made it possible for any organisation to enjoy the benefits of collaborative communities. Given the benefits these communities offer, my analysis also suggests that collaborative communities are now a competitive necessity.

ISSUES, CONTROVERSIES, PROBLEMS

This section present a perspective on the issues, controversies, and problems related to collaborative communities and the role they play in E-Novation. To this end, a number of inter-related domains are explored including:

- Decision making and governance
- Motivational models
- Performance management
- Cultural and behavioural norms
- Technology
- The role of constraints
- Communication and internal marketing
- Businesses and business relationships
- Management techniques and philosophy
- Policy
- Business strategy

Decision Making and Governance

In any community there is a natural tension between the different goals of different community members. Further, community members who contribute more generally expect to get more in return, including a larger say in the direction of the community. These dynamics are also present in E-Novation collaborative communities. The tension can be heightened when a specific corporation acts as a sponsor. After all, corporations are run by capitalists. They expect any investment to generate a return. So do the rest of the community members, who after all make significant contributions and are keenly aware of it. These tensions turn governance and decision making into a delicate balancing act.

Motivational Models

Governance and motivational models are intertwined in collaborative communities due to the simple fact that decision making authority is itself an intrinsic reward. Money is no longer the strongest motivator. Management theory has long acknowledged that money is a mere hygiene factor. Now a new generation of workers is requesting different forms of recognition and reward. E-Novation collaboration encapsulates many of the incentives and benefits that appeal to these individuals (Table 2).

As you can see from the list of benefits, money is by far not the primary motivation. In many cases the primary reward is derived from, and defines, the mission of the community. In order to stimulate the greatest performance, E-Novation communities need effective, new motivational models.

Performance Management

Any discussion of motivation inevitably leads to a discussion of the other elements of any performance model. The greatest challenge is probably in the area of performance measures. Even without E-Novation, leaders struggle to measure the performance of knowledge workers. In part, this reflects the fact that knowledge work is work shared across projects, processes and cross-functional teams. It also reflects the fact that the outputs of knowledge work are frequently both unstructured and intangible. The interactive, in fact collaborative, nature of work in E-Novation further complicates the challenge of measuring output. And as the saying goes, you cannot manage what you cannot measure.

Table 2. How e-novation collaboration rewards people

Personal, primarily financial, benefits	Personal, primarily non-financial, benefits
- earn advancement / promotion - earn compensation - get control / power - improve career opportunities / prospects - satisfy a direct need for community products - build relevant / valuable expertise - professional development / learning	- improve society or the environment - influence the future - hobby / personal passion - chance to do something different - intrinsic pleasure / enjoyment of the activity itself - personal learning / self improvement / self help - delight in novelty
Social & psychological benefits - improve community standing - gain respect of peers / community - recognition / respect as an expert - improve reputation / personal brand image - meet interesting people - ego gratification - social interaction	**Reciprocity benefits** - civic obligation / sense of responsibility - creating good karma - giving back / paying forward - have to go along to get along - what goes around comes around - safety in numbers - opportunity to contribute

Cultural and Behavioural Norms

The role of climate and culture are widely acknowledged to have a significant impact on any Corporation. The impact is higher, as are the stakes, in any collaborative community. To complicate the situation, managing climate and culture is an art form, not a science, today. What complicates the situation even further is that techniques of this art form do not lend themselves to the distributed milieu of a collaborative community.

Technology

The press has paid much attention to the promise of Web 2.0 technology and tools. They appear to play a role, but just how much of a role? Technology is often hyped as "the solution". Yet past experience teaches us that technology plays a supporting role. How important is technology to collaborative communities?

The Role of Constraints

No corporation has unlimited resources. Skilled people are scarce. As are funds. Time is the scarcest resource of all. So if resources are scarce, how does a corporation make decisions about the level and mix of resources to invest in a community.

How much is too much? How much is too little. How much is enough? Under what conditions do resource constraints represent a barrier, and under what conditions do they stimulate ingenuity?

Communications and Marketing

Communities have great promise as an inbound channel for the voice of the customer. They also work as an outbound channel for distribution. How do community organisers and sponsors harness E-Novation communities to support marketing and communications? Conversely, how do community organisers harness marketing and communications to support E-Novation communities? After all, communities need to be visible to grow and prosper.

Businesses and Business Relationships

The traditional, vertically integrated enterprise is a thing of the past. Rapid change requires flexibility and variability in the procurement and management of all resources. Do collaborative communities represent the ideal future state, or just one more option? In the past, contracts defined any business relationship. Given the rarity of traditional contracts within collaborative communities, how do corporations manage business relationship.

Management Techniques and Philosophy

Work has moved to the edge of the organisation. When people on the edge, community members, make decisions in real-time based on the information and tools available in the moment, then the quality of work and decisions improves. E-Novation collaboration emphasises the contributor as much as the content. Every community member is active and has a voice. This creates a new form of business intelligence capability. The collective wisdom of the crowd can find the best approach; there is no need for a select few people to be entitled to promulgate "the answer". This challenges the traditional hierarchies of authority. What will rise to replace them?

Policy

Corporate law dictates that a corporation's directors owe fiduciary duty to the corporation. he decision to leverage a collaborative community does not negate these duties, of which the duty of care is arguably foremost. This makes some amount of new policy inevitable where E-Novation collaborative communities are concerned.

E-Novation communities generate and consume enormous quantities of information. This makes it critical to effectively manage the quality and sensitivity of the information. This is this sort of challenge that policies typically address. However, given the unstructured and transient nature of the information, it is a significant challenge to create effective policies. Given that ineffective policies generally do more damage than the absence of policy does, what does a responsible corporation do?

When it comes to Web 2.0 in the public space, there are macro legal restrictions, which tend to mirror country laws. If you bring Web 2.0 into the corporate world then many more restrictions — like the SEC restrictions — apply. Social networking in the corporate world may eventually be limited to internal wiki's. Organisations have to be very careful about what they share outwards. There is every possibility of eventually ending up in a situation where auditors join E-Novation collaborative communities in order to monitor communications to customers just as they review public presentations today.

Regulations and restrictions can throttle collaboration. In the US, the Securities Exchange Commission (SEC) states you cannot promise a customer future functionality as part of current purchase. If you do promise future functionality you cannot recognise the revenue from the sale until you deliver the functionality. So once upon a time firms could be open about what-will-happen-when and publish product roadmaps. These days a firm has to hide product roadmaps because once these are exposed they become part of a commitment to the market. And those commitments have an impact on the recognition of current revenue. Collaboration is bi-directional by definition, but firms cannot collaborate too freely as it gives a window into the firm's plans. You can take customer input but can only reciprocate to a limited degree. Again, what policy response is called for?

Business Strategy

The performance of a given organization is the net result of its own efforts plus those of its suppliers, the suppliers to the suppliers, its channels to market, its customers, and its customers' customers. It is these collective ecosystems that compete, rather than individual organizations. How then does a corporation leverage collaborative communities in search of competitive advantage? What impact do these communities have on business strategy? How do choices of community structure compliment a business strategy?

SOLUTIONS AND RECOMMENDATIONS

There are many challenges to building a successful community: Fostering collaboration within an E-Novation community requires a number of inversions of traditional management thinking. The philosophy of management shifts from control to influence. In parallel, leadership comes not from telling but from doing, and doing well. Thus traditional hierarchies, which are based on authority, are replaced by hierarchies of trust. The philosophy of quality shifts from "right the first time" to "release early release often" coupled with stringent peer review. Because projects live or die based on community interest and needs, corporate politics are subject to the forces of natural selection. This means that innovation for its own sake yields to innovation as demanded. Each demand comes from one individual community member rather than a market segment, so mass market thinking yields in favour of uni-casts to address the long-tail. This shifts priorities away from completeness of product, in pursuit of something-for-everyone, and toward simplicity of product. Since many of the products are information, or significantly based on information, the reflex to protect products evolves into the decision to share those products. The desire to share reduces the value of subscriptions in favour of the value of advertising as a revenue model. This in turn drives out the pursuit of stickiness in favour of syndication. The use of specialist editors of content is replaced by reliance on using the wisdom of the crowd to find the answer. And because the crowd ultimately trusts itself more than formal institutions, corporate speak is replaced by the power of personal voice. Taken all together, these inversions are so far outside the operating parameters of most corporations that they comprise a paradigm shift, or rather an interconnected series of paradigm shifts (Table 3).

The remainder of this section discusses insights on dealing with these paradigm shifts, as well as

Table 3. Significant paradigm shifts with e-novation collaboration

From	To
management control	*management influence*
Completeness	*simplicity*
mass audience	*long tail*
Protect	*share*
Subscribe	*advertise*
Stickiness	*syndication*
Correctness	*early availability*
Editor	*wisdom of the crowd*
corporate speak	*personal voice*
Product	*participation*

recommendations for responding to the issues and problems presented in the preceding section. These are examined according to the appropriate domains:

- Decision making and governance
- Motivational models
- Performance management
- Culture and behavioural norms
- Technology
- The utility of constraints
- Communication & internal marketing
- Businesses and business relationships
- Management techniques and philosophy
- Policy
- Business strategy
- Starting a community of your own

Recommendations on Decision Making and Governance

Governance is central to the success of any collaborative community. Because collaborative communities are by definition a multi-enterprise endeavour, the rules about rule making and enforcement must be well understood by all. Executed effectively, the right governance structure tangibly contributes to success. Governance has a direct impact on any leader's ability to ensure that their strategic objectives are achieved. Therefore one must consciously define a structure for the "power" dimension of b-web life: who makes the rules; how the rules are made; and how compliance with the rules is monitored and enforced.

How does one structure effective governance in a collaborative community? A dynamic, no-entitlement, community approach provides a high degree of individual autonomy. In this milieu, people are encouraged to contribute to any project in any facet they wish. Thus, community contributors play their best role in each one of the projects they involve themselves in. With this broad based "free-for-all" approach, solutions have a higher degree of leverage, creativity and effectiveness mainly because they are not encumbered by predefined models of governance and management. This does require sharing power among participants. The usual and useful protocol is that contributions generate the opportunity for influence and power. As a consequence, sharing power actually enhances leadership credibility. It also brings relevant stakeholders into the decision making processes, thereby making these processes better informed.

As a counter-weight to general community members, governance can provide an entry channel for business stakeholders. Here too, influence reflects direct contributions to community outcomes. In this context, the term *direct contributions* means personal investments of time, ideas and energy. Other contributions — especially in the form of corporate resources like funding, people and time — do matter, but are perceived as less personal and so garner lower levels of respect from community members.

Some traditional rules of thumb for governance also apply to E-Novation collaborative communities. Governance works best when roles, responsibilities, processes and decision criteria are all defined and communicated clearly. Role clarity is greatly enhanced when individual community member responsibilities — especially for

quality reviews — are documented and published. Transparency of decision making enhances the credibility of the decision makers. Poor rules encourage people to disrespect all decisions, whereas good decisions encourage people to respect all decisions.

Recommendations on Motivational Models

The motivation model for E-Novation Collaboration takes a disruptive approach. The objective is to create a collective motivation across the community as well as stimulate individual contributions to the collaborative community. Thus, it is necessary to trigger deep motivations to engender change behaviours. Money is not the strongest motivator. Management theory has long acknowledged that money is a mere hygiene factor. E-Novation collaboration puts that theory into practical use. In E-Novation collaboration, the motivation plan is built according to the following rules:

- People are driven by multiple motivations, so look for ways to offer multiple benefits linked to community participation.
- People are also driven by multiple combinations of motivations, so recognise and reward contributions primarily through public recognition, secondarily through enhanced authority, and finally through financial rewards.
- Both individuals and groups of individuals contribute to outcomes, so both individuals and project teams are rewarded.
- Challenges are a spur to creativity, so make rewards meaningful, visible and difficult to earn.
- Collaboration and the wisdom of the crowd are powerful tools, so campaigns and projects are a good way to organise work.
- Recognition is a powerful motivator, so intertwine peer recognition and community recognition.

- Any system must be internally consistent in order to function, so tune the motivation plan to the values of the community.
- Influence is its own reward, so award stature on the basis of contributions rather than rank or entitlement.
- Balancing contributions and rewards turns community participants into genuine stakeholders, so involve relevant stakeholders in the rewards process.
- The opportunity to participate in decisions about rewards is a form of stature, so make this opportunity an explicit part of the reward system.
- Becoming a contributor is easy and apparent to all, so structure rewards such that they creating a genuine sense that right behaviours are recognised and rewarded.

The objective is to create a collective motivation balanced with the recognition of individual contributions to the community.

Recommendations on Performance Management

One of the first steps in performance management is to identify useful measures of performance, along with targets against each measure. Measuring real business value in collaborative communities is not much different from measuring it in a classic corporation. Products are either generated or not. Quality is acceptable or not. Market growth is strong or not. Customers are satisfied or not. The collaborative communities, described earlier in this chapter, measured their own performance in these and similar categories.

Communication contributes to effective performance of a collaborative community. Use both formal and informal channels to promote a healthy level of communication that is focused on the performance of the community. People need to now how they are performing in order to improve that performance.

Convert participants into stakeholders by aligning leadership with contributions, through effective governance. This increases the motivation to contribute strongly to the performance of the community.

Role clarity directly promotes performance in that it helps people understand what their "job" is. Role clarity is greatly enhanced when a documented outline of individual community member responsibilities is readily available. It is particularly useful to clarify the responsibility of community member for quality reviews. User support is another area that benefits from clear roles and rules of engagement.

Recommendations on Cultural and Behavioural Norms

Tune the structural elements of the community to compliment the cultural and behavioral norms that make communities productive. Collaboration requires common ground and a common understanding. Thus, good relationships produce a community culture which stimulates knowledge sharing and consensus building. Avoid fragmentation, which generally weakens the community. Keep communications active, and promote a healthy level of professional conflict in order to reduce tensions.

Community relationships are a prerequisite to mutual trust. Trust is a factor of: capability, commitment, and comprehension. Visible demonstrations of professional capabilities build respect, which is the prerequisite for respect. Equally, visible demonstrations of commitment build trust and respect. Each member's comprehension of the community's goals, and their responsibilities to the community, enables that member to be more productive.

Similarly, the transparency of decision making reinforces the credibility of the decision makers. It also contributes to the level of trust that community members have in those decision makers.

Recommendations for Technology

Tools aren't everything but the right tools can solve coordination and collaboration challenges in any community or distributed team. Start with the challenges and then pick the tools, not the other way around. When looking for challenges, look beyond the day-to-day processes of the community. For example, most community members will value career management tools. Favour tools that are easy to use, participate in, navigate through, and work with. In general, more functionality does not make for a better tool.

Involve community members in both the selection of any tool and the deployment. Respect their ability to make informed choices. Harness their "user-focused" perspective to find the best way to enable people to just do their work simply and easily. If you put constraints on the technology then the way you do business won't change.

Community based teams present a special challenge since these teams are usually formed around projects that might have a defined beginning, but in many instances have the goal of ensuring there is no ending. Community projects are usually created by and around the user community for a particular entity, and have as their primary goal the continued support of this entity.

Recommendations on the Utility of Constraints

The utility of resources displays a step function. The actual thresholds vary from community to community so it is difficult to give a quantitative rule of thumb. Some minimum level of resources is needed to get the community started and keep it growing. Sponsoring and staffing a core team, even small, is a most effective approach to community and project start-ups. If you have launched a community or project and growth has been slow, then it's likely that more resources — especially people with appropriate skills — will help. Once strong growth is under way you will probably be

able to increase the resource level at a slower pace than the overall growth of the community. Finding the optimal level of resources is a balancing act.

Within reason, constraints on resources — especially time and money — lead to smart and efficient solutions. Setting aggressive target dates for a release has the effect of constraining the time available. Moderate time pressure has the effect of motivating people to work more quickly than they might on their own. At the other end of the spectrum, setting release dates that are impractically soon will have the opposite effect, discouraging people and reducing their commitment. Similarly, when financial rewards are meaningfully large and difficult to obtain they produce higher motivation to contribute. Remember that money is not the primary motivation for many community members, but that does not mean it is without any value at all.

Recommendations on Communication and Internal Marketing

Communication is of primary importance to a functional and effective community. Foster communication at a community level through formal channels such as scheduled community meetings and project status reports. Also foster communications at an individual level through informal channels.

Provide community members, and most especially leaders, with tools that help them effectively communicate what they offer to any project, including any previous project experience. It is equally important for project leaders to communicate the value of the project itself to the community. Internal marketing plays a key role in building support and enthusiasm for new projects.

Internal marketing also plays a role in building community spirit. Celebrating success stories raises the morale of the community, whether the successes relate to client support, projects completing on time or improved quality. Celebrating successes add to the buzz of excitement. Excitement lifts the performance of current community members and attracts new members to the community. New members bring new skills. New skills lead to new successes.

Communities also play a role in out-bound communications. Community members, especially those not in the employ of the community sponsor, can openly advocate the community's products. Speaking in their own personal voices, they have a level of credibility that is no longer available to the corporate voice.

Recommendations for Businesses and Business Relationships

Business models are changing faster but more traditional organisations are adopting them more slowly. Thus there is often a 'gap' between what the technologies permit, and the adoption of emerging business models. Business models need to be flexible and have in-built mechanisms to evolve and respond to changes in the environment. Sometimes models lag too slowly behind changing technologies, Web 2.0 being a prime example.

Processes should be in place to facilitate business and organisational requirements, but sometimes have become ends in and of themselves. Processes need to be constantly questioned and reviewed as new technologies emerge and market dynamics change. If you put constraints around how technologies change your processes then your business will change very slowly indeed.

No matter how many smart, effective people you have in your employ, there are many more smart, effective people outside your organisation. So if you want to have the best people working for you then you need to attract them to your community. Once you attract them, remember to treat community members as partner not employees. They are participating because they want to, not because they have to.

Recommendations for Management Techniques and Philosophy

Management needs to be flexible. Continually look for new ways to manage business processes and technology to serve community goals. This requires managers to be well versed in the opportunities afforded by new technologies. Many managers are not so well versed. If your managers are not well versed in the latest technologies then you have an opportunity for improvement.

In collaborative communities, management acts by influence rather than authority. By and large community members are volunteers. They participate in the community because they want to. Similarly they contribute to the community because they want to, or rather because they believe that contributing to the community's objectives helps them achieve their own objectives. You will find it difficult to get their cooperation unless you know what their objectives and expectations are. Clarified and rationalized stakeholder expectations are a must. Once you know member's expectations it becomes practical to align them across the larger community and ecosystem.

When you involve relevant stakeholders in decision making, you add their credibility to the decisions. You also gain their support, and can leverage their influence to persuade others to embrace the decision. Awarding stature on the basis of contributions helps make certain that the most valuable community members are also the most influential.

Recommendations for Policy

Fostering successful E-Novation communities involves a number of policy considerations for managing risks. While these considerations are critical, they are also simple and straightforward. In the main you will be extending your existing policies into the E-Novation community space. Or rather, you will be educating your employees on the fact that your existing policies also apply to the E-Novation community space. In particular, pay attention to policies relating to:

- Acceptable use of corporate assets, especially technology-related assets
- Confidentiality and privacy of information, especially your standard classifications of information
- Transparency and professionalism in public venues
- Security related policies

Recommendations for Business Strategy

Both in terms of community members and community-generated content, economies of scale are critically important to the success of any community. Content attracts more members. Members generate more content. And because this is so, the strategic play revolves around standardization, adoption and market penetration of technologies. This is true for the technologies that form the enabling infrastructure of your community. It is also true for the content that comprises the outputs of your community, whether that content is technology products, like open source software, or not. When in doubt, make the choice that facilitates growth.

Optimise your ability to attract, retain and motivate community members: suppliers, partners, channels, customers, regulators, standards bodies, and even competitors. This is as much as matter of quality as it is a matter of quantity. More community members and, especially, more diversity of community members improves quality by reducing the likelihood of group-think. It also heightens the number of smart people in your community which increases the value of peer review.

Take a deliberate approach to building the market profile and brand image of the community. These are important enablers to community growth. Until a given community reaches critical mass, it is in danger of losing momentum and

fizzling out. A larger community, that one in your competitor's ecosystem for example, may lure away your community members. Given the impact of community size on community attractiveness, the target of sufficient scale can prove elusive, especially in demand-supply matching communities. The same is true for supply-side communities. By contrast, demand-side communities can benefit from an image of exclusivity. This is almost always inversely proportional to perceived community size. Ultimately the exact scale that is desirable is a factor of the community archetype, the degree of exclusivity desired, and the opportunity for economies of scale in supply or demand. This is more art than science. Learning by doing is a powerful tool, and creates first mover advantages.

The efficiency and effectiveness of business processes — from product innovation through to customer service — is as important to communities as it is to corporations. Business processes, in turn, are impossible to separate from the technologies that enable them and the people that operate them. Unfortunately, the difficulty of designing and optimising processes is more difficult in communities. Most community members own and operate their own production technologies, i.e. PCs, creating significant heterogeneity. And heterogeneity of technology always drives cost up. With employees you can recruit and train for the ideal set of values, attitudes, skills, knowledge and education needed to do the job. Unfortunately, all community members bring their own values, attitudes, skills, knowledge and education to the party. And you will struggle to shift any of them.

Ultimately, E-collaboration appeals to corporations because communities can contribute directly to any corporation's strategic focus. Getting the right contributions from the community depends on first selecting and customising the appropriate generic mission for the community, Table 4. It also depends on identifying the most helpful community architecture.

Table 4. Relationships between corporate strategy and community mission

Strategy focus:	Productivity	Growth
Possible contribution of community:	• increase staff productivity • increase staff job satisfaction • retain and reuse enterprise knowledge / assets • improve corporate / shared service efficiency • improve execution capabilities • increase integration efficiencies • overcome organizational boundaries • increase business adaptability • foster collaboration and consensus • facilitate problem solving	• acquire new customers • retain current customers • improve customer relationships • improve customer profitability • improve employee-- customer interaction • improve brand equity • improve innovation abilities • increase business agility • improve knowledge of customers • implement informal sales channel • implement informal distribution channel
Generic missions for community	• provide a non-hierarchical, outbound distribution channel for content and products • coordinate large-scale activity on particular issues, processes, or problem solving • provide a non-hierarchical in-bound channel for the voice of the employee • facilitate focused discussion and knowledge sharing on particular topics • solving industry ecosystem-wide problems	• accelerate creativity and product innovation • accelerate market growth • facilitate collaborative design, production or creation of products • provide a non-hierarchical in-bound channel for the voice of the customer • support grassroots movements or address social responsibilities • promote system lock-in by expanding the range of value-adding partners
Community architecture	↑ Supply-side	↖ ↗ Demand-supply matching ↑ Demand-side

Setting aside social networking sites, discussed in the Introduction to this chapter, typical E-Novation collaborative community architectures include:

- supply-side communities
- demand-side communities
- supply-demand matching communities

Supply-Side Communities

Supply-side communities typically include the employees of the firm and of its suppliers. The value proposition is to improve customer service by giving the customer service team – like field engineers and product evangelists – faster, more comprehensive access to subject matter experts like product engineers. Supply-side communities either support or comprise assisted service channels. Symantec's SymIQ is an example of an assisted channel. It supports the more than 3000 sales engineers Symantec has in the field. EDS, like other large high tech firms, has dozens of

such communities, which are variously organised around technologies like.NET and Java, industries like banking and retailing, and service offerings like testing and strategic technology consulting. For example, EDS-Source is devoted to generating and leveraging open source code, whereas EDSipedia serves broad technical community. Supply-side communities lend themselves to the support of productivity strategies (Table 4).

Demand-Side Communities

Demand-side communities are typically focused on current customers and/or the industry at large. The value proposition is stimulate demand and general industry growth. This typically involves driving community involvement and disseminating information to the market. Demand-side communities are by definition direct-access channels for customers. The range of examples is quite broad. Microsoft's Channel 9 stands out as a shining example of digital marketing. Jonathan Schwartz, the Chief Executive Officer and President of Sun Microsystems, Inc, blogs at www.blogs.sun.com/jonathan. Jonathan's blog helps Sun's customers, prospects, the community at large (including Sun's competitors) to follow the thinking and strategies of Sun's management. It is also a strong vehicle for feedback, such as when Sun changed its stock ticker from SUNW to JAVA. These range from code snippets, to complete sets of code, to usage guidance tailored to Visual Studio or other developer environments. Demand-side communities lend themselves to the support of growth strategies (Table 4).

Supply-Demand Matching Communities

Supply-demand matching communities typically have a value proposition of facilitating customer service. These communities often aim to provide a one stop shop for customers. Supply-demand matching communities are by definition direct-access channels for customers. A typical example is Microsoft's CODEPLEX, which provides the developer community, including both suppliers and customers, a collaborative environment to enable sharing of development artefacts. Tibco's power.tibco.com is a one stop shop for customers to find tech forums, download software, enter problem tickets, and contact product engineers. By contrast, Tibco's developer network – Tibco.com/devnet – is more narrowly tailored to the needs of developers and enables them to interact with one another directly. Supply-demand matching communities lend themselves to the support of both productivity and growth strategies (Table 4).

Recommendations on Starting an Open Community of Your Own

Building an open community from a distributed and disparate group of professionals is a challenging task. Pioneering E-Novation communities have shown – by doing – that there are some valuable techniques to community start-up. Here is a generic process:

1. Identify how you want the community to contribute to your strategy.
   a. Analyse your current performance against your strategy to identify key gaps.
   b. Select 1-2 mutually-reinforcing, archetypal missions for the community that will fills the gaps. Customise them to your situation.
   c. Identify the appropriate community architecture (Table 3).
2. Identify the focus of the community.
   a. Trying to build communities *de novo* is extremely difficult, unless you have a subject people are passionate about. Begin by identifying a need, an issue, an itch to scratch, to create energy and enthusiasm.
   b. It is far easier to identify an existing community and provide accelerators to the leaders of that community. Helping people become heroes also helps to build a community.
   c. Explore the viewpoint of each category of stakeholders. Make sure you can answer their question, what's in it for me?
3. Identify sponsors and other key stakeholders.
   a. Sometimes a community start-up project may need to be "under the radar" in a large organisation but will still need business sponsors to enable it to survive.
   b. Support both the planning and start-up with funding and staff a dedicated core team. A core team is vital, especially community leaders who will take the lead, drive activities, keep the team together, and set the agenda. This frees up other team members to get on with their key roles.
   c. Deliberately include participants that bring a breadth of new perspectives and diversity of opinions. Decision

making within a community amounts to consensus building. Too narrow a range of views leads to narrow "group think". Find ways to integrate other contexts and sources of information as a way of enriching decision making.

4. Define the key types of rules, and the philosophy on rule compliance.
   a. Trust the community. Putting in a lot of rules will drive the community to other spaces or other tools.
   b. The fact that your community will be distributed in space and time — operating 24 hours a day on a global basis — creates the opportunity for higher quality through diversity. Be clear in your own mind how your rules will foster the "wisdom of the crowd".

5. Determine the approach to sharing of control.
   a. Because collaborative communities are by definition a multi-enterprise endeavour, the rules about "how we make rules" and "how we enforce rule" must be well understood by all.
   b. Foster open discussion and debate on values, rules, rule making, and value sharing.
   c. Treat community members as part of the solution, not part of the problem. The more empowered they feel, the more they contribute.

6. Define initial structures, processes, and roles within the community.
   a. Enable efficient communication. It underlies all and community building efforts in the beginning and all collaboration thereafter.
   b. Carefully align the reward processes with community norms, culture and climate.
   c. Plan to maintain a community capability in both supply and demand. Communities are at their healthiest when the volume of value-exchanges is high.

7. Set governance priorities and roles.
   a. Governance is central to the success of any collaborative community. Executed effectively, the right governance strategy tangibly contributes to success.
   b. Plan for just enough adjustment to policies to satisfy *duty of care*.
   c. Clarify how governance will help the community become a trusted supplier, a trusted voice, or the benchmark in quality

8. Summarise and communicate the "big rules".
   a. The distributed nature of E-Novation communities increases the value of clear communications about roles, processes and expectations. Documentation removes doubt.
   b. Be transparent about the goal of creating real business value. Be equally transparent about the need to measure that value in meaningful ways.

9. Plan the launch.
   a. Focus on content and community first, on technology and tools second. Content draws people and people generate content.
   b. New communities rarely have the level of familiarity needed to engender an optimal level of trust. Team members normally default to a lower level of trust as a matter of self preservation. For this reason it is important to start early on activities that promote familiarity.

10. Supply resources and kick off the launch project.
    a. Lead by example. It helps when executives are visible members of the community.
    b. Maintain a high level of attention until the communities reaches a critical mass of digital capital (people and content). Until that point the community's prospects are uncertain.

FUTURE TRENDS

E-Novation collaboration will continue to grow in importance to corporate strategy. Corporations that master the art and science of collaborative communities will prosper at the expense of those who are slow to embrace the opportunity. Eventually, collaborative communities will become a standard part of every industry ecosystem.

Over time corporations will master the community domains of people, content and collaboration. Then emphasis will shift to the domains of process and technology, as the search for competitive advantage continues.

CONCLUSION

Open Source taught us that communities are a powerful tool for harnessing collaboration. That power has been reconfirmed by the pioneering efforts of a few early adopters who have sponsored new communities within their industry ecosystems. A number of interesting examples of E-Novation through collaborative communities are profiled following this conclusion. The strategic use of collaborative communities is now crossing the chasm into the early majority category of adopters.

Research and analysis has revealed the issues, controversies, and problems related to collaborative communities and the role they play in E-Novation. It has also revealed useful insight about, and solutions to, many of these challenges. Business leaders can benefit by learning from the insights offered by these pioneers. This chapter goes one step further by offering a process by which business leaders can leverage to add a community of their industry ecosystem.

Harnessing E-Novation through collaborative communities is now a strategic opportunity for any organisation. However, a not of caution is also in order. E-Novation Communities, like the Web 2.0 tools that power them, are a means to an end not an end in themselves. The reader is cautioned

against the temptation to build E-Novation communities where no community-of-interest already exists. The effort will be costly and protracted. The return on investment will be disappointing.

At the same time, the reader is also cautioned against ignoring the opportunity to leverage an existing community-of-interest into E-Novation Collaboration communities. The opportunity for strategic advantage is too significant to ignore, as demonstrated by the communities profiled next.

PROFILES OF SAMPLE COMMUNITIES

E-Novation Collaboration Profile: Sun OpenSolaris Community

Theme: we're all in this together.

In 2005, Sun open sourced over 10 million lines of code with the OpenSolaris project. Sun continues to sponsor the project by employing hundreds of software engineers who work on OpenSolaris, and by hosting the community site, www.opensolaris.org. Through the site, OpenSolaris provides community members with access to documentation, user groups, blogs, announcements, events, news, downloads, forums and public mailing lists (referred to as "discussions') that cover a variety of subjects. The ethos of the community is reflected in the statement of "can-do" attitude and approach to governance by the OpenSolaris Governing Board of 2008, "We value openness and transparency, we prefer delegation and empowerment, we will strive to be enablers, facilitators and behind-the-scenes trouble-shooters, and we intend to focus on making things work and getting things done."

Governance has evolved gradually. On Wednesday February 8th 2006, the OpenSolaris Community Advisory Board approved the OpenSolaris Charter. On Friday February 10th 2006, Sun Microsystems also approved the Charter. The OpenSolaris Charter established the OpenSolaris Governing Board (OGB), granted powers to the OGB, and assigned to the OGB an initial membership (the members of the CAB) until the adoption of the OpenSolaris Constitution that was specified in the Charter. The initial OGB presented the Constitution to the OpenSolaris community for ratification, and it was approved in the March 2007 election.

Open Solaris operates as a community of communities. As stated in the Constitution: "The OpenSolaris Community is structured as an organization of volunteer participants in which Members are given the right to vote on Community-wide decisions, the most significant of which is to elect an OpenSolaris Governing Board (OGB) to be responsible for overall day-to-day operations and representation of the organization to third parties. The OGB, in turn, delegates the organization and decision-making for specific OpenSolaris activities, such as product development and marketing tasks, through the creation of Community Groups. Each Community Group consists of participants and contributors, a subset of who become long-term Core Contributors and are given the responsibility for governance within the Community Group. Finally, the set of all individuals that have been named by one or more Community Groups as Core Contributors are the Members who are given the right to vote on Community-wide decisions." (OpenSolaris Governing Board, 2007).

Under the Constitution, various terms are used to describe the people who are involved in the OpenSolaris Community efforts, based on their recognized contributions, length of commitment, and current activity. The OpenSolaris Community recognizes four levels of involvement: Participant, Contributor, Core Contributor, and Emeritus Contributor.

Participant

Any registered person who participates in the OpenSolaris Community, either through general discussion areas or within one or more Community Group efforts, shall be termed an OpenSolaris Participant.

Contributor

A participant who has been acknowledged by one or more Community Groups as having substantively contributed toward accomplishing the tasks of that Community Group, or by the OGB for at-large contributions, shall be termed an OpenSolaris Contributor. Such designation is permanent and persists regardless of the person's current level of activity or status within the Community. A Contributor may request that their status not be published or published only in the form of a pseudonym that is unique within the Community.

Core Contributor

A Contributor who is an active and sustained contributor to any Community Group and accepts designation as such by said Group shall be termed a Core Contributor for said Group and granted the status of Member for the OpenSolaris Community as a whole.

Emeritus Contributor

A former Core Contributor whose prior grants of Core Contributor status have all expired, or who has voluntarily resigned from Core Contributor status by declining all grants, is termed an Emeritus Contributor. Emeritus Contributor is a designation of respect for Core Contributors who have moved on to activities outside the OpenSolaris Community or who are temporarily unable to perform the duties of a Member. An Emeritus Contributor can return to Core Contributor status by acquiring and accepting new designations of Core Contributor status.

E-Novation Collaboration Profile: Sun Solaris Community

Theme: communities first, then customers

Sun has been working very hard to build the community, and the momentum, around the Solaris operating system. Why invest in the collaborative community? As is the case with few other products, Sun's overall market is defined by how big a community of skills, applications and developers it can build around Solaris (and its younger sibling, OpenSolaris) - and only then, by how many customers Sun can generate. Why Solaris? As a systems company, the operating system (OS) is among the most important lenses through which Sun's microelectronics, software, systems and service innovations are seen by the marketplace. If the lens is cloudy, you can't see much.

The work to build that developer community was begun in earnest in January of 2005. That is the date on which Sun made the first source code to Solaris available under a free software license. But the investment in innovation (the main reason people care about source code, after all) began far earlier, with projects like ZFS and DTrace beginning about 2000. Other enhancements were more recent - like Sun's embrace of the Postgres community, the evolution of Glassfish (which has a similarly long history), and even the inclusion of CIFS (which allows Solaris to be a first class file server for Microsoft Windows machines).

The developer community surrounding Solaris - as opposed to the user community - is best measured by Open Solaris. Like its brethren in the Linux community, OpenSolaris is always the most up to date release of Solaris innovations. That's why it is used by those who not only tolerate changes to the underlying OS, but eagerly anticipate it in hopes of eking out incremental performance, features or functions.

What are the results? A recent Forrester report showed that of the European financial services firms surveyed, 44%consider Sun Solaris to be strategic. This bodes well for Sun's capacity to

grow, and the early return on what's been a long innovation cycle, not solely in features and performance, but in community too.

E-Novation Collaboration Profile: Sun NetBeans Project (*NetBeans IDE 6.9 Features,* 2008)

Theme: anyone can do it.

The NetBeans project is an open-source project. With some exceptions, the software and other content is licensed under the Common Development and Distribution License, which complies with the Open Source Definition. The NetBeans (Integrated Developer Environment (IDE) is a free, open-source Integrated Development Environment for software developers. You get all the tools you need to create professional desktop, enterprise, web and mobile applications, in Java, C/C++ and even Ruby. The IDE runs on many platforms including Windows, Linux, Mac OS X and Solaris; it is easy to install and use straight out of the box.

The NetBeans community has a very flat, lightweight governance structure. Decisions are made in public discussion on public mailing lists. There are no formal roles - an individual's word carries weight in accordance with their contribution to the project. Decisions are made by consensus, rather than voting - most decisions are of interest only to members of the community who will be affected by them. The combination of public mailing lists and consensus ensures that any person who could be affected by a decision both finds out about it, and has a voice in the discussion.

In the case of an irresolvable dispute, there is a governance board. The board consists of three people, who are appointed for six month terms. Two of the members are appointed by the community, by consensus or vote on the public mailing lists. The third is appointed by Sun Microsystems, which started the project and funds the web site and a large number of developers who work on NetBeans full-time. The board is a voting body, but in practice, a dispute that cannot be resolved and needs its intervention is extremely rare.

If one were to break down the forms of participation in the NetBeans project into a set of roles, the result would look something like this: Users -- Contributors -- Developers -- Maintainers -- and finally, "The Board".

Users

Users are the people who use the Platform or the Integrated Developer Environment (IDE). Users use the software, report bugs, and make feature requests and suggestions. This is by far the most important category of people - without users, there is no reason for the community. Anyone can become a user by downloading the IDE and using it to write code, or downloading the Platform and using it to build an application.

Contributors

Contributors are individuals who contribute to netbeans.org, but do not have CVS write access to the source tree. Contributions can be in the form of source code patches, new code, or bug reports, but could also include website content like Articles, FAQs or screenshots. A contributor who has sent in solid, useful (source code) patches on a project can be elevated to developer status by the maintainer.

Integration of contributors' contributions is at the discretion of the project maintainer but this is an iterative, communicative process. Note that for code to be integrated, a completed CA is required from each contributor. See the CA policy page for info.

Anyone can become a contributor by participating on Mailing Lists; by adding a small NetBeans icon to their site or RCP application's About screen, and linking to netbeans.org; or by simply talking about NetBeans strengths, and weaknesses, on blogs, industry mailing lists, print magazines and forums.

Developers

Developers have CVS write-access to the source tree, either for the individual modules they are working on, or in some cases global write permissions everywhere in CVS. A developer must complete and send in a Contributor Agreement form to commit code. Anyone can become a developer by submitting some patches via email, and asking the maintainer of the code you've patched for commit access.

Maintainers

Each module has one maintainer, who has check-in permissions (either for that module or global), and "manages" a group of developers. They are responsible for merging contributors' patches, bug fixes and new code from the development branch of the source tree onto the stable branch. Maintainers are responsible for making sure that these contributions do not break the build. For module projects the person who started that project or currently maintains it is the maintainer. If you start a project, you are the maintainer of that project. Anyone can become a maintainer: by starting a module project; or by having responsibility for that module handed over from the current maintainer; or by taking over an abandoned project.

The Board

As mentioned above, the Board consists of three members, made up of one Sun appointed representative and two at large representatives. The Board has the high-level duty to ensure that the netbeans.org project is being run in a fair and open manner. The Board exists as a last resort to resolve disputes and grievances. Every effort should be made to solve disputes at the community level before turning to the Board.

The NetBeans project seeks to maintain as-lightweight-as-possible governance procedures. Above all, it invites all interested developers to take part in the enhancement of this project and seek input from all. The governance procedures should never become an obstacle to the momentum of any group or individual within it who seeks to create software as part of the NetBeans project. As Robert's Rules of Order were not written in order to create the fillibuster, so the community seeks to avoid complexity in governance in order to avoid the perverse incentives complexity can give rise to.

To become a board member, one must be nominated by fellow community members on the public mailing lists. Any participant in the community is eligible for membership on the NetBeans board.

E-Novation Collaboration Profile: Sun MySQL Community

Theme: what's mine is yours.

The Sun MySQL collaborative community is organized around the MySQL database. MySQL database is the world's most popular open source database because of its fast performance, high reliability, ease of use, and dramatic cost savings. The community is a virtual organization that subscribes to the Open Source philosophy. MySQL Community leadership is provided by a line up of "rock stars" from Sun Microsystems like Simon Phipps, the Chief Open Source Officer. In terms of governance and policy, the MySQL community is significantly more informal that the OpenSolaris community.

The E-Novation community site http://dev. mysql.com/ offers community members easy access to tool and software downloads, documentation, articles, forums, bug information, a Forge, training, newsletters, job postings and blogs. MySQL engineers, along with the MySQL community, can read and respond to postings on the developer forum pages. MySQL Meetup's offer MySQL developers the opportunity to meet nearby MySQL users and developers to talk about the open source database, get great tips and share

new ideas. The Meetup site provides opportunities for help-wanted and services-available postings. Speaking formally, this facilitates demand-supply matching. Speaking from the practical perspective of the community members, it meets the need for recognition and opportunities for both immediate work and long term career advancement. Message boards provide the opportunity for conversations around topics of particular interest.

E-Novation Collaboration Profile: EDSource

Theme: forging new approaches to Open Source Software.

The EDSource project represents EDS' vision for leveraging the concepts of the Open Source community development process to create a new way of developing internal EDS Assets as well as influencing how EDS delivers to customers. The EDSource project provides an environment that is channelling the power of the EDS industry eco-system including clients, partners, suppliers and competitors. By leveraging the thought leadership of a large and diverse community, EDSource is demonstrating leadership in the adoption of Open Source principles to deliver value to EDS and its customers. EDSource supports both the creation and maintenance of solution. EDSource creates assets in the field to address issues from the field. It is thus a formidable tool to understand – and leverage - what is important in the field of application development. This global, collaborative community includes virtual teams all around the world, across different time zones, with broad cultural diversity. EDS has 35,000 developers out of 150,000 employees who are all able to participate in EDSource.

EDSource is not a public Open-Source initiative. Nor is it an effort to promote Open-Source products. Nor is it a production facility for delivering revenue generating, time critical, customer driven projects. EDSource is an internal, community based, development environment characterised by the principles of the Open source communities. Project management control is low, technical control is high. Quality assurance is based on stringent peer review and community testing. Consequently, the principle of full disclosure applies. All source code is open and available for review. Initiatives, projects and work are all needs driven. In fact, survival of the fittest is the protocol: projects live or die based on the interests, needs and participation of the community. The community is driven from the bottom up based on meritocracy — the best ideas and people, as defined by the community itself.

EDSource promotes peer recognition as the fundamental reward mechanism for members and projects. The EDSource Governance Committee handles the final decision through a voting process. For the prizes, the EDSource approach is to reverse the way incentives are defined by asking people first and thus create an incentive catalogue where the awarded person could choose. This approach is becoming strongly embedded within EDS' overall strategy with high level communication focusing on the goals and potential benefits for EDS and the positive impact for EDS employees.

What are the results? EDSource has delivered a range of tangible business value. The community has supported collaborative sourcing projects where EDS, clients, partners and competitors all work together on the same project for major clients. It has supported efficient reuse, minimizing the cost of reuse by creating shareable assets thanks to sound design and strong technical rules. It has rationalised and expanded the reuse portfolio based upon interest in the field. EDSource provides an integrated community feedback and participation model for EDS offerings, capabilities and frameworks. It harnesses and coordinates the passion and interests of technical leaders along with the day-to-day needs of the developer community. It contributes to the EDS brand image as an employer-of-choice. Most of all, it has delivered

practical innovation that works and is used in the field — a tangible expression of EDS knowledge.

In the EDSource community, governance is based on the principle of influence rather than control. EDSource governance positions are published within the leaders' forum wiki. The use of a wiki allows EDSource Forum members to add their own views. Moreover, a forum dedicated to EDSource Governance has been created to provide a channel for governance discussions. There are two main bodies: the Governing Committee and the EDSource Forum.

EDSource Governance Committee

EDSource Governance Committee is a staffed committee dealing with:

- strategy
- funding
- communication & events
- sponsorship of campaigns
- defining & improving governance
- solving issues that have been escalated
- rewards

All members of the EDSource Governance Committee are also members of the EDSource Forum by definition.

EDSource Forum

Membership in the EDSource Forum is voluntary. Typically, members include EDSource participants, especially project and / or campaign leaders. In addition to governance responsibilities, the EDSource Forum also deals with operational activities related to the EDSource Forge, including:

- gathering best practices
- providing guidance and mentoring for project leaders

- identifying and resolving any bottlenecks in operational processes on a day to day basis
- identifying and setting priorities for improvements based on "field demands"
- making recommendations on recognition to EDSource Governance Committee based on peer reviews, polls

EDSource Forge was instituted to establish and deploy the tools necessary to sustain the community. It is based on GForge. It can be used by any EDS employee to create assets through projects. The rules for participation are:

- Participants agree to embrace EDS community basic values (volunteerism, ethics, respect, sharing…)
- EDSource assets are free for use within EDS
- EDSource assets are available to all EDS employees
- Participants agree to provide feed-back through channels such as surveys

E-Novation Collaboration Profile: Microsoft MVP Program (*Microsoft Most Valuable Professional Program*, 2008)

Theme: it takes an "A player" to spot an "A player"

The Microsoft MVP program recognizes exceptional technical community leaders worldwide who actively share their real world expertise with others. Inclusion in the program is by award — the MVP Award — is a prestigious form of public recognition. Membership in this E-Novation collaborative community helps MVPs connect with each other and with Microsoft, enhance their technical skills, and stay abreast of the latest product developments. Other prerogatives include a thank you gift, an MVP certificate, and a variety of resources to help them make the most of their experience as a Microsoft MVP.

The Microsoft MVP Award recognizes exceptional technical community leaders from around the world who voluntarily share their high quality, real world expertise with others. Microsoft MVPs are a highly select group of experts representing technology's best and brightest who share a deep commitment to community and a willingness to help others. Worldwide, there are over 100 million participants in technical communities; of these participants, there are fewer than 4,000 active Microsoft MVPs. The MVPs offer great leverage to Microsoft. Any given MVP has greater credibility and a lower cost than the same person would have as an employee of Microsoft. The credibility is stronger because peer viewpoints are more influential than the corporate voice. Turning an MVP into an employee can actually reduce their credibility in the community. MVP performance is measured through surveys of developers (like DevTracker) especially developers working for ISVs, product recommendations in public forums, blogging activity, presentations at non-Microsoft conferences, and so on.

Microsoft believes that technical communities enhance people's lives and the industry's success by providing users with the opportunity to have conversations about technology that catalyse change and innovation. Technical communities help users adopt new technologies more quickly and more effectively. Also, they help Microsoft product developers understand the "pulse" of users and better meet customers' needs. As the most active, expert participants in technical communities, MVPs are recognized and awarded for their inspirational commitment to technical communities. In fact, one of the significant motivators of MVPs is the desire to be seen as an expert. Fame leads to interesting work today and interesting job opportunities tomorrow. MVPs all love technology, so another motivator is the sheer joy of personally making the technology better. This can even be articulated, by the MVPs themselves, as a desire to change the world. They take great pride if one of their recommendations becomes a product feature.

In order to receive the Microsoft MVP Award, MVP nominees undergo a rigorous review process. Technical community members, current MVPs, and Microsoft personnel may nominate candidates. A panel that includes MVP team members and product group teams evaluate each nominee's technical expertise and voluntary community contributions for the past year. The panel considers the quality, quantity, and level of impact of the MVP nominee's contributions. Active MVPs receive the same level of scrutiny as other candidates each year.

MVP Award recipients reflect Microsoft's global customer base and the breadth of Microsoft's technologies. MVPs have been awarded in new categories such as Windows Live, Xbox, VSTO, Microsoft Dynamics, and Visual Developer Team System. A significant portion of new MVPs represent emerging markets in China, Russia, and Korea, as well as smaller markets like Ghana, Nepal, Macedonia, and Macao.

MVPs also represent the diversity of today's technical communities. Respecting the user's desire to get technical information in a variety of ways, Microsoft recognizes both online and offline community contributions. Reviewers consider the contributions that nominees make to traditional communities such as public newsgroups and third-party Web sites, as well as emerging community venues such as forums and blogs. By sharing their knowledge and experiences and providing objective feedback, MVPs help people solve problems and discover new capabilities.

Microsoft Most Valuable Professionals (MVPs) are exceptional technical community leaders from around the world who are awarded for voluntarily sharing their high quality, real world expertise in offline and online technical communities. Microsoft MVPs are a highly select group of experts that represents the technical community's best and brightest, and they share a deep commitment to community and a willingness to help others.

MVPs represent a broad spectrum of Microsoft product users. They occupy many different professions including accountants, teachers, artists, engineers and technologists. MVPs reside in over 90 countries, represent 30 different languages, and cover more than 90 Microsoft technologies.

MVPs tend to be early adopters of new technology and actively communicate their experiences to millions of other technology users. Through their extensive community activity, MVPs help others solve problems and discover new capabilities, helping people get the maximum value from their technology. However, unlike the open source model, Microsoft does not incorporate software from MVPs into its products. Instead when Microsoft sees brilliant code they try to hire the brilliant developer and then redevelop the code within the Microsoft product architecture.

Microsoft offers a variety of dedicated resources to help Microsoft MVPs maximize their MVP Award experience, expand their personal networks, and increase their technical expertise. This includes: MVP Academy, Downloads, Microsoft Learning Opportunities, Knowledge Base Resources, MVP Private Newsgroups, MVP Product Feedback, SearchOff , MVP Source Licensing Program, Technical Support, Technical Subscriptions, and MVP Webcast. All MVP community members have an MVP Lead, a Microsoft employee who is the MVPs' dedicated point of contact with the Microsoft MVP community. The MVP Lead is the MVPs' advocate, keeping them informed of news, events, and opportunities within the MVP Award Program and in Microsoft, both locally and around the world. MVP community members also have exclusive access to a Web site that provides access to MVP Award benefits, information, and updates. This Web site enables MVPs to meet and collaborate with each other easily. And finally, MVP community members also enjoy a range of global, regional, local and virtual events.

Governance is a balancing act. Rule making is a blend of highly autocratic (the role of Microsoft) and highly participative (the roles of the community spokespersons). Rule compliance is voluntary for the MVPs. Microsoft imposes constraints on employees in the community, like the rule against criticising competitors in blogs, which it does not impose on MVPs.

E-Novation Collaboration Profile: Microsoft STEMD MVP Program

Theme: developing tomorrow's technology leaders

The Microsoft STEMD MVP program strongly parallels the Microsoft MVP program but targets students in the Science, Technology, English, Math, and Design disciplines. Members are students who act as the voice of Microsoft on campus. Thus the program gives Microsoft additional leverage in reaching future business users of technology. The STEMD MVPs get free Microsoft products, cool gadgets, special training, and special tools like blogs. They even have the opportunity to generate financial benefits for themselves, for instance through selling advertising space on their blog. To put it simply, they get fame and money.

In return, Microsoft has strong performance expectations. It expects student downloads to be two to four times higher where STEMD MVPs are active, compared to where they are not active. It looks for higher use of Microsoft tools outside the classroom setting. It follows Academic Tracker surveys for evidence of impact.

E-Novation Collaboration Profile: TibCommunity

Theme: strengthening the voice of the customer

Community membership is available to developers in organisations with customer, partner or supplier relationships to Tibco. The benefits of community membership include participation in

multiple, technology-oriented or product-oriented online discussion Forums; access to technical libraries, tools, best practices guidance, etc.; access to webinars; access to professional training and certification; software downloads; etc. TibCommunity members get access to materials from Tibco or Tibco customers. They get access to expertise or expert services that are difficult to get through standard business means. And they get the opportunity for social connections between Tibco partners (Integrators) and Tibco customers.

TibCommunity supports an open, social networking aspect of collaboration between Tibco and its customers. In Tibco's point-of-view a community can help address two types of important connections. The first is the technology connection – you want something or want to know something. The second is the social network side of connections. The social networking aspect is particularly important because the community is small due to Tibco's strategic focus on Global 500 organisations.

Community members play a key role because customers can share information with one another more freely than Tibco can. For example, if Tibco shares performance data if might be viewed as "corporate speak". After all the reality with performance data, unless it comes from third parties, is that real world scenarios don't match the lab environment. Every customer's situation has unique performance characteristics. This makes performance difficult to replicate outside the lab. As a result vendors tend to limit statements about performance but customers can share their own performance information with each other freely.

TibCommunity was formed recently to subsume developer.tibco.com and power.tibco.com. These "walled communities" — participation is limited to existing customers — were launched five years ago to give customers a voice into Tibco. In hindsight, Tibco made decisions that turned out to be limiting. First was the decision to make them walled communities, which made it difficult for people to get in. It turns out that there are more readers than posters so limiting participation limits both the content and the number of visitors, in a vicious cycle. Tibco envisioned the communities as perpetual motion machines but walled gardens need gardeners, which is to say community managers. Tibco is addressing this need with three to four community managers for TibCommunity.

Tibco has a tool called accept 360, for collaboratively refining customer requirements which come in from a variety of mechanisms. Using this tool, Tibco product managers become customer advocates. Yet they have to hide product roadmaps because once these are exposed they become part of a commitment to the market. And those commitments have an impact on the recognition of current revenue (as discussed under Issues, Controversies, Problems in this chapter). Ironically, while collaboration is bi-directional by definition, high-tech firms like Tibco cannot collaborate too freely as it gives a window into the firm's plans. In the high-tech sector, these constraints complicate a rapid cycle of collaboration.

The project started 12 months ago when the head of marketing and the CEO got together and talked about FaceBook. The CEO prompted the head of marketing to consider how Tibco could leverage FaceBook. To make it the firm's primary community is difficult without direct control of the community. So instead, Tibco is launching a "FaceBook in a box" approach. This will enable Tibco to make more personal connections to customers and customers to make personal connection to other customers. The community was launched with a light layer of functionality: blogs, forums, document publishing. Phase 2 will accelerate community interaction. The phasing reflects the challenges of managing personal profiles, and dealing effectively with legal issues like privacy vs. publicity. In these kinds of communities, you cannot separate the individuals from the company that employs them. Tibco is still working out the policy issues, but the area of process needs the most work, and technology is lagging both.

With respect to governance of TibCommunity, rule making is highly autocratic, controlled by Tibco. Rule compliance is mandatory, at least to the extent technology will allow with enforcement mechanisms. Tibco has not implemented an approval process checking posts, preferring to rely on people's professionalism. In phase two when profiles are implemented then there will be rules around posting and content, and those rules will be enforced by technology.

E-Novation Collaboration Profile: TIBCO User Groups

Theme: we few, we proud few

TIBCO User Groups are local communities of customers, partners, and resident experts of TIBCO and its technologies. They create an opportunity to connect with IT peers and TIBCO executives. Regularly held meetings foster the exchange of ideas and the sharing of technology best practices, and also offer sneak peeks of new and upcoming TIBCO products.

The leadership and governance model is simple. TIBCO User Groups are governed by a Steering Committee formed by 3 to 5 group members, including an elected Committee Chairperson. Leadership terms are determined individually at the group level, but are generally between six months to one year.

TIBCO provides a range of resources to help in starting and sustaining User Groups. Local TIBCO contacts help in setting the agenda, coordinating logistics, and promotion. Communication resources promote User Group meetings, including newsletters and event flashes. Online community sites and calendars promote meetings, archive content, and extend User Group discussions beyond the physical meetings. Some modest funding is available to cover expenses.

User groups can often be leveraged as the "seed" of an E-Novation collaborative community. Thus there is a high probability Tibco User

Groups will evolve steadily toward greater and greater leverage of Web 2.0 technologies.

E-Novation Collaboration Profile: Australia.NET Community (Saifar, 2008)

Theme: giving everyone a fair go

Australia.NET is an ICT Industry community initiated by a number of industry stakeholders and supported by the Australian Government, Microsoft and other local stakeholders. The aim of the community is to bring together Australian Software organisations to engage in co-operative activities, achieve collective competitiveness and develop new opportunities for the Australian software Industry as a whole. Microsoft's Windows operating system is the basis of commercial software solutions and services developed by many of the small and medium sized ICT companies in Australia. Australia.Net is a unique way to assist these companies to develop innovative software, access new markets, and achieve global reach. This community-of-communities includes communities (clusters) at the state level including Canberra, Victoria, New South Wales, Queensland, and Northern territory.

The community's philosophy is simple: that ICT Small and Medium Enterprises (SMEs) can work with other complementary companies to overcome limitations, generate new ideas and ways of doing business and ultimately expand their market reach and penetration. Cross industry and cross business collaboration is one of the most practical ways for organisations to effectively negotiate today's competitive global market place. Members enjoy a range of benefits, including knowledge transfer opportunities, access to an extensive industry network and exposure to partnership prospects. Many community members have used the community to establish partnerships with one another, and /or forge alliances with multinational corporations. Knowledge sharing and resource pooling is frequent.

What are the results? The Australia.NET community now includes more than 800 member organizations, collectively employing more than 9,600. NET specialists. The community has facilitated more than 5,100 known.NET projects, with an estimated total value of more than AUD$1 billion.

E-Novation Collaboration Profile: ARC Research Project Community

Theme: knowledge shared is knowledge grown

The ARC Research Project community is undertaking research into Semantic Technologies. The community is formed around a virtual team of interested parties, including Fuji Xerox and researchers at RMIT University and internationally. The community is set up o be able to expand, and to collaborate along the principles of Open Innovation.

Governance and rule making is somewhere in between highly autocratic and highly participative. Rule compliance is voluntary, based on self-interest. The primary measures of performance for the community include: sharing of knowledge and information; facilitation of discussion and interrogation of ideas; project management for specific tasks and pilots; and document management among the group. Although Fuji Xerox is supporting the community, the outputs of the community will not be direct inputs to Fuji Xerox's business. Some of the outputs include: strategic information, planning knowledge, process knowledge, and technical knowledge that flows around the core-product value creation process. These outputs are embodied in genuine research papers, regular reports, outcomes of pilot projects, some technical knowledge, and business process knowledge.

For community members, the motivators are: sense of community, community development of identity and loyalty, linkage beyond the community to other various stakeholders, diversity of perspectives and new ideas. The community was self-launched by community members. The community members sought a cost-effective and efficient way of sharing knowledge. The members have tried a number of content management systems and are exploring new ones now, but budget and efficiency were definitely key drivers, as was the interest to experiment with these tools.

E-Novation Collaboration Profile: SymIQ

Theme: peer pressure drives higher performance

SymIQ is a closed community that serves the customer-facing technical personnel at Symantec. Members include more than 3,000 field service personnel, consultants, and other support professionals. SymIQ provides community members with all of the tools and information they need to be effective and productive. This includes the ability to rapidly find, share and update any information needed. The information is classified, as regards allowable distribution, to facilitate controlled, out-bound sharing when appropriate. SymIQ leverages sub-communities built around special interests like specific solutions and product groups.

The community makes significant use of peer review in the form of a ratings and comments system, similar to the Amazon.com model of stars and comments. In SymIQ this is an iterative approach since the community recognition of an individual reviewer shapes the perceived value of the stars and comments. This peer review approach echoes, and reinforces, the Symantec practice of using peer review as part of the formal career progression process for senior roles in technical job families. In this gated process the manager recommends a promotion, which is reviewed by a formal, peer review board chaired by the CTO. The peers, on the review board, judge the individuals fitness for promotion based, among other things, on contributions to SymIQ. Or rather SymIQ offers a highly visible venue within which to contribute to the business.

The complimentary duality of informal yet explicit peer review of contributions to SymIQ coupled with formal peer review in career advancement provides a powerful mechanism for assuring quality. As a result, SymIQ does not have a protocol requiring community postings to be reviewed in advance. It's a very Darwinian approach; the people that do a good job and contribute high quality content are the people who prosper in the community.

The community also leverages discussion forums as a search mechanism. Typically a product team will initiate the establishment of a discussion forum for a new product, as a way of providing a stronger level of support to the field services team during this critical go-to-market phase. One prerequisite for launching a discussion forum is the naming of "authoritative responders" for that forum. These SMEs are expected to respond within 24-48 hours to all queries requesting an authoritative response. This is a cultural norm rather than a Service Level Agreement, because peer pressure gets the job done. Different product teams handle the responsibility for "authoritative response" differently.

Beyond the discussion forums, there are no formal expectations or service levels related to things like content reviews. Thus there is a theoretical risk of misinformation being posted on the community's portal since different community members submit content. This risk is addressed through the philosophy of "community-governed content". The built-in governance processes (peer pressure again) promote rapid review by an advisory team and by designated subject matter experts, typically product team members. As a result, content quality is high even when there isn't a 100% consistent look-and-feel. The opinion of peers is very important in an E-Novation community like SymIQ. People want to achieve the level of community respect and recognition that comes with asking and answering insightful questions.

SymIQ has a hybrid governance model. Overall governance and rule making authority is vested in an Advisory Council. Authority over sub-community/sub-site administration is distributed within the community. This approach builds on the fact that a community proliferates when members feel comfortable they have a chance to contribute and participate. One key tool that aids governance is a performance dashboard. The automatically generated performance metrics include: the adoption rate for SymIQ; reduction in time spent looking for information; number of wiki subscribers; number of visitors to the community portal, etc. In addition, SymIQ surveys 40% of the field technical population on matters such as the quality and timeliness of information.

The SymIQ community launch has gone one step at a time. The first step was to attract a critical mass of content. The second step was to leverage the content to attract community members. The third step was to implement comments and ratings to drive recognition, an intrinsically rewarding style of feedback. The fourth step was to leverage the rewards of recognition to stimulate new content. The whole exercise takes time and the sponsors advise to others seeking similar results is, don't sweat the ups and downs.

Meanwhile, despite the strong focus on community dynamics and on content, the tech-savvy users are pushing new technologies into use on their own initiative. The community portal offers access to a field technical repository, product technical information, discussion forums, dynamic search, comprehensive document annotation & comments, two-way technical discussion forums between field and product teams, sharing of best practices, blogs. It is already clear that the use of Web 2.0 technologies has enabled the creation of a larger community that transcends time and location constraints. The combination of global diversity and a community that works 24 hours a day produces higher quality.

The results? In the spirit of peer recognition I'll let community members speak for themselves. One executive said, "As you can see we really adopted SymIQ and it is an essential part of our daily business. This portal rocks." A Principal Solutions Specialist remarked, "Let me extend my kudos and thanks for the incredible job you spearheaded with the SymIQ project. I use it every day for numerous things. It is invaluable to facilitating an SE's ability to do their job efficiently."

What's next? The sponsors are exploring the issues related to opening the community to outsiders. The complication is that some content is meant for internal audiences only. There is a degree of caution due to regulatory concerns, discussed elsewhere in this chapter, over content related to product future directions. Simple mechanisms may prove useful, like a carefully selected set of "shadow content" hosted on a physically separate machine for an external (i.e., demand-side) community. Separately, the sponsors are exploring plans to implement incentives based on content that receives good rating stars and comments, and on ratings and comments that are themselves judged as useful.

E-Novation Collaboration Profile: CodePlex

Theme: helping developers help themselves

CodePlex is a collaborative environment to enable the developer community to share and contribute development artefacts. This includes: code snippets; complete sets of code; guidance, packaged for storage into Visual Studio or other developer environment; peer reviews and reputation information. It uses a rating system & reviews to drive quality and attribution for contributions. A moderator function is an informally recognised way to maintain focus on goals and outcomes. The CodePlex community is highly self-organised. It's a kind of FaceBook for software engineers. Anyone can start a new project, join an existing one, download software created by the community, or provide feedback.

Microsoft sponsors CodePlex as a web site for hosting open source projects. Microsoft does not control, review, revise, endorse or distribute the projects on CodePlex. Microsoft sponsors the CodePlex site solely as a web storage service to the developer community.

REFERENCES

Fine, C. H. (1998). *Clockspeed, winning industry control in the age of temporary advantage.* New York, NY: Perseus Books.

Microsoft. (2008). *Most valuable professional program.* Retrieved June 17, 2008, from http://mvp.support.microsoft.com/gp/mvpawardintro

NetBeans. (2008). *IDE 6.9 features.* Retrieved June 17, 2008, from http://www.netbeans.org/features/index.html

OpenSolaris Governing Board. (2007). *OpenSolaris constitution – Current version.*

OpenSolaris Governing Board. (2008). *Statement of the OGB class of 2008's "can-do" attitude and approach to governance.* Retrieved June 17, 2008, from http://www.genunix.org/wiki/index.php/OGB_2008/001

Oracle. (2008). *Sun sponsors open source community $1M innovation award.* Retrieved from http://www.sun.com/software/opensource/awards/index.jsp

Saifar, D. (2008). *Community statement of intent.* Retrieved June 16, 2008, from http://www.australiadotnet.com.au/

Tapscott, D., Ticoll, D., & Lowy, A. (2000). *Digital capital: Harnessing the power of business Webs.* Boston, MA: Harvard Business School Publishing Corporation.

ENDNOTES

[1] Between 1 January 2008 and 1 August 2008, a number of executives and community organizers were interviewed for this chapter. They included: Michael Gill, Cisco Systems; Mathew Quinn, Tibco Software; Domenic Ravita, Tibco Software; Mark Bregman, Symantec; Jose Iglesias, Symmantec; Sophia Abramovitz, Symantec; Lars Kongshem, Symantec; Angus.McDonald, Sun; Anna Liu, Microsoft; Norbert Haehnel, Microsoft; Anni Rowland-Campbell, Fuji-Xerox; Razmik Abnous, EMC; Mark Wilkin, Borland.

These interviews were supported by direct experience of using many of the community websites as a registered community member.

[2] Examples include: GlassFish, GNOME, Grid Engine, JavaDB, java.net, Jini Network Technology, JXTA Technology, Linux, Mobile & Embedded, Mozilla, MySQL, NetBeans, OpenDS, Open ESB, OpenJDK, OpenCDS, Open Media Commons, Open MPI, OpenPrinting, OpenPTK, OpenOffice.org, OpenSPARC, OpenSSO, OpenSolaris, OpenxVM, Portal, PostgreSQL, Project Darkstar, Project Fortress, Project Looking-Glass, Project Woodstock, Roller, X.Org and others.

Chapter 8
Online Branding

Jennifer Rowley
Manchester Metropolitan University, UK

David Bird
Manchester Metropolitan University, UK

ABSTRACT

This chapter contributes to the active debate about the significance of branding in the online channel, by exploring the opportunities and challenges associated with online branding. A discussion of online branding objectives and how they might be achieved is complemented by an exploration of the unique facets of online branding. Case studies of successful brands with interesting approaches to branding in the online channel provide interesting illustration. Finally, some thoughts on the future of online branding conclude the chapter.

INTRODUCTION

Brands communicate with customers; they capture key values and messages, relating, for instance, to quality, excellence, consistency, reliability, modern, traditional, exciting, socially responsible, or entertaining. Brands are a means of making an immediate impact on new customers, and reminding returning customers. Strong brands have high brand equity and make a significant contribution to business performance and organizational success. In an increasingly networked economy and environment, messages about what an organization or its products and services mean, and the value that they offer increasingly needs to be communicated remotely, through the organization's web site. The web site is not just another channel designed to increase visibility and access. It is a shop window, through which the organization delivers marketing communication, purchase opportunities, information, advice, customer care, service, and experiences. The website has the potential to deliver the company's identity, products and service in the space of a few screens and within seconds; the whole experience comes together for the user, or, if not managed properly, it falls apart. The web site experience defines the brand experience of the online brand.

DOI: 10.4018/978-1-60566-394-4.ch008

The growing importance of online branding and advertising is demonstrated by the investment that many organizations are making in branding and advertising through digital media. In the UK, online advertising spend has reached £2.6bn p.a (2007), and is projected to rise further. US expenditure on online advertising is $21bn p.a., 7.4% of total media expenditure, and this is projected to rise to 15.4% by 2012 (www.eMarketer.com). Increasing investment in online advertising and branding is associated with higher levels of activity and interest in relation to online branding. The novelty and continuing evolution of digital channels requires ongoing innovation from both businesses and advertising and media agencies, not only in how they present and represent their brand online, but also in how they manage brand communication and the brand experience. Indeed, Chapman (2001), when discussing the rapid rise of Internet brands, such as Yahoo! and Amazon asserts that the role of the brand has changed dramatically, such that brand has become a key competitive weapon in gaining market dominance.

Despite the increasing investment and activity in the area of online branding, the debate about whether brands are more or less important in the online channel continues. Some argue that in a digitized world, with information overload, brands are becoming ever more important, because they save the customer time by reducing their search costs and helping them to make choices in a world that is replete with choice (Rubinstein and Griffiths, 2001; Ward and Lee, 2000). For those product categories in which it is difficult to judge product or service quality through the Internet, branding may be an important signifier of quality, reliability and consistency. And further, in rapidly changing marketplaces, in which many purchases are for products or services that are new to the consumer, the continuity and reliability of brands will become all the more important to consumers. There is also evidence that experienced consumers return to the same sites rather than 'surf the web' (Carpenter, 2000). The alternative point of view is that with a wealth of information at their fingertips, coupled with sophisticated search engines and comparison sites, which help in locating information, products and services, consumers can free themselves from the shorthand of brand. Instead they can gather detailed information, including expert and user opinion, on products and services and make their own judgments on the suitability of a product, service or organization, such that brands become superfluous (Rowley, 2004). As Ward and Lee (2000) suggest that there may be a declining role for brands as consumers gather more experience on the Internet, and their search proficiency rises. In summary, the jury is still out on the importance of branding in and through digital channels, but this has not deterred major brands from devoting considerable attention to building brand presence online.

Those who believe that branding 'matters more on the Internet' argue that the Internet is fundamentally changing how companies manage their brands, with the emphasis being placed on the 'branded experience', not only through digital channels, but also through all other channels through which the organization, and therefore the brand, interacts with customers. This may well be the case for some brands, but for other brands the impact may be less significant. The importance and impact of online branding may depend on product category, with online branding being more important for high risk and high involvement products. Danaher et al (2003) found that in the online world, brand loyalty was related to market share, with high market share brands attracting a higher level of loyalty than those with smaller market shares. In addition, Jiang (2004)'s exploration of the relationship between online brands and customization offers some interesting insights into the role of brands online. They found brand name to have more impact on purchase choices in customization scenarios where quality information is not available for facilitating customer choices. Recognizing that the availability of quality information to a customer in the choice process is dependent on a number of factors suggests that the impact of brands online will not only vary between product and service categories, but also between customer segments.

Before advancing the discussion of online branding further, it is useful to propose a definition of online branding. Interestingly, such definitions are scarce, but a useful practitioner definition is offered by Chaffey (2008). He suggests that online branding is:

'How online channels are used to support brands, which in essence are the sum of the characteristics of a product or service as perceived by a user'

Online branding, then, is a process of brand building, or the creation of online brand value or equity. An online brand is a brand that has an online presence. As we shall discuss later, the objectives, extent and nature of that presence may vary. In particular, there is an important distinction to be made between pure play brands, such as Amazon, and eBay where online branding is the central brand building process, and click and brick (multi-channel) brands where online branding complements branding through other channels. Any discussion of online branding needs to embrace both pure-play and multi-channel brands, as is evidenced by Revolution's top forty UK digital brands, which includes, for example, Google, eBay, and Amazon.co.uk, alongside BBC, Curry's, Tesco.com, John Lewis, and Times Online (www.brandrepublic.com).

In some respects, online branding is the same as branding through any other medium (as demonstrated through the case studies in Meyers and Gerstman (2001)), but in specific and practical respects the online channel poses new and different challenges for branding. This means that discussions of online branding, whether they involve academic analysis or practical advice and tips tend to be strange hybrids of branding concepts, practice and strategy, and the design and delivery of e-service and e-commerce experiences. Online

branding, or as others might call it, e-branding, digital branding, internet branding, or i-branding, as a concept is slippery and difficult to disentangle. The academic literature is limited and is in a formative stage with little integration (Ibeh et al, 2005; Merisavo and Raulas, 2004; Murphy et al, 2003; Simmons, 2007). The academic literature is complemented by a range of professional practice books, articles and web resources. This chapter draws on a wide range of these sources, and seeks to offer insights that make a useful contribution to our understanding of online branding.

This chapter then, discusses the opportunities and challenges associated with online branding. The sections in the chapter are:

- **Branding concepts:** draws together key concepts on the nature of brands and branding, as a platform for the later sections of the chapter.
- **Delivering on online branding objectives:** explores a range of different perspectives on what an organization might seek to achieve through its online branding strategy and actions.
- **Facets of online branding:** identifies a number of key issues and opportunities associated with online branding.
- **Examples of successful digital brands:** complements examples offered throughout the chapter with carefully selected case studies of successful brands with interesting approaches to branding in the online channel.
- **Future trends:** summarizes a number of key areas which are central to capitalizing on the full potential of branding through digital channels.

BRANDING CONCEPTS

This section briefly reviews and summarises some key branding concepts and principles that are an important foundation for understanding online brands and branding. Effective online branding is based on an appreciation of the role of brands and the processes that can promote brands, coupled with an appreciation of the specific opportunities for branding offered in the digital channel. Specifically, this section explores concepts such as branding, brand image and reputation, brand meaning, corporate branding, and co-branding.

Brand strategy is the overall approach, in terms of plans and tactics, that an organization deploys in order to create long term brand equity and competitive advantage from branding. Branding is essentially the process of creating value through the provision of a compelling and consistent offer, (the brand promise) backed by a positive customer experience (the brand experience) that will satisfy customers and encourage them to return. This provides an opportunity for building brand relationships, which, in turn, deliver repeat business, allow the business to charge premium prices, and make it more difficult for competitors launch a challenge (Aaker, 1991; DeChernatony and McDonald, 1992; Doyle, 1998). Branding is the relationship between the company and the customer; every form of contact that a company has with a customer contributes to that relationship. Branding is about how a company makes a customer think and feel. The branding process builds the value of the brand to the business, or its brand equity.

Brand image and reputation are central to driving customer purchases, engagement and recommendations. Brand identity is how the organization and its management want the brand to be perceived. In developing brand identity an organization will consider the brand's positioning, and emphasise its distinctive characteristics that make it different from its competitors and appealing to the public (Kapferer, 2004). Positioning is based on established the What (promise and benefit), Whom (target audience), When (which occasion), and Against whom? (competitors) of branding. Through marketing communication,

managing the brand experience, understanding and listening to customers and delivering on brand promises, organizations seek to align their brand image with their brand identity.

Brands can be perceived, interpreted, and managed at a variety of different levels, as shown in Figure 1. First and foremost, a brand is signified by a brand mark, and therefore has a basic function associated with recognition, and association. All documents, products and web pages carrying a common brand mark can be seen to emanate from the same source. Brand marks when registered as trademarks may also be used to protect brands from copying and sabotage.

Brands can also be viewed as representing a cluster of attributes, such as 'organized', 'durable', 'reliable' and 'pleasurable'. Such attributes can be communicated through web site design and online service delivery, although some attributes are easier to communicate through a web page than others. For example, Disney captures the sense of 'fun' through 'where the magic comes to you' on a web page that provides access to movies, music, TV, live events and travel. Tesco captures 'every little helps' through online discounts and offers, and price comparison, but representing 'reliable' or 'socially responsible', whilst not impossible, is a little more challenging.

Figure 1. The brand meaning pyramid

125

Brand attributes are typically translated into a brand value proposition by considering brand attributes from the perspective of the benefits that they deliver to the customer. The brand value proposition is the collection of functional, emotional and self-expressive benefits delivered by the brand that together provide value to the customer. One way of enhancing the potential for identification with a brand is to endow the brand with a personality. Brand personality is the brand image or identity expressed in terms of human characteristics. For example, consumers might visualize a Mercedes as a wealthy, middle-aged business executive. The personality of a brand may be communicated through its online presence. For example, the site for Saatchi & Saatchi, an advertising agency, uses the latest technologies in an imaginative way to show that they are creative and innovative. On the other hand, NatWest, a banking and financial services provider, uses a lot of blue and black to suggest that they are trustworthy and the emphasis is on text not images for providing information. However, communicating brand personalities online is not easy; Opoku and Hinson (2006) conducted an analysis of place branding through the official web sites of ten African countries, and found that none of them communicated a clear and distinct brand personality.

Increasingly, the concept of brand as experience has been promoted; this concept emphasizes that the consumer's brand image is formed not just by a brand's attributes, benefits and values, or personality characteristics, but by the total experience that they associate with the brand.

Importantly, given the multiple meanings that may be associated with the concept of brand, any one brand may be understood as a sign for recognition by one person, as a set of attributes, benefits, values, or personality characteristics by another, and as an experience by a third person. The brand is a complex symbol, and the challenge of branding is to develop a set of meanings or associations for the brand that can resonate with the variety of different perspectives that consumers might adopt in formulating a brand image.

Many of the basic definitions of brands and branding, including that of online branding offered by Chaffey (2008), privilege product and service brands. Corporate brands (such as Nestle, Virgin, HSBC, and Amazon) are becoming increasingly important, because investing in the brand equity of corporate brands offers an opportunity to extend the brand over a wide range of products and services, and is therefore more efficient. Balmer (2001) defined a corporate brand as:

'the conscious decision by senior management to distil and make known attributes of the organization's identity in the form of a clearly defined branding proposition'.

Xie and Boggs (2006) explain this in terms of the opportunity for building enhanced trust and relationships:

'Corporate branding facilitates customers' desire to look deeper into the brand and evaluate the nature of the firm. Trust in the products and brands the firm offers predisposes customers to accept its claims about other products and services.'

Corporate branding is significant in the online channel since many organizations use a corporate brand website as the anchor to their online branding strategy. For example, Kellogg's corporate site is central to their online branding strategy, although they also have product brand sites, such as www.all-bran.com. Especially online, a corporate branding strategy is both more helpful to customers and makes for more straightforward brand management. Accordingly it is important that online branders understand that for successful corporate branding:

- The brand is communicated through all of the organizations' communications and actions

- The values embedded in the corporate brand (such as 'excellence', or 'customer-focussed') must reflect the core values of the organization and the way it works internally as well as the way it does business
- Corporate brand decisions must be viewed as strategic decisions
- Corporate branding requires integrated marketing and brand communications (Balmer and Gray, 2003).

Another facet of branding that is important in the online channel is co-branding. Co-branding is a strategy of brand alliance. Grossman (1997) views co-branding as the pairing of two brands in a marketing context. In the context of corporate co-branding, co-branding is concerned with the integration or merging of corporate brands and the creation of a viable linked or joint identity (Motion *et al.*, 2003). In online environments, through links between websites, sponsorship, and affiliate marketing, organisations are engaging in product and corporate co-branding. In so doing, brands are building and seeking to capitalise on each other's brand equity, but they risk negative image transfer (Lei et al, 2008). In addition, for co-branding to be credible, brands must have shared brand values, such as, say commitment to social responsibility, or service excellence. Co-branding has consequences for brands and their management. Unfortunately, co-branding is one of the under-researched fields of marketing and little is known about the factors that determine a successful co-branding strategy (Chang, 2008).

DELIVERING ON ONLINE BRANDING OBJECTIVES

The success of online branding depends on what the business seeks to achieve through its online branding strategy, and on clear online branding objectives. After some discussion of the need to acknowledge the range of different online branding objectives that an organization might adopt, this section focuses on three main groups of branding objectives, viz, building brand awareness and recall, delivering the brand experience, and, building and promoting brand loyalty and relationships. In each of these areas we discuss tools and approaches in the online environment which can support the achievement of online branding objectives.

Perspectives on Online Branding Objectives

Businesses have different objectives for their online channel, in terms of its contribution to the business. The online channel can be variously used for information and presence, communication and interaction with customers, service delivery, performing commercial transactions, and the delivery of digital products (such as photographs, software and music). These functions have implications for branding possibilities and objectives.

One way of looking at branding objectives is in terms of the brand promise. Dayal et al (2000) identify the range of options for branding objectives in terms of the different types of brand promises that businesses can make through the online channel:

- **The promise of convenience:** making a purchase experience more convenient than the real world, or than rivals
- **The promise of achievement:** to assist consumers in achieving their goals, such as managing their finances, or making decisions about investments
- **The promise of fun and adventure:** through an online experience that is more than functional, but also extends to being fun or engaging through, for example, games, gambling, or interaction with other people.
- **The promise of self-expression and recognition:** through personalised services,

127

and opportunities for consumers to build their own web site.

- **The promise of belonging:** as provided by membership of online customer clubs, and social networking communities.

No one online brand can expect to deliver on all of these promises. Indeed, the best online brand campaigns do not try to convey too many messages (Sweney, 2007). An online brand must choose the promises on which it seeks to deliver in a way that is consistent with its brand identity and image and taking into account its business sector, audiences, messages, and budget.

Another way of looking at branding objectives is to view the development of online branding in terms of the stages of brand building, starting with brand awareness, and moving on to the delivery of the brand experience, and finally seeking to promote brand relationships and loyalty. De Chernatony and Christodoulides (2004) suggest that many organizations undertake a phased development of online branding, starting with a basic site that secures online presence for the brand, and then gradually evolving their web site through offering greater opportunities for engagement with the brand through greater interactive opportunities, transaction facilities, and online communities. Table 1 summarises this evolution in terms of e-business objectives and online branding objectives. The online branding objectives and the

Table 1. Evolution of e-business and online branding objectives

Stage	E-business objective	Online branding objective
1	Online presence and information provision	Building brand awareness and recall
2	Interaction and trans-actions	Delivering the brand experience
3	Communication and community	Building and promoting brand loyalty and relationships

tools and approaches that can be used to deliver on those objectives are discussed below.

Building Brand Awareness and Recall

One of the key purposes of even the most basic website is to establish a presence in the online domain, and thereby to offer an opportunity to capitalise on enhancing brand awareness through an additional channel. Once people are aware that the brand exists, the next objective is typically to remind them of the brand sufficiently often to achieve recall of both the brand logo, and its meaning. But, just having a web site does not create awareness and recall; people also have to find that website. In other words they have to be directed to the website. This involves engaging in all of the different approaches for driving traffic to the website, such as:

- *Search engine optimization* to ensure a high ranking in search engine outputs in response to searches using pertinent search terms,

- Search engine or *pay per click marketing*, again leading to presence on search engine websites.

- Building *affiliate networks* and partner programmes through which traffic is driven between the sites of those organisations who have agreed to the reciprocal placement of links on each others web sites.

- *Email, e-newsletters* and other types of communication to remind customers of the brand and inform them of new products and service developments. In order to avoid such communications being viewed as spam, targeting should be precise and permission should be sought.

- *Advocacy marketing* or viral marketing, through which organizations seek to encourage recommendations from satisfied customers, using incentives, such as discounts, and loyalty points and easy-to-use tools, such as web-based e-mail forms, and pass-along email newsletters (Datta et al, 2005).

- *Offline promotion* of the website through other channels such as billboards, radio, posters, flyers, and television.

Good traffic management will enhance traffic, awareness of web site presence, and, in turn, brand awareness.

The role of brands as search keys also deserves specific mention. Unique brand names that are widely known and that are not generic terms (such as Nike, WWF, Disney, Virgin, and, Primark) can be very effective as key words in searches. Brand names are particularly useful for those customers who know the brand that they are looking for, but do not know the web site address. They are also useful in facilitating channel switching.

Even more important is the link between domain name and brand. Consistency between domain name and brand name can reinforce familiarity with the brand, and strengthen the message link between channels. Domain names should be unique, easy to remember or guess and appropriate to the products and service available through the website (Hanson, 2000; Ilfield and Winter, 2002).

Delivering the Brand Experience

'On the world wide web, the brand is the experience and the experience is the brand'. (Dayal et al, 2000)

In the online channel, marketing communication, service, and relationship building can all be delivered simultaneously. Customers have brand experiences when they engage with the brand through the website. Websites with a high level of usability and usefulness and that are convenient and appropriate to the task are a must. Flexible and effective navigation is also a prerequisite.

But, building the brand presence involves more than web site functionality. It is also important to communicate the brand through the web site design. Brand values and messages are, for example, communicated through the following aspects of web site design:

- *Logo* and its presence on every page on the site to act as a reminder of the of the brand throughout the site and increase brand recognition and recall.
- *Graphics and images*, including animated mages and video clips, which are visual representations of brand values and personality. Images make more impact than words and can be a differentiating factor in online branding
- *Text and copy* which sets the tone of voice, and helps to define the brand's personality; text is the site talking to the customer. The words determine what it says, whilst the typeface determines the style of the communication
- *Shapes* of boxes, menus, buttons, images, textboxes etc are key to both readability and communicating the brand visual identity.
- *Currency* through new images and text is important to communicate a live and dynamic website. This may seem obvious, but Doherty et al (1999) found evidence of websites that had not been updated for a long time.
- *Colour*, its shades and the way it is used, conveys values, such as peaceful, trust, excitement, or warning. The brand colour palette is a key consideration in web site design
- *Layout of the web page* can be used as a metaphor linked to brand values. Thus, for example the BBC News website (www.news.bbc.co.uk) has a 'front page' which is arranged in columns to simulate a print newspaper.

Other features of the web-site also offer opportunities for building and promoting loyalty and relationships, as discussed below.

One of the very real challenges in delivering an online brand experience is that the Internet is a self-service medium. The experience is constructed by the customer, using the tools designed into the web site; the e-service experience is self-service (Meuter et al, 2000; Zhu et al, 2002). The quality of the experience is not only determined by the web site design, but also by the competence of the customer. Existing customers are likely to have a more positive experience than new customers, because not only are they more familiar with the processes that they wish to undertake, but are more confident and at ease. Other factors, such as personality, values, attitudes, culture, and perceptions of control, may also impact on the brand experience (e.g., Bradley and Sparks, 2002; Yen, 2005; Zhang and Prybutok, 2005).

Building and Promoting Brand Loyalty and Relationships

Building on awareness of the brand and its values, reinforced through brand experience, offers a platform for intensifying customer's engagement with the brand. Positive brand experiences are likely to affect customer's allegiance to the brand, and the wider and more frequent their experience is with the brand, the greater will be the customer's brand knowledge. The Internet is an additional channel through which a customer can interact with a brand, and indeed, a channel through which that interaction can be conducted at a time and location to suit the customer. Unfortunately there has been limited research into loyalty through the online channel (Rafiq and Fulford, 2005) although Harris and Goode (2004) claim that online loyalty is dependent upon consumer trust in the procedural rigour and operational abilities of the supplier.

Web sites can be designed to offer opportunities for enhancing the depth of engagement with the brand. This might be achieved through:

1. *E-mail and other communications* both in the form of e-mails and e-newsletters to the customers, and also in the form of opportunities for the customer to talk to the organization to resolve specific problems, to offer feedback on service performance, or to raise more general issues. Merisavo and Raulas (2004) discovered that regular e-mail marketing had a positive effect on brand loyalty; loyal customers appreciate regular communication and other information content, more than direct brand offers.

2. *Content*, such as information and advice, may not only provoke more frequent web site visits and thereby more frequent engagement with the brand, but can also engender trust and influence attitudes and behaviour.

3. *Full integration of channels* in a multi-channel environment. For example, Jessops (www.jessops.com), a photography retailer, supports online purchase of cameras and other equipment, but if there are any difficulties with the online process, a telephone number for a local store is available. The store can then assist with the ordering process, advice on availability, and delivery.

4. *Trust building approaches and tools* Trust is the commodity that makes people and organizations comfortable and prepared to share information, do business, and participate in communities. Trust is arguably even more important in the virtual world than it is in the real world, because the parties to a transaction are not in the same place and there is no personal interaction (Ibeh et al, 2005; Ratnasingham, 1998). On the other hand, the bond of trust, in the depersonalised setting of the Internet is very fragile (Hodges, 1997; Varadarajan and Yadav, 2002). Security and privacy polices and practices form a platform for the development of trust. Registration with Trust agencies such as TRUSTe and TrustUK is another useful step. Wang and Emurian (2005) propose a number of trust-

inducing interface design features within the categories of: graphic design, structure design, content, and social-cue design, whilst Shankar et al (2002) offer a more detailed proposal of the components, antecedents and consequences of online trust.

5. *Online brand communities* can be used to build engagement with the brand. They offer a virtual context in which brand tribes, the informal groups of consumers who share awareness, passion and loyalty for a brand, can interact. Tesco, for example, has online clubs for Wine and Baby & Toddler, whilst Kellog's invites you to participate in 'The All-Bran Day 10 Club'. The willingness of customers to engage in brand communities depends upon the value that they derive from the community, either through exchange of useful information and advice, access to informative content, or the availability of special discounts. From the business's perspective, the higher level of engagement with the brand can lead to enhanced brand knowledge and brand loyalty. It may be possible to use an online community to enhance and enlist customer knowledge, through surveys, dialogue, and co-creation. Rowley et al (2007) demonstrate the way in which interaction through an online community can be used to enhance physical community involvement, and to engage users in the co-creation process associated with the development of the products and experiences in sport kiting. Organizations that have products and services associated with hobbies, professions or other general interest topics (politics, health, cars, investments, or houses) are most likely to be successful in creating online brand communities.

FACETS OF ONLINE BRANDING

This section identifies a number of key issues and opportunities associated with online brand-ing. These include: the constraints of a web site for brand communication, multi-channel brand management, consistency v customisation, global v local branding, appealing to advertisers, organization of branding, protecting domain names, and online reputation management.

Communicating a Brand Message through a Web Site

Organizations may not only fulfil a range of business objectives through their web-site but they are also seeking to fulfil a range of branding objectives. This is a lot to ask of a web-site, which is viewed through a small screen; the screen is even smaller on mobile devices. It is imperative to enlist all of the components of the web site for brand building as discussed earlier in this section, and to avoid viewing branding as an add-on. Not only must the web site communicate and deliver on several fronts, but it must also differentiate the business from its competitors and capture attention. This requires innovative design, but design that delivers under the constraints of the brand's visual identity and customers' technology platforms. Early studies (e.g. Leong et al, 1998) suggested that whilst the website is highly suitable for communicating rational messages, it is more challenging to communicate the emotional values of brands.

Multi-Channel Brand Management

Now that the initial era of Internet euphoria and the mushrooming of unsustainable dotcoms has passed the majority of brands have both online and offline presences. Initially, some organizations were unsure about whether to migrate existing brands online. A new online brand offered the opportunity for a fresh start, to do things differently, and to build a new identity. It also limited the risk of damage to existing brands through exposure in the new uncertain digital marketplace. On the other hand, building a new brand requires significant investment, and does not capitalise on the brand equity of existing brands. Degerau et al (2000) found that known brand names become more valuable online because information on those brands is readily accessible from memory. Further, use of the existing brand online can also help to drive overall brand awareness and engagement (Chen 2001). Some organizations, such as the Co-op bank, with smile.co.uk, have separate online brands. Such organizations need to manage the relationships between the brands in their brand portfolio carefully. However, for most organizations the dilemma is how to create a sense of *'the same credibility, but a different presentation'*. The challenge is to achieve consistency of both brand message and experience through different channels, whilst engaging with the customer in different ways. This requires careful and ongoing attention to integrated marketing communications, or more specifically integrated brand communications (Interbrand, 2004).

Consistency vs. Customisation

Brand consistency is central to ensuring brand impact and the building of brand equity, and in the previous section we have emphasised the importance of consistency in branding between channels. However the 'consistency' rhetoric needs to be balanced against the dynamic nature of a brand. Brands evolve and undergo re-branding. They subtly adapt and shift their messages and visual identities to embrace social and cultural trends. In the Internet environment, particularly for pure play brands, such as Google and Amazon, it is very easy to change a brand identity by re-designing a logo or a web site. Further, such organizations, are constantly incrementally improving the functionality of their web sites, and thereby changing, and seeking to enhance the brand experience.

Another challenge to brand consistency across channels is that a key aspect of multi-channel strategy is to differentiate channels by function, and sometimes by audience. This means that some brands may have different audiences online and offline. There is plenty of evidence to suggest that online shoppers are different from in-store shoppers (e.g.Donthu and Garcia, 1999; Lynch and Beck, 2001). Different audiences may seek different brand messages and experiences from the one brand. The challenge is to balance the expectations of the different audiences, whilst maintaining a core brand identity. Tools for customization or personalization of web sites that permit users to design their own home page for the site (e.g. myYahoo) offer them the opportunity to dilute the brand message and re-construct the brand experience, whilst on the other hand, 'making the brand their own' (Stuart and Jones, 2004). Whilst there is evidence that the take up of such tools may be variable, and dependent on the consumer's trust in the online organization (Chellappa and Sin, 2005), the consequences of providing such tools for the consistency of the brand image and communication of the brand identity need to be considered.

Global/Local

The global nature of the Internet also presents some challenges for organizations. The actual audience for online brands is less predictable and more diverse than the brand audience for many other channels. Language, symbols, messages, and colours often do not translate across countries and cultures. Global brands have long recognised that they need attributes, values, and personalities to appeal to different communities.

Organizations hoping to sell to markets outside of their own country need to design their website accordingly. For example, Yan (2001) discusses how New Zealand companies, recognising that their largest market would be the US, were careful to avoid *'pushing a stereotypically antipodean image'* (p.9). Global corporations, such as McDonalds and IBM have a corporate website complemented by national websites. The corporate website typically provides corporate information and establishes the core brand identity. The country websites speak more directly to their specific audiences, and whilst, for example, retaining the logo and many of the brand colours and messages adapt these to accommodate local languages, consumer behaviour and cultures (e.g. Rowley, 2004b). With the Internet, the relationships between these various brand representations become much more transparent, and coherence is even more important. For further discussion of this issue see Murphy and Scharl (2007).

Appealing to Advertisers

Many pure play and digital content web sites rely heavily on advertising revenue for their business success. Successful branding for consumers makes the site more attractive to advertisers. Organizations need to be clear about the advertising objectives that can be fulfilled through their site, and the means for evaluating the success of any advertising investment from commercial advertising contracts with third parties. They need to be proactive in understanding the brand building objectives of advertisers.

Authority, Responsibility and Organization

An organization's ability to deliver on the online brand promise involves a wide range of different people. The question is '*who is responsible for online branding?*'. To the forefront in this process are likely to be information systems, marketing, and communications departments and professionals. Such groups will have responsibility for formulating brand messages, designing web sites and ensuring a safe and secure online presence. In the background, but equally important to the brand experience, are customer service, finance, and logistics departments and professionals. Importantly, also, especially for e-commerce sites, delivery is likely to be through a sub-contractor and payment mechanisms may also be managed

by an external agency. The total brand experience may also depend on suppliers, distributors and other contractors. Most organizations understand the need for coordination between departments in theory, but too many have not mastered this in practice. Some wrestle with inappropriate organizational structures, organizational cultures and values that reward behaviours that are irrelevant in today's dynamic marketplace, and poor osmosis of customer knowledge. Strebinger and Treiblmaier (2004) discuss the interdependencies between organizational structure, brand structure and IT structure, within the context of other forces such a corporate strategy, corporate culture and organizational processes. They illustrate some of the complexities of brand strategy and management within organizations, especially those exercising multi-brand strategies.

Protecting Domain Names

A key aspect of online branding is associated with promoting, and most significantly, protecting the domain name. Certainly in the early days of online branding, weak regulation and easy registration of domain names encouraged the abuse of brands as domain names. The classic example is that of General Motors, who failed to register generalmotors.com sufficiently promptly such that an individual in Georgia was able to make a registration. Failure to register relevant and obvious domain names leaves the brand's image and thus the brand's equity susceptible to sabotage by competitors, adversaries and proactive entrepreneurs (Hanson, 2000). Ensuring registration and protection of domain names can be a complex process. Brands need to consider registration under the appropriate global domain,. com,. org, or,. net, as well as registration in an appropriate range of the 200 country domains. Many UK fashion retailers have registration of both. com and. co.uk domains, and automatically direct searchers between these domain names. However, there are exceptions; for example, the Mosaic group has registered www.principles.co.uk to support their Principles brand, but www.principles.com is a website with ethical and religious content. Rules and fees for registration vary between countries (Murphy et al, 2003). Whilst top brands have 'learnt from their mistakes', and are now more careful to protect their brands through domain name registration, many smaller businesses and businesses in developing countries remain vulnerable, as illustrated by Hashim and Murphy's (2007) study of Malaysian hotels.

Look-alike and sound-alike brands seek to capitalise on brand the equity of major brands by registering brand name variations (Reis and Reis, 2000). The global nature of online brands makes it difficult to regulate, leading to online brand confusion. Categories for these brand abusers have been proposed:

- **Cybersquatters:** register famous brands to attract consumers to their site, or to sell the site to the highest bidder – which is often the well-known brand.
- **Gripe sites:** add a derogatory word to the domain name, as in IBMsucks.org, or Googlesucks.com.
- **Typosquatters:** take advantage of user typing errors to claim hits. United Airlines, for example, did not register untied.com, but on the other hand Yahoo have registered yahop.com. The website, hotmale.com redirects intending hotmail.com users to a porn site, and hoymail.com re-directs to gambling sites.

Brand owners need to be alert to such potential abuse and take appropriate action.

Online Reputation Management

Online reputation management presents specific challenges because it is easy for people to publish their thoughts and distribute comments on brands. Online bulletin boards, forums and consumer review sites, such as Ciao (www.ciao.co.uk) have been joined more recently by consumer-to-consumer interactions through blogs and social networking sites. Facebook, for example, has a web page for brands. Anti-brand sites are a further forum for exchange of comment. It is easy for people to share negative (or even positive) brand experiences or opinions. Kucuk (2008) describes this as 'negative double jeopardy', suggesting that the most valuable brands attract more anti-brand sites, whilst less valuable brands do not have such 'hate attraction' on the internet. In recognition of the need to manage the potential for negative brand equity, a number of online reputation management services have grown up. Also free alerting tools, such as Google Alert (www.googlealert.com) can be used as a basis for monitoring comments on specific brands.

Another aspect of online reputation management relates to the proactive use of the web site to manage potentially negative publicity. Not only can the web site be used to respond either directly or obliquely to brand challenges on the Internet, but it can also be used to disseminate apologies, congratulations, and thanks, and to keep people informed during a crisis. Whenever an event attracts negative publicity, the organisations' website is the public's first port-of-call. The web site is an important channel of communication in a crisis or disaster, and needs to be fully utilised in such circumstances.

EXAMPLES OF SUCCESSFUL DIGITAL BRANDS

In this section we offer some examples of brands that have been successful online, and describe briefly their approach. As discussed above, brands may seek to deliver different objectives through the online channel. Accordingly, for the purposes of this section we propose a framework of four different types of brands, and discuss examples that represent each of the following categories:

- **"Non-sales"**: Globally branded organisations that use digital branding to build brand awareness and communicate directly or indirectly with customers but that do not actually sell from their web site (i.e. the company "sells" only in offline environments)
- **"Pureplay"**: Brands that exist only in a digital environment/channel
- **"Mix-of-Clicks"**: Brands that exist in a multi-channel environment.
- **"Innovators"**: Brands that have made *"particularly innovative"* use of either regular web and/or social media environments. Innovators may be either Pureplay or Mix-of-Clicks.

Non-Sales

Good examples of brands which have really taken on the non-sales role of a digital presence are automobile brands. Automobile manufacturers all have a heavily developed (and financially invested) traditional sales channel through dealer networks, so the role of the automobile web site is purely to create brand awareness and *"the-product-as-a-brand"* awareness. Of particular note are the digital presences created for Fiat, Volkswagen and BMW, and Audi. Volkswagen created an intriguing "Night Driving" site to promote the Volkswagen Golf, but it has no direct sales rapport. A strange quirk of these global organizations and their digital presences is that each presence is more often than not localized to individual countries due to the localised nature of the product; individual motor car products are often specific to a country (or a continent as a minimum). Few automobile brand sites are truly global, more *"glocal"* in nature.

Despite the fact that no purchase transactions can be made through these sites an enormous effort is made to ensure usability and (more important) memorability. Sometimes the web site is part of a wider multi-channel campaign. For example, the Volkswagen Night Driving site supported a much larger awareness campaign created in traditional media channels, with TV adverts used to encourage viewers to visit the site, and engage in an interesting brand experience.

The best non-sales sites not only provide information but also entertain. Automobile manufacturer's sites are highly interactive, and the entertaining digital proposition often comes in the ability to create and customize a car. Brand values are often transmitted in the way that the sites are created. Strong corporate brand themes are evident in all of the automobile manufacturer sites.

Pureplay

Both Amazon and eBay are widely recognized and acknowledged pure play brands. Both organizations have resilient approaches to search engine marketing. Casual search for products on Google or MSN will often reveal an organic search listing and a paid-per-click listing of one or either firm and the related product. Both organizations rely heavily on affiliate marketing approaches. Both organizations have a network of sellers and resellers. And both have spawned an array of complementary business services that both rely on and support the survival of the two firms. As a result, they have a global brand recognition envied by firms with a longer heritage; eBay ranks 43rd in Interbrand's Best Global Brands 2010 listing, and Amazon is ranked at 36nd. (www.interbrand.com). Both logos are immediately identifiable with the specific service they offer. eBay's digital brand has gone on to dominate all offline promotional media (TV adverts, the eBay University etc) for its auction proposition, yet its Paypal brand is not dominated by the eBay brand and neither is its Skype brand. This suggests that each of the services requires its own distinctive brand identity in order to deal with the unique service propositions that they operate (financial transactions and VOIP telephony, respectively).

Mix-of-Clicks

Ministry of Sound (MoS) has become an extremely powerful, global brand in the music and entertainment sector with a mix of channels to market for the brand and a huge combination of products and services. There has been a huge growth in TV, radio, mobile and web services for MoS since 2005 with a concurrent growth in global audience. MoS syndicates its content to a variety of other platforms in a both a branded and white-label format, but its particular current strategy is to develop "made-only-for-digital" content for digital partners such as Bebo (in order to continue to attract a youth audience) as well as to develop a digital web-based TV channel whose branded content (news, film, music and downloads) is syndicated to a variety of aggregator sites.

The online brand is dominated by the original offline corporate identity, and so it can be seen as a brand extension rather than a unique proposition in its own right. The site is not used necessarily to communicate brand values but is actually a further channel to a sophisticated marketplace. The brand here is used to communicate trust to the specific target audience. This audience would probably tend to already be committed MoS consumers and would regard personal association with the brand to have some value. A digital brand extension could conceivably add to credibility that the consumers seek from association with MoS.

Innovators

The category 'innovators' has been proposed to provide a focus for discussion of really different approaches to online branding, whichever of the previous three categories might also apply. The two examples discussed below focus on the use of social media.

Current TV is an emerging *non-sales* brand that demonstrates that the use of user-generated content can help create a well-defined and recognized digital brand whilst at the same time remaining close to its core business of developing quality TV programming. Whilst the programming itself may not be to every consumer's taste, they have developed an approach that allows them to create, distribute and promote their programming. The social nature of Current TV allows users to choose what will be aired.

This social brand could create significant loyalty. The audience associates the brand with some level of ownership, either through user generated content or through programming choices, and so users could now start to associate the brand with being something that belongs to them.

O2 made particularly clever use of Facebook towards the end of 2007 with a sponsored Facebook group (The Great University Race) offering thousands of UK students the chance to win a party at their University. This brand awareness raising campaign was a real early adopter initiative and particularly caught the flavour of Facebook use at its growth period at that point. Tens of thousands of students, the particularly attractive segment for O2, joined the group in an effort to win the prize, providing O2 with enormous brand exposure for relatively little outlay. This interesting experiment could expose potential consumers to a positive experience of the brand, which in the long run could affect future sales (to a specific segment noted for its heavy use of mobile services) when such consumers consider their next mobile services purchase.

FUTURE TRENDS

There is plenty of evidence to suggest that investment in online advertising continues to escalate. Organizations will increasingly be seeking to understand how they can successfully build their brand awareness, recall, relationships, experiences, and most importantly, equity, through the online channel. Online or digital branding is set to become much more important over the next few years. In many sectors, online branding is currently relatively conservative, focussing on brand visual identity as exemplified through website design. The case studies in the previous section offer some examples of more innovative approaches, but these are the exception rather than the rule. Rubinstein (2002) argues that the principles of branding have changed very little as a result of the internet and also that online branding needs to build on and integrate with branding through other channels. On the other hand, there has been a shift in emphasis from the belief that 'branding is all about communication' to the belief that real branding is about creating relationships with customers and delivering positive brand experiences. Over the next few years, the digital channel will not only become increasingly significant as a branding channel, but the opportunities that it offers for engagement with customers may herald a revolution in branding and the role of brands.

In order to fully capitalise on the potential of branding through digital channels we speculate that organizations are likely to need to become increasingly proactive in:

1. **Protecting their brand capital and reputation online:** including managing domain name registrations, co-branding, managing and representing their brand architectures, and undertaking a host of other actions to protect and promote their brand name online. Across the brand portfolio, organizations may need to re-visit the relationship between product and corporate brands. A possible scenario is that corporate brands will have a key role in managing and retaining customers, whilst product brands might be the main tool in customer acquisition.

2. **Understanding how customers use brands online:** In addition to understanding the implications of the ongoing debate about whether the opportunity to product search online makes brands more or less important, organizations will need to understand how their customers use brands online. For

example, a consumer seeking to purchase a pair of Adidas trainers is likely to be searching on the 'Adidas' brand, and looking for the retailer offering the lowest price. The consumer chooses the retailer primarily on price and not brand, but may, for example, avoid any retailer brands on the basis of poor delivery and reliability reputations and experiences. As in this small example, the roles of the manufacturer brand and the retailer brand are different. Nevertheless, there may be increasing competition for brand attention and loyalty between product and retailer brands.

3. **Brand positioning online:** whilst it is important to consider the merits of brand consistency between channels, businesses will need to consider the extent to which positioning should be aligned across channels. Some brands may reach different audiences and communities through different channels. Further, the dimensions of positioning may be different between channels. For example, Revolution (www.brandrepbublic.com) rank digital brands on the basis of innovation, recognition, customer care, longevity, reliability, and value.

4. **Communicating brand values:** Many retailers have been surprisingly reticent about communicating their values and position explicitly through the online channel. For example, in a recent study of UK fashion multi-channel retailers, Rowley (2008) found very little evidence of brand values or brand strap-line on home pages. All businesses with an e-presence need to recognise that some potential customers will first encounter their brand through the online channel, and be proactive about communicating brand positioning through their 'online shop window'.

5. **Brand communication and experience online:** There is some evidence that e-mail communication, and relevant web site con-

tent can build brand loyalty and commitment. This suggests that organizations need to develop an understating of the types of content and communication that are valued by customers. In their consideration of content, organizations need to give attention to the sensory aspects of their web presence, including the quality and resolution of any images, zooming options, and 3-D display. Marketsentinel (2007) discusses how Avis have proactively engaged in a two-way dialogue with customers; they used consumer comments to understand who was talking about them and in what terms, and who was talking about car hire/rental in general and the authorities with whom they needed to connect. This helped them to identify the influencers, establish what they were talking about, and the language that they were using, and to respond by developing their products and communications accordingly. This process, they suggest places the brand where it should be: *'the place where you solve problems for your customers'*. Finally, online brand experiences should, as appropriate, extend beyond the functional to the provision of excitement and fun.

6. **Brand communities online:** If the brand web-site provides a venue which offers customers resources and communication opportunities that they value, then it is a small step to seek to explore the potential for use of the website to build brand community. A brand community is a community of people who are enthusiastic about a brand; the brand is a key consideration in future purchase decisions, and they act as advocates for the brand. They also enjoy discussing their experiences with the brand with other brand enthusiasts, may participate in co-creation of product, services or experiences, and may be important in refuting anti-brand online communication. The increasing availability and use of social networking tools is generating greater quantities of comments about brands and organizations, to which organizations need to listen, learn, and react.

7. **From online to digital branding:** As indicated at the beginning of this chapter there are a number of terms currently used for branding in digital channels. In this chapter, we have preferred the term 'online branding' because it is the term used in much of the previous literature in this field, and where the focus has primarily been on branding through the Internet. Nevertheless, there is increasing use of the terms 'digital brand' and 'digital branding' to reflect that branding can be delivered through a range of digital channels, including digital television and mobile devices. In recent years there has been increasing interest in the potential of advertising though mobile channels, but only limited research on mobile brands and branding. Early contributions in this area tend to focus on creating value for customers, and customer relationship development (e.g. Pura, 2003; Nysveen et al, 2005). In addition to the need to develop expertise in relation to each new digital channel and its contribution to branding, the diversification of digital channels will present an ever greater challenge to brand management. Brand management is set to become increasingly important and interesting, but all the more challenging.

CONCLUSION

Online branding and advertising is growing in importance and significance. Organizations need to develop their understanding of, and competence in, online branding. Researchers can support practitioners through enquiry and model-building. In this chapter, we have suggested that it is important to remember and continually re-visit the basics of branding as a platform for both theory and practice in digital branding. Most significantly, organizations need to be clear about their objectives for branding in the online channel. Whilst there is a case for arguing that digital branding has much in common with branding through other channels, there are also a range of strategic and operational considerations that need special attention for successful online branding. Going forward, organizations will be seeking to build brand awareness, recall, relationships, experiences and equity through the online channel. Different organizations are at different stages of development in relation to online branding, but across many sectors there is considerable scope for development of practice and knowledge.

ACKNOWLEDGMENT

The authors would like to thank Assia Grazioli-Venier at FLYPAPER.TV, Alex Paris at Brand Communications Group, Barry Christie at JWT, Simon Polovina at Sheffield Hallam University, Andrew Hyatt at Bernard Hodes Group, Raja Baradwaj at Mediaedge:cia and Chris Pistorious for comments and insights on online branding.

REFERENCES

Aaker, D. A. (1991). *Managing brand equity*. New York, NY: The Free Press.

Balmer, J. M. T. (2001). The three virtues and seven deadly sins of corporate brand management. *Journal of General Management, 27*(1), 1–17.

Balmer, J. M. T., & Gray, E. R. (2003). Corporate brands: What are they? What of them? *European Journal of Marketing, 37*(7/8), 20–33. doi:10.1108/03090560310477627

Chaffey, D. (2008). *What is online branding?* Retrieved from www.davechaffey.com/ E-marketing-Glossary

Chang, W.-L. (2008). OnCob: An ontology-based knowledge system for supporting positions and classification of co-branding strategy. *Knowledge-Based Systems, 21*, 498–506. doi:10.1016/j.knosys.2008.03.007

Chapman, M. (2001). Branding.com: Building brand leadership in the new economy. *Corporate Reputation Review, 4*(3), 200–208. doi:10.1057/palgrave.crr.1540143

Chellappa, R. K., & Sin, R. G. (2005). Personalization versus privacy: An empirical examination of the online consumer's dilemma. *Information Technology Management, 6*, 181–202. doi:10.1007/s10799-005-5879-y

Chen, S. (2001). Assessing the impact of the Internet on brands. *Brand Management, 8*(4-5), 288–302. doi:10.1057/palgrave.bm.2540029

Danaher, P. J., Wilson, I. W., & Davis, R. A. (2003). A comparison of online and offline consumer brand loyalty. *Marketing Science, 22*(4), 461–476. doi:10.1287/mksc.22.4.461.24907

Datta, P. R., Chowdhury, N., & Chakrabrty, B. R. (2005). Viral marketing: New form of word-of-mouth through Internet. *Business Review (Federal Reserve Bank of Philadelphia), 3*(2), 69–76.

Dayal, S., Lanesberg, H., & Zeissberg, M. (2000). Building digital brands. *The McKinsey Quarterly, 2*, 42–51.

De Chernatony, L., & Christodoulides. (2004). Taking the brand promise online: Challenges and opportunities. *Interactive Marketing, 5*(3), 238–251. doi:10.1057/palgrave.im.4340241

De Chernatony, L., & McDonald, M. (1992). *Creating powerful brands*. Oxford, UK: Butterworth Heinemann.

Degeratu, A., Rangaswamy, A., & Wu, J. (2000). Consumer choice behavior in online and traditional supermarkets: The effects of brand name, price, and other search attributes. *International Journal of Research in Marketing, 17*(1), 55–78. doi:10.1016/S0167-8116(00)00005-7

Doherty, N. F., Ellis-Chadwick, F., & Hart, C. A. (1999). Cyber-retailing in the UK: The potential of the Internet as a retail channel. *International Journal of Retail and Distribution Management, 27*(1), 22–36. doi:10.1108/09590559910252685

Donthu, N., & Garcia, A. (1999). The Internet shopper. *Journal of Advertising Research, 39*(3), 52–58.

Doyle, P. (1998). *Marketing management and strategy* (2nd ed.). Harlow, UK: Prentice Hall.

Grossman, R. P. (1997). Co-branding in advertising. *Journal of Product and Brand Management, 6*(3), 191–201. doi:10.1108/10610429710175709

Hanson, W. (2000). *Principles of Internet marketing*. Cincinnati, OH: South Western College Publishing.

Harris, L. C., & Goode, M. M. H. (2004). The four levels of loyalty and the pivotal role of trust: A study of online service dynamics. *Journal of Retailing, 80*(2), 139–158. doi:10.1016/j.jretai.2004.04.002

Hashim, N. H., & Murphy, J. (2007). Branding on the Web: Evolving domain name usage among Malaysian hotels. *Tourism Management, 28*(2), 621–624. doi:10.1016/j.tourman.2006.09.013

Ibeh, K. I. N., Luo, Y., & Dinnie, K. (2005). E-branding strategies of Internet companies: Some preliminary insights from the UK. *Journal of Brand Management, 12*(5), 355–373. doi:10.1057/palgrave.bm.2540231

Ilfield, J. S., & Winter, R. S. (2000). Generating website traffic. *Journal of Advertising Research, 42*(5), 49–61.

Interbrand. (2004). *Integrated brand communications*. Toronto, Canada: Interbrand Canada.

Jiang, P. (2004). The role of brand name in customization decisions: A search vs. experience perspective. *Journal of Product and Brand Management, 13*(2), 73–83. doi:10.1108/10610420410529708

Kapferer, J.-N. (2004). *The new strategic brand management: Creating and sustaining brand equity long term*. Boston, MA: Kogan Page.

Kucuk, S. U. (2008). Negative double jeopardy: The role of anti-brand sites on the Internet. *Journal of Brand Management, 15*(3), 209–222. doi:10.1057/palgrave.bm.2550100

Lei, J., Dawar, N., & Lemmink, J. (2008). Negative spillover in brand portfolios: Exploring the antecedents of asymmetric affects. *Journal of Marketing, 72*(May), 111–123. doi:10.1509/jmkg.72.3.111

Leong, E., Huang, X., & Stannersa, P.-J. (1998). Comparing the effectiveness of the website with traditional media. *Journal of Advertising Research, 38*(5), 44–49.

Lynch, P., & Beck, J. (2001). Profiles of Internet buyers in 20 countries: Evidence of region specific strategies. *Journal of International Business Studies, 32*(4), 725–748. doi:10.1057/palgrave.jibs.8490992

Market Sentinel. (2007). *Online brand building – A case study from Avis Europe*. Retrieved from www.marketsentinel.com

Merisavo, M., & Raulas, M. (2004). The impact of email marketing on brand loyalty. *Journal of Product and Brand Management, 13*(7), 498–505. doi:10.1108/10610420410568435

Meuter, M. L., Ostrom, A. L., Rountree, R. I., & Bitner, M. J. (2000). Self-service technologies: Understanding customer satisfaction with technology-based service encounters. *Journal of Marketing, 64*(3), 50–64. doi:10.1509/jmkg.64.3.50.18024

Meyers, H., & Gerstman, R. (2001). *Branding at the digital age*. Toronto, Canada: Interbrand. doi:10.1057/9781403905468

Motion, J., Leitch, S., & Brodie, R. J. (2003). Equity in corporate co-branding: The case of Adidas and the All Blacks. *European Journal of Marketing, 37*(7/8), 1080–1094. doi:10.1108/03090560310477672

Murphy, J., Rafa, L., & Mizerski, R. (2003). The use of domain names in e-branding by the world's top brands. *Electronic Markets, 13*(3), 222–232. doi:10.1080/1019678032000108310

Murphy, J., & Scharl, A. (2007). An investigation of global versus local online branding. *International Marketing Review, 24*(3), 297–312. doi:10.1108/02651330710755302

Nysveen, H., Pedersen, P. E., Thorbjornsen, H., & Berthon, P. (2005). Mobilizing the brand: The effects of mobile services on brand relationships and main channel use. *Journal of Service Research, 7*(3), 257–276. doi:10.1177/1094670504271151

Opoku, R., & Hinson, R. (2006). Online brand personalities: An exploratory analysis of selected African countries. *Place Branding, 2*(2), 118–129. doi:10.1057/palgrave.pb.5990050

Pura, M. (2003). Case study: The role of mobile advertising in building a brand. In Mennecke, B. E., & Strader, T. J. (Eds.), *Mobile commerce: Technology, theory and applications* (pp. 291–309). Hershey, PA: Idea Group Publishing. doi:10.4018/9781591400448.ch017

Rafiq, M., & Fulford, H. (2005). Loyalty transfers from offline to online stores in the UK grocery industry. *International Journal of Retail & Distribution Management, 33*(6), 444–460. doi:10.1108/09590550510600861

Ratnasingham, P. (1998). The importance of trust in electronic commerce. *Internet Research, 8*(4), 313–321. doi:10.1108/10662249810231050

Ries, A., & Ries, L. (2000). *The 11 immutable laws of Internet branding*. London, MA: Harper Collins.

Rowley, J. (2004). Online branding. *Online Information Review, 28*(2), 131–138. doi:10.1108/14684520410531637

Rowley, J. (2004b). Online branding: The case of McDonald's. *British Food Journal, 106*(3), 228–237. doi:10.1108/00070700410528808

Rowley, J. (2008). Online branding strategies of UK fashion retailers. *Internet Research, 19*(3).

Rowley, J., Kupiec-Teahan, B., & Leeming, E. (2007). Customer community and co-creation: A case study. *Marketing Intelligence & Planning, 25*(2), 136–146. doi:10.1108/02634500710737924

Rubenstein, H. (2002). Branding on the Internet – Moving from a communication to a relationship approach to branding. *Interactive Marketing, 4*(1), 33–40. doi:10.1057/palgrave.im.4340161

Rubenstein, H., & Griffiths, C. (2001). Branding matters more on the Internet. *Brand Management, 8*(6), 394–404. doi:10.1057/palgrave.bm.2540039

Shankar, V., Urban, G. L., & Sultan, F. (2002). Online trust: A stakeholder perspective, concepts, implications, and future directions. *The Journal of Strategic Information Systems, 11*(3/4), 325–344. doi:10.1016/S0963-8687(02)00022-7

Simmons, G. J. (2007). "I-branding": Developing the Internet as a branding tool. *Marketing Intelligence & Planning, 25*(6), 544–562. doi:10.1108/02634500710819932

Strebinger, A., & Treiblmaier, H. (2004). E-adequate branding: Building offline and online brand structure within a polygon of interdependent forces. *Electronic Markets, 14*(2), 153–164. doi: 10.1080/10196780410001675095

Stuart, H., & Jones, C. (2004). Corporate branding in marketspace. *Corporate Reputation Review, 7*(1), 84–93. doi:10.1057/palgrave.crr.1540213

Sweney, M. (2007, 16 July). Top 10 online brand campaigns named. *The Guardian*. Retrieved from www.guardian.co.uk/ media

Varadarajan, R. P., & Yadav, M. S. (2002). Marketing strategy and the Internet: An organizing framework. *Journal of the Academy of Marketing Science, 30*(4), 296–312. doi:10.1177/009207002236907

Wang, Y. D., & Emurian, H. H. (2005). An overview of online trust: Concepts, elements, and implications. *Computers in Human Behavior, 21*(1), 105–125. doi:10.1016/j.chb.2003.11.008

Ward, M., & Lee, M. (2000). Internet shopping, consumer search and product branding. *Journal of Product and Brand Management, 9*(1), 6–20. doi:10.1108/10610420010316302

Xie, H., & Boggs, D. (2006). Corporate branding versus product branding in emerging markets: A conceptual framework. *Marketing Intelligence & Planning, 24*(4), 347–364. doi:10.1108/02634500610672099

Yan, J. (2001, March 17). Online branding: An Antipodean experience. *CAP Online*. Retrieved from www.jyanet.com

Yen, H. R. (2005). An attribute-based model of quality satisfaction for Internet self-service technology. *The Service Industries Journal, 25*(5), 641–659. doi:10.1080/02642060500100833

Zhang, X., & Prybutok, V. R. (2005). A consumer perspective of e-service quality. *IEEE Transactions on Engineering Management, 52*(4), 461–477. doi:10.1109/TEM.2005.856568

Zhu, F. X., Wymer, W., & Chen, I. (2002). IT-based services and service quality in consumer banking. *International Journal of Service Industry Management, 13*(1), 69–91. doi:10.1108/09564230210421164

Chapter 9
E–Novation Curriculum (Communication and Education):
Who Should Care?

Daphne Freeder
University of Technology, Australia

ABSTRACT

Marketing techniques need to reflect the era that they operate in, match customer needs, environmental dynamics such as social media, and evolve through educative processes to enhance ethical and expert practice. The future will reflect a scenario where customers become sparser than capital (Rogers, 2007), and if dissatisfaction levels in surveys can register highs of 70%, marketing approaches need to change (Jaffe 2007). Marketers are still fixated on labelling and attributing general characteristics to different generations and groups of people so that marketing can be targeted "appropriately." For example the exposure of Generation Y to technology is unequivocal but the descriptions of people in this generation elevate this to levels where somehow these consumers have become genetically modified human beings, without the same frailties, emotional responses, and foibles because of their exposure to technology. Images from YouTube could be collected everyday to provide us with ready examples of Generation Y consumer frailties.

Generic labelling of consumers does not demonstrate sophisticated marketing and does not reflect the level of analysis that can be done to target appropriate or one to one marketing. On an ethical level, marketers need to focus on permission based marketing and apply co-creation models which have the potential to address the bottom line and shareholder returns without compromising the interests and wellbeing of consumers. Emotion remains the key brand response from consumers, but the new online research environment offers opportunities for marketers to apply analytical diversity and the use of

DOI: 10.4018/978-1-60566-394-4.ch009

creative and lateral thinking (Cooke & Buckley, 2007), rather than just intrusive marketing practices enhanced by technological capabilities. Improved practice, together with ethics, should be represented in marketing and business training and in the profession. All of this is influenced by technology and its flawed or decent application reflects human intervention as always. How much protection or care then should marketers exercise towards consumers in their environments especially since consumers are deemed to be more sophisticated? Educative systems should also ensure that sustainability practices are a promise of future marketing.

INTRODUCTION

Each new technology in our world is greeted with enthusiasm by some, fear by others, disdain, acceptance or just acquiescence. Technology provides us with great freedoms and tools. Imagine life without the discovery of electricity, the invention of the wheel, radio, phone, computer, camera or the iPod. Yet with the freedoms that technology provides come concomitant responsibilities and traps for the unwary, the crowd followers, the sophisticates and the thinkers. The pace with which technology develops is less fearful when you are immersed in it but future trend discussions often resonate with the more fearful scenarios that technology can promise to affect, even when that is not the intention of the futurists discussions. As both a positive and a negative, human intervention in the form of individuals, companies or marketers stands in between as a variable that will influence the uses of technology with varying levels of control, with positive and negative intentions and with beneficial or harmful uses. Marketers need to ensure that their applications of technology are responsible and ethical.

Organisations reflect our human frailties and marketing through its creations reflects the intent of those organisations to promote quality products and services or formulates a fiction as a means to an end. These fabrications or product or service untruths reflect the less palatable forms of marketing which engender distrust in consumers who find them frustrating and harmful. Unethical practices should also resonate with others in the marketing profession as unacceptable. Marketing

permeates all of our lives and so its conduct is very important.

What does "marketing" mean? Marketing is described as advertising, promotion or a function of the process of buying and selling. At a fundamental level is it about transferring and communicating information. So simple a premise and yet there is nothing simple about the way people process information, gather it and then use it to best effect.

It is very easy for some to condemn and dismiss marketing and yet ironically not be able to avoid relying on it in some form or another. The pervasiveness of marketing means that how it is taught both professionally and via curriculums needs to match the demands of the era that it reflects. In a world with so much data to hand, consumers expectations high, fragmentation of segments, social media networks, opportunities for new forms and methods of cooperative research and creation of products and services, marketing can evolve into very sophisticated forms. The Obama presidential campaign is a clear example of this. Co-creation models where consumers and companies work together to enhance product or service development appeal for their potential to address company and shareholder returns without compromising the interests and wellbeing of consumers.

However sophisticated consumers or marketing becomes some traits remain unchanged. In this technological age we retain our need for human contact, the fundamental sense of the need to belong to a group. In allowing us to achieve this in some forms online we have become even more vulnerable. Tangible alternative worlds/cultures can reflect how lonely, stressed and overwhelmed people are and highlight that the web is not just the positive options of being creative, sourcing information, finding escapism and learning. Equally online environments provide another avenue for seamier and unpalatable human behaviours. Marketing needs to separate itself from these less positive aspects and reflect this in its marketing training environments.

Specifically this chapter explores the so called academic professional divide, aspects of the E-Novation curriculum of the future, ethical marketing practices, permission marketing and social media and the options they provide for research. Most importantly the focus is on the needs, responses and welfare of consumers.

BACKGROUND

Starting with the premise that the future will reflect a scenario where customers become less available than capital (Rogers, 2007) and surveys continue to register results where 60-70% of respondents feel more negative about advertising and would adopt products that would allow them to block advertising (Jaffe, 2007) the organisational focus of companies and the nature of their approach to marketing needs revisiting.

Economic conditions and the costs of goods and services always test customer loyalties in the buying process. The web also makes cost comparisons available in a matter of minutes. So a key point of differentiation that can be used is the development of a relationship with a customer which provides value to customers and makes the option of swapping to other companies inconvenient and without incentives. The added imperative for a company to pursue this goal is the knowledge that retention of existing customers is cheaper than trying to acquire new ones. Realising the level of relationships required in the future will happen with the development of strong trusting relationships between an organisation and its employees. There is a two way link between customer and employee satisfaction with happy employees making for happy customers (Peppers & Rogers, 2005). In a research brief of a study by Luo and Hornberg, Wells (2007) writes that happy customers also influence employee satisfaction to the extent that employees are encouraged to remain with the organisation they work for. On another level if customers are satisfied, their loyalty and promotion of the company by word of mouth may also decrease the amount of investment a company needs to make in future advertising and promotion while still achieving the required sales. Customer satisfaction metrics should be promoted both to prospective employees and customers to ensure retention of both (Wells, 2007).

Customers are looking for constants: self help options, products and services they can trust and dependable sources of information to serve their best interests. Interestingly part of the influence dynamic has changed from expensive marketing campaigns to potentially strangers wielding more sway. The rating system of buyers and sellers of each other on EBay provides a perfect example of this.

So how do we market to societies of people that have become more fragmented with less people available to target for doing or purchasing the same things and where the mindset of companies still focuses on mass marketing (Cooke & Buckley, 2007)? The object of mass marketing is to achieve a percentage of sales by targeting enough people to warrant the approach used.

Age is another generic targeting model. Marketers are still obsessed with generic descriptions of different generations of consumers and are determined that successful marketing needs to be targeted on that basis. For example the exposure of Generation Y to technology is distinctive but the descriptions of people in this generation elevate this to levels where somehow these consumers have become genetically altered human beings, without the same frailties, emotional responses and foibles because of their exposure to technology.

An article in Time Style and Design by van Dyk (2008) reported on the results of market research by Resource Interactive an Ohio based marketing company. A blanket assertion was made that millennials have a closer parent child relationship in contrast to any other generation that preceded them evidenced by their sharing of vacations and multiple texting during the course of the day. It is also observed that millenials can absorb twenty hours of information in a seven hour period. Again the characteristics are represented in a way which does not reflect the technological capacities now available but extends to a perceived genetic change in a generation. In reality this again becomes a rationale for a one size fits all approach. It is interesting that newer research indicates that irrespective of age groups those with an inclination for technology retain this trait throughout their lives (Stroud, 2005). Essentially marketers are their own worst enemies because unlike the consumers they are meant to represent they have not evolved and are using out of date marketing practices to develop and manage marketing offers. This is detrimental to individual organisational marketing and also does nothing to improve the status of marketing overall.

Emotion remains the key brand response but the new online research environment offers opportunities for analytical diversity, the use of creative thinking to the point of fuzzy logic in marketing approaches (Cooke & Buckley, 2007). It was refreshing that in the van Dyk (2008) article reference was made to the retailer Scoop NYC very successfully applying psychographics rather than demographics to its customers. Mothers and daughters were targeted together. The opportunities for cross generational emotional marketing were also applied by Trinny and Susannah in their Undress the Nation series (ITV Productions, 2007) where older women were encouraged to purchase fashion from fashion houses on the High St in London. Normally these stores target younger markets and yet the older women were very successfully attired and had a great emo-

tional experience. Similarly the virtual mirrors in boutiques in New York aimed at young women wanting to try clothes and then get immediate feedback from friends from images sent to them Venkatraman (2008) have value for all shoppers. These are examples of marketers thinking outside the square. Clever use of technology affords marketers many opportunities but it has to be done with care. In 1997 Huisman was already writing about our paradoxical society where six degrees of separation between human beings was being taken to new levels with technology. Increasingly distance was a non issue

between people but marketers also began to have unprecedented access to consumers. These same consumers benefiting from the communication elements of the technology began wanting to block unwelcome marketing communications. Information that consumers had revealed about themselves for specific purposes began to be used by marketers to push other products and services. This raised the counter customer concern of privacy. Privacy remains a key concern with new technologies providing even more scope for abuse.

The very fact that technology allows us capabilities for collecting information about consumers and communicating with them far more comprehensively than before does not mean that it should happen without getting permission from the customer to collect such information and to make contact. The principles of permission marketing are very important here. A company can collect information from its customers with their consent and then apply appropriate and targeted marketing to suit those individual customers.

Trust is a key building block in relationships and the advantage of consensually collected information is in the trust that it implies. So why is relationship building between companies and their customers important? Maintaining company differentiation just through pricing is unsustainable (Turner, 2007) except where consumers have restricted incomes.

Gathering permissions may seem to be an onerous task but others have demonstrated that it is achievable. Jack Ewing wrote in 2007 about the Danish Marketer Come & Stay which obtained permission based email for blue chip level customers, 270 million plus of them and then extended this to mobile advertising with incentives of reduced or free mobile services. Responsible use of data is an obligation all companies should abide by and the whole market benefits from holistic approaches. The Danish example also illustrates that ethical processes can be put into effect for large scale consume groups.

The additional benefit of permission marketing is that it is a more cost efficient option in an era of customers directing organisations rather than products just directing customers because it is based on accurate information. Information collected solely using cookies or based on past transactions does not give a context to the consumers reasons for buying. Amazon which is a leading light as an example of marketing also makes the mistake of pushing content to customers based on past purchasing even though the purchase may be a one off for a gift.

Consumers have opportunities to innovate with available technology rather than being told how to use it (Barley, 2002) and marketers can learn from this.

Using consumer insights to test product and service offerings and their value should be a focus of marketing. Poor strategic decision making is not due to a lack of data regarding consumers but to poor hypothetical's (Bullmore, 2004). In summary more customer specific information is available and it should be reasonable for customers to anticipate that this will be used intelligently to furnish them with future information and to facilitate future transactions.

The other area that needs to be investigated is the question regarding "care" of customers.

Martha Rogers (2008) holds that customer care is the new focus of marketing. Should this not have been the case always and what level of customer self care needs to be factored into the equation in an era of sophisticated consumers? Social media and online worlds are elevating this as a discussion point and highlighting that levels of customer care may have to be escalated.

Permission marketing focuses on one on one relationships with individuals but some marketers are now presenting that the focal point in dealing with consumers is as part of tribes of people where situational factors determine the persuasion influences (Cooke & Buckley, 2008). In other words people group together at different stages and for different lengths of time and the circumstances that brought them together can be used to pitch specific marketing. Current events which prompt people to communicate via a particular blog is an example of this. As people we always retain intuitively the need for belonging to a herd what ever our levels of sophistication (Mackay, 2007). Online social networks also demonstrate this. Social Networks are said to contain three types of people: those that provide the social connections, those that gather information from the network and assess its value and those that spread the word and make the messages pervasive (Clarke, 2007).

In 2004 Faith Popcorn predicted that people would turn to their friends to tell them who and what to trust (Mack, 2005). Innovative changes in society always link to forms of technology. Web 2.0 technologies are creating grass root developments of self governing communities with communal sharing of information (Cooke & Buckley, 2008). This ability to connect has a counter side which is seen as a drawback. Content people share with "friends" can also be viewed by other parties with different vested interest such as prospective employers, government agencies or worse intruders. The level of self governance online is also an ethical issue for marketers to explore with their new product offerings. Again is this a case of requiring customer care or self care?

E-NOVATION CURRICULUM

Deficits in marketing practice have to be in part attributable to how and what marketers are taught. Not all marketers will be taught formally through educational institutions but will learn their approaches through on the job training. Both have their place in the development of professionals. The aim should be to see them complement each other and reinforce higher levels of marketing practice but each has factors which impinge on their capacity to do so.

Advertising as one form of marketing is highlighted as a professional area where there is a greater divide between academic and professional practice in contrast to areas such as law, medicine or engineering (Nyilasy & Reid 2007). On one level perhaps this is understandable as these professional areas have higher legally enforceable levels of customer care that is required for obvious reasons. That is not to say that there isn't room for more forced care in business and marketing more specifically.

Part of this "divide" between teacher and professional is acknowledged as a natural contrast between theory modelling in any discipline and the practical application of those concepts (Nyilasy & Reid, 2007). Evidence regarding the divide is not conclusively supported with experimental or experiential facts and figures (Nyilasy & Reid, 2007) but the discussion remains ongoing. McDonald (2008) uses as evidence, that the Marketing Science Institute cited ten issues as being critical to the profession but only four of these issues were reflected in the top rated academic journals over a two year time frame. Marketing academics are described as being unable to communicate effectively with their professional colleagues, and due to the nature of academic environments are more focused on the number of times they are published and the type of journal in which this happens rather than the professional relevance factor. Their peers in the profession are said not to read academic journals. Responsibility for this is ascribed to the approaches in marketing education. It is also attributed to academics choosing to concentrate on obscure topics and issues with limited scope coupled with their writing in language that is difficult to understand(McDonald, 2008).

Environmental imperatives of publishing are not unique to marketing academics and any blanket coverall assumes that marketing academics are not practitioners as well and that the practitioners are not pursuing ongoing academic studies. We also know that it is a truism that a modern imperative of education is as a means to an end not an end in itself.

Holbrook (2005) is even more damning is his assessment of academic environments accusing them of formulaic and dumbing down approaches which make education more palatable, engaging, simplistic and saleable to students who are looking for ready made tools and solutions that they can apply in their workplaces even if those predetermined solutions can never really fit. There is the added fiction says Holbrook (2005) that Harvard case studies that are used, actually reflect real life business dilemmas and scenarios. Their usefulness is severely limited because real data is removed. Prescriptive approaches also do not allow for individual academics to challenge the "norms" based on their own professional experience and then potentially to have those viewpoints debated between students and academics across all of their classes. The other consequence is compromising the integrity of academic staff (Holbrook, 2005). There have to be opportunities for pragmatic learning rather than memorising content in order to pass exams (Nonis et al., 2005). Students need to be able to undertake reflective learning and think about the transfer processes that they use in problem solving. It is probably reasonable for Ramocki (2007) to assert that this should be a mandatory component of student assignments. Students would be forced to articulate how they came to their conclusions and how they used knowledge transfer. The educational price being paid now is loss of intellectual rigour and lateral solutions for individual scenarios as they occur.

It is craziness if real life problems with all the real facts and figures cannot be used for analysis by students particularly concerning past events in companies. This would be a cheaper option for companies to assess future risk and allow for more in depth analysis of problem based research by marketing academics. The analysis would then hopefully spark the interest of professionals. If the difference between academia and professionals is to achieve what reflective learning is all about then viva la difference.

There is surely the need for more cooperation between professionals and academics which will also benefit students by allowing them access to the benefits of real life scenario planning. This may also help to improve students' motivation in learning which operates as a key factor in academic success (Nonis et al., 2005).

Innovative, intelligent marketing and communication approaches are required combining the intuitive with the rational. Scenario planning training better mirrors the level of intellect required in this new playing field. All of this needs to be reflected in the training and curricula for marketers so that the profession can move forward and not be typecast as superficial or employing one dimensional techniques of marketing and marketing research.

ETHICS

Ethics in marketing operates on several levels. At the highest it is about truth in the messages being delivered. At another level it is about practices which involve marketing that shows a lack of respect for consumers and evokes their distrust about the motives of marketing.

There is a claim that irrespective of its history of research, marketing, of all the business disciplines is less accountable for its actions (Nyalisy & Reid, 2007).

There is no doubt that there are cynical and poor applications of marketing in all disciplinary spheres but marketers as the conduits and creators of the public face of organisations, their products and services also pay the price of association with poor business strategies and unethical business practices without necessarily having the control to stop them. We all know that funny things are done in the name of marketing. International call centres have been established and employees are taught to speak in unfamiliar accents, learn familiar expressions and phrases of specific segment markets and pretend empathy about local weather conditions when they are half way around the other side of the world. All this to affect subterfuges that call centre staff are based just around the corner!

Television is an another example of the cynical application of marketing which has the potential to contribute to overall negative public perceptions of the profession but worse have more social impact than anyone would care to own. A television programme is developed. The marketing of the characters and the show goes into over drive with the intent of making the characters an integral part of the television audience's lives. Ratings and television budgets depend upon it.

The cynicism articulates in several ways. Successful shows that start to wane in the face of competition are axed with not even an attempt in many cases to finalise story lines for an audience that has been a loyal customer base, that has adopted the characters into their lives and cares about them and that has bought the marketing.

Other customers are deemed so loyal or so oblivious at the end of a working day that television practice allows marketing and promotion of a "new" series of a favourite programme which has old episodes interspersed with the new ones throughout the season.

Now clearly you could argue that the business decisions being put into practice here are not the fault of marketers who simply have the job of promoting the television product but if anything is clear from the era that we are in the role of the marketer is paramount to an organisations success and the customer has to count.

Marketing has to matter at the top levels of an organisation not just at a departmental level. It has to be a fundamental driver of organisational strategy.

Socially we have skirted around the impact of marketing and the influences it has for good or ill but in reality there is no question that marketing owns a social responsibility for its actions and approaches. Imagine a world where J.K. Rowling had killed off Harry Potter. For loyal customers and supporters of the Harry Potter story losing key characters like Dumbledore, Dobby and Sirius were hard enough to take. It could be argued that J.K.Rowling acted responsibly in a marketing sense anticipating the consequences and impact of her writing.

Similarly organisations need to satisfy customers that they have customers' welfare in mind in order to satisfy their needs. Each customer contact with any part of an organisation needs to reinforce this and contribute to the organisations' learning.

As a matter of course ethics and ethical practices should be part of business training and yet the inclusion of these varies from institution to institution even where recognised accreditation such as AACSB applies. AACSB rather than being prescriptive denotes that ethics is included in curriculums but not how that is to be achieved (Evans et al., 2006). Interestingly in their study Evans, Trevino and Weaver (2006) found those Business schools with larger cohorts of marketing and management academics paid ethics more consideration in their curriculums. The impetus for reflections on the need for ethics should not be as a consequence of media coverage of an organisation, board members, or CEO being found out for their unethical practices. Equally the impetus should not be discoveries of faulty products and poor or negligent service. Realistically for ethics to be a routine part of an organisations fibre, requires leaders within the organisation championing the cause beyond symbolic compliance with the law

and governmental imperatives. The same also applies to ethics in curriculums (Evans et al., 2006). In the context of curriculums ethics is often listed as one of the "desirables", graduate attributes that are so important they should be imbued and integrated throughout subjects with in reality no real measures of how and if these are achieved.

The counter argument is made that if ethics is not integrated into subjects; the contexts of where ethical decisions are called for are lost but equally with no overarching framework how do we measure how much ethical training students actually have been given (Evans et al., 2006)? This needs to change. There is a line of reasoning which says if customers are becoming more sophisticated then they are also in a position to take responsibility for their actions. This notion would align with the theory that technology savvy equates automatically to less vulnerable consumers. If that is the case why are phishing sites still able to "reel" in targets? Not everyone from our technology era is proficient or comfortable with technology. Any contact with an undergraduate class would affirm that. More importantly, the potential vulnerabilities of all of us as consumers with the interconnectedness of systems and the nature and depth of online information about people should evoke in all marketers the need for ethical approaches. A measure of ethics may well be the day when a student or a marketer or business does not think that the application of ethics should differ when they think about the marketing approach from the perspective of the business or from themselves as customers. To achieve that, integration of ethics as core units in business studies is necessary.

MARKET RESEARCH

To produce forecasts and strategy directions to suit the current era research methods and communication need to change. One of the short comings in existing marketing research includes categorising consumers just on the basis of demographics. This results in some very ageist approaches at both ends of the maturity scale. Consumer research needs to be done in context and in real life settings so that it becomes clear which variables are linked to specific behaviours (Husiman, 1997). Leading researchers are writing that long established models of market research are not providing the consumer intelligence expected by clients. Fuzzy logic or addressing more random patterns in the information gathered about consumers gives marketers scope for coming up with creative approaches. The long established model has been to categorise information about consumers on a hierarchical or sequential basis e.g. a consumer is this age, has this level of assets and therefore is automatically interested in x.

This approach to research doesn't provide the level of analysis of more flexible models. In the past researchers were satisfied to profile consumers on the basis of archetypes and "predictable consumption" (Cooke & Buckley, 2008). The one size fits all approach. There is still a concentration in research on consumer reasoning without taking into account the emotional and sub conscious elements. The loading of personal information and images in Facebook or sent via mobile demonstrate that consumers often act before they think about the consequences of their actions. Marketing has a role in protecting consumers from being their own worst enemies.

Consumers still act in response to conditioning but what is influencing that behaviour is more ambiguous to define because it has to have a more individual focus. (RutterSmith, 2002) Now consumers are defining technology uses rather than being on the receiving end of directions as to how to apply finished products (Barley, 2002). The notion of researchers operating in partnership with end consumers and clients waits to be adopted more widely (Cooke & Buckley, 2008). Orchestrated research environments can be replaced with real time observations and real time testing of products resulting in information that is

better targeted and customer specific. Contrived contexts like focus groups can be replaced with natural context options (RutterSmith, 2002). Conversely it would be naïve to assume that all online consumers represent themselves with complete authenticity and accurate data quite apart from those who deliberately create other personas in societies lived online. The same issues apply to the offline environment and survey instruments. What are the incentives for customers not to lie unless their responses are directly invested in product or service gains?

RutterSmith (2002) was of the view that research can be gathered without complex permissions and via intelligent automation. Yes this can be done but if marketing is to change both in the perceptions of the profession and the accuracy of its data collection then research by stealth is not the answer. Cookies are a prime example of this. The technology options are at a level to implement far more sophisticated approaches and actually communicate in context and collaboratively with consumers. On a positive note the responsiveness of the marketing research industry to the technology era is evidence of an industry that is thriving and coping and one third of US marketing revenues moving from offline to online research are a practical articulation of that (Cooke & Buckley 2008).

Another deficiency identified in marketing research is limiting primary research analysis to centralised research hubs. Clients can link to global research networks and get cost effective analysis of their own primary research. The issue here is that price efficiencies are bad substitutes for more insightful, intuitive and cross platform integrations of information (Cooke & Buckley, 2008). In other words patterns are looked for in the data and matched to the old consumer category models which suited homogenous markets and now the process has to focus on fragmented and heterogeneous consumers (Cooke & Buckley, 2008). The themes that govern marketing thinking today are that emotion rules in branding, intuitive and unconscious decisions are made and consumer behaviours and mindsets alter with different situations. A preparedness to handle left of field signals from the market place in a research context is also needed (Cooke & Buckley 2008).

Web 2.0 is providing a dynamic avenue and source for collaborative practices and professional marketers are demonstrating how this can be achieved. Experiential learning was a technique employed in a UK graduate training programme in preparation for work in a market research agency (Cooke & MacFarlane, 2007). Formerly the GfK NOP programme encompassed five weeks of intensive training in research skills through lectures and classroom activities. This was changed to on the job training combined with an internal training programme. The aim of the programme was to change from a push approach to active learning which involved students in co creation of knowledge through the use of Web 2.0 tools. The students were given a list of sixteen social media that they could work with. The students had to analyse which social media would enhance existing notions of market research and to demonstrate how the research should be done. The students also had to articulate the training process goals and aims and put them into practice. Students conducted interviews as avatars in virtual worlds became members of social network sites, read blogs, joined online forums, used wikis and rss feeds. The programme was supported by volunteer mentors who gave both time and resourcing to the project. The process operated on the community practice/knowledge models where informal groups of people cooperatively share their learning and expertise to evoke news ways of problem solving. At the conclusion of their research the graduates advocated research on virtual worlds and social networks and so they were given the task of building an online brand. Cooke and Macfarlane (2008) indicate that a failing of the community practice model they used was how it operated in tandem with the formal processes and infrastructures of the rest of the

business. They recommend specific support of such programs be assigned and the process be integrated into the business.

The model above displays how research can be done effectively by observing consumers as they participate in online environments rather than asking them in a focus group to talk about their experiences.

There are also good examples of co-creation research methods. Recently Starwood Hotel group has used second life as a test site for the design and architecture for its loft style hotels (Cooke & Macfarlane, 2008). Facebook in an upgrade and relaunch of its profile pages allowed customers access to the beta testing phase to trial them and then give feedback (Sydney Morning Herald, 2008).

The opportunities for different research methods continue. Marketers are also using language analysis to study content from the discussions of online focus groups. The words used by consumers are examined for what they demonstrate about consumer opinions on topics. The words are then given a code and analysed using computing software. The purpose of the software is to eliminate bias and ensure qualitative and quantitative analysis (Mason & Davis, 2007).

PERMISSION MARKETING

Permission marketing provides a point of differentiation for companies competing for their share of customers and also helps to enhance perceptions of marketing. It serves the dual purpose of businesses not wasting money on unwanted, ignored or irrelevant marketing and customers being satisfied that marketing messages delivered to them are relevant.

Access to information and to people can now happen on a twenty four hour time scale but from a marketing perspective access and communication with consumers will have to be on the basis of value to the consumer not just on the basis that you have the means to do it (Huisman, 1997). The dichotomy marketers face is balancing consumers expectations and right to privacy.

Consumers anticipate that ongoing transactions with a company will be facilitated with appropriate levels of information about them (Huisman, 1997) but also protect their privacy. For the future integrity of the profession the emphasis will have to be on the basis of permission marketing. Marketers need to expand their concept of permission marketing. It should be applied to all levels of the marketing mix and not just in the context of getting permission from consumers to send them electronic newsletters says Jim Stengel (AdAge. Com, 2004) Consumers will certainly not give their permission if they are not confident that the information they exchange with a business will not be used to their benefit (Godin, 1999). Permissions can be achieved even on larger scales. Norway has one of the highest densities of Internet usage of European countries. It is also a country where unsolicited marketing emails are legislated against. Loyalty cards are a big market in Norway encompassing 37% of households. All registered members must be contacted by companies through an alternate communication channel to ask customers of they do wish to receive emails.

Legitimate marketing continues to compete with poor practices with at least half of emails sent daily qualifying as spam (Sales Leader, 2007). A point to remember is that even with clever technology legitimate permission based emails can trigger spam alerts and so end up being blocked. A quarter of permission emails never make it to consumer inboxes (Sales Leader, 2007). This is usually because the permission emails emulate characteristics of spam emails such as too much punctuation in the subject lines, headings that use all caps in the font and the use of trigger words (Kent, 2003). It would be false to declare all spam email as unproductive but it is a false economy when permission based emails generate higher click throughs, result in more purchases and overall are more effective (Kent, 2003).

The use of permission marketing is not new and it is growing and it can be applied in small and large scale contexts. Even welcomed messaging can be overdone and it needs to be done with sensitivity and good judgement.

SOCIAL MEDIA, THE INTERNET AND TECHNOLOGY

Venkatraman (2008) sees the focus of the network age as redefining our notions of what products, offerings and experiences are and as swapping vertical integration with virtual. For this analogy Venkatraman (2008) writes about how currently we can obtain components and operating systems to create a functional computer without sticking to brand specific components and how in the future similarly our preferred transport has our favourite engine from Jaguar but Mercedes Benz does the servicing of our vehicle. In this sense Business models move from products to a set of capabilities that can be selected from. Social media provide us with tools to develop those capabilities as do co-creation campaigns.

Traditional marketing is suffering from a lack of trust by consumers and brand identity is defined by consumer experiences. A very successful campaign balancing company and consumer input includes the Red Bull campaign which gave consumers an opportunity to create artwork using the Red Bull Can. In the Adidas campaign white trainer shoes were coupled with a paint pallette for decorating the trainers. The campaign became an online social event in the form of a competition. The best decorated pair of trainers was voted on by 60 000 people. Fifty pairs were made of the winning design with twenty five pairs given to the winner and the other twenty five sold in New York (Cherkoff & Moore, 2007). These campaigns highlight what can be achieved with creative marketing. Risk taking also has to be factored into the equation. In the interest of creating bona fide relationships with customers companies can make public mistakes, show that they are not infallible, be forgiven and then proceed.

Attempts to create perfection before launching with new ideas will only serve to hold back creativity and innovation (Cherkoff & Moore, 2007).

The message being trumpeted loud and clear is consumers are outlining the terms in new media options. Testimony to this is the popularity of YouTube and Flickr which reflects a market where consumers pick and choose content to consume and are not limited to what a broadcaster deems newsworthy. This is all "true" but now rather than follow the herd of the broadcaster consumers are following other situation specific tribes. The types, forms, numbers and locations of the tribes may have changed but we still have the scenario where some lead and others follow. Clarke (2007) has identified three types of significant role players in social networks. The connectors are able to build large numbers of social contacts, the mavens evaluate and gather information from the network and then pass on their assessments and the salespeople are the messengers who sway people through their natural personas. Consumers don't really function as lone entities but as members of tribes and membership is fluid (Cooke & Buckley, 2008). Clarke (2007) advocates that we think about those that influence decision making and separate them according to product categories so that we understand the notion that in one situation one person exercises more influence and in another someone else persuades us. (Turner, 2007) takes this further with advocacy for the cooperative approach. All product evaluations need to stem from consumer insights and all new ideas need to be matched against the benefits acting on the ideas will provide.

Technology is always the major driver of change and innovation in societies. It is also interesting how technology now can on one hand give you virtual access to the whole world and at the same time create more isolation (Cova, 2001). Socially we are now more fragmented and

individualistic and then in another reversal we have the opportunity to regroup in informal online groups which have more power to influence our behaviours because we have selected groups with norms we identify with. These tribal groupings are not permanent and when they are no longer meaningful participants can move on. To achieve communal links consumers may adopt products and services purely because of the community they link them to. Likewise marketing can target products and services that are relevant in the time of the tribe. Marketers who adopt this philosophical approach say it is not possible to group consumers beyond micro level groups. These micro groups share comparable feelings and experiences in loose webs of interrelated communities. Group profiles of consumers based on segments and niches are based on consumer profiles that are improbable (Cova, 2001).

Web 2.0 has made socialising through technology devices more intuitive and is providing a diverse range of options for consumers. Friends can communicate and strangers can share using Web 2.0 (Venkatraman, 2008). Online profiles can be created. These profiles can be for the purpose of seeking work or as starting points for dating. In the United Kingdom online profiles operate like currency and are the new business card. There is room too· for online voyeurism or natural curiosity with people able to seek out information about colleagues, acquaintances etc. The software is facilitating the development of grass roots communities with members determining acceptable practices. Trust is the right of passage earned through appropriate participation. Democracy rules OK and this signifies a liberal use of media without precedent (Clarke, 2007). There is a natural appeal to these "non rules" and yet we do need to ask the question about where safeguards and levels of control should rest. Is self governance adequate? Tacit ground rules that mirror broader society norms don't prevent sordid uses like animated paedophilia or "virtual" rape and so in these instances legal interventions are called for. Even Raymond (2001) in his anti authority stance recognises that criminals need to be controlled.

Hacking in its open source context represents all of the positive elements we can value in people's behaviour: creativity, information sharing and learning (Raymond 2001). Hacking that infringes privacy should be viewed differently. The right to privacy has to be defined as your right to control it except where it harms others.

Spenser Kelly (2008) a presenter on BBC click wrote a piece on how their technical staff created application software for people to add to their Facebook suite. The application was called Miner and chameleon like it could appear as a jokes or games application while in reality it was skimming for customers and their friends personal details. The information that they were able to retrieve was then transferred via email to BBC clicks email. BBC click was illustrating how the addition of applications to profiles exposes both the profile owner and their friends to the hazards of skimming unless the option to disallow this is taken up. Deactivating this option means that applications will not work. Applications on Facebook, games, quizzes etc. unlike its competitor MySpace operate by way of third party servers hence creating the potential for skimming of Facebook customer details (Kelly, 2008). Authors who want to change the code of their applications on MySpace are subject to manual checks. The BBC click programme was not able to replicate the same exercise via MySpace. Privacy options and statements should be honest and in your face obvious in any media.

The following is an ironic example. A recent direct mail from a key consumer group in Australia "CHOICE" invited people to subscribe to their publication and included a privacy assurance that guaranteed subscribers that their details would not be made accessible to anyone else. The subscription card asked for title, name, address, email, and phone number. (Choice, 2008) Here's the punchline. The reply paid form came with

no envelope! To be fair it should be noted that the return response was also available via fax or registering via the website.

Discussion of social media, online and connected environments would not be complete without discussing the negative elements associated with our networked and technology ridden world. They are relevant because they demonstrate elements of the consumer psyche which need to be taken account in the context of responsible and ethical marketing.

Being switched on and always connected has become compulsive behaviour for people across the world (Serjeant, 2008). Initial studies estimate that in the USA ten percent of people employ technology in a way that creates problems: for their health, in their work and private lives. Examples of this are visible everywhere and include things like people never being able to switch off their phones whether during driving or having a meal.

In some personal reflections I will take the example of two female undergraduate students from an e-business class. One is an international student and the other local. In a class discussion both admitted to sleeping with their mobile phones on and in very close proximity. Both admitted to a fear factor playing a role in this.

From the perspective of the international student who is away from family and friends in a strange city separated by major distance and different time zones the need for feeling connected is understandable. For the other student who is in the parental home and others like her I despair. This student is playing out a behaviour that is not unique to her or her age group. Her mother always asks whether she has her mobile phone with her and other members of the class admitted to feeling like the world would end if they left their mobile phones at home but surviving the experience nevertheless. Together with house keys, purses or wallets mobile phones are now required before leaving the house.

"Today there is a growing fear of being untethered in the world without the security blanket of a mobile phone" (Johnson, 2008, p1). Our social cosmos is contained in them and periods of deliberate disconnection are non compliance with the norm and almost a sign that things are not quite right with you (Johnson 2008). The technology that we use to remain connected, that by all intense and purposes is supposed to make our lives more flexible and to serve us is also playing such an intrusive role because we feel compelled to be captive to it. Now we have a growing group of people who have to make the effort to switch off for a night, weekend or designated days throughout the year and encourage those in their networks to do the same (Serjeant, 2008).

For people living in more privileged societies one of the luxuries of being human is to step back from the business of surviving and take time to reflect. Increasingly opportunities for quiet reflection on life and people we care about are being consumed by technology intrusions. The diversions they offer range from work to games to filling the space by contacting someone.

Data transmission is also being confused for communication. SMS, social media and email are perfect for organising get togethers, self promotion, sharing and quick exchanges. On their own they do not equate to communicating or real friendships. Negative behaviours are also facilitated through the convenience of technology. School bullying now has another vehicle with children being victimised via their mobile phones. Reputations are being destroyed with malicious online postings with stories and photos. Life mistakes are made publicly and instead of fifteen minutes of fame they become fifteen minutes of infamy for example hundreds of party goers are messaged or online networked about a party location, then trash the venue and neighbouring houses which results in police intervention. The party organiser is then approached by a publicity agent who wants to capitalise on the situation. A radio broadcaster is jailed for soliciting a 16 year old girl for sex in an internet chat room in exchange for an iPod.

Fortunately in this instance the 16 year old was actually a police officer NineMSN (2008).

Marketers through their organisations promote the use of all of these technologies. It would seem reasonable to suggest that organisations also promote responsible usage, highlight privacy protections and where possible employ technical means to enforce it.

BLOGS

Blogs are increasing in multiple millions and as an alternate online media for consumer to consumers they are making considerable impacts on both the newspaper and advertising industries. To date systematic studying of bloggers and their motivations by marketers in no way matches the observable fact that is blogging (Huang et al., 2007). Blogs are providing people the opportunity to create online memoirs of their lives which can then be shared interactively through technology mediated environments. So far information that has been articulated about bloggers is that they do not make up the majority of internet users, as individuals they use the internet a lot, they socialise through technology use, most of their blogs target very small groups of people and for the majority their blogs are for individual expression and a hobby and pastime rather than the greater social good (Huang et al., 2007). Motivations guiding bloggers variously include self expression and commentary and to establish an identity in virtual communities. Bloggers who gather content through this medium are motivated to use blogs as a podium for social commentary, developing community forums and information seeking (Huang et al 2007). In advertising blogs have been used for dedicated campaigns, targeted advertising in niche segment blogs and placing ads in blog RSS feeds. In media environs blogs are causing further fragmentation of the market place and in a very positive outcome the media no longer have a monopoly on news generation and coverage and control. Consumers have control over what they take on board and in what form (Vogt, 2007). The merging of layperson and professional content is changing ownership to facilitation a fact highlighted by citizen contributions to the BBC after the bombings in July in London in 2007 (Cooke & Buckley, 2008). After a comprehensive overview of other blog studies and conducting a study of their own Huang, et al. (2007) concluded that the communication approaches and focus of marketers needs to match the motivational factors of the bloggers. Huang et al., (2007) also detail the need for identifying the generic motivations of bloggers, combined with standard consumer demographic approaches for identifying target segments and placement of campaigns should follow accordingly. Non complex campaign messages can then be directed to bloggers who provide a network to other bloggers and more complex and prolonged marketing campaigns can be focused towards bloggers who are content oriented users of blogs. Apart from the viral marketing these approaches appear very much like a direct marketing approach just via the different media of blogs. Surely the opportunity is here through technological means to open up a cooperative dialogue and to talk to consumers so that "campaigns" can be more targeted on intellectual and emotional levels rather than the more narrow focus of trying to find generic typecasts for different groups of consumers. To that end the Nielsen Research group established its online community "Hey! Nielsen, which is extending its analysis of market share beyond statistics and sales data to more of the emotional dynamics.

The company Phillips Design based in the Netherlands has a design brief that spans offline products and services to web services and technology mediated interfaces. The concept of co designing and cooperative research has been employed by Phillips Design for some time. A research approach that they use provides an opportunity for consumers to record their reflections through text, photos, multimedia and blogs. Their

research projects vary in length from a week to months (Reinhold & Bhutiaia 2007). The strength of Web 2.0 technologies as they see it is that they allow interactions between people using intuitive multimedia formats and as such provide an avenue to conduct research through interactive communication and information exchange. Participants are not asked questions. Instead the research is contracted out to the participants by getting them to undertake activities, either individually or through collective group discussions where all have access to the blog and can comment. The researchers act only as moderators. Compilations by the participants of text, pictures, blogs etc. are available for analysis and the insights that these elicit.

ELEMENTS OF OUR FUTURE AND THE IMPLICATIONS FOR MARKETING

Canton (2007) lists many options open to us in the future for example DNA profiling for dating and embedded DNA chips into our arms. RFID chips have already been placed in the arms of two employees at Watcher.com to control access to a security control room. (Wireless Report, 2006) Science fiction movies and books have always foreshadowed some glimpses into the future with accuracy because they reflect creative thinking.

Some of these options are very sobering but even more so when you contemplate that the technologies so many celebrate is still inaccessible. The digital divide exists.

Education costs and accessibility will need to be another social focus in the future so that the gaps don't widen any further.

Many noble causes, charitable works and fund raisers validate the better sides of marketing. One of my wishes for the future is that in serving one good cause we don't do disservice to another. Aside from the global cooling/warming debate consumption and the creation of unnecessary waste should hit the radar of marketing. Pick any great fundraising event which is raising money for research. It would be wonderful if public support didn't mean having to donate by buying another plastic object which has no functionality except that it is a fun way to present the campaign. At least if these items for purchase could be made biodegradable or have a useful purpose that extends into the future the positives of these campaigns would be enhanced.

RECOMMENDATIONS

Marketing is an elementary part of people's lives and so the way it is managed lays the groundwork for how on professional levels it is perceived. The following recommendations include fundamentals which should underpin the development of sound marketing practice.

- Any real or perceived divide between academics and professionals needs to be eliminated. This could be facilitated through cooperative networks of academics and professionals which could then work to provide real business problems for students to work on. This has be a fundamental part of the essence of business training
- Students do need to be able to undertake reflective learning and think about the transfer processes that they use in problem solving. As Ramocki (2007) suggests consideration could be given to making this mandatory.
- Ethics training should be firmly established as core training in business courses
- Marketers and business have to stop collecting research and information on customers by stealth
- Permission marketing should be pursued in all avenues of marketing
- Companies allow for creative mistakes in their risk management strategies to encourage innovation

- Sustainability should be an important focus of marketing.

CONCLUSION

Our era is affording us an opportunity to work in creative and unique ways and yet fixed into the fabric of marketing and business are philosophical approaches which undermine the chance to change. Most specifically the propensity to collect research by covert means is indefensible. Why would there be a need to do this if products and services provide real value and marketers and businesses move past pushing consumer herds in one direction or another? There will always still be room for marketing campaigns with more fun and fluff rather than substance without deceiving customers. Restrictive company budgets can be mediated with clever and efficient use of technology options. Martha Rogers (2008) is correct. Consumers will become sparser than capital and the threads that will bind them to business offerings will be price, trust, service, quality and at other times sheer expediency.

Each of the above are issues that need to be dealt with.

The solution is to try and affect more permanent changes to the marketing/business ethos through the educative process for future marketers and all business people. To make this education worthwhile real case studies and business problems need to be analysed and students do need an opportunity for reflective learning.

Marketing represents the face of organisations and to do this effectively marketers cannot be treated as islands and their place in organisations and business needs to reflect the consumer co-creation model. Simply put marketers need to be included in the concept planning and implementation stages and not just presented with poorly conceived end products and services to market to consumers. Similarly consumer reflections on potential products and services and or possible improvements to existing ones need to be factored in. Marketers cannot continue to take the blame for poor business strategies and lack of scenario planning, particularly when their input to products and services is only called on when these are presented to them as a fait accompli to then be promoted. Another solution lies in the overall focus of organisations. Ethical practice is a reasoned and reasonable expectation by professionals and customers alike. Companies that have concentrated their energies on profit making over their customer needs have paid the price with their businesses (McDonald, 2008) and this will continue to be the case. The use of products to signify individualism and importance is part of the human condition and so on different occasions all consumers are vulnerable to marketing messages however authentic or reasonable and no matter how intelligent the consumers. Markets can be made from the simplest of things. Today children purchasing individual dial tones for their mobiles are already an industry worth five billion dollars. (Venkatraman, 2008) The emphasis marketing should strive for is not to instil a lack of confidence or insecurity where individualism can only be expressed through outward symbols and the use of products. This is particularly true where the promises are unobtainable such as the imitation of supermodels and their airbrushed perfection in magazines.

While technological changes will continue, a constant remains the fallibility and strengths of people. Marketing as a profession can benefit from the technological advances without compromising the wellbeing of consumers.

A sea change for marketing is being called for. Clever marketing campaigns, done with integrity get their due recognition. The focus now has to be on raising cleverness levels and truth in professional marketing in all businesses.

REFERENCES

ADAge.com. (2004). *P&G marketing boss slams ad industry for foot-dragging.*

Barley, N. (2002). Information Technology grows up-Five predictions for 2010. *Market Leader*, Spring. Retrieved from www.warc.com

Canton, J. (2007). *The top trends that will reshape the world in the next 20 years.* New York, NY: Plume Penguin Group.

Cherkoff, J., & Moore, J. (2007). *Co-creation rules: The new realities of marketing in a networked world.* Market Research Society Annual Conference. Retrieved from www.mrs.org.uk

CHOICE. (2008). *Choice reply form.* Sydney, Australia: CHOICE.

Cognos. (2007). *What's your return on customer? An interview with Martha Rogers.* Retrieved April 1, 2008, from http://www.cognos.com/newsletter/business/st_071017_01.html?mc=web_ns_rss

Cooke, M., & Buckley, N. (2008). Web 2.0, social networks and the future of market research. *International Journal of Market Research, 50*(2), 267–292.

Cooke, M., & MacFarlane, P. (2007). *Training the next generation: It's market research, but not as we know it.* Esomar Annual Congress, Berlin.

Cova, B., & Cova, V. (2001). Tribal marketing: The tribalisation of society and its impact on the conduct of marketing. *European Journal of Marketing, 36*(5-6). Retrieved from http://visionarymarketing.com.

Evans, J. M., Trevino, L. K., & Weaver, G. R. (2006). Who's in the ethics driver's seat? Factors influencing ethics in the MBA curriculum. *Academy of Management Learning & Education, 5*(3), 278–293. doi:10.5465/AMLE.2006.22697017

Ewing, J. (2007). Denmark's Masters of e-mail marketing. *Business Week Online.*

Holbrook, M. (2005). Marketing miseducation and the MBA mind: B******t happens. *Marketing Education Review*, 15.

Huang, C. Y., Shen, Y.-Z., Lin, H.-X., & Chang, S.-S. (2007). Bloggers' motivations and behaviors: A model. *Journal of Advertising Research, 47*(4). doi:10.2501/S0021849907070493

Huisman, D. (1997). *Information Technology brings us back to the basics.* Esomar Information Technology.

Jaffe, D. (2007). *Do not disturb.* The Advertiser.

Johnson, C. (2008, May 20). In praise of silence. *Sydney Morning Herald.* Retrieved 23rd May, 2008, from www.smh.com.au/news/technology/in-praise-of-silence/2008/05/20/1211182807058.html

Kelly, S. (2008). *Identity "at risk" on Facebook.* Retrieved May 14, 2008, from http://news.bbc.co.uk/2/hi/programmes/click_online/7375772.stm

Leader, S. (2007). Send marketing emails that boost responses. *Sales Leader, 12*(24), 1.

Mack, J. (2005). Tribal Marketing. *Pharma Marketing News, 4.* Retrieved January 14, 2008, from www.news.pharma-mkting.com/pmn411-oped.html

Mackay, H. (2007). *Advance Australia... where? How we've changed, why we've changed, and what will happen next?* Sydney, Australia: Hachette Livre.

Marketing, P. (2005). Tribal marketing. *Pharma Marketing News, 4*, 1-2. Retrieved January 14, 2008, from www.news.pharma-mkting.com/pmn411-oped.html

Mason, P., & Davis, B. H. (2007). More than the words: Using stance-shift analysis to identify crucial opinions and attitudes in online focus groups. *Journal of Advertising Research, 47*(4). doi:10.2501/S0021849907070511

McDonald, M. (2008). Viewpoint-After 50 years of IJMR, the state of marketing. *International Journal of Market Research, 50.* Retrieved from www.ijmr.com

Nine, M. S. N. (2008). *DJ jailed for luring teenager for sex.* Retrieved May 26, 2008, from http://news.ninemsn.com.au/article.aspx?id=569408

Nonis, S. A., Philhours, M., Syamil, A., & Hudson, G. I. (2005). The impact of non-intellectual variables on the academic success of business students. *Marketing Education Review, 15*(3).

Nyliasy, G., & Reid, L. N. (2007). The academician-practitioner gap in advertising. *International Journal of Advertising, 26,* Retrieved from www.warc.com.

Productions, I. T. V. (2007). *Trinny and Susannah undress the nation.* United Kingdom.

Ramocki, S. (2007). A critical challenge awaiting marketing education. *Marketing Education Review*, 17.

Raymond, E. S. (2001). *The cathedral & the bazaar-Musings on Linux and open source by an accidental revolutionary.* Sebastopol, CA: O'Reilly Media Inc.

Reinhold, N., & Bhutiaia, K. L. (2007). *The virtual home visit: identifying people insights in the virtual world.* Esomar Qualitative Research Paris. Retrieved from www.esomar.org

Report, W. (2006). *Surveillance company implants workers with RFID chips.* Retrieved August 1, 2008, from http://www.thewirelessreport.com/2006/02/13/surveillance-company-implants-workers-with-rfid-chips/

Serjeant, J. (2008, May 20). Why the switched on are switching off. *Sydney Morning Herald.* Retrieved 22nd May, 2008, from www.smh.com. au/news/technology/why-the switched-on-are-switching-off/2008/05/20/121118

Sydney Morning Herald. (2008). *Facebook unveils more minimalist look.* Retrieved May 22, 2008, from www.smh.com.au/news/web/facebook-unveils-more-minimalist-look/2008/05/22/121118296460

Venkatraman, N. V. (2008). From the industrial age to the network age. *Market Leader*, Spring. Retrieved from www.warc.com

Wells, R. (2007). Outstanding customer satisfaction: The key to a talented workforce? *The Academy of Management Perspectives*, 87–89. doi:10.5465/AMP.2007.26421243

Chapter 10
E–Novation Customer Relationship Management

Othman Boujena
Rouen Business School, France

Wesley J. Johnston
Georgia State University, USA

ABSTRACT

In the early 1990's, marketing theory experienced a paradigm shift from a transactional approach focusing on sales to a relationship one. This shift was due to several limits of traditional mix marketing based on the "four P's" and to the change in the market business models. In fact, the growing role of branding in mass markets, the development of services marketing, and the importance of network and human interactions in business are some of the main reasons behind relationship marketing emergence. Relationship marketing is then aimed at developing and maintaining mutually profitable relationships with customers and even stakeholders. In the era of technology evolution and Internet, customer relationship management (CRM) is moving forward to better manage, drive, and keep value-added relationships. However, CRM is, first of all, a company strategy and a shared vision that involves organization, people, and processes in satisfying and retaining customers. This chapter deals with the concept of customer centricity and its development, customer lifecycle with acquisition and retention, and finally the issue of CRM implementation.

CUSTOMER CENTRICITY

The aim of CRM strategy is the development of customer-centric business culture in the hope of achieving two results – improving the customer's experience and lowering sales and marketing costs. Relationship marketing consists in acquiring and maintaining customers by creating and providing better value than competitors do (Naumann 1995). Then it seems to be at the heart of a successful CRM initiative. The process begins with the development of a clear relationship market-

DOI: 10.4018/978-1-60566-394-4.ch010

ing strategy (Godson 2009; Peppers and Rogers 2004). This requires the definition of roles for customer facing functions like sales, marketing and customer service. Once the roles are defined within the relationship marketing strategy the processes have to be reengineered to operationalize the cited strategy. Finally, the appropriate level of technology needs to be acquired to support the customer centric approach now in place. In globalized markets and while products and services offers become standardized, customer knowledge represents the imperative key to drive markets and gain a competitive advantage. From a marketing point of view, customer should be the center of marketing decisions. In other words, customer centricity is the result of the evolution of marketing from a transactional approach to relational paradigm supported with knowledge of the customers and their preferences and behaviour. Marketing has moved from being a company's function dedicated to simply promote products to shift inventory to playing a major role in customer satisfaction and retention.

However, some marketing scholars call for a broader relationship and centricity approach that goes beyond the customer to reach a balanced centricity (Gummesson 2008; Gummesson 2009). The main idea is to align the service-dominant logic with marketing development by integrating a complex relationship approach based on all stakeholders' network under many-to-many marketing (Vargo and Lusch 2004). Consequently, the value chain should be processed and analyzed by keeping in mind the satisfaction of all intermediaries needs from the supplier to the customer. The case of a company adopting ethical raw material sourcing to meet its customers' philanthropic motivations represents clearly the question of stakeholders' interdependence. Also, a pure player that tries to build valuable relationships with its logistics and fulfilment suppliers to ensure a better delivery service quality to the end customer is a typical example.

Customer-centricity is more than a simple slogan or mission statement but should be a company's strategy based on the alignment of resources to effectively meet the evolution of customers' needs while creating mutually profitable relationships (Buttle 2004). In concrete terms, implementing a customer centric approach consists in internalizing basic marketing values that involves a number of measures (Grönroos 1990). First of all, the company should build a customer oriented corporate culture and ensure employees' adherence. Then, the company should demonstrate this empathic customer orientation. That's to say, that management should try to play the customer role and to put himself instead of the customer to understand his way of thinking. The objective is to be able to better serve the customer and meet his or her expectations. The concept is simple, however, implementation is very difficult in an ongoing firm. Success in building customer centricity is easier in start-up companies. The reason is that the success of a company is found in its systems, processes, and knowledge of its employees. Moving from a transactional marketing system to a customer-centric system requires the destruction or reform of most of the existing transactional system. And, it is very difficult to do this in a gradual approach. Early CRM system implementations failed at high rates because of the resistance of the established organization to a new philosophy of customer centricity.

While customer centricity may refer to a common principle, there are some differences in the way of applying it between business-to-consumer and business-to-business markets. In facts, these markets don't adopt systematically the same means to build their customer centricity. For instance, business-to-business relationships used to be built around personal interactions through the critical role and customer orientation of sales force and sometimes engineering staff members. Salespeople should enjoy empowerment to manage customer relationships (Crosby et *al.* 1990; Johnston 1997). The study of Homburg and

Rudolph (2001) shows that the sales force interaction quality influences significantly customer satisfaction. Moreover, Bennett, Kennedy and Coote (2000) found the positive impact of trust and commitment to the salesperson on attitudinal brand loyalty.

Business-to-consumer companies are more used to develop the relationship through the brand. Now with CRM, and especially e-CRM, BtoC companies are also building the relationship through personal interactions via websites and more one-to-one direct marketing techniques. However, business-to-business market has recognized the importance of branding and has a number of initiatives in branding: corporate branding, product branding, ingredient branding and co-branding. Then, both BtoB and BtoC marketers have become customer centric and are looking for ways to improve it. Therefore, the increasing need for CRM solutions. Global consumer goods companies like P&G or Unilever modified more than ten years ago their business models to reinforce customer focus. It's the same case for the world retail companies like Metro or Tesco that implemented strong online loyalty programs. In the same vein, Wal-Mart implemented the *community concept* store to show its customer care through delivering a regionally grounded experience to everyday customers.

In general, we can identify three main levers for building customer centricity strategy: building customer knowledge, brand offer and communications design and customer service and experience quality. (Figure 1)

Customer centricity shows through the way brands try to build customer knowledge through a holistic and comprehensive view of customer data (Kumar and Werner 2005). Thanks to IT capabilities, companies are more able to collect, process and diffuse information about customers and market. CRM solutions allow through database marketing proceeding to customers' segmentation so as so to better satisfy customers' specific needs by bringing to market relevant, unique and dif-

ferentiated selling propositions. At this level, it seems important to emphasize that collecting data is not sufficient, companies should turn data into tangible and valuable business intelligence and insight. Companies could use the appropriate segmentation criteria and types to approach their markets and consumption habits (socio-demographic, psychographic, RFM (Recency, Frequency, Monetary value), customer lifetime value, etc.). To do so, statistical software applications permit classification, hierarchical clustering or segmentation trees operation. Then targeting policy is facilitated by identifying customers' profiles on the basis of data collected. In addition to that, company's interest for customer data represents itself a way to express customer centricity. In fact, marketing information system relies on market studies, sales force feedback but should also lead regularly customer surveys to evaluate satisfaction, measure attitudes, improve experience, identify decision drivers, apprehend product launch opportuneness, etc. Also, call centers contribute to collect data on customers, answer their requests and ensure follow-ups. For example, SAP company rationalized its inbound telemarketing processes to improve its responsiveness and customer orientation. The process consisted of routing product and services requests as

Figure 1. Customer centricity levers

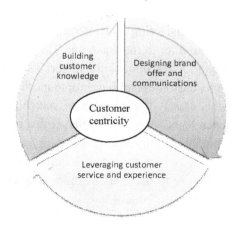

well as emails from the "Contact SAP" link on the SAP website.

In the same line, marketing managers should communicate with the sales force who is a key informer on customer attitudes and behaviours towards product or service, brand or ads. Management should then ensure and promote sales force empowerment to make customers feels that the company is really willing to satisfy their needs and to meet their expectations. Marketing decision makers can also organize shops visits to better understand consumer behaviour and apprehend the impact of situational factors. In addition to that, marketers can use mystery shoppers to make salespeople experience different situations and to have more objective feedback on sales territory.

Customer centricity is demonstrated also by leading customer surveys aimed to collect consumers' opinions and measure satisfaction. The results should be then internally shared between all partners, even outside marketing department and then integrated to decision making process. Companies should then communicate to their customers the extent to which the survey results have been taken into consideration in decision making and at which levels. In the same line, while declarative surveys have shown some limits especially in understanding customer behaviour and emotions, observation techniques seem to be useful. The objective is to observe consumer non verbal cues and sometimes emotions in different situations: products consumption at home, online navigation experience, shopping in store, service encounter, etc. This is a way to move beyond the classical methods of collecting data on customers that focus only on verbal or declarative cues. Finally, a sustainable benchmarking activity is supposed to help marketing decision markers to better understand competitors' strategies and the way they manage to satisfy customers.

In terms of communication, the way brands get in touch with consumers is very important for the future of the relationship. Brand communication style should be transparent and informative. In fact, consumers are increasingly skeptical to traditional ads promoting products and services only for sale. Nowadays, consumption is not only based on an utilitarian motivation but customers are looking for ways to give a sense to their buying decisions, to rid them of complexes by purchasing fair trade products like Max Havelaar labelled products, green products or supporting offers of militant companies like United Colors of Benetton or those committed to sustainable development. Relationship marketing literature emphasizes the crucial role of communication in building and favouring attitudes through critical, accurate, real-time and opportune information delivery.

Virtual communities and brand blogs increase brand awareness, loyalty and advocacy and consequently the effectiveness of target customers. Red Bull launches its online community after insights from research among fans that indicate their willingness for a space on the web where they could share content about the brand and its sponsored events like Formula 1. The examples of Harley-Davidson Owners Group (HOG) or Apple evangelists illustrate also these brand engagement initiatives.

On the other hand, being customer-centric implies also recognizing customer loyalty and rewarding it. In fact, loyalty programs must be well thought to increase behavioural loyalty through consumer conditioning and dependence but also by working on and improving attitudinal loyalty which is more relevant. Most of loyalty programs focus only on repeat purchase and neglect developing attitudinal loyalty which guarantees strong resistance to competitors' offers (Unlces et *al.* 2003). Loyalty programs should also cultivate customer membership, brand values sharing, aspirational needs and service distinction.

Customer centricity is also materialized by a service quality level which conveys brand positioning. Customer service experience and participation is an opportunity to generate perceptions that contribute to the whole satisfaction. To create a favourable image of service and influence shopping perceived time, communication efforts may be oriented toward sensorial and experiential marketing. In fact, operations management that makes changes to reduce actual waiting time is not really sufficient to influence customer service evaluation. Sensorial marketing consists of influencing consumer senses to generate positive attitudes, purchase and retain customers in the shop. In retail environment, brands develop attractive ambient and environmental conditions in store to increase shopping pleasure and enjoyment. For this reason, Marks and Spencer propose their "Cafe Revive" concept which consists of in-store coffee shop allowing customers to have a break and enjoy a range of drinks and snacks in family-friendly context.

In addition to that, brands can alter product attributes to influence customer senses. Lush is a good example of sensory branding. The brand epitomizes sensory stimulation through valorizing its handmade cosmetics based on product color, shape, ingredients or odour. On the other hand, experiential marketing attempts to connect consumers with brands through personally relevant and memorable contexts. Customer-experience marketing can be applied even in a store environment or through brand website like Procter & Gamble or Hermès Group. Most of psychological studies show that activating reason leads to deduction while addressing emotions generate behaviour. Therefore, the increasing interest for emotional branding. HSBC life insurance company uses the slogan "Insuring Your Emotions" and introduce itself as brand dedicated to the development and providing of innovative and unique products based on market and customers needs understanding.

Participatory marketing is indeed a way to make consumers involved in different marketing decisions. Thanks to CRM 2.0 capabilities, companies could favour embracing among customers by involving them in marketing development. For example, brands can request customers to study the opportunity of launching a new product or service. Consumers could then participate by

defining some products components or organoleptic attributes, most suitable product name, price sensitivity, marketing campaigns concepts etc. By the way, mobile marketing allows brands to get in touch with consumers, inform them about products attributes, promotions or store locations, increase membership database, etc. On the other hand, brand can increase customer participation and commitment by resorting to customization. Offering the customer the opportunity to personalize his or her product or service like on the NIKEiD website demonstrates brand's capacity of meeting customers' expectations and leads to improved satisfaction and strengthens the brand relationship. The Japanese retailer Muji holds the *Muji Award International Design Competition* to encourage consumers and studios to design a creative object for the minimalist brand.

To summarize customer centricity is about company's philosophy, resources and processes orchestrated with stakeholders and aimed at making each customer touch point a satisfaction opportunity.

CUSTOMER ACQUISITION

The life cycle of CRM is based on three phases: customer acquisition, customer retention and customer portfolio development. When companies adopt an offensive relationship strategy, their goal will be mainly oriented towards customer acquisition. In concrete terms, customer acquisition refers to the passage from the prospect status to the customer one. Since, this conversion is often associated with high costs, relationship marketing recommends to cultivate profitable customers' loyalty once they are acquired (Reinartz, Thomas, and Kumar 2005). In addition to that, customer acquisition initiatives have never been so challenging since customers are nowadays more knowledgeable, empowered and demanding. The framework below mentions the implicit issue of balancing acquisition and retention resources to ensure customer profitability (Figure 2). The authors' findings indicate, for example, that a suboptimal spending on retention will have a greater impact on customer profitability than suboptimal acquisition expenditures. In addition to that, interpersonal and interactive communication channels seem to be more useful for long term customer profitability orientation.

When brands try to initiate or develop relationships with customers, the first objective concerns customer acquisition. Two cases can be then considered, acquiring new customers, for the first time, or aiming to substitute lost customers due to a high churn rate. In terms of marketing policy, customer acquisition will be implemented in cases like creating new usage situation of an existing product, brand repositioning, new business start, identifying nostalgic connotation of a product, or new product or service launch. Some sectors like health services, travel and hospitality, education or retail banking have permanently to face the customer acquisition challenge.

The famous and meaningful rule of the three Ts: Track, Target and Touch summarizes the process to be followed for acquisition. This process implies the existence of a market multichannel

intelligence system inside the company and a database marketing approach. In order to draw up their customer acquisition plan, companies need to carefully handle the process by identifying the leads or customers to target, the channels by which these customers can be touched and the type of products or services offer that is the most adapted for them. In other terms, the plan consists of tailoring the right offer to the right customer in the right place and at the right time. Companies can then leverage their campaigns effectiveness by examining indicators like response rate, channel affinity rate, period related performance, or cost per response. Furthermore, it's very important to keep in mind the retention objective while setting customer acquisition plan. To maintain the customer lifecycle, customer acquisition should develop mechanisms that are supposed to enhance customer knowledge, follow needs evolution and reward purchase through the different channels (stores, web, call centers, etc.) and facilitate customer retention afterwards (Buttle 2004).

For example, customer acquisition in banking sector represents a real challenge for brands. Competition is intensive, consumer behaviour in retail banking is often fluctuating and customer value

Figure 2. Linking customer acquisition, relationship duration and customer profitability (Reinartz, Thomas and Kumar 2005)

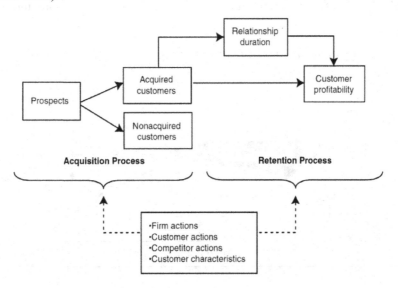

creation is critical. Then, banks need to develop analytical models that ensure accurate and low cost targeting. Then, a segment who tends to spend heavily using credit cards, take out insurances offers (home, travel, etc.) and that maintain a reliable account balance can be interesting to approach. Acquisition channels are decisive and can be based on word-of-mouth campaign by bringing referrals from existing customers. This target is likely to represent a profile similar to current customers in terms of banking behaviour, leisure activities, lifestyle, etc. This acquisition approach allows costs optimization in sense that the bank will be able to get new guaranteed customers and to strengthen loyalty by rewarding customers who have referred. Furthermore, banks can reinforce acquisition process by resorting to communication event through sponsoring or corporate patronage to favour brand awareness.

Consequently, customer acquisition strategy addresses the issue of matching channels selection with profitability through customer equity growth. According to Lewis (2006), customer value generation capacity depends on his or her acquisition channel. In fact, when looking for new customers, companies can rely even on marketing efforts (mailing campaigns, web marketing, advertising, etc.) or on referrals (word-of-mouth). Also, the digitization of word-of-mouth through Internet and social networks offers new opportuni-

ties and challenges for brands to monitor feedback mechanisms (Dellarocas 2003). While examining word-of-mouth theory, Kozinets et al. (2010), identify a progressive shift to three models: the *organic interconsumer influence model* (consumer to consumer exchange), *the linear marketer influence model* (the impact of marketing practices on consumers) and *the network coproduction model* (favoured by internet, it refers to directly managing and influencing WOM and dealing with market messages that are exchanged between consumers) (Figure3).

The *network coproduction model* implies, for marketers using social media marketing, to develop new methods to analyze networked narratives.

On the other hand, Villanueva et al. (2008) found that customer life time value depends on the acquisition mode (Figure4). Their results indicate that if companies are to enlarge their customer database rapidly, they will have to mobilize heavy initial investments and foresee high retention budget to maintain new customers' contribution value. Inversely, firms that choose to invest in developing and using referrals to acquire customers will have to spend less on retention.

To some extent, relying on internet as a channel of favouring positive WOM diffusion seems to be profitable. This is due to the fact that customers tend to attribute more credibility and

Figure 3. The network coproduction model (Kozinets et al. 2010)

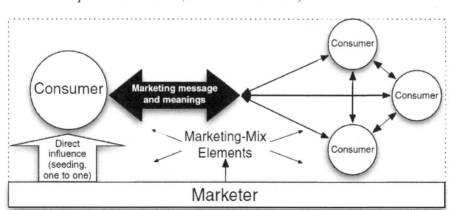

Figure 4. Customer acquisition and value generation (Villanueva et al. 2008)

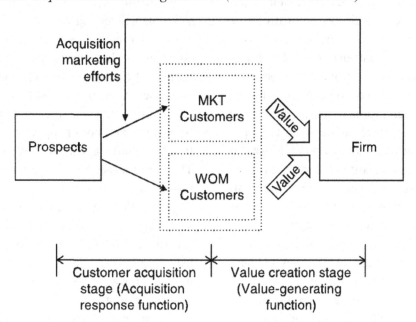

persuasion to other customers recommendations than to conventional advertising (Brown and Reingen 1987). Moreover, since customers are aware of the wilful influencing role of brand advertising, they try to keep distance from it and are more receptive to viral marketing (Friestad and Wright 1994). Finally, WOM allows for a costless communication on the brand. One of the recent examples is the launch of the Ford Fiesta that used mainly social media to help diffusion. After selecting volunteers to participate to the test drive program, they were asked to engage in social media conversations about their experience. The return on investment was very positive and the brand managed to generate online buzz and to optimize marketing budgets.

Acquisition situation raises the question of customer newness. Customer newness can be related either to a product category or to the company. Concerning customers new to a service or product category, they might have recognized a new need or a new solution for an existing want. For example, consumers reaching senior age level express new needs related to activities like leisure, travelling and cruises or plastic surgery. This is

due to the will of filling spare time or fighting ageing. In business-to-business context, a company that aims to engage in sustainable development processes will start to be interested in green raw materials and then to be a potential customer for the concerned suppliers. In the market of coffee machines for domestic use, customers can choose a new coffee machine because it allows them to prepare and obtain a hot beverage that is more suited to their needs and expectations. Finally, product usage context or situation can sometimes be dictated by customers. It's the case for several food goods that are, for example, used by consumers as cooking recipes ingredients. Consequently, brands communicate the new usage contexts and try to increase product buying probability by mentioning some recipes on product packaging for example. Nestlé company has a dedicated space on its brand relational website to stimulate recipes exchange among the brand community and provide advices.

On the other hand, customers can also be new to the company which means that they are acquired or recovered from competitors. Customers can shift to new brands because they consider that they manage to better satisfy their needs, meet their values or because of variety seeking or innovativeness. This shift means also that switching costs were not enough high to prevent relationship disruption. Acquiring customers from competitors depends on the market lifecycle and the type of relationships established between customers and the competing brands. When markets reach the maturity phase, offensive measures consisting of enticing customers from competitors is often the most favoured option since there are no new customers integrating the market. Differentiation levers are then the main key to facilitate customers shift. They can be based on service quality dimensions, improved customer experience, product attributes, enhancing brand identification by improving brand image, etc. Recovering customers from competitors addresses the issue of loyalty building approach. Two loyalty dimensions are always important to develop: attitudinal and behavioural (Dick & Basu 1994). As mentioned above, the main problem is that the majority of loyalty programs are based on repeated purchase improvement. This limited approach of loyalty increases the risk of switching when competitors propose interesting offers. In addition to that, relationships' strength between consumers and brands or customers and suppliers will influence the customer acquisition process. The more the consumers' attitude towards the competing brand is positive and the more they are committed, the more difficult it will be to convert them. In industrial markets, the more the company is dependent on its current supplier and benefiting from specific advantages, the more the switching costs will be higher and the relationship difficult to disrupt.

Thanks to CRM databases, customer knowledge has been largely improved and acquisition efforts more accurately planned towards identified segments. Companies should carefully handle the multichannel approach to ensure customer data synchronization otherwise, CRM benefits won't be reached and customer service not improved (Payne and Frown 2004). The main question is about identifying the right customers for the acquisition plan. Selecting the potential customers that must be targeted should be based on their value contribution. In other terms, companies should estimate the margins earned from the customer's purchases over a given period. Companies should also consider the customer propensity to switch from current brands or suppliers. Once this stage fulfilled, marketers must move to prospection. This step consists of looking for ways to convert prospects into customers. Prospects represent the output of the segmentation process that generates segments, clusters or individuals based on specific and relevant criteria that aims to result in homogeneous groups that are likely to respond in a similar way to companies marketing actions.

In business-to-business context, the sales force is often in charge of the prospecting activity. The objective is to identify leads, in other words, companies that might be worth approaching. CRM applications and data mining capabilities help in identifying customer profiles that are interesting for targeting or cross selling. Then, the identified lead needs to be qualified through several questions related to the extent to which the lead expresses a need for company's offers, lead's solvency (credit rating) and the authorization to buy for the lead. Once leads qualification accomplished, companies must consider the best channels to approach the selected prospects. Customers can either be contacted directly through salespeople, call centres or mailing or emailing campaigns or indirectly by other partners or intermediaries. In consumer markets, brands rely more on other tools like advertising to influence attitudes, sales promotion, internet and merchandising.

In order to measure customer acquisition plans efficacy, CRM practitioners should define relevant indicators (Ang and Buttle 2006). The main concern is about the volume of acquired customers, estimated customer acquisition cost and acquired customer value. The objective must be to maximize the profit in terms of customer value compared with acquisition costs. Acquisition costs will depend on marketing expenses and adopted channels to approach prospects. Finally, companies need to propose the right offer to the prospects based on their needs and records in the database.

Customer acquisition is then a relational strategic approach to the market that should take into consideration and rely on multichannel management. Customers' selection is decisive for the company relationship strategy success and sustainability.

CUSTOMER RETENTION

Once customer acquisition is accomplished, the following step in the relationship lifecycle consists in customer retention, especially in a digital economy and high competitive markets (Peppers and Rogers 2004). Customer retention planning aimed at first maintaining relationships with the customers who already belong to the company's database through churn rate mastering and second increasing contribution value of customers (Ang and Buttle 2006; Reichheld and Sasser 1990). The retention strategy must be totally integrated to the relationship marketing policy and be adapted to the business context (Ahmad & Buttle 2001). The principle at this level should be to focus efforts on customers that are supposed to generate more value than relational investments mobilized by the firm. This principle refers to the notion of lifetime value (LTV) which is a reliable metric of the cumulative cash flow a customer brings to the company during his or her life-term (Blattberg et *al.* 2001; Jain & Singh 2002). LTV allows the identification of the customers to target for the retention plan. Only customers with high LTV will be considered and their LTV compared to the costs associated to their retention. In fact, relationship strategy should look out for mutual benefits realization and maintenance through effective retention that allows financial objectives achievement. In terms of time and efforts'

allocation, companies should more focus, in their retention plan, on the profitable customers who express low positive attitude toward the brand or a low brand commitment. To do so, emailing marketing campaigns seem to be, when adapted, a smarter, effective and costless way to retain customers by ensuring a valuable ROI.

Retention process implies tracking customer disruption signs or behaviors. The earlier the company detects defection intention of the customer the easier and costless the retention will be (Reichheld and Sasser 1990). For this reason, companies need to pursue customers' records and behavior to identify rapidly any sign that precedes defection. Consequently and according to a customer centric strategy, companies must keep listening to customers and taking into consideration their feedback, especially in critical moments of truth, to ensure that their satisfaction level is improving significantly. To do so, brands can lead satisfaction surveys, ask salespeople to make regular reports about customer remarks and shopping behavior or send marketing managers to stores to observe customers.

Customer willingness to disrupt will depend on the stage reached in the relationship cycle. Generally, disruption refers to a process with a variable duration that is characterized by a progressive alteration of customer behavior. Consequently, the longer the relationship between the customer and the brand or the supplier the less sensitive he will be in case of failure and the lower the defection probability will be. In fact, this is due to the memorization and interactions accumulation process. When customers have a long experience with the company they may try to compensate their occasional dissatisfaction by previous memorized pleasurable experiences (Bolton 1998; Caruabna 2002). However, if the customer is new to the company, he or she will be more likely to break the relationship in case of dissatisfaction since there is no interaction memory. Then, brands should improve and valorize permanently customer experience to generate and strengthen attitudes. Nowadays, the main challenge for brands is not only to integrate customers set of consideration by memorization but also to generate brand preference.

In addition to that, brands should consider channel choice and migration when working on retention (Thomas & Sullivan 2005). As a gravitational media, internet allows interactive and intensive social interactions and facilitates retention through CRM 2.0. Companies relying on social CRM are able to track and monitor information exchange between business partners or buzz among consumers on brand corporate blogs or communities' websites (Boehm 2008). In fact, relational websites content should generate valuable conversations between customers to favor content sharing about emotions and common experiences that are supposed to lead to strong relationships. Moreover, relational websites content represent a valued source of customers' perceptions, evaluations and consumption trends. Finally, CRM 2.0 could help brands to boost their sales in sense that it allows the most loyal and motivated customers to promote and recommend products under a CtoC scheme through advices (problem solving), rankings, testimonies or ratings.

All these scenarios and contents' types represent a major challenge for brands that will have to deal with structured and low quality or unstructured data to drive satisfaction and generate delight through permanently exceeding customer expectations. For example, brands can define some metrics or indicators to examine social CRM informational output effectiveness. Companies can measure (1) conversations spread on the basis of the number of answers and initiated online discussions a topic manages to generate, (2) demographic profile of online consumers based on answers that contain age, location, job, etc, (3) consumers leadership based on the number of people answering to them, agreeing with their comments, his/her social network size, (4) information diffusion speed based on the number of people answering in a limited period, etc.

However, companies must be careful when they manage customer relationships by avoiding to be only led by satisfaction objectives. They should also pay attention to retention scores. In fact, increasing customer satisfaction by trying to overpass his or her expectations can be very expensive. Then, some companies will look only for some costless aspects that can influence satisfaction but that don't ensure competitive advantage and repurchase behavior. For this reason, the approach of customer satisfaction should be based on retention criteria. In addition to that, CRM practitioners can also try to build and maintain switching barriers to make it dissuasive or risky to move to competing brands or suppliers (Keaveney 1995). To do so, companies can use different levers according to the market and their resources like technological sustained innovation, low price policy, service dominant strategy, etc.

Driving customer retention supposes setting metrics to leverage its effectiveness. As for any ROI measure, the company should refer to the main objective of retention which is about keeping profitable customers. Since time notion is critical for retention, managers should take a reference period to calculate the number of remaining customers compared with those at the beginning of the period. Reference period selection can be different according to type of product category, marketing operation, industry and customer ownership behavior. Since repeated purchasing behavior is correlated with relationship durability, this factor has also to be taken into consideration. However, some customers can be wrongly considered as retained or defecting. In the case of insurance services market, some customers can terminate their contracts because of situation change like after selling their cars, house, etc. According, to a CRM multichannel architecture, information about termination must be centralized and shared thanks to synchronization. However, if synchronization doesn't operate correctly, the customer will be considered as defecting and if the same customer is to take out an insurance policy again, he will count for a new customer. Consequently, companies should design their customer retention dashboard to consider industry type, customer behavior and purchase cycles.

As mentioned above, retention strategy should focus on profitable customers that express low brand attitude level. Consequently, companies will identify, by the way, the customers that are not interesting to keep. It's a critical issue that companies should handle carefully in sense that it's directly related to the brand image and reputation. In fact, the way the brand tries to disrupt its relationship with unprofitable customers can also influence potential or profitable existing ones. This process can be significantly amplified online because of large scale dissemination capacity. Some brands use common measures like raising prices, allowing less easy terms, modifying product or service offers or associated conditions or decreasing service quality, sales force visits' frequency or customer care towards unprofitable customers.

Cultivating customer retention refers to a central relational concept which is commitment. Commitment is defined as the customer willingness to maintain the relationship with the brand or the supplier over time (Morgan and Hunt 1994). Then, commitment represents a strong relationship quality indicator like trust, satisfaction and loyalty. In other terms, by building and developing customers' commitment toward the brand, the supplier or the salespeople, brands will ensure an important resistance of customers to competitors' offers. However, while dealing with customers that are mainly regular brand switchers, variety seeking driven or who simply don't express a predisposition to initiate an in-depth relationship with the brand, companies should avoid retention emphasis or insistence.

Once the retention plan implemented, companies should set some indicators to assess its efficacy. These indicators can be based on the number of customers retained compared with the beginning of the reference period, the cost of retention plan, the variation of the attrition rate, the share of requirements, price sensitivity, recommendation, the contribution of retained customers in terms of sales or margin, etc.

To conclude, customer retention is a value driven process that should be adapted to the company context and product category. Retention should favor customer loyalty and commitment and be oriented toward mastering defection.

CRM ADOPTION AND IMPLEMENTATION

An ocean away an executive education seminar on relationship marketing is taking place. The instructor is talking about the greatest changes is marketing concepts over the last twenty years. "Relationship marketing is clearly one of these." The instructor discusses how the emphasis of marketing strategy has shifted from primarily being concerned with customer acquisition to placing more and more weight on customer retention. "Customer Relationship Management or CRM is being used by more and more companies to examine the value of each customer and determine the appropriate amount of marketing, sales and customer service for that customer. CRM will soon be essential to an effective marketing strategy."

One of the executives starts thinking about the recent implementation of a brand name CRM system at his bank. Everything was working well during the first month. The account managers had all been well trained. The implementation consultant the bank hired had the system up and running flawlessly. Everybody was using the system to manage their clients. In the second month usage started to drop off, however. And, in the third month almost none of the account managers were using the system. An investment of millions was slowly grinding to inactivity and the executive did not know why.

During the refreshment break of the seminar the executive approached the instructor and shared the problem with the instructor. The conversation went something like this:

Executive: "My bank, (well known and large), just implemented a CRM system provided by (leader in the industry) but there seems to be a problem."

Instructor: "What seems to be wrong? Is there a glitch in system?"

Executive: "No everything is fine with the hardware and software. It was running well when we started, but people have stopped using it."

Instructor: "Are the users familiar with the system? Have they been trained?"

Executive: "Yes, we had an excellent training program."

Instructor: "Tell me about the intended purpose of the system. What is it used for?"

Executive: "Our account managers use it to manage their relationships with their clients. Before they contact a client they log on to the system and analyze the bank's relationship with the client – what products the client is using and what level of relationship the client has with us for each product. Then the account manager contacts the client and does some bonding and rapport building before he/she starts suggestive selling to either add new products to the clients portfolio or increase the level of relationship with already existing products. Then, after the call, the account manager updates the data in the system and moves on to the next client."

Instructor: "That sounds like a good use of CRM."

Executive: "I know, but people have stopped using the system."

Instructor: "Why do you think that is happening?"

Executive: "The account managers believe the system takes up thirty percent of the time they have to spend with customers. They have gone back to just calling up customers and suggesting changes in the customer's portfolio."

Instructor: "Have you changed the incentive system for the account managers?"

Executive: "No."

Instructor: "Have you done anything to require the managers use the system?"

Executive: "No."

Instructor: "Does management check the entries into the system against changes in the customer's portfolio?"

Executive: "No."

Instructor: "Your problem is pretty common in the implementation of CRM systems. There are some things you need to do in the way of change management. I am pretty sure I can help. Let's get back to the seminar and we can talk afterwards."

This discussion actually took place and is representative of the problems found in the implementation of CRM systems.

With the increasing utilization of computers in all business areas the 1990s saw the emergence of special software to support sales and then marketing. These tools were aimed at measuring and managing customer relationships. At first they were called "sales force automation" and then "customer relationship management." Thus, CRM software became the narrow and computerized version of a phenomena – customer relationship management – that had existed since there were customers. At first CRM implementations failed miserably. This was because it was about installing the software across the entire enterprise and then adapting all marketing and sales processes to suit the software. In some studies 70% of all implementations failed to accomplish the basic objectives of improving the customer experience or lowering sales and marketing costs. Today, after 15 years of experience, CRM is still risky but more implementations are finding success.

The fact that customer relationship management can have both broad and narrow meanings is important to the entire field of marketing (Crosby 2002). Early views of relationship marketing felt that the idea was to use the tools of marketing to raise every customer relationship to a higher and stronger and deeper and longer connection. "Marriage" was often used as a metaphor for the goal of relationship marketing between supplier and customer. The fact that not all customers wanted to be in a monogamous, long-term, contractual relationship with a supplier was ignored. With the advent of the term customer relationship management in the narrow sense, relationship marketers began to come to their senses and realized it was better to think of the appropriate level of relationship with each customer. Some customers would be strategic accounts and other would not. How to serve each customer best while maintaining profitability became the goal of relationship marketing and marketers began to think in terms of a customer portfolio of relationships. One dissertation found that the average level of customer satisfaction went down after firms implemented customer relationship management systems. Upon closer examination it was determined that the level of satisfaction for larger customers went up while satisfaction for midsize and smaller customers went down due to the firms prioritization of support and services to customers based on importance of the customer. Customer relationship management in the broadest sense now encompasses all of the areas marketing used to be responsible for. For firms that truly adopt a customer centric focus, customer relationship management can include all of the business functions. Thus, a phenomena that began in the academic area of industrial marketing has spread to all areas of marketing and now threatens to be the umbrella under which all business functions can be classified.

CRM IMPLEMENTATION

Implementing CRM systems has been largely studied especially when more than 70% of projects fail or don't manage to achieve objectives. Some authors examined the leading factors to CRM/ SFA adoption (Jelinek et al. 2006; Jones et al. 2002; Parthasarathy and Sohi 1997; Rangarajan et al. 2005; Schillewaert et *al.* 2005; Speier and Venkatesh 2002). They identify two main categories of adoption determinants: individual and organizational. The individual factors are related to the users' characteristics (age, previous experience with IT, attitude toward IT, etc). On the other hand, organizational factors refer to company size, industry type or competition intensity. However, it seems that we should move beyond these factors to have a more global approach of the CRM project. In other words, the CRM project should be repositioned in a strategic orientation and led under a communication policy. In fact, the advent of CRM solutions in the company often generate cognitive dissonance among users especially salespeople (Zablah, Bellenger and Johnston 2005). Moreover, the solution is perceived as a mean of increasing precariousness, role ambiguity and stress. The CRM project is quite different from other projects undertaken by companies in sense that it contains not only a financial constraint but also a behavioural one related to the integration of the solution in the daily tasks (Becker, Goetz and Sönke 2009; Boujena et *al.* 2009; Johnston et *al.* 2003).

ALIGNING CRM AND THE COMPANY STRATEGY

CRM is not a about technology or process but first about company strategy. Likewise, CRM shouldn't be approached as, a nice to have solution, competitors' imitation measure or a question of blind faith in an effective technology. CRM strategy consists of putting the customer in the center of all companies decisions in manner that all the interactions will have as an objective to develop and maintain relationships with the customer (Boujena et *al.* 2009). Second, in a globalized context where offers are becoming increasingly standardized, CRM remains a crucial mean to gain competitive advantage through customer centric strategy and service differentiation. Also, this strategy allows the improvement of customer interaction processes as opportunities to set strong relationships. However, while CRM strategy is built around the customer, the CRM project should be also sales force minded in sense that it is in the halfway between the company and its customers and the salespeople are the most concerned users and important information source of CRM in the company. In the same line, the CRM project should be positioned in a cost reduction and time saving approach. In fact, by rationalizing information and communication processes in the company, CRM leads to economies in terms of task accomplishment required time and operations costs. Finally, since information is power and that CRM concerns different company's departments a part from sales and marketing, the implementation requires company's reorganization. This reorganization should fall into line with the new information sharing and tasks redefinition scheme.

THINKING THE CRM PROJECT

As cited above, the CRM project must be thought in line with company's strategy and by considering salespeople's objectives (Boujena et al. 2007). For this reason and according to the participative approach, management should implicate salespeople in problems detection process and needs assessments. The sales force is in direct interaction with customers and is then able to provide insights on ways of developing and maintaining customer relationships. The first step is about making an inventory of customer interactions types according to the company industry and salespeople assigned role. The second step will consist of being data centric by listing essential data needed and collectable. Companies should account at this stage for data quality and integration issue since it's decisive for the CRM effectiveness afterwards especially in terms of customer service quality,

sales force adherence and operating costs (Peikin 2003). On the basis of that, management can start setting specifications for CRM solution acquisition. This process allows CRM solution choice optimization and influence salespeople involvement by increasing solution usefulness perception. Finally, the company can initiate benchmarking and technological intelligence to find the most suited solution as regards specifications set. Some criteria are relevant to choose the more suitable CRM solution: platform accessibility (web based or not), solution features, adaptability and degree of solution customization, ergonomics, solution compatibility with the current operating system, durability, solution power and capacities in terms of data storage, solution evolutionarity, implementation cost per duration and users' number, after sales service, training offer, etc.

CREATING AN ACCOMPANIMENT STRUCTURE

As stated above, CRM implementation relates to an innovation process that requires leading change strategy to succeed. For this reason, the management should create an accompaniment structure which will be in charge of following solution integration steps inside the company. Consequently, top management must constitute a common project pilotage or monitoring board assembling both users and technicians. In addition to that, company should appoint a CRM project sponsor who commits political capital as well as resources and personal time. The sponsor will be in charge of different tasks like empowering project management, apprehending project complexity, approving plans and schedules or reviewing project's progress. Finally, the integration of CRM/SFA solution requires efforts in terms of users' time allocation. For this reason, management and the sponsor should ensure in addition to user manual diffusion an optimal programming of training sessions adapted to users' adoption rhythm and profiles difference. Training is one of the factors influencing ease of use perception which is considered with solution usefulness as the main determinants of adoption according to the technology acceptance model (Davis 1989; Venkatesh & Davis 1996).

Then CRM should move from the strategic level to the operational one by becoming a grounded culture among employees and a used application as a technology. For this reason, management should be committed to a persuasion process aimed to arousing employees' adherence to CRM project. In the following figure, we provide an illustration of the persuasion process based on the theory of planned behaviour (Ajzen 1975) and that is intended to sales force as a major using target.

In fact, companies should adopt a relevant, credible and efficient communication policy to sell the CRM solution inside the organization before promoting it for the customer (Figure5). Communication is the main tool to deal with users' perceptions and attitudes. Furthermore, communication is able to weaken or to face rumours and internal interpretations that can impede CRM implementation. In addition to that, communication has an important role in accompanying solution integration by a adopting a progressive persuasion according to salespeople and users' behaviour. The communication strategy can be articulated around three main axes: valuing investment in CRM decision, mobilizing users around the CRM project and valuing salespersons' performance (Figure6).

VALUING INVESTMENT IN CRM DECISION

While investing in CRM is mainly a decision emanating from the hierarchical summit, company should communicate investment motivation and implementation objectives to the salespeople. In fact, the project must be sold first inside the company to ensure users' adherence. For this reason,

management should not only position the CRM project as an answer to the company orientation, me too strategy or productivity seeking but also as sales force needs satisfaction. In other words, management must stress the match between CRM objectives and salespeople expectations meeting. This supposes that the company should adopt a participative project approach to make salespeople feel that CRM/SFA is not only about achieving the top management objectives or increasing control over them. Users should become aware of change need or opportunity and integrate innovation in their behaviour (Beyer and Trice 1978; Nord and Tucker 1987; Tornatzky and Fleischer 1990). Then the adoption is a process which ends once usage becomes routine. Finally, CRM should be the opportunity to create or strengthen the company's innovation culture. In fact, matching company's customer orientation and innovation with CRM will heavily influence project intelligibility and efforts' federation from the future users' perspec-

Figure 5. Sales force persuasion process

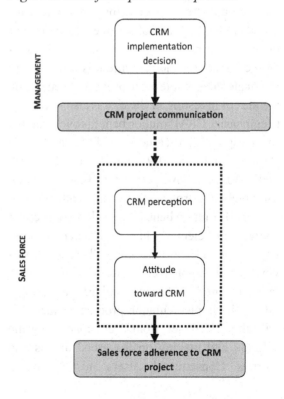

Figure 6. CRM project communication axes

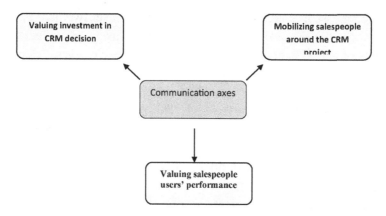

tive. Another consequence deals with value sharing improvement and belonging to company feeling increase among salespeople.

MOBILIZING USERS AROUND THE CRM PROJECT

To ensure solution integration and a large diffusion of technology inside the company, management should stress the contribution of CRM for users. Given the fact that salespeople are one of the major users of CRM system, we will focus on the impact for them. While it is important to implicate salespeople in the process of generating the idea of investing in CRM, it is also necessary to emphasize CRM solution benefits over features for salespeople (Ahearne and Schillewaert 2004; Barnes and Engle 1995; Hunter and Perreault 2007). As cited above, perception of CRM solution usefulness is a strong determinant of adoption. In fact CRM solution benefits for salespeople cover a large set of elements like: improving customer knowledge, decision making, call planning, service quality, responsiveness etc. In addition to that, management should keep listening to salespeople during the implementation process. In fact, this will allow feedback from users concerning the solution and making up for users' dreads and worries. Consequently, users must appoint a

representative group in charge of communication with the project monitoring board.

VALUING SALESPERSONS' PERFORMANCE

In order to improve CRM solution usage and to promote performance, management should play an important role by first cultivating management leadership. CRM implementation is often perceived as a hierarchical and mandatory decision. For this reason, management involvement in solution usage and diffusion is beneficial. In addition to that, management can push IT usage by setting online applications for holiday demands or communicating by electronic mail for meeting planning. Moreover, CRM/SFA usage will affect task accomplishment in sense that the automation of information and communication processes influences roles and consequently means of achieving objectives. Then, management should communicate the revision of performance evaluation criteria to fall in line with the new tasks' configuration (Ahearne and Schillewaert 2004; Sundaram et al. 2007). This process includes tasks redefinition, appraisal grids, etc. In the same line, performance criteria should be indexed to CRM solution capacities. Also, management must promote the usage and the reward of salespersons' performance. Colleagues represent a subjective norm that influences CRM adoption. Then, a regular or intensive usage by colleagues is the best evidence for hesitating salespeople of solution ease of use and usefulness. This is due to the fact that salespeople give more credibility to colleagues' word of mouth and behaviour than to managers' speech. Moreover, diffusion of usage among colleagues can create a dynamic competition to achieve goals. Companies can reward users' performance through awards or prizes ceremonies, appointing the confirmed users to coach the others, organizing thematic meetings, etc.

In sum, as any information system, CRM is based on people, organization and technology. CRM is first of all a company strategy that should be integrated by all collaborators. CRM implementation should be designed as a participative process driven by customer orientation and people involvement.

REFERENCES

Ahearne, M., Srinivasan, N., & Weinstein, L. (2004). Effect of technology on sales performance: Progressing from technology acceptance to technology usage and consequence. *Journal of Personal Selling & Sales Management, 24*(4), 297–310.

Ahmad, R., & Buttle, F. (2001). Customer retention: A potentially potent marketing management strategy. *Journal of Strategic Marketing, 9*(1), 29–45.

Ajzen, I. (1985). From intentions to actions: A theory of planned behavior. In Kuhl, J., & Beckmann, J. (Eds.), *Action control: From cognition to behaviour* (pp. 11–39). Heidelberg, Germany: Springer.

Ang, L., & Buttle, F. (2006). Managing for successful customer acquisition: An exploration. *Journal of Marketing Management, 22*, 295–317. doi:10.1362/026725706776861217

Ang, L., & Buttle, F. (2006). Customer retention management processes: A quantitative study. *European Journal of Marketing, 40*(1/2), 83–99. doi:10.1108/03090560610637329

Barnes, M., & Engle, R. (1995). Can sales force automation help you be a more effective manager? *Sales Process Engineering and Automation Review*, (September), 16-19.

Becker, J. U., Goetz, G., & Sönke, A. (2009). The impact of technological and organizational implementation of CRM on customer acquisition, maintenance, and retention. *International Journal of Research in Marketing, 26*(3), 207–215. doi:10.1016/j.ijresmar.2009.03.006

Bennett, R., McColl-Kennedy, J., & Coote, L. (2000). Trust, commitment and attitudinal brand loyalty: Key constructs in business-to-business relationships. *Proceedings of ANZMAC Conference: Visionary Marketing for the 21st Century: Facing the Challenge.*

Beyer, M. J., & Trice Harrison, M. (1978). *Implementing change: Alcoholism policies in work organizations.* New York, NY: Free Press.

Blattberg, R. C., Getz, G., & Thomas, J. S. (2001). *Customer equity: Building and managing relationships as valuable assets.* Boston, MA: Harvard Business School Press.

Boehm, M. (2008). Determining the impact of Internet channel use on a customer's lifetime. *Journal of Interactive Marketing, 22*, 2–22. doi:10.1002/dir.20114

Bolton, R. N. (1998). A dynamic model of the duration of the customer's relationship with a continuous service provider: The role of satisfaction. *Marketing Science, 7*(1), 45–65. doi:10.1287/mksc.17.1.45

Boujena, O., Johnston, W., & Merunka, D. (2007). *Sales force automation benefits: A comparative study of sales managers and salespeople's perceptions.* Relationship Marketing Summit, Universidad Torcuato di Tella, Buenos Aires, December 13-15.

Boujena, O., Johnston, W., & Merunka, D. (2009). The benefits of sales force automation: A customer's perspective. *Journal of Personal Selling & Sales Management, 29*(2), 137–150. doi:10.2753/PSS0885-3134290203

Boujena, O., Johnston, W., & Merunka, D. (2009). *The impact of sales force automation on customer-salesperson relationship quality: A conceptual model.* The 24th Annual National Conference in Sales Management, Norfolk, VA, 25-28th March, 2009.

Boujena, O., Merunka, D., & Johnston, W. (2009). *The impact of CRM on customer: Expected benefits and implementation issue.* The 8th International Congress Marketing Trends, ESCP-EAP, Paris, 16-17th January.

Brown, J. J., & Reingen, P. H. (1987). Social ties and word-of-mouth referral behavior. *The Journal of Consumer Research, 14*(3), 350–362. doi:10.1086/209118

Buttle, F. (2004). *Customer relationship management: Concepts and tools.* Oxford, UK: Elsevier Butterworth Heinemann.

Caruabna, A. (2002). Service loyalty. The effects of service quality and the mediating role of customer satisfaction. *European Journal of Marketing, 36*(7/8), 811–828. doi:10.1108/03090560210430818

Crosby, L. A. (2002). Exploding some myths about customer relationship management. *Managing Service Quality, 12*(5), 271–277. doi:10.1108/09604520210442056

Crosby, L. A., Evans, K. R., & Cowles, D. (1990). Relationship quality in services selling: An interpersonal influence perspective. *Journal of Marketing, 54*, 68–81. doi:10.2307/1251817

Davis, F. D. (1989). Perceived usefulness, perceived ease of use, and user acceptance of Information Technology. *Management Information Systems Quarterly, 13*(3), 319–339. doi:10.2307/249008

Dellarocas, C. (2003). The digitization of word of mouth: Promise and challenges of online feedback mechanisms. *Management Science, 49*(10), 1407–1424. doi:10.1287/mnsc.49.10.1407.17308

Dick, A., & Basu, K. (1994). Customer loyalty: Towards an integrated conceptual framework. *Journal of the Academy of Marketing Science, 22*(2), 99–113. doi:10.1177/0092070394222001

Friestad, M., & Wright, P. (1994). The persuasion knowledge model: How people cope with persuasion attempts. *The Journal of Consumer Research, 21*(1), 1–31. doi:10.1086/209380

Godson, M. (2009). *Relationship marketing.* Oxford, UK: Oxford University Press.

Grönroos, C. (1990). Relationship approach to marketing in services contexts: The marketing and organizational interface. *Journal of Business Research, 20*(1), 3–11. doi:10.1016/0148-2963(90)90037-E

Gummesson, E. (1999). *Total relationship marketing. Rethinking marketing management: From 4Ps to 30Rs.* Oxford, UK: Butterworth Heinemann.

Gummesson, E. (2008). Extending the new dominant logic: From customer centricity to balanced centricity. *Journal of the Academy of Marketing Science, 36*(1), 15–17. doi:10.1007/s11747-007-0065-x

Homburg, C., & Rudolph, B. (2001). Customer satisfaction in industrial markets: Dimension and multiple role issues. *Journal of Business Research, 52*, 15–33. doi:10.1016/S0148-2963(99)00101-0

Hunter, G. K., & Perreault, W. D. Jr. (2007). Making sales technology effective. *Journal of Marketing, 71*(1), 16–34. doi:10.1509/jmkg.71.1.16

Jain, D., & Singh, S. S. (2002). Customer lifetime value research in marketing: A review and future directions. *Journal of Interactive Marketing, 16*(2), 34–46. doi:10.1002/dir.10032

Jelinek, R., Ahearne, M., Mathieu, J., & Schillewaert, N. (2006). A longitudinal examination of individual, organizational and contextual factors on sales technology and adoption and job performance. *Journal of Marketing Theory and Practice, 14*(Winter), 7–23. doi:10.2753/MTP1069-6679140101

Johnston, W. J., & Hite, R. (1997). *Managing salespeople: A relationship approach.* Cincinnati, OH: Southwestern Publishing Co.

Johnston, W. J., Zablah, A. R., & Bellenger, D. N. (2003). *Understanding user acceptance of CRM technology.* In 12th International Purchasing and Supply Education Research Association Conference.

Johnston, W. J., Zablah, A. R., & Bellenger, D. N. (2005). *Organizational innovation and change dissonance: Understanding user acceptance of CRM technology.* (Working paper series, Centre de Recherche de Bordeaux Ecole de Management, 73-04).

Jones, E., Sundaram, S., & Chin, W. (2002). Factors leading to salesforce automation use: A longitudinal analysis. *Journal of Personal Selling & Sales Management, 22*(3), 145–156.

Keaveney, S. M. (1995). Customer switching behavior in service industries: An exploratory study. *Journal of Marketing, 59*(April), 71–82. doi:10.2307/1252074

Kozinets, R. V., De Valck, K., Wojnicki, A., & Wilner, S. (2010). Networked narratives: Understanding word-of-mouth marketing in online communities. *Journal of Marketing, 74*, 71–89. doi:10.1509/jmkg.74.2.71

Kumar, V., & Werner, R. (2005). *Customer relationship management: A data-based approach.* Chichester, UK: John Wiley & Sons, Inc.

Lewis, M. (2006). Customer acquisition promotions and customer asset value. *JMR, Journal of Marketing Research, 43*(May), 195–203. doi:10.1509/jmkr.43.2.195

Morgan, R. M., & Hunt, S. D. (1994). The commitment-trust theory of relationship marketing. *Journal of Marketing, 58*, 20–38. doi:10.2307/1252308

Naumann, E. (1995). *Creating customer value: The path to sustainable competitive advantage.* Cincinnati, OH: Thomson Executive Press.

Nord, R. W., & Tucker, S. (1987). *Implementing routine and radical innovations.* Washington, DC.

Parthasarathy, M., & Sohi, R. S. (1997). Sales force automation and the adoption of technological innovations by salespeople: Theory and implications. *Journal of Business and Industrial Marketing, 12*(3), 196–201. doi:10.1108/08858629710188036

Payne, A., & Frow, P. (2004). The role of multichannel integration in customer relationship management. *Industrial Marketing Management, 33*(6), 527–538. doi:10.1016/j.indmarman.2004.02.002

Peikin, D. (2003). Data quality: The foundation for effective CRM. *Target Marketing, 26*(2), 49–50.

Peppers, D., & Rogers, M. (2004). *Managing customer relationship: A strategic framework.* Chichester, UK: John Wiley & Sons Inc.

Rangarajan, D., Jones, E., & Chin, W. (2005). Impact of sales force automation on technology-related stress, effort, and technology usage among salespeople. *Industrial Marketing Management, 34*(4), 345–354. doi:10.1016/j.indmarman.2004.09.015

Reichheld, F., & Sasser, W. (1990). Zero defects: Quality comes to services. *Harvard Business Review*, (September-October): 105–111.

Reinartz, W., Thomas, J. S., & Kumar, V. (2005). Balancing acquisition and retention resources to maximize customer profitability. *Journal of Marketing, 69*(January), 63–79. doi:10.1509/jmkg.69.1.63.55511

Schillewaert, N., Ahearne, M., Frambach, R. T., & Moenaert, R. K. (2005). The adoption of Information Technology in the sales force. *Industrial Marketing Management, 34*, 323–336. doi:10.1016/j.indmarman.2004.09.013

Speier, C., & Venkatesh, V. (2002). The hidden minefields in the adoption of sales force automation technologies. *Journal of Marketing, 66*(3), 98–112. doi:10.1509/jmkg.66.3.98.18510

Sundaram, S., Schwarz, A., Jones, E., & Chin, W. (2007). Technology use on the front line: How Information Technology enhances individual performance. *Journal of the Academy of Marketing Science, 35*(March), 101–112. doi:10.1007/s11747-006-0010-4

Thomas, J. S., & Sullivan, U. Y. (2005). Managing marketing communications with multichannel customers. *Journal of Marketing, 69*, 239–251. doi:10.1509/jmkg.2005.69.4.239

Tornatzky, L. G., Eveland, J. D., & Fleischer, M. (1990). Technological innovation as a process. In Tornatzky, L. G., & Fleischer, M. (Eds.), *The processes of technological innovation* (pp. 27–50). Lexington, MA: Lexington Books.

Uncles, M., Dowling, G., & Hammond, K. (2003). Customer loyalty and customer loyalty programs. *Journal of Consumer Marketing, 20*(4). doi:10.1108/07363760310483676

Vargo, S. L., & Lusch, R. F. (2004). Evolving to a new dominant logic for marketing. *Journal of Marketing, 68*, 1–21. doi:10.1509/jmkg.68.1.1.24036

Venkatesh, V., & Davis, F. D. (1996). A model of the antecedents of perceived ease of use: Development and test. *Decision Sciences, 27*(3), 451–481. doi:10.1111/j.1540-5915.1996.tb01822.x

Villanueva, J., Yoo, S., & Hanssens, D. M. (2008). The impact of marketing-induced vs. word-of-mouth customer acquisition on customer equity. *JMR, Journal of Marketing Research, 45*, 48–59. doi:10.1509/jmkr.45.1.48

Zablah, A. R., Bellenger, D. N., & Johnston, W. J. (2004). Customer relationship management implementation gaps. *Journal of Personal Selling & Sales Management, 24*(Fall), 279–295.

Chapter 11
E–Novation Deployment:
Creating New "Spaces" and Distribution Using E–Novation

Stephen Dann
Australian National University, Australia

ABSTRACT

Space is the final frontier for e-marketing. Advances in storage space, digital data transmission, and infrastructure development have created a near limitless marketspace that exists over the contemporary physical marketplaces, and as an independent market of ideas, data, experience, and content. This chapter overviews a series of key issues in the use of the new "space" for e-novation with attention given to the rise of user generated content through prosumer activity. This chapter is based on exploring how companies and individuals are currently co-creating value in the dynamic marketplace of the new collaborative platforms, and how these new concepts such as the "home shopping channel", digital rights management, and user generated distribution channels can factor in the future success on and offline for marketing.

INTRODUCTION

E-Novation refers to a process of combining innovation, e-marketing, and the new collaborative platforms into an entrepreneurial mindset that views the blurring boundaries of the marketspace and marketplace as a series of opportunities, rather than a range of threats. E-novation incorporates an approach to innovation which involves the strategic use collaborative platforms in an e-marketing environment as a driving force for change in markets, business processes and consumer behaviour. Functionality in the e-novation framework places distribution as the cornerstone of this new market-

DOI: 10.4018/978-1-60566-394-4.ch011

ing practice. Historically, distribution has been the unglamorous workhorse in the marketing stable, whether concerned with the movement of physical objects from producers to consumers, interchange of data through distributed networks or the flow of benefit to, from and between customers, marketers and the marketplace. E-novation requires a revision of the role, importance and priority given to the distribution channel as the host, enabler and venue for the contemporary e-marketing practice. This chapter covers the use of the internet as a collaborative platform for customer and organizational developed value, the rise of user generated channels, and the use of software shop fronts to capitalize on e-procurement and physical distribution.

BACKGROUND

Marketing's history with the distribution channel can be succinctly encapsulated in one of the earliest definitions of commercial marketing. In 1937, the fledging American Marketing Association defined marketing as the direction of the flow of goods and services from producers to consumers (Gundlach, 2007). Seventy years and four definitions later, the American Marketing Association (AMA) definition marketing has evolved into a more complex system of business management which engages multiple stakeholders in the process of creating, communicating, delivering and exchanging offerings of value. The AMA (2007) definition of marketing reads as "the activity, set of institutions and processes for creating, communicating, delivering, and exchanging offerings that have value for customers, clients, partners, and society at large" (Keefe, 2008). Fundamentally, the nature of marketing depends on distribution as the cornerstone to manage the multi-directional flow of offerings of value among the range of actors in the marketplace.

E-Novation deployment is one facet of the management of the multi-directional flow of value offers through the wired and unwired electronic networks which interconnect consumers, prosumers (producer-consumers) and producers into a global marketspace of value exchange.

Prosumption is a form of consumer behaviour whereby the individual gains benefit from combining consumption and production of products through co-creation of value which is redistributed to other consumers via user generated marketspaces. It occurs through the creation of a derivative offering of value based on the individual's consumption experience as a transformative experience of redistributed co-production. Offerings that can have value are reprocessed through consumption into derivations that have value for the original consumer, and a market of secondary tiers. The key to prosumer behaviour is that benefit is derived from both the consumption and production experience, and that product consumption can be a means to access the personal benefits to be gained from the production process. Deployment is the use of marketplace and marketspace technology to distribute an initial value offer by a marketer, or, as outlined later in the chapter, the use of the self-same technologies by the proonsumer to redistribute their personalized reversioning of the initial value offering. Marketspace is the "virtual realm where products and services exist as digital information and can be delivered through information based channels" (Rayport and Sviokla, 1995 in Blois, 1998). Although the origin of the marketspace concept is grounded in the AMA (1985) definition of marketing, with its reliance on the digital goods and services mix, the digital product concept is best suited to the contemporary framework of "offerings that have value". (Keefe, 2004; 2008). Indeed, the development of service dominant logic (SDL) which views the role of goods as a physical embodiment of a service function (Vargo and Lusch, 2004), and the expansion of the SDL framework to value-in-use (consumption) rather than value-in-exchange (ownership) (Ballantyne and Varey, 2008) emphasizes the non-corporeal, transient nature of the modern marketing offering. Features have given way to benefits as the central platform of the marketing offer, even if features still have the top billing in the promotion of the marketing producer-created product.

Products in the digital world are predominantly service orientated in that they can be consumed without the transfer of ownership. The paradox of the digital world is the continued existence of goods in an electronic form. Although the use of a website based service does not result in the transfer of ownership of a product an mp3 file purchased from iTunes requires storage, movement and inventory management in a manner akin to its physical world predecessors (CDs, tapes, vinyl albums). Whilst the physical size of the object has changed, making it possible to transport a mid 1990s radio station's library worth of CDs in your pocket, it still takes a mid-1990s radio station library management system to make the music collection useful to the listener. Although the software as service model has been subject to considerable debate with the success of web-based software delivery, consumers have expressed a preference for goods-like ownership of software on their personal physical devices. Microsoft Office is perceived as a digital good whereas use of Google Documents is seen as accessing a digital service, and while both address related but dissimilar markets of consumers. Either way, both software-as-goods and software-as-services both depend on the consumer accepting the digital product (pdf files) as the substitute for the atom-based products (printed paper).

Beyond the classic goods/service divide in the digital framework is a third category of information product (Freiden et al, 1998). The information product is the near perfect case study of the value in use paradigm (Ballantyne and Varey, 2008). In a raw state, digital information products exist as data which can be transferred, copied and replicated to a near infinite number of times with no loss or degradation of the original data

source (Frieden et al, 1998). However, from the consumer's perspective, data is not information – 0110010101100111 is no substitute for an e-mail, mp3 or virtual world experience. Data must be converted into a meaningful format through its use as an information product. The information product in turn is bounded by the level to which it will create, communicate, deliver or be part of the exchange of value between information product producer and information product consumer. The information product itself is capable of supporting an embedded service as it represents a separated form of product removed from both goods and services (Vargo and Lusch, 2004). This separated form of product is classically identified by AMA (1985) definition as "idea", and as either knowledge (Dann and Dann, 2004) or experience outcomes (Arnould 2008). That said, these conceptualizations are usually focused on the outcomes of physical experience of a good or service, rather than interaction with the information product.

The increased interest from marketers in the embedded service within a physical good, alongside the development of the co-creation of value as the central platform of the marketing exchange, has created a stronger market for the distribution of the intangible experiential information product. If marketing is no longer dependent on the physicality of goods, or the co-location of services, but instead focuses on the development of an offer of value which is co-created in the exchange between company and client, then the non-physical realm of the marketspace is better suited to marketers than the physical marketplace. As Friedman (2007) notes with the widespread availability of "world flattening" technologies, the movement of idea, experience and knowledge products is considerably easier than in previous points in history. That said the Gutenberg press functioned as a similar device for distribution, with similar statements regarding the rapid increase in the ease of idea distribution. The key to both historical distribution and contemporary e-novation deployment is in how the technology's capacity is applied to provide the value offering to the desired end-user. Whereas Gutenberg's technology became a mechanism for broadcast, the current e-novation deployment framework is far better suited to collaborative means of value development and value re-deployment.

"Value deployment" is the assumption that customer co-creation can occur wherever and whenever the customer is available to interact with the value offering. Building on the principle of service dominant logic which assumes all products to be some form of actual or embedded service, the co-creation of value presumes the customer will engage in an active self-service role to self-produce a desired outcome using the available tools (goods), staff (services) or knowledge (information). Customer co-creation of value also alters the dynamic of the marketplace in a fundamental albeit subtle way insofar as the consumption of the embedded service depends on the participation in production of the final outcome. (Ballantyne and Varey 2006) Consequently, the mass markets of previously passive consumption are now microcosms of self-produced product variants, each subtly different and customized to meet the specific needs of consumer. Although the marketplace has always engaged in this form of behaviour, it has previously thought very little of the consequences of generations of mass market tinkering, tailoring and user-generated candlestick making. However, traditionally, barriers to entry to the marketplace have been perceived as greater than most consumers would be willing to overcome – from the financial costs of distribution, through to the psychic costs of independence from the mainstream.

An unintended consequence of the new world view of marketing which acknowledges, respects and depends on the customer's contribution to the creation and consumption of products has been the massive decrease in barriers to entry for

the consumer self-produced content. In addition to the declining production costs for consumer self-produced embedded services is access to the internet which provides a viable mechanism for the self-producer to distribute their experience to the wider marketspace (Friedman, 2007). Returning briefly to the concept of the information product as a separate form of co-created experience, ideas were usually only as viable as the extent to which they could be accurately replicated and distributed. Word of mouth involves imprecise replication which gradually degrades the original content to the point of becoming more noise than signal. Printed distribution depends on finite resources which are consumed through the replication process. Digital deployment greatly reduces both replication issues (distortion and resource consumption). Consequently, the consumer is now in a position to develop an experience which they can encode into information, replicate, duplicate and distribute as part of their engagement with the co-creation process. Witness the rise of YouTube videos of the "unboxing" process of unpacking a new product, and detailing the recently acquired device as an example of the ease of encoding the experience of "new product joy". Widespread access to digital deployment has created a wide array of prosumer (producer-consumer) opportunities which are now forming the backbone of consumer-to-consumer marketspaces.

A counter point to the lowered barriers for deployment of co-created content is the maintenance of the mental cost of co-creation. The psychic costs of independence is exhibited through risk-aversion and the desire to conform to the majority view, group norm or socially approved "mainstream" practice. Drawing on the Rogers (1995) innovation adoption framework as a key indicator of the preference of the majority of a population for mimicry and conformity, the need to individually personalize a product does result in an increased risk of non-conformity which is viewed positively by the innovator and early adopter categories, and negatively by the early and later majority groups. Consumers who make decisions based on majority opinion, social norms and group-level support for an idea or product are faced with increasing uncertainty as market fragmentation decreases the level of confidence an individual can feel in a product being "the right" socially endorsed choice. Increased choice also increases the risk of making the wrong choice either by supporting the "wrong" product, or failing to identify and support the fashionable 'right' choice. The rise of Apple's market power mirrors the decline of its "Think Different" mantra as the target moved from the innovative and creative elite to the mass marketspace more content with "Think Similar".

Additional risks arise for the individual who engages in the co-production and re-deployment of the co-created product insofar as they have invest ego, time, effort and reputation in the redistribution of the idea as they believe it has a value to others. Consequently, if the re-deployment of the value offer is unsuccessful, criticized or met with loss of social prestige, this can increase the total social price faced by the individual for attempting to engage in the practice again, and raise the price for those people in the social circle who have observed the consequences of the failure.

The need for conformity is also an e-deployment perspective insofar as the long-tail phenomena where a small number of highly influential figures attract the majority of traffic can result in an identifiable 'leader' for the market to follow. The advantage for the e-marketer is the capacity of the marketspace to produce a series of social microcosms where the long tail effect occurs within smaller communities guided by self-interest. However, the advantage of the fragmentation of the marketplace is also the weakness inherent in the complexity of either becoming the market leader for first mover advantage, or finding the market leader for second mover advantage and 'me-too' product innovations.

CONSUMER TO CONSUMER: NEW COLLABORATIVE PLATFORMS FOR VALUE DEPLOYMENT

The development of a C2C marketspace has created a new space for commercial and non-commercial content to co-exist as the prosumer market develops a range of use innovations for existing products through their co-creation activities (Toffler, 1980; Berman et al 2007; Griffiths, 2007). User generated content has become increasing recognized by marketing as a companion to the professionally produced marketer controlled materials, and, more importantly for marketing, as an integral part of the value offering for key influencer target markets.

PRINCIPLES OF USER GENERATED CONTENT

User generated content pre-dates the e-novation movement. As user generated content is only as visible and viable as the reach of the consumer generated distribution channels, it has been less able to capture large shares of the market. That said certain traditional mechanisms have had significant impacts – from the church doors distribution approach in the Reformation period through to hand to hand underground distribution channels for music fanzines in the post-Xerox era. However, as with all physical networks, capacity constraints reduce the impact of the average user generated content product to the users localized social networks or physical geography (Griffiths, 2007).

In discussing the creation of new spaces resulting from the e-novation, and world flattening technologies, it is important to note that rise of the prosumption movement coincides with the market's ability to combine consumption, customer co-creation, and the customer-produced user generated content. To that end, the new marketspace of the e-novation deployment is seen through the consumer's active engagement in the new marketing process whereby the creation, communication, delivery and exchange occurs within and between the marketer, customer, partners and society at large. The AMA (2007) definition respects and recognizes the rising prosumption movement by acknowledging the "offerings that have value" flow through a more complex network of interactions than was acknowledge in the predecessor definitions. From this world view, prosumption becomes the active involvement of the market (customers/clients) in the activities and processes of creating, communicating, delivering and exchanging offerings which have value through the use of the new e-novation marketspaces and marketplaces.

APPLICATIONS OF USER GENERATED CHANNEL

For the purpose of the chapter, prosumption is defined as consumption and production based on user generated co-creation of value which is redistributed to other consumers via user generated marketspaces, or through the access to the distribution networks provided by the electronic marketspaces and marketplaces. The chapter outlines a user generated marketing mix which explores how user generated content uses new technologies to develop marketspaces to create opportunities for C2C and B2C marketing activities. The user generated mix is based on the four process elements of the AMA (2007) definition which form a de facto marketing mix in the form of "create, communicate, deliver and exchange". These four elements are explored in depth; however each must be seen in the context of marketspace-information product dynamic. All forms of user generated content can, and probably do, exist without the intervention of e-distribution channels. However, the user generated content mix discussed below is biased towards the use of

e-deployment as the facilitator for the offerings of value. Without this backbone technological framework, virtual offerings of value could not be created, knowledge of their existence would be limited to traditional word of mouth networks, and, most critically, the market entry barriers would remain higher than the ordinary consumer would be willing to accept simply to share their co-created experience with like minded others. Flattening the world through ease of access to global deployment channels lowers the cost barriers for the consumer, and makes entering the marketspace to share their experiences a valued experience as part of prosuming co-creation behaviour.

Although user generated content is most visibly associated with the advertising and promotion, the strength of the process comes from the user generated distribution networks which use the unique elements of the internet to cluster into communities of like-minded consumers. One of the highest profile user generated networks is Livejournal (www.livejournal.com) which started as a non-commercial network of social diaries between the founding developer Brad Fitzpatrick and his personal social network. As the social network grew through friends of friends, Livejournal used the advantages of e-deployment to create a service based around the duplication and replication of information product (diaries) and the network capacity of the internet to develop a networked community hosting service. Livejournal evolved beyond a user-generated distribution channel into a commercial service provider and now hosts a range of user generated communities and micro channels which are developed around shared interests, fandoms, and more recently, by commercial marketers seeking to engage their consumers in a co-created community atmospheres. Similar co-created social networks can be produced across a diverse range of platforms which provide infrastructure for community hosting, consumer-created groups, and the areas which cluster consumers around key themes, sites or product use experiences.

A second tier of user generated distribution channels occur through the use of the peer to peer networks protocols such as Bittorrent, USENET, (or in the old language Napster and Gnutella). Without regard to the legality of the content being transmitted, the peer to peer protocols create ad-hoc networks between the individual users and frequently depend on the individual members of the network to provide content to be shared across the whole of the community structure. Peer to peer systems also create the unusual dynamic of load sharing within the community whereby the strength of the whole network is dependent on each member contributing bandwidth, costs, energy or content. This is a reversal of the traditional business network whereby the host organization produces the core value offer to be consumed by the members. Blizzard Software's World of Warcraft update systems are delivered through a combination of server-side push delivery (classic download) and peer to peer file transferring which shares the download distribution between players in nearby sections of the internet. The end result is a faster delivery of the mission critical patches and updates to allow the World of Warcraft playing community to reconnect with their virtual world on an equal level.

Peer to peer structures have physical equivalents through concepts such as Open Mesh Wireless Networks which is where wireless internet connections are hosted by a series of users who share infrastructure load, and either contribute by hosting a hub or repeater node to create the mesh network. Devices such as the Meraki (http://meraki.com/) allow for private broadband connects to be securely shared as public wireless space insofar as the Meraki owner can't view the traffic over their public wireless point, and the public user can't view the contents of a private LAN using the Meraki wireless signal.

Open Mesh internet access creates a new level of public commons where individual users contribute broadband access to their community to form a wireless shared commons. This form of community wireless space will becoming increasingly valuable to the offline and online business sector with widespread diffusion of wireless internet capable handheld devices such as the iPhone able to tap into the public wireless commons. Increasing the coverage of wireless networks through community engagement also increases the rate at which public and private networks will provide the multiple redundancy level saturation coverage necessary for the wireless handheld devices to reach their full e-commerce potential.

THE ONLINE/OFFLINE DISTRIBUTION

In addition to the ad-hoc value distribution networks created by the C2C marketspace, traditional value delivery channels also co-exist with the new delivery mechanisms. The classic top-down implemented networks are examined in the following section.

The "home shipping channel" has emerged through digital product distribution of ideas, experiences and services designed to ship to individual desktops, set tops and handheld devices. Software such as iTunes (www.apple.com/itunes) and Steam (www.steamworks.com) on the computer and the proprietary networks of the Sony, Microsoft and Nintendo console platforms provide retail store level supply lines right into the desktops and living rooms of the consumer. To some extent, downloadable content is now easier to access than the equivalent physical products on DVD or CD. However, network congestion, bandwidth charges and the technical limitation of providing continuous high speed data movement have not eliminated the value of physical shipping as a supplement to online ordering.

Expansion of network capacity, consumer technologies and home ownership of high end computer or gaming platforms have developed the capacity to deliver a second layer of virtual worlds into the homes around the world. This in turn allows for the development of a second layer of virtual community structure that creates a series of market places and distribution channels independent of the physical location of the consumers.

The internet is the third channel after radio and television that allows for home delivery of services and experiences without reliance on atoms or physical delivery. Radio was the first home shipping channel that brought the experiential product to the customer under a distributed exchange subsidy scheme – consumer received "free" entertainment in exchange for advertising sponsorships, license fees or related indirect payments. The first phase of home shipping channels, products were largely shipped at the discretion of the supplier. Radio station determined playlists were influenced by music sellers' interests (and the payola scandals). Early developments in television mimicked the radio station model. With limited channel choice, television was a producer's marketplace. To a lesser extent, the global similarity in television program offerings indicate radio and television's producer orientated pedigree remains a viable means for product offerings to be distributed at an audience through the media channels (EurodataTV, 2007)..

A second phase of home shipping emerged through the widespread distribution of cable television, and the promise of interactive television including concepts such as movies on demand and 24 hour licences for "Box Office" movies. These offer a restricted demand side structure for consumers to request product from a preset menu of options. That said the current "movie on demand" structure for home television viewers is only a generation or two advanced from the widespread "in-room" movie systems of the average hotel chain. In many respects, the ideals of the home shipping network were equally parodied and predicted by The Jetsons cartoon series where a push button future promised anything and everything could be shipped to the user's house with varying levels of satisfactory perfor-

mance. The Jetsons creators understood the future would suffer quality control problems equally as frustrating as their present. However, whilst the physical world's push button era failed to arrive on schedule, an alternative one-touch home shipping network developed with the widespread access to broadband and cable internet.

The third phase of the home shipping channel has emerged through the integration of the PC, internet and a range of household appliances to create viable pull-based market structures. Unlike movie on demand which is based purchasing a time limited "access pass" to one of a limited selection of movies playing on loop, the home shipping options of the current systems allow for digital content delivery to a range of different platforms from such as the home computer, games console for PC, and handheld devices such as the iPad and iPhone. The Valve Corporation (http://www.valvesoftware.com/) proprietary digital distribution platform "Steam" (http://www.steam-powered.com) will be showcased as an innovative form of e-marketing channel creation which has been expanded for access by any marketer with a video game product.

Steam was initially used as a form of rights management to ensure copies of Half Life 2 were legitimately owned and registered. From this starting point, the software was also used to push updates and patches to the registered users, and progressively, the software has upgraded into a fully fledged virtual games store. Currently, Steam offers several hundred retail video games, and other digital products ranging from demonstration versions, add-ons and expansion packs, through to videos and trailers for forthcoming game releases. Inbuilt community options include the capacity to manage a social network within the Steam software, and access to a range of game play based matching services – server management, player versus player skill matching, and related services. Steam also maintains a set of sports-style achievements, records and statistical data on each player as part of their community profile – the digital equivalent of a personalised trading card for every Steam player.

Steam still functions as a rights management system. Game ownership is tied to the account login rather than the host machine, allowing Steam users to access the games they own across a range of machines (some downloading required). This form of ownership-right recognition greatly expands the value of Steam, and encourages legitimate game ownership with recognition that the company provides an insurance policy that if the machine is lost, damaged or destroyed, the virtual assets (games) can be recovered from Steam. This form of digital rights management operates in reverse to the usual trend where DRM is used to lock a virtual good to a specific piece of hardware. From a marketer perspective, Steam is one of the quintessential channel mechanisms for e-novative distribution. Valve has elected to open the marketspace it developed for shipping its own products to any game producer through the SteamPowered program. In addition, Valve shares a large amount of the data gathered by Steam's access to its 15 million gamer user base to partners in the SteamPowered program (www. steampowered.com). The Valve system is based on a collaborative value creation platform whereby increasing the volume of products available through the Valve store improves the value of Steam for the organisation by improving the net value of having Steam software installed on the consumer's computer.

Steam represents a classic distribution channel model whereby efficiencies and competencies created by the Valve Corporation in their own channel are leveraged to provide a wholesale/retail outlet for competitor and partner organizations. Whilst top down in nature, the strength of the channel has been the value provided to the consumer through key decisions such as recognizing product ownership for the user rather than the hardware, and allowing the recovery of lost digital assets through the Steam client. In addition, the social network functionality of connecting players in game, and community structures provide additional levels of value which encourages loyalty to the Steam platform.

The Steam model is interesting in its acceptance and engagement of the competitor gaming companies as allies for the development of the distribution channel. With a 15 million strong marketplace, Valve has leverage over competitors, yet simultaneously, Valve is dependent on the flagship products from the competitor companies to deliver the value for the customer. In contrast, a range of other organizations have developed mono-product or mono-organization channels to lock competitors out of access to their market. For example, Apple's steadfast refusal to allow non-iPod devices to have recognized access to the iTunes library has limited the channel options for the non-iPod devices. Although device exclusivity has yet to harm Apple, it has made the prospect of an alternative to iTunes an item of significant interest to developer-entrepreneurs.

However, not all mono-channel software devices are based on trade restriction or device protection. Several virtual specialty stores have been developed as part of the software shop front movement. One particularly beneficial application of software shop fronts is where the organization is the provider of a specific physical product range, and can utilize a combination of e-procurement and physical distribution. The Lego Company has released a virtual Lego software package that allows the user to create Lego toys from a range of original component parts. Whilst fan-based versions of the Lego CAD software such as LDraw (www. ldraw.org) predate the official package by many years, the Lego Digital Designer's competitive edge comes from operating as a micro-toy store. At the completion of the design and development of the virtual model, the user can elect to upload the model to the Lego Gallery site, receive a quote for the parts and pieces, and order the custom kit to ship in an official Lego designed box. In essence, Lego have developed the penultimate combination of user-generated content, and just-in-time inventory management through the use of a sanctioned CAD software package that will create a customized product within the limits of the organization's available asset base. The e-novation lesson from the Lego Digital Designer is based on combining the inventory management capacity of the virtual value chain with an online shop front where purchase transactions are hosted on the Lego website through standard credit card ordering. Essentially, the Lego Digital Designer is an offline procurement software system refined for customer use both as a shopping cart and as a standalone virtual toy kit. The combination of organizational value (ordering, procurement, customized sales) and equal levels of customer enjoyment (virtual Lego kits) produce a unique point of customer and organization co-creation of value.

FUTURE TRENDS

Three trends have been identified within the chapter - the rise of the user generated channel through peer to peer networks online and mesh wireless offline; development of e-procurement/physical shipping in the form of software storefronts such as the Lego Digital Designer; and, the virtual vending machines of iTunes and Steam. These three forms of distribution are in their infancy, and as such, may result in this chapter providing a historical snapshot of a failed venture into the e-deployment. Alternatively it may provide recognition of the forerunners of more sophisticated co-production and deployment mechanisms.

There are two potential hurdles on the horizon for e-deployment. First, digital rights management has been a major barrier to the ongoing success of a range of home shipping options. The collapse of MSN Music and Yahoo! Music stores with their DRM laden music has resulted in the customers who paid for legitimate copies of digital music products being informed that their products would cease functioning. It's hard to imagine a good scenario arising from the marketplace realizing that they can only lease digital objects, and that the lease can be revoked because of the failure of the retailer. , The dominant use of DRM systems seems to have been to hinder the use of legitimately purchased products rather than to increase their value to the customer (Valve's insurance, auto-update and recommended added content network stands out as an isolate case of good DRM in a sea of bad decisions by other firms). Customers may perceive lower risks of DRM and rights revocation from physically distributed objects (even if those can be controlled remotely through DRM systems). This perception will reduce the overall effectiveness of the electronic distribution channels. The market should rightly question the value of product that only works in the store where you bought it, and fails to function once you try to take it home.

Second, there are serious concerns regarding the environmental impact of the virtual world. Whilst early discussion of Second Life included romantic notions of virtual worlds replacing face to face meetings, the energy drain of maintaining these environments may create a larger per person carbon footprint than the various forms of travel it was supposed to supplant. Carbon neutral computing is an issue that will experience increased interest as the environmental impact of the virtual marketspace comes under increased scrutiny by businesses seeking to reduce energy costs, and by environmentalists looking to reduce energy consumption overhead. It should be noted that Google's movement towards sustainable energy use is both corporate social responsibility (environmental impact) and corporate survival (financial impact) as energy costs increase. Finally, the contemporary virtual world environments are still inherently primitive in their interface, visual construction and tolerance for nuanced customization. The promise of the immersive virtual marketplaces of people, goods, services and experiences is still well removed from the current reality of limited graphics and lagged communications.

However, there are also several new technological developments that can greatly increase the potential of the e-deployment. Existing systems such as the Meraki wireless sharing platforms allow for plug and play level simplicity for creating mesh networks that can allow small, medium or large businesses to allocate a portion of their bandwidth to the public domain. Shopping centres, cafes and other locations can use these simple platforms for rolling out a wider wireless network which can in turn increase the value of the physical space by augmenting it with a marketspace capacity. Similarly, peer to peer software currently allows networked computers to share bandwidth loads, and distribute content in a more efficient manner than single source downloads. Given the current technology in mobile phones, Blackberries and iPhones, and the theoretical capacity of Bluetooth to provide short distance ad hoc peer to peer networks, it will be a matter of time rather than technological breakthrough before handheld devices were able to start forming mesh networks with each other to share data broadcasts. As the capacity of standard mobile handsets increase to equal or better the iPhone or iPad or other palmtop devices, the potential for physical spaces to be augmented with an e-deployment network is greatly increased. If the market combines the generation of ad hoc network structures with social networking systems such as Facebook, the augmentation of the virtual social network with physical proximity creates an entirely new marketspace for customer, partners and marketers. This is not necessarily a utopian outcome as social, ethical and legal issues surrounding consumer privacy are yet to be fully realized in the current wired and limited networked spaces. Given the gap between the capacity of a network to reveal intimate details of the user's location, habits and activities and the debate over the ethicality of accessing and using this information skews towards the technology, there are many unresolved issues if "Should we?" to be addressed after the market has already demonstrated that "Could we?" is not

longer an issue. The exploration of these issues is beyond the scope of this chapter, and is an area for further research and debate.

Future developments in areas of 3D rapid prototyping can also lead to advances in converting virtual models to physical products. If the rapid prototyper is considered the equivalent of the photocopier rather than the personal printer, then the opportunity exists for Kinkos, Officeworks and other office supply store chains to add a prototype printer alongside the colour photocopier services provided to the public. Whilst not quite the Star Trek replicator in sophistication, rapid prototype machines and 3D printers bridge the gap between the virtual and physical worlds by producing hardcopies of the intangible. Although Lego currently draws on pre-existing stock to assemble their custom kits, potential exists for the customer to design a custom product in a software shop front, and send it to print at local store for collection, or physical mail out to the end user.

CONCLUSION

The internet provides an unusual set of opportunities for marketers with regards to channel creation, channel management and retail outlets. The open nature of the system, including the dominance of non-proprietary open standards, allows more opportunities to create spaces, venues and channels than can be afforded by the offline world. The internet bypasses planning regulations, space restrictions and other physical world considerations that limit physical goods distribution. At the same time, physical limitations such as data transfer speed limits over optical fiber or twisted pair copper creates a new layer of restrictions for the digital environment. The pros and cons of the e-deployment channels are also subject to change as the network technology develops and evolves, and the transfer protocols adapt to fill the space available in the bandwidth. E-deployment presents an unstable field of marketing technology where promising future developments run into insurmountable obstacles (physics, chemistry, venture capital shortfalls), or where the logistics of the physical world shipping (rising fuel prices) negate the cost-savings of the virtual environment. Currently, the gap between the physical and the real is felt in two opposite directions – shipping costs that exceed the price of the original product by a factor, or download/shipping time costs that exceed the value of the desired experience. Movies on demand which take longer to download than to watch alters the costs of the movie. Pipeline issues such as bandwidth speed, filtering and bandwidth quotas alter the extent to which some of the e-deployment ideas, particularly the Steam style clients, can compete against a physical world store. Physical DVDs which provide the buy-once, own forever access to a movie are still more price competitive than video on demand systems 24 hour leases, or the time limited storage of movies and TV shows on TiVO like devices.

However, as demonstrated by several markets, including the Steam software, digital rights management systems can be used to enhance distribution channels, improve customer trust in the distribution networks, and encourage reliance on the virtual product. As barriers to entry to virtual distribution networks continue to decrease, and customer generated channels arise where likeminded individuals cluster in ready made market segments with self provided distribution channels, the role of the e-marketer in the e-deployment may move back toward the classic AMA (1937) understanding of marketing as the guiding force from producer to market. The only certainty for e-deployment is that the Internet (like radio, television and telephony) has a long period of development before the technology can be considered to have reached stability and maturity.

REFERENCES

American Marketing Association. (1937). *American Marketing Association: An association for the advancement of science in marketing: Proposal for constitution and by-laws*. Chicago, IL: AMA.

American Marketing Association. (1985, March 1). The definition of marketing. *Marketing News, 2*.

American Marketing Association. (2004, September 15). Definition. *Marketing News*.

American Marketing Association. (2007). *Definition*. Retrieved from http://www.MarketingPower.com

Arnould, E. J. (2008). Service-dominant logic and resource theory. *Journal of the Academy of Marketing Science, 36*, 21–24. doi:10.1007/s11747-007-0072-y

Bagozzi, R. (1975). Marketing as exchange. *Journal of Marketing, 39*(October), 32–39. doi:10.2307/1250593

Ballantyne, D., & Varey, R. (2008). The service-dominant logic and the future of marketing. *Journal of the Academy of Marketing Science, 36*, 11–14. doi:10.1007/s11747-007-0075-8

Ballantyne, D., & Varey, R. J. (2006). Creating value-in-use through marketing interaction: The exchange logic of relating, communicating and knowing. *Marketing Theory, 6*(3), 335–348. doi:10.1177/1470593106066795

Berman, S., Abraham, S., Battino, B., Shipnuck, L., & Neus, A. (2007). New business models for the new media world. *Strategy and Leadership, 35*(4), 23–30. doi:10.1108/10878570710761354

Dann, S., & Dann, S. (2004). *Strategic Internet marketing 2.0*. Chichester, UK: Wiley.

Eurodata, T. V. (2007). One television year in the world – 2008 edition. *Media Metrie*. Retrieved from http://www.mediametrie.com/news.php?news_id=48

Freiden, J., Goldsmith, R., Takacs, S., & Hofacker, C. (1998). Information as product: Not goods, not services. *Marketing Intelligence & Planning*, *16*(3), 210–220. doi:10.1108/02634509810217327

Friedman, T. L. (2007). *The world is flat: The globalized world in the twenty-first century – Expanded and updated edition*. London, UK: Penguin Books.

Griffiths, M. (2007). Oxygen: Social intranets, collective intelligence, and government practices. *The Electronic. Journal of E-Government*, *5*(2), 177–190. Retrieved from www.ejeg.com.

Gundlach, G. T. (2007). The American Marketing Association's 2004 definition of marketing: Perspectives on its implications for scholarship and the role and responsibility of marketing in society. *Journal of Public Policy & Marketing*, *26*(2), 243–250. doi:10.1509/jppm.26.2.243

iTunes. (n.d.). *iTunes*. Retrieved from www.apple.com/itunes

Keefe, L. M. (2004, September 15). What is the meaning of marketing? *Marketing News*.

Keefe, L. M. (2008, January 15). Marketing defined. *Marketing News*, (pp. 28-29).

Ldraw. (n.d.). *Home page*. Retrieved from www.ldraw.org

Livejournal. (n.d.). *Home page*. Retrieved from www.livejournal.com

Meraki. (n.d.). *Home page*. Retrieved from www.meraki.com

Rayport, J. F., & Sviokla, J. J. (1994). Managing in the marketspace. *Harvard Business Review*, *72*(6), 141–150.

Rogers, M. R. (1995). *Diffusion of innovations* (2nd ed.). London, UK: MacMillian.

Steampowered. (n.d.). *Home page*. Retrieved from www.steampowered.com

Steamworks. (n.d.). *Home page*. Retrieved from www.steamworks.com

Toffler, A. (1980). *The third wave*. New York, NY: Bantam Books.

Valve Software. (n.d.). *Home page*. Retrieved from www.valvesoftware.com

Vargom, S., & Lusch, R. (2004). Evolving to a new dominant logic for marketing. *Journal of Marketing*, *68*, 1–17. doi:10.1509/jmkg.68.1.1.24036

Section 4
E–Novation Business Development

Chapter 12
E–Novation and Start–Up Companies

Suresh Sood
University of Technology Sydney, Australia

ABSTRACT

Author experiences from working jointly and within startups inform this chapter. Emphasizing the importance of employees achieving unprecedented productivity through working collaboratively and supported by flexible roles and social technologies cannot be understated. Startup employees led by the entrepreneur are masters of embracing complexity. This means the startup team understands cause and effect follow a non-linear relationship with the subtlest of changes potentially resultant in producing chaotic behavior and surprise. For the startup, especially in recessionary times, this means counterintuitive thinking wins the day. In light of this, small expenditures can have a greater impact on developing new business compared with the large budgets available to incumbent players.

The startup employee prefers not to be constrained by the old broadcast model of email instead exploiting social technologies. This includes the use of wikis as an enabler of both interactive communications and repository of company knowledge. A founding myth helps drive new hires and can underpin a service centric focus creating unique customer experiences based on the vision of the entrepreneur and storytelling. A startup is a learning organization improving processes and results on an ongoing basis mirroring entrepreneurship as a learning process. Within a startup, limited processes exist, and core employees embrace next practice to help drive a major source of competitive advantage. Startup employees realize success goes beyond consideration of product functionality or a track record of existing customers. Each business development opportunity for the startup is driven by experience co-created with the customer.

By 2010 the potential to launch a "startup-in-a-box" with an E-Novation framework (Pattinson and Low 2008) supported by social technologies to foster intense collaboration among core employees will become both a reality and essential. Only through a combination of framework and social technologies can startups and founding employees keep pace with the changing business landscape and generate a rapid amount of knowledge to sustain sufficient advantage in the market.

DOI: 10.4018/978-1-60566-394-4.ch012

INTRODUCTION; THE STARTUP DEFINED AND COMPLEX SYSTEMS

Startup company categories (Luczkiw 2005) include self- employed independent consultants, small business owners (franchisees and mom & pop operations) and entrepreneurs. The entrepreneurs see themselves as "dream merchants" (Purewal 2001), formulating plans intuitively (Mintzberg 1983), building emerging businesses rather than extending and defending existing businesses (Baghai and Coley 2000). Most importantly, the entrepreneur capitalizes on opportunities arising from "market transitions and business model shifts" (Fryer and Stewart 2008) in advance of the overall marketplace. The primary focus of this chapter is the entrepreneurial driven company (startup).

Central to the fabric of the startup is the notion of a startup as a complex system and a key property of the entire system, "emergence". A startup behaves as a complex system composed of numerous agents (parts), which can each interact with each other through artifacts including home offices, laptops and mobile phones. The system complexity relates to the unexpected or surprise behavior of the overall system stemming from the interaction between agents arising from connectivity. This system characteristic otherwise known as "emergence" can never be predicted from the individual agent behavior nor understood by decomposition of the system. Therefore, in a complex system cause and effect follow a non-linear relationship with small changes potentially having a big impact and large changes having minimal impact. To this end, complexity has been dubbed the "science of surprise" (Casti 1994) and startups on numerous occasions demonstrate surprises in a variety of markets leading to leadership positions in markets where established players have been operating for decades including the Apple iPhone and the incumbent mobile phone players or Google and advertising agencies.

Arising from author experiences working within and interacting with startups, the key concepts and tools of a startup as a complex system are illustrated in Figure 1. These concepts and tools are now discussed in more depth.

Figure 1. Startup as complex system

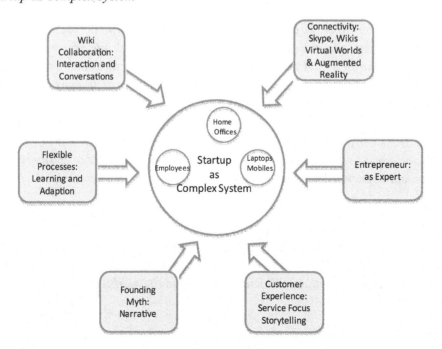

COMPLEX SYSTEMS, SURPRISE AND ENTREPRENEURSHIP

Through the startup stage of a company, entrepreneurs are driven beyond the pursuit of self-interest and are not beholden to traditional macro economic decision-making but a higher calling moving a founding vision to reality. Against this backdrop, complex systems theory offers bystanders a lens to better understand entrepreneurial interactions with employees, learning and processes. Complexity regards the actors (e.g. employees or mobiles) less important than the actual interactions themselves. The interactions between employees provide the organization with the structural capability to achieve resilience in turbulent environments or sustain competitive threats. The interactions represent a feedback loop fueling the complex system or organization. Given the agents are intelligent human beings double loop feedback takes place with agents learning from the results of actions and altering behavior together with other agents to get closer to achieving business objectives. In this manner the startup can be seen as a complex adaptive system (CAS).

Startups when commencing operations are reliant on customer feedback from the outside to provide the voice of the customer and guide product designs. Web forums and email are no longer the only mechanisms for customer feedback a plethora of social tools including Twitter, Forum, Wufoo.com, GetSatisfaction and CrowdSound (a social feedback widget) allow startups like Bump Inc to participate in customer conversations with these tools requiring minutes to setup and ensure "a startup feeds off feedback" (Mckay 2008).

The distinction between complicated and complexity needs to be clear when thinking about applying the notion of complex systems to startup organizations with an understanding "complicated is not simple, but ultimately knowable…complex is not simple and never fully knowable. Just too many variables interact" (Moore 2005). Complicated problems are predictable like assembling an engine or sending a rocket to the moon requiring some degree of expertise in addition to being able to follow instructions. Once a complicated problem has been solved although the solution may comprise a large number of components the approach can be applied to similar problems. On the other hand, a complex problem calls for limited application of recipes or experience with one type of solution providing little or no guarantee of future success in similar situations. Complexity is at best steeped in uncertainty when seeking solutions. An engine of many parts is complicated but predictable in behavior the stock market or weather is complex and the behavior highly unpredictable.

From the perspective of the entrepreneur "organizations are complex social processes, not complicated machines. Organizational outcomes emerge from the ongoing process of conversation and interaction between people"(Rodgers 2006). An entrepreneur understands "Managing humans will never be complicated. It will always be complex. So no book or diagram or expert is ever going to reveal the truth about managing people" (Moore 2005). Hence, the startup employees are less likely to require handholding or written objectives. This compares markedly with traditional organizations with the prevalence of micro-management and central control.

A key hallmark of startups is the dynamism exhibited amongst employees, changing business plans and business models against an evolving landscape of competitors. The startup is a complex adaptive system (CAS) always in motion continuously adapting to changing environments otherwise "It's essentially meaningless to talk about a complex adaptive system [CAS] being in equilibrium: the system can never get there. It is always unfolding, always in transition. In fact, if the system ever does reach equilibrium, it isn't just stable. It's dead."(Waldrop 1992). Whilst the startup can operate in a wide operating range from being balanced to unstable the ideal position is between these two extremes otherwise referred to as chaos.

The entrepreneur is key to ensuring the startup continuously pushes away from equilibrium by creating ambiguity and having internal development groups competing against each other. This avoids the risk associated with a single idealized strategy in a new marketplace and instead explores multiple strategies building on the capacity of the employees and organization to adapt from learning and creates new opportunities. Paradoxically, the startup as a CAS has no command and control structure but is self organizing. Entrepreneurs encourage self-organization to aid the devolution of strategy as well as creating new behavior. John Chambers the CEO of CISCO's learning from a previous employer supports self-organization in that "One person cannot anticipate a market transition. At Wang, we transitioned four times, but we missed the fifth, from mini computers to PC and software. If you don't catch them [all], you leave your company behind " (McGirt 2008).

Managers need to understand "neither managers nor anyone else can control the outcomes that ultimately emerge, even where they have the formal authority to command certain actions along the way…"(Rodgers 2006). Entrepreneurs as "experts" can be successful in a startup by recognizing patterns, seeing the big picture, noticing subtle differences, recognizing leverage points, improvising and both capturing and transferring knowledge using storytelling (Klein 1999). Leverage points provide the entrepreneur with the ability "to create a new course of action, notice something that may cause a difficulty because there are obvious signs of trouble, and figure out what is causing the difficulty"(ibid).

BUSINESS PROCESS AS EXECUTION

Franchise operations and "mom & pop stores" have well defined and documented processes and roles either through the systems offered by the franchisor or the sheer simplicity of the operation allowing ready duplication of similar such businesses. This contrasts with the development of a startup, which behaves as a complex system following a chaotic process of discontinuous growth (Bygrave 1989; Stacey 1996; Mckelvey 2004) making the vision of the entrepreneur essential for guiding the activities of employees.

The startup tends not to have access to readily available processes, as by definition the business has neither been conducted previously or elsewhere unlike franchises or small businesses. Allowing the initial core of employees to conduct business on the fly as well as make things up drives the approach of "execution as learning" (Edmondson 2008) to become the glue for startup culture and processes.

The startup imperative is not to have a fixed mindset (Dweck 2006) and consider execution for efficiency's sake in order to getting things done right the first time but instead a growth mindset (ibid) prepared to take risks and reliant on execution as learning resulting in improvement and evolution. A startup is a learning organization improving processes and results continuously, through sharing new knowledge and expertise reinforcing the notion of entrepreneurship as a learning process based on past experiences of the entrepreneur (Minniti and Bygrave 2001). This is very different to organizations with well-defined business processes but forced to finding only limited opportunities where the already defined process is well suited. The key to business process as execution is learning and adaption through the execution of the process. Building blocks to help cement this notion include individual and collective intelligences, employee collaboration and information. These building blocks help create a learning infrastructure to improve execution and evolve the process in accordance with Edmondson (2008) following the cycle illustrated in Figure 2.

The approach outlined in Figure 2 is refined for the startup. In reality, a startup does not have the luxury or desire to follow best practice focusing on today and enshrined in policy. Instead

Figure 2. Learning infrastructure

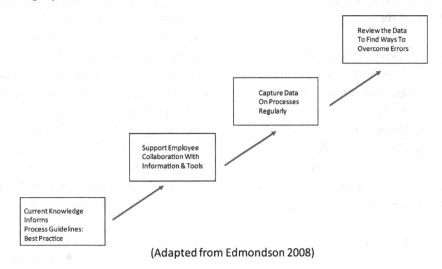

(Adapted from Edmondson 2008)

rather than employees focusing on best practice the focus is on next practice representing "disciplined imagination" (Prahalad 2008) offering the potential to disrupt industries by taking a future focus driven by the mindset of a practitioner to find new ways of doing things. With a company where limited processes exist the core employees embrace next practice to help drive a major source of competitive advantage. This provides the driver to introduce totally different ways of doing business relative to competitors or existing players. Two very different startups serve to illustrate next practice and how the approach is extensible to meeting unforeseen opportunities companies may face in the future.

Zappos a Billion dollar E-commerce company selling shoes and other accessories online with a customer service orientation like no other organization is well beyond startup but serves as an exemplar of execution as learning and next practice. Today, Zappos retains the same company culture, which helped the organization startup. Employees actually write the company handbook (Zappos 2007) consisting of hundreds of employee and partner stories. Beyond the handbook, the company encourages new employees to challenge the prevalent culture and brainstorm new ideas to

keep the Zappos culture "fun and a little weird" (Zappos 2008).

TIBCO like Zappos is an established company with the feel of a startup but in the business of software knitting together legacy and new customer applications. The core values of the company are simple and do not require an employee handbook to communicate these values. Simple rules are the hallmark of a complex system with simplicity driving complex behavior. The TIBCO values are considered to be part of the company "DNA" (TIBCO 2008) and are:

- Focus on the customer
- Demand excellence in everything we do
- Make innovation a way of life
- Focus on individual initiative in a team environment
- Act with integrity
- Have fun!

To support the TIBCO values and the Zappos desire to have the company rule book entirely written by employees both these very different companies can only be successful by tightly collaborating on new ideas and problem solving within their organizations.

CORE EMPLOYEES AND COLLABORATION

Within a startup, the initial half dozen or so employees using a military analogy are commandos who "Work hard, fast, and cheap.... Their job is to do lots of damage with surprise and teamwork, establishing a beachhead before the enemy is even aware that they exist." (Cringley 1996). This first wave of employees " simply put, they create something out of nothing, turning an idea into a product. A commando can literally do the work of a hundred normal employees when they've got the right problems to work on. A start-up without commandos has nothing to sell."(Ibid). Clearly, the importance of supporting these core employees cannot be overstated. This group of employees has flexible roles owing to the variety of tasks required at startup. This includes providing demonstrations during fund raising presentations, developing new business channels including partner sign ups, hands on involvement with product modifications, testing and market launch events.

By their very nature entrepreneurial startup companies have a garage or kitchen heritage launching from a home with little capital and access to barely more than personal computers and mobile phones. The core employees operate in a variety of time zones and are faced with the necessity to improvise and create processes "on the fly" whilst not only having to move beyond launching the business to the identification of opportunities but all of these activities are associated with a sense of urgency (ibid).

The requirement to collaborate (work jointly on new activities) rather than just communicating (exchanging information using any media) amongst employees needs to be very high as "only those companies that build collaboration into their DNA by tapping into the collective expertise of all employees – instead of just a few select leaders at the top – will succeed…" (Fryer and Stewart 2008).

The degree of collaboration in a startup directly ties to the amount of new product innovation as interaction between the entrepreneur who embraces risk and drives growth, collective knowledge and experience of the firm regarding new markets, customer requirements and technology expertise and technology whether from internal R&D efforts or from external technology providers (Park 2005).

How then is a startup beyond commencing operations to conduct business and facilitate high levels of collaboration amongst a handful of employees in times of scarce capital?

THE DEATH OF EMAIL AND RISE OF WIKI COLLABORATION

Without employees having the ability to be highly interconnected, the startup, as complex system is unable to survive and doomed to failure. The connectivity is directly responsible for allowing new thinking to surface across the organization including innovations as well as disseminating learning to allow employees to adapt to behavior based on new knowledge. Not all connections need to be tightly bound as weak ties (Granovetter 1983) have the potential to bridge to the outside world and provide early warning of changing strategies by competitors.

Unlike the traditional established organizations the startup avoids the significant costs of creating a secure email focused communications infrastructure using software vendors or telecommunication services. Importantly, the basis of moving away from email is supported by the previous discussion regarding complex systems. Email continues to underpin the traditional model of the communications process source-message-receiver. This model misses the concept of a feedback loop instead supporting a "push" model. What is required is an ability to facilitate interaction between all stakeholders through supporting conversations. The new startup thrives on collaboration and social technologies seeing email as an outdated form of communication basically using the metaphor of a printed page and the hallmark of centralized control and middle management working in hierarchical organizations established last century.

The use of wikis in a startup supports ongoing conversations through interactivity freeing up considerable time in communicating and preparing supporting documents when directly compared with using email alone.

Wikis allow multiple authors to edit and create documents to build up a body of knowledge. The wiki is participatory in that the formal roles of content creators and consumers do not exist with all participants geographically dispersed. Content is not structured in a hierarchy but instead tagged and any order arising is emergent from the interactions of the users. Wikis have search engines and all attachments as well as pages become immediately available to consumers via the search engine without any formal indexing. The wiki overcomes major problems associated with circulating different versions of documents amongst a group by maintaining an automated version control system.

Looking at the normal usage of email sent with attachments, individual recipients make changes and email back to the sender who collates all the inputs together and creates yet another document. Unlike email, which sends mail to each person, the wiki is born collaborative from day one. The wiki invites people to come together and work on the same text instead of separate copies for everyone. The time saved over logistics associated with using email can be put to practical use in spending more time on creativity. Wikis also allow access to fine levels of granularity allowing security to be set down to the page level.

Another example usurping the use of email is the development of a company directory. Updates are normally emailed to a central group or individual. Allowing directories to be created on a wiki means updates by the people who own the personal information saves considerable time

and ensures the entries are up to date. Rather than emailing agendas and taking inputs from potential attendees the agenda can be placed on a wiki page and everyone can provide inputs along with contributing to the recording of the minutes of the meeting. All that is required to be emailed is the wiki page link so everyone can provide inputs. Employee handbooks with direct inputs from employees as illustrated by the Zappos case study can be generated in the same fashion using wikis rather than developing a handbook with one or two people who might have vested interests. Only through such an approach will a simplification of policies occur e.g. rather than having complex rules an expenses policy may just say any reasonable expense on business will be reimbursable.

Urbis a specialized Sydney based professional services consulting group uses wikis to maintain a knowledge base of projects (Step Two Designs 2009) which have been previously executed and helps save time when generating proposals. Many existing organizations rely upon tacit knowledge held by employees, which is lost when employees finish work for the day or leave the company completely. An unintended benefit of the knowledge base is new employees can come up to speed much more quickly than the previous two weeks allocated for induction and rather than chasing up individuals on email. Sundia a ten person fruit company documents every procedure on the wiki including finance, inventory and marketing procedures (Copeland 2006).

Email is not totally old school and dead. This still provides an appropriate mechanism for 1:1 communication when the recipient is not immediately available or requiring feedback as in the case of a broadcast message. Only when email is used in the types of scenarios discussed in this section do problems arise along with trying to use email incorrectly as a synchronous mechanism expecting to find an immediate reply which creates interruptions resulting in "knee jerk" reactions and a fear of information overload by many consumers.

FREE COLLABORATION TOOLS AND SERVICE

The startup platform of choice uses the Internet, open source and freely available collaboration tools from consumer centric companies including Google, eBay or Yahoo.

Turning our attention to the mass adoption of the Internet free telephony Skype service from eBay, two key differences exist over placing a traditional voice call, presence and directories. Presence lets a consumer know the availability of the party being called whether they are offline, online or away. Thus presence helps contacts and fellow employees know when a party is available to talk or just busy to chat. Directories are no longer white or yellow pages but attached to each user and customized by each user.

Initially Skype provides the ability to make telephone calls across the Internet. A Skype conference can be either a voice or video call and users can automatically start a chat using the instant messaging (IM) capability. Messaging technologies focus on getting information from one individual to one or more others. With regard to IM all participants must be available to achieve real time communications between 2 or more parties.

Automated translation services allow communication with other Skype users without the need to know their language, translating voice calls and chat pretty close to real-time. Chat notification settings alert users when specific words are used and chats can be archived for compliance reasons. Additional capabilities include multi user whiteboards. Startups understand an average Skype user prefers making calls rather than relying on email communication. Traditional organizations continue to prefer employees for reasons of security not to use Skype. Increasingly, Skype has become a mechanism for directly tapping feedback from customers.

VIRTUAL WORLDS AND AUGMENTED REALITY

Employees working continuously using Skype or other collaboration tools from home or in remote offices away from the central office incur psycho-emotional barriers to collaboration by missing out on the social atmosphere of the office (Johnson 1995) overhearing nearby conversations, attending a fellow employee birthday party or participating in a chance meeting with a new customer visiting the R&D team. Many serendipitous opportunities normally arising from such physical encounters can be completely missed. Seeing a fellow employee or overseas visitor can be a reminder to pass on information or setup a future meeting.

Virtual Worlds (VWs) represent computer-generated realities where each user represented by an avatar can explore and interact with other users and compliment video conferencing environments in which fellow employees and customers can meet, greet, socialize, build trust and informally learn. The best resources of the startup can be enlisted to become involved in bootstrapping a team through active learning (Johnson 1995) in a VW in which the team actually engages with customers using the most experienced person to actually help rather than participants in a traditional teaching model. Startups have understood this approach very well in the real world allowing the initial employees to be highly mobile but now VWs potentially makes this very cost effective through orchestrating previously discussed stories of successful customer experiences with different customers and new employees in VWs.

Whilst active learning deals with real time opportunities simulations can prove to be a very pragmatic use of VWs. The Simulated Loss Review (SLR) helps establish the critical success factors (the things that must go right) regarding a concept or sales activity. This is a walk through of a scenario identifying all the things that could go wrong and for each of these an action plan is established that avoids or preempts the issues.

This simulation approach can be equally applied to both B2B & B2C scenarios. Rather than just using online whiteboards to generate the SLR a three dimensional virtual world environment captures contributions to the scenario based on touching, walking, teleporting, quizzes, wikis and forums. Sloodle (www.sloodle.org) combines the multi-user 3D immersive capabilities of Second Life (www.secondlife.com) with the Moodle (moodle. org) learning management system making the vision of active learning a reality for startups.

Innovative organizations are putting VWs to use including Market Truths a New Zealand market research company who has used VWs to source research panel members as well as solicit interviews for research and conduct focus group sessions (Wilson 2009). Gronstedt Group in Austria conducts weekly meetings with customers as well as all internal meetings and project reviews in VWs (ibid). Enormous savings in money from overcoming the tyranny of distance and time allow startups to consider the potential of VWs a reality.

Augmented Reality (AR) converges the physical world with virtual objects augmenting our view of the physical world with streams of information from the Web. Whilst associated with VWs this technology is yet to play an important role in the workplace of startups. However, indirectly this technology has spawned innovative firms stretching talent to the fullest in coming up with innovative uses of AR and mobile technology. Mobilizy develops the Wikitude in which a mobile user holds the Google Android phone camera against a building and Wikitude will provide location and contextual information by linking global positioning co-ordinates to previously geo tagged Wikipedia articles (Mahoney 2008). Yet another "… small team of analysts at a startup called Sense Networks" (Baker 2009) analyses real time movements of people from mobile phone data to predict consumer behaviors.

FOUNDING MYTH

Founding myths are the stories shared by employees regarding the founding of the company, entrepreneurial vision and important sales and milestones in the early history of the company.

The term myth is very appropriate, as these early stories become part of the identity of the employees and are often regaled at annual customer meetings, training courses and employee meetings explaining in some cases why the startup behaves as it does. In the case of priceline.com, the power of the idea was so compelling even for financiers "When I met Jay Walker of priceline.com there was no business plan - there was an idea and there was Jay. In 20 mins I was sold."(Wallis 2000).

Some sense of super achievement beyond what the average person can do associates with the myth and involves beating the competitors against all odds. By contextualizing the myth in everyday activities employees consider the stories to be real and even possible. Vivek Ranadive a well known Silicon Valley entrepreneur and founder of TIBCO relates how he delivers a presentation to his first customer Goldman and key executives over breakfast. He recalls being interrupted by a man who would walk in every time he would began his presentation."The third time this happened, Bob Rubin [the ex-US treasury secretary] leaned over to me and said: 'everytime you tap your foot, it summons the waiter'." (Purewal 2001).

The myth serves an important purpose of providing a model for new employees to follow. This is similar to the hero's journey (Campbell 1949) of setting out on a task and returning home with riches after having overcome superhuman challenges en route. If the myth contains promises of the future when times get tough the stories help good employees to think twice about changing employers. Using the social technologies of wikis, blogs, podcasts along with word of mouth storytelling allows the rapid dissemination and assimilation of startup myths within the company, amongst customers and partners. The founding myth represents an important knowledge transference mechanism in a complex system (startup) rather than using data (Glouberman & Zimmerman 2002).

SERVICE AND CUSTOMER EXPERIENCE

Startup employees realize sales cannot be based on product functionality or a track record of existing customers. Each business development opportunity for the startup is driven by experience co-created with the customer as the starting point (Hills and Shrader 1998) rather than just focusing on product or innovation. Experiences go beyond the commodity-product-services value chain (Pine and Gilmore 1999) allowing customers and stakeholders to experience through emotion i.e. doing, feeling and interacting the product or service being offered. Experiences are not simply entertainment nor do they try to establish the features and benefits of what is being sold. To provide an experience the startup endeavors to do something beyond presenting information making every client event memorable and authentic. Customer experiences encapsulate the knowledge and skills of the startup applied to real customer problems breaking away from traditional goods or "service as product" paradigm transforming to a service dominant mindset (Vargo and Lusch 2004). iTunes exemplifies the ability of a service platform to achieve market dominance with over 4 billion song downloads (chicagotribune.com 2008). In reality, the iPod/iPhone taken together with iTunes represents a hybrid model of service and product (Fryer and Stewart 2008).

Startups recognize large established companies rarely achieve customer focus owing to conflicting requirements. However, the recipe for both large and small companies to achieve value rests with a future of co-creating customer experiences individually whilst globally sourcing talent and resources (Prahlad and Khrishnan 2008) further

reinforcing the notion of a startup as a complex system participating in "many to many marketing" (Gummesson 2004) underpinned by networks, interactions and relationships (Gummesson 2006).

E-NOVATION AND THE STARTUP IN 2010

This chapter introduces a different way of thinking about startups as a complex system of multiple interacting parts and subsystems exhibiting a behavior greater than the sum of parts not unlike the emergent patterns of bees swarming, birds flocking or a school of fish. This approach recognizes the importance of communication not as a traditional means of pushing messages between parties A & B but a conversational interaction between all parties and stakeholders including customers. The startup continually experiments, adapts and evolves in an ever-changing complex networked world through flexibility in processes. Storytelling about the foundation of the startup, stories shared by the entrepreneur and consumer-generated stories about customer experience further inform the complex system as a whole through word of mouth and social technologies including Twitter and Facebook.

"Startup-in-a-box" refers to the provision of an E-Novation framework (Pattinson and Low 2008) supported by a platform of social media technologies including wikis and blogs to allow employees to rapidly build knowledge and collaborate. Industries on a global basis are undergoing structural change and transformation stemming from changing customer demographics, deregulation, globalization and the credit crunch. In order to support the changing need of the marketplace and capture the tacit knowledge of employees before they walk out the door each evening the platform needs to be readily customizable for each employee and extensible to include the provision of audio, video and images.

By 2010 social networks, Virtual Worlds and an integrated learning management system will come preconfigured with the platform to help dramatically improve the on the job learning efficiency of new employees. The "startup-in-a-box" is not an abstraction but a reality and as a minimum when unpacked includes:

1. Skype with messaging to handle connectivity and conference calls with any member of the team anywhere.
2. A Wiki to allow collaboration between employees and an ability to capture the company culture and knowledge from day one.

This minimal capability provisions a startup to be born global from day one. Sundia "the fastest growing produce brand in North America" (Sundia Corp 2009) is a startup having commenced operations with a two person headquarters in San Francisco, marketing offices in London and Singapore and a CFO in India (Copeland 2006). Currently, the Linkedin social network lists nine employees with Sundia. Collaboration technologies allow this new type of startup to commence operations worldwide with minimal effort. Apart from a good idea, an entrepreneur, core employees, wiki technology and adherence to an E-Novation framework what else does the startup require but an ability to harness surprise from complexity?

REFERENCES

Baghai, M., Coley, S., & White, D. (2000). *The alchemy of growth*. New York, NY: Basic Books.

Baker, S. (2009, February 26). Mapping a new, mobile Internet. *BusinessWeek*.

Bygrave, W. (1989). The entrepreneurship paradigm (II): Chaos and catastrophes among quantum jumps? *Entrepreneurship Theory and Practice*, *14*(2), 7–30.

Campbell, J. (1968). *Hero with a thousand faces* (2nd ed.). Princeton, NJ: Princeton University Press.

Casti, J. (1994). *Complexification: Explaining a paradoxical world through the science of surprise*. New York, NY: Abacus.

Chicago Tribune. (2008, December 27). Stopping music piracy. *Chicago Tribune*. Retrieved from www.chicagotribune.com/ news/ opinion/ chi-1227 edit1dec 27,0,7536586.story

Copeland, M. (2006). How startups go global. *Business 2.0*, July, (pp. 107-112).

Cringley, R. (1996). *Accidental empires*. New York, NY: HarperCollins Publishers.

Dweck, C. S. (2006). *Mindset*. New York, NY: Random House.

Edmondson, A. (2008). The competitive imperative of learning. *Harvard Business Review*, (July-August): 60–67.

Fryer, B., & Stewart, T. (2008). The HBR interview: Cisco sees the future. *Harvard Business Review*, November.

Glouberman, S., & Zimmerman, B. (2002). *Complicated and complex systems: What would successful reform of Medicare look like?* Institute of Health Services and Policy Research Discussion Paper, July, No. 8, (pp. 1-37).

Granovetter, M. (1983). The strength of weak ties: A network theory revisited. *Sociological Theory*, *1*, 201–233. doi:10.2307/202051

Gummesson, E. (2004). From one to one to many to many. In B. Edvardsson, et al (Eds.), *Marketing service excellence in management: Interdisciplinary Contributions, Proceedings from QUIS 9 Symposium*, (pp. 16-25). Sweden: Karlstad University.

Gummesson, E. (2006). Many-to-many marketing as grand theory: A Nordic school contribution. In Lusch, R. F., & Vargo, S. L. (Eds.), *The service-dominant logic of marketing: Dialog, debate, and directions* (pp. 339–353). Armonk, NY: M.E. Sharpe.

Hills, G. E., & Shrader, R. C. (1998). *Successful entrepreneurs' insights into opportunity recognition. Frontiers of Entrepreneurship Research.* Wellesley, MA: Babson College.

Johnson, M. (1995). *Managing in the new millennium.* New York, NY: Butterworth Heinemann and Management Centre Europe.

Klein, G. (1999). *Sources of power: How people make decisions.* Cambridge, MA: MIT Press.

Luczkiw, G. (2005). *Jazzin' in the vineyard – Entrepreneurial education in an age of chaos, complexity and disruptive change.* OECD's International Conference Fostering Entrepreneurship: The Role of Higher Education, June 23.

Mahoney, J. (2008, December 26). The 10 best Android apps of 2008. *Gizmodo.*

McGirt, E. (2008). *How Cisco's CEO John Chambers is turning the tech giant socialist.* Retrieved March 2, 2009, from http://www.fastcompany.com/magazine/131/revolution-in-san-jose.html

McKay, L. (2008). *A startup feeds off feedback.* Retrieved on March 1, 2009, from http://www.destinationcrm.com/Articles/Columns-Departments/Secret-of-My-Success/A-Startup-Feeds-Off-Feedback-51751.aspx

Mckelvey, B. (2004). Toward a complexity science of entrepreneurship. *Journal of Business Venturing, 19*(3). doi:10.1016/S0883-9026(03)00034-X

Minniti, M., & Bygrave, W. (2001). A dynamic model of entrepreneurial learning. *Entrepreneurship: Theory and Practice*, Spring.

Mintzberg, H. (1983). *Structure in fives: Designing effective organizations.* Englewood Cliffs, NJ: Prentice Hall.

Moore, A. (2005). Simple ideas lightly held. In Sattersten, T. (Ed.), *More space: Nine antidotes to complacency in business, astronaut projects.*

Park, J. S. (2005). Opportunity recognition and product innovation in entrepreneurial hi-tech start-ups: A new perspective and supporting case study. *Technovation, 25,* 739–752. doi:10.1016/j.technovation.2004.01.006

Pattinson, H. M., & Low, D. R. (2008). *E-novation: An offbeat view of innovation, e-marketing and a new collaborative information platform.*

Pine, B. J., & Gilmore, J. H. (1999). *The experience economy: Work is theater & every business a stage.* Cambridge, MA: Harvard Business School Press.

Prahalad, C. K. (2008). *Inaugural address.* Special Conference of the Strategic Management Society, December 12-14, Hyderabad, India.

Prahalad, C. K., & Krishnan, M. S. (2008). *The new age of innovation: Driving co-created value through global networks.* New York, NY: McGraw-Hill Professional.

Purewal, S. (2001, June 27). This entrepreneur makes you laugh. *The Tribune India.* Retrieved December 27, 2008, from http://www.tribuneindia.com/2001/20010627/biz.htm

Rodgers, C. (2006). *Informal coalitions: Mastering the hidden dynamics of organizational change.* New York, NY: Palgrave Macmillan.

Stacey, R. (1996). *Complexity and creativity in organisations.* San Francisco, CA: Berrett Koehler.

Step Two Designs. (2008). *Intranet innovations 2008.* Retrieved March 1, 2009, from http://www.steptwo.com.au/products/iia2008

Sundia Corp. (2009). *Sundia true fruit website.* Retrieved March 3, 2009, from http://www.sundiafruit.com

Tibco. (2008). *Tibco culture.* Retrieved December 27, 2008, from http://www.tibco.com/ company/ recruiting/ tibco_culture.jsp

Waldrop, M. (1992). *Complexity: The emerging science at the edge of order and chaos.* New York, NY: Simon & Schuster.

Wilson, N. (2009). *Virtual qorlds for business.* Clever Zebra, Q2.1.

Zappos. (2007). *Zappos 07 culture.* Retrieved December 27, 2008, from http://zapp.me/z7427746

Zappos. (2008, December 5). *Inside Zappos culture class.* Retrieved December 27, 2008, from http://au.youtube.com/ watch?v=vq2VZH3jZ7U

Chapter 13
E–Novation in Large Corporations

Michael Conlin
EDS Applications Services Asia Pacific, Australia

ABSTRACT

This chapter explores the lessons learned by large corporations that have been pioneers of e-novation. These pioneers have much to teach us about the opportunities for competitive impact and business value. These are explored within the framework of Porter's Five Forces model. The impact of e-novation on employees and, especially on the employee-employer relationship is explored to reveal possible insights. Although a significant portion of these pioneers are in the high tech sector, many of the insights are broadly applicable to all sectors of the economy. A case is made that e-novation is well on its way to broad adoption in the business community. Recommendations are offered for those wishing to take up the challenge of e-novation.

INTRODUCTION

Pity the poor CIO confronted with a raft of decisions. Is Web 2.0, just a fad? Is this new collaborative platform the real deal or is it a flash in the pan? Are the examples cited throughout this book real? And if so, are they expressions of business and end users driving traditional IT decision making or subverting it? How do you take control of technologies that appear to have little underlying structure, few contractual controls, and costs approaching zero? Are these dangerous developments? Are they inevitable? Is IT losing control over its traditional domain? Is this a business revolution or a train wreck waiting to happen?

For many CIOs, the answers are not self-evident. What's worse, sometimes the technologies themselves are often not evident to executives. A lot of these new technologies are entering the enterprise through the backdoor, with little or no

DOI: 10.4018/978-1-60566-394-4.ch013

executive awareness. Approvals? What approvals? Many of these technologies are free or nearly so, available on a single-user subscription basis. Anyone with a web browser can get access, and they do.

Consider this scenario at a hypothetical consumer products firm.

A product development team is in the final stages of preparing a product for launch. Some team members, who began using Second Life at home, convinced their colleagues to use it for team meetings at work. Because it compensated for the geographic dispersion of the team, Second Life has become their de facto collaboration tool. They use it extensively in their meetings to review product performance, efficacy and safety.

They supplement Second Life with mash-ups of geospatial data sourced free online, combined with Census data (ditto), weather and climate data (ditto) and their own internal testing data from the field and labs. The results all show that a few worrisome incidents can be accounted for by environmental factors. They decide to release the product, and target distribution for those geographic regions where there won't be any complications.

Meanwhile, a few months later…product liability claims begin to come in from the field. A staff attorney from the legal affairs department meets with the research team. Here's how the meeting goes:

Attorney: Please start by walking me through the meeting minutes of your final reviews.

Team: We don't have any meeting minutes. We met in Second Life.

Attorney: What's that?

Team: You know, Second Life. On the web. The meetings were so much more fun that we didn't want to get bogged down in taking minutes.

Attorney: You didn't take any minutes?

About 30 minutes later…

Attorney: You know what, forget Second Life. Just show me your data.

Team: OK, Give us a couple a hours to recreate the mash-ups.

Attorney: Mash ups? What are…hey did you just say "recreate"?" You mean you don't have the original data you worked from? And you can't show me the supporting audit trail?

Team: Heck who needs to store this stuff? It only took us a few minutes to pull it together. The only real delays were the web searches.

Attorney: Please tell me you didn't use uncertified data from the internet.

Team: But it was free! And it's updated everyday.

Attorney: So you can't retrieve the actual data you mashed up in your meetings?

Team: No. hey, where are you going?

Attorney: I'm going to the CIOs office to have a very unpleasant conversation!

Team: Why would you do that? We didn't work with the IT department on any of this. Who needs them anyway? They don't know much about these new tools.

To repeat, pity the poor CIO. In large corporations the CIO either controlled or directly influenced all major spending on IT until now. Web 2.0 technologies are a marked departure from this control, and this stuff is everywhere. Depending on the survey you look at, somewhere between 5% - 10% of employees in large organisations are already experimenting with the WEB 2.0 technologies that make up the new collaborative information platform. If you've got 50,000 people in your organisation then 2,500-5,000 of them are playing with these new technologies now.

Meanwhile, the edge of the enterprise will create an exponential growth of new content and context information. The early signs of this flood are everywhere. Leading companies, who successfully harness this information, will create competitive business advantage. Others will simply drown in the data. So how the heck do you manage a deluge of unstructured, transient information? And while it's fine to claim there will be competitive advantage, what are the real sources of that advantage? Where should CIOs spend their time and energy?

BACKGROUND

Throughout the history of IT there have been periods of innovation and growth followed by periods of refinement and digestion (where the real value is extracted from the innovation). The dot com era was one of those periods of innovation and growth. Based on past performance, the world is nearly through the trailing period of refinement and digestion. Traditional cost savings techniques are losing their effectiveness. Industry best practices, process streamlining, rationalization and reorganization have all been exploited for maximum effect.

Are you wondering what will come next? Here's a hint, the world is entering a new period of innovation and growth that will make the dot. com boom look like a recession. This new phase is being driven by the metamorphosis of the World Wide Web into a powerful multimedia, multipurpose, multipoint, multi-country vehicle for the development and delivery of new products (throughout this chapter the term products is used to include both goods and services).

What's going on here? In "The World Is Flat", Thomas Friedman, (2005) conceptualized and discussed a "flat world" which he characterised as "Globalization 3.0". In Freidman's view, ten "flatteners" are combining with a triple convergence to amplify the competitive pressures faced by businesses, individuals and countries. These competitive pressures are evident in the harsh realities facing executives today:

- Globalization will accelerate.
- Business ecosystems will dominate
- Where, how, when and by whom work gets done is shifting
- Edge technologies and access will explode
- Legacy systems and processes are barriers to survival, let alone success

Globalization will accelerate. Third world nations — from China to India to Russia to others — are challenging first world powers with increased innovation, robust economies and less expensive manpower. Exponentially accelerating advances in information technology capabilities and decreases in costs will continue to fuel the acceleration. There's even exponential growth in the rate of exponential growth (Kurzweil 2001). New competitors and new markets are emerging from this change. In turn, the future will see changes in business from products to processes to business models.

Business ecosystems will dominate. The 'flat world' will amplify the effects of the levelled playing field, severely distorting economics and driving immediate worker dislocation and "leap-frog" strategies. The traditional, vertically integrated enterprise is a thing of the past. Rapid change requires flexibility and variability in the procurement and management of all resources. The performance of a given organization is the net result of its own efforts plus those of its suppliers, the suppliers to the suppliers, its channels to market, its customers, and its customers' customers. It is these collective ecosystems that compete, rather than individual organizations. The literature refers to industry ecosystems by a variety of interchangeable terms including: the Electronically Extended Enterprise, B-Webs (Tapscott, Ticoll, & Lowry, 2000), Digital Business Networks (Cameron, Orlov, & Bright, 2006), and Customer Fulfilment Networks, (Lowry & Hood, 2004). Web 2.0 provides an enhanced platform for collaboration within these ecosystems, thereby making them more productive compared to traditional stand-alone businesses.

Where, how, when and by whom work gets done is shifting. The dislocation of work is evident everywhere. The work force, and work itself, is increasingly mobile. Work is performed in the office, at home, on the road and in the field. Collaboration and teamwork have moved into 3-D virtual reality worlds. The lines between work and play are blurring. Customers are creating products, providing one another with support, and doing back-office work like order entry. In other words, many of the individuals performing work for the firm are no longer necessarily employees of the firm. Nor are they necessarily using the firm's assets to perform that work.

Edge technologies and access will explode. Corporations are spending enormous money on the edge — first contact of IT with practical application — to satisfy the needs of increasingly sophisticated and demanding customers, and increasingly sophisticated and mobile staff. More and more semi-autonomous devices — from PDAs to iPods to RFID chips to memory spots to remote sensors — are being connected to the enterprise and generating a flood of both content and context data. For example, the number 32 is content. The fact that it is the temperature (in C) of the container that a "frozen chicken" is in and that it has been in this container for 5 hours – that's context. The combination of content and context enables leading enterprises to create competitive advantage and superior execution. As this value is realised, the edge will continue to expand creating an exponential growth of new content and new context information to be harnessed for value creation.

Legacy systems and processes are barriers to survival, let alone success. The average business process involves 5-7 different applications. The knowledge worker has to shift from one application to another, transposing information as they go, and all the while remembering where they are in the business process. Forget exception handling be-

cause the reality is when there is no formal process everything is an exception. And the real reason things are in such a mess is that legacy systems are just too hard to change. Legacy systems are also hard to implement in the first place, which creates a significant gap between the capabilities of an organisation's IT portfolio on the on hand and the ever changing needs of the employees on the other hand. In turn the gap entices employees to leverage their consumer-oriented technical tools and services — from iGoogle to SecondLife to Gizmodo —for use on the job. Even in the realm of B2B purchases,

Although Friedman never uses the term Web 2.0, he refers again and again to the underlying concepts and tools. He discusses collaborative concepts such as "in-forming" which he defines as "the ability to build and deploy your own personal supply chain — a supply chain of information, knowledge, and entertainment…. It is about seeking like-minded people and communities." (Friedman, 2005). He discusses the impact of tools under the heading of "The Steroids", citing the impact of digital, mobile, personal and virtual tools for collaboration that enable an organisation to reach farther, faster, wider and deeper. Regardless of the name — from "flatteners" to "steroids" to Web 2.0 — technologies are increasing the pressure to change.

A collaborative information platform, the cloud, is emerging from the traditional E-Business techniques and technologies. The World-Wide Web has metamorphosed into a powerful multimedia, multipurpose, multipoint, and creative platform for development and delivery of new, emergent products and services. Incorporating many new technologies —ranging from teamwork & collaboration to messaging to social computing to special content to mobility and edge — this collaborative platform for E-Novation promises to be critical to businesses who aim to be new industry leaders in the coming decade. The cloud is the next evolution of the Internet.

The new E-Novation collaborative platform is characterised as:

- Mobile: with support for individuals wherever they are, even on the go
- Personalised: for everything from content to interaction to goods and services
- Contextual: adapting to everything from the user's role to their geographical location to their time of day
- Graphical: with information presented visually when that is superior than numbers and text
- Seamless: providing information and tools with a common look and feel even though they come from a wide range of sources
- Collaborative: where team work replaces individual effort and the social aspects of working together are catered for

This platform appears to be leading to a new wave of innovation which can be seen at both well established and emerging internet firms. Household names like Amazon, Google, eBay, and Yahoo have raised their game with a range of new capabilities and services. Wholly new market niches have emerged in response to new internet players like Second Life, YouTube, and Wikipedia. What's more, new technology vendors have emerged — from Skype to VisiblePath to Flickr to Leverage Software — to propel adoption of Web 2.0 technologies — from blogs to wikis to RSS to mashups to 3-D virtual worlds to podcasting to telepresence.

THE CIO'S DILEMMA

Other technology fads have come and gone before. Other innovations have been hyped to similar levels but failed to reach their promise. There have been many promising technologies that failed to deliver tangible business value. And there is no question that what works spectacularly well for one organisation can be a spectacular failure in another organisation. With all this hype, and all this opportunity, what is a CIO supposed to do? For that matter, what should any "C-level" executive do?

Business leaders need to understand if Web 2.0 technologies provide competitive advantage, and if so business leaders also need to understand the real sources of that advantage. With this understanding, business leaders can help other organisations leverage this new technology as well.

Issues, Controversies, Problems

The effort, to assess whether or not the promise of E-Novation is backed by real business value, was informed by interviews of key executives in significant firms in the IT sector – from Microsoft to Sun to Symantec to EDS to BEA to Fuji Xerox to Cisco. These firms were selected because they are pioneers in the E-Novation space. The interviews explored several key analytical dimensions:

- Do Web 2.0 technologies provide competitive advantage, and if so what are the real sources of that advantage?
- How did the pioneers get started on their E-Novation journey?
- What impact has E-Novation had on employees and, especially, on the employee-employer relationship?
- What implications does E-Novation have for policies and processes?
- What was the role of the CIO in realising the promise of E-Novation?

Do Web 2.0 Technologies Provide Competitive Advantage, and If So What Are the Real Sources of That Advantage?

Michael Porter's well known Five Forces model was used to assess the competitive impact of E-Novation. In the 28 years since its original

Figure 1. Porter's five forces model (Porter, 2009)

publication, the model has been validated as the most insightful framework for analysing competitive advantage, under the rationale that competitive advantage is a most useful indicator of business value. The assessment examined how E-Novation affects the bargaining power of suppliers and customers. The assessment also examined whether E-Novation fosters or retards the threat of new entrants as well as the threat of substitute products. And ultimately the assessment led to a view on whether E-Novation stimulates or dampens competitive rivalry within an industry (Porter, 1980).

How Did the Pioneers Get Started on Their E-Novation Journey?

The interviews explored a range of issues and questions: the impact today's E-Novation is already having on employees, employers, and the overall business landscape; how deeply Web 2.0 technologies have penetrated the typical large corporation; how early adopters got started with Web 2.0 technologies, and the typical scenarios for the use of Web 2.0 technologies in E-Novation;

and finally, have the pioneers been able to demonstrate tangible business value.

What Impact Has E-Novation Had on Employees and, Especially, on the Employee-Employer Relationship?

Another way to assess the reality of E-Novation is to explore it's impact on employees and especially on the employer-employee relationship. To this end, the analysis examines the impact of Web 2.0, and the free flow of information it enables, on the traditional balance of power between employer and employee. The analysis examined the effect of Web 2.0 technology on overall employee engagement, particularly how employees spend time on the job, how much they accomplish, and how they feel about their job and their organisation. After all, today's employees are much more knowledgeable and empowered by virtue of the availability of information — inside and outside the company. Leaders need to understand the extent to which they can and should try to manage or control this new "architecture of participation and democracy".

To the extent E-Novation is real, there should be strong implications for organisational leadership. In the past, "leadership" was more often a function of your position than of your ideas. Because of today's evolving technologies, ideas are seen as becoming simultaneously more ubiquitous and more central to leadership. To understand this, the analysis examines what E-Novation means for the next generation of workers and the next generation of leaders. The analysis also examines what impact Web 2.0 and the free flow of information are having on the profile of today's and tomorrow's business leaders.

What Implications Does E-Novation Have for Policies and Processes?

In the event E-Novation is a reality, then one should see implications for changes to policies and processes, which leaders will need to understand. For all its promise, E-Novation technology will likely come with its own set of challenges. The analysis examined some of the potential risks and downsides for organisations. For example, are Web 2.0 technologies a distraction from the business at hand? If so, how does one maintain employees' focus on the company's business amid so many potential distractions? To what extent should companies try to control this new technology? Can they succeed?

The relatively unstructured and uncontrolled nature of E-Novation communications raises concerns for the corporation's "right to operate". When any employee can communicate publicly, who speaks for the corporation? How does the corporate voice retain the same credibility in an era of unfettered expression? Does traditional branding and marketing activity lose relevance, remain relevant, or take on new power?

Further, leaders need to understand what impact these new technologies comprising the "electrical umbilical" — especially the increasing use of mobile phones, handheld devices, emails and instant messaging — have on the quality of communications and decision making. How can executives respond creatively to these issues?

What Was The Role of The CIO in Realising The Promise of E-Novation?

With all this hype, all this opportunity, and all these questions, what is a CIO supposed to do? For that matter, what should any "C-level" executive do? The analysis explored the role of the CIO and the IT Department with respect to the Web 2.0 technologies that underpin E-Novation. Over the last 20 years, each wave of new technology has generally been embraced by the business departments first. Then when the spend has amalgamated to a material level, the CIO has been given the challenge of getting the wave under control. This generally means hardening, scaling, and then supporting the technologies. With that in mind, if E-Novation is real then one needs to understand the best way to approach this collaborative information platform. Or, to put it another way, one needs to understand which aspect is most important: the collaboration or the technology platform? The analysis examined where on the CIO's agenda one ought to find both E-Novation and Web 2.0 technologies. The analysis also gathered some advice to offer CIOs seeking to maximise the value from E-Novation in their own organisation.

Do Web 2.0 Technologies Provide Competitive Advantage, and If So What Are the Real Sources of That Advantage?

The early examples of E-Novation – from the LINUX and Open Source communities to Cisco's breakthrough website – involved broad participation from the entire industry ecosystem. By contrast, many of the new examples, from large high-tech organisations, have been purpose built to serve specific stakeholder communities which are functioning as a subset of the industry ecosystem. Typical community archetypes include:

- supply-side communities
- demand-side communities
- supply-demand matching

Supply-Side Communities

Supply-side communities typically include the employees of the firm and of its suppliers. The value proposition is to improve customer service by giving the customer service team – like field engineers and product evangelists – faster, more comprehensive access to subject matter experts like product engineers. Supply-side communities either support or comprise assisted service channels. Symantec's SymIQ is an example of an assisted channel. It supports the more than 3000 sales engineers Symantec has in the field. EDS, like other large high tech firms, has dozens of such communities, which are variously organised around technologies like.NET and Java, industries like banking and retailing, and service offerings like testing and strategic technology consulting. For example, EDS-Source is devoted to generating and leveraging open source code, whereas EDSipedia serves broad technical community.

Demand-Side Communities

Demand-side communities are typically focused on current customers and/or the industry at large. The value proposition is stimulate demand and general industry growth. This typically involves driving community involvement and disseminating information to the market. Demand-side communities are by definition direct-access channels for customers. The range of examples is quite broad. Microsoft's Channel 9 stands out as a shining example of digital marketing. Jonathan Schwartz, the Chief Executive Officer and President of Sun Microsystems, Inc blogs at www.blogs. sun.com/jonathan. Jonathan Schwartz's blog helps Sun's customers, prospects, the community at large (including Sun's competitors) to follow the thinking and strategies of Sun's management. It is also a strong vehicle for feedback, such as when Sun changed its stock ticker from SUNW to JAVA. These range from code snippets, to complete sets of code, to usage guidance tailored to Visual Studio or other developer environments.

Supply-Demand Matching Communities

In supply-demand matching communities the typical value proposition is to facilitate customer service. These communities often aim to provide a one stop shop for customers. Supply-demand matching communities are by definition direct-access channels for customers. A typical example is Microsoft's CODEPLEX, which provides the developer community, including both suppliers and customers, a collaborative environment to enable sharing of development artefacts. Tibco's power.tibco.com is a one stop shop for customers to find tech forums, download software, enter problem tickets, and contact product engineers. By contrast, Tibco's developer network – Tibco. com/devnet – is more narrowly tailored to the needs of developers and enables them to interact with one another directly.

None of the three community archetypes favour any particular Web 2.0 technologies. Blogs, wikis, instant messaging, virtual reality, etc, all play a role. E-Novation is about more than the Web 2.0 technologies it utilises. All technologies are valueless until applied with specific business use in mind. That application begins with people, process and policy. Web 2.0 technologies then provide the final element of the solution delivering real time information and collaboration. Nevertheless, each of these E-Novation community archetypes can have a different effect on Porter's five-forces.

How E-Novation Affects the Bargaining Power of Suppliers

In the past, competition was played out on a firm-to-firm basis. Although inter-firm rivalry has not vanished, competitive rivalry now plays out on a broader, more strategic scale as rivalry between industry ecosystems. This dynamic links the fortunes of all members of an industry ecosystem, right across the value chain. This linkage provides suppliers with a direct incentive to cooperate and collaborate with the firm, thereby reducing the bargaining power of suppliers. In addition, any well managed firm will carefully stimulate competitive tension between its own suppliers.

E-Novation is being harnessed to enable the cooperation and collaboration, thereby linking the fortunes of suppliers to the larger industry ecosystem. Any firm benefits from having the other firms in the industry ecosystem aggressively selling the ecosystem's products and contributing to technological development. It also reduces technological uncertainty by legitimising the ecosystem through sheer strength of numbers. These dynamics broadly, if only slightly, reduces the bargaining power of suppliers. E-Novation also provides an excellent vehicle for stimulating competitive tension. Electronically published supplier scorecards enable each supplier to see its own relative ranking, based on contributions to the end customer, and thus strive to improve in order to earn a larger share of the business. This concentrates bargaining power into the hands of the supplier that makes the strongest contribution to the industry ecosystem, directly benefiting the customer. It simultaneously makes it less likely that any one supplier will retain that bargaining power indefinitely. For example, any casual visitor to the Microsoft corporate web site can readily find and join dozens of active communities. These communities represent a large, rather ridiculously large, number of suppliers in the Microsoft ecosystem. As long as the firm carefully manages E-Novation, it offers the opportunity to reduce the bargaining power of suppliers.

How E-Novation Affects the Bargaining Power of Customers

For a number of years there has been is an increasing tendency for consumers to react negatively to large corporations. This tendency has been especially visible on the web. The web has changed how people communicate, the speed of communications, the speed and effectiveness of organisation of groups. E-Novation has taken this to a new level of consumer social activism. Customers want to get a view into an otherwise faceless corporation, which used to be a big black box. What's more, customers want a chance to have a voice to the big black box. The ultimate exercise of that voice comes when the customer says some variant of, "you can have my business if you just…". E-Novation can be a strong enabler of that voice, especially when it is used as a means for individuals to organise into large groups that speak with one voice. When a large corporation harnesses E-Novation for an ongoing dialog with customers, E-Novation provides the opportunity to be as responsive as smaller competitors. Without the responsiveness of E-Novation, large companies will be less able to secure their base against small competitors.

Customers have been exchanging views and swapping customer services tales in off-line venues for decades, and in on-line venues for more than ten years. There are several significant differences with E-Novation. First, it enables the firm to directly observe what people are saying about the firm and its products, including both customer and partner feedback. Second, E-Novation enables the firm to put out ideas and invite feedback. This makes it possible to shape the direction of products without having to go to the expense to turn the idea into a product first. E-Novation provides a mechanism for the firm to give people outside the firm a voice so they can articulate their views of key issues. This provides the firm's executives with business intelligence on the wider customer community, which in turn facilitates s a thoughtful, effective and transparent response by the firm. E-Novation also provides a mechanism for the employee voice, thereby giving executives intelligence on what's happening inside the firm. By giving a voice to people inside and outside the firm, and allowing them to have that voice to articulate their views of key issues, E-Novation provides executives with the best business intelligence of the wider market. By providing insight on product defects and brand sentiment this intelligence further facilitates a coordinated, and therefore coherent, response to the market. Taken together, these dynamics improve the firm's bargaining power relative to that of customers as a class.

Perhaps the strongest impact of E-Novation on the bargaining power of customers is seen in the way E-Novation raises switching costs. (Remember that the higher a customer's switching costs, the lower that customer's bargaining power.) The impact varies between direct channels and assisted channels, with some characteristics in common. I'll discuss the common characteristics first.

E-Novation, especially the use of Web 2.0 technologies, improves the customer experience by enabling more interactivity, more flexibility, and more self-directed navigation. Without E-Novation, the customer experience in either channel is pre-programmed, inflexible, and regimented. Typically, the channel support system will have been developed by programmers with little direct experience with the product, and even less experience with customers. The combination delivers a poor customer experience. With assisted access channels the experience of awkwardly designed, automated call menus, coupled with customer service assistants who have no direct experience with the product, is maddeningly inefficient. Exploiting the wide range of Web 2.0 technologies available can significantly improve the customer service experience in assisted channels by making customer service representative simultaneously more effective and more efficient. E-Novation thereby provides a superior customer experience.

In E-Novation-enabled direct channels, customers can conduct product inquiries, enter their own orders, and raise their own service requests all in an interactive, intuitive manner supported by self-navigation. E-Novation can also be leveraged to offer customers more different kinds of direct access channels than was possible prior. All this raises customer satisfaction, and with it raises barriers to switching. An additional advantage accrues since E-Novation makes it possible for the firm to monitor customer's activities, thereby gaining significant insight into customers' true wants, needs and interests. This information can be used to continuously improve both the products and the direct access channel. These improvements represent opportunities to provide value added services to each individual customer. Adding value equates to higher switching costs.

Despite the personal effort involved, many customers strongly prefer direct access channels, especially in the high-tech industry. This is because direct access channels are both more efficient and more effective to use than is the experience of working through an assisted access channel. Over time, repeated use builds familiarity, which makes the customer reluctant to switch to other suppliers because of the effort needed to learn a new direct access channel.

A further advantage to the firm is that direct access channels lower costs because the customer is performing the work that would otherwise be performed by employees. And the customer is, at least subtly, aware of their own investment of time and effort in the direct access channel. Presuming a well designed direct access channel, and therefore a satisfying user experience, the awareness of the investment combines with the effect of cognitive dissonance to raise the customer's perceived value of the channel and the firm. There are limits to this of course; when the self-serve load crosses a threshold then it can become overwhelming and counter-productive. This too tends to create switching costs, at least to the extent that learning one more supplier's system becomes unappealing.

All of these factors raise switching costs thereby reducing the bargaining power of customers.

The economics of using E-Novation for business are compelling, but E-Novation demands that the firm understand the changed sociology for dealing with web-based customers. There is increasing evidence that customer loyalty is substantially lower for those customers who the firm interacts with mainly via the web, compared to face to face customers. What's not clear is whether the web causes the reduction in customer loyalty, or merely makes it more visible and easier. If your use of web technology is problematic or unsatisfying for a customer, they will "vote with their click" and go somewhere else. The early evidence from my surveys suggests that the strong community component of E-Novation attracts more loyal customers, and works to strengthen that loyalty.

E-Novation has also fostered the emergence, and the bargaining power, of two specific classes of customers: customer apostles and customer owners (Kaplan & Norton, 2004). Customer apostles are those customers who are so delighted with a firm's products (whether goods or services) that they actively promote them to potential customers. Customer apostles go one step further. Their identification with the firm is so strong that they actively collaborate with the firm to shape the direction of new releases and new products. Customer owners are particularly important in identifying the ideal new functionality to introduce. And in examples like open-source, customer owners actually contribute direct inputs to the production process. E-Novation provides both customer apostles and customer owners with a powerful, purpose built venue in which to contribute to the industry ecosystem. Their activities improve the firm's products, thereby increasing demand from both existing customers and new products. This has the impact of increasing the bargaining power of these few elite customers. However, customer apostles and customer owners are few in number. And since they tend to strongly identify with the industry ecosystem itself, or at least its products,

they are less likely to exploit their bargaining power to increase the value they extract from the firm. Presuming attentive management by the firm, the reduction of the bargaining power of customers in general more than offsets the increased bargaining power of customer apostles and customer owners. The net effective is to reduce the bargaining power of customers.

How E-Novation Affects the Threat of New Entrants

E-Novation has a mixed impact on the threat of new entrants, as shown the breadth of the themes which emerged from the interviews. On the one hand E-Novation facilitates new entrants into every market. E-Novation makes it easier to gather market intelligence, ranging from market size to significant trends and dynamics to competitive insights to the identities of influential customers and channels. E-Novation also makes it relatively inexpensive to establish a market presence through lost cost Web 2.0 direct channels to market. If you look at eBay, MySpace, Facebook, YouTube and the like, it becomes evident that a business can be architected by a hand-full of individuals around Web 2.0 technologies. While a decade ago you needed considerable funds, a bright idea and a business plan to find a backer then start a new company, today you can do it on a shoestring to start - provided the good idea is a winner. And any idea can be copied rapidly by others. In this way E-Novation raises the threat of new entrants. Unfortunately for incumbents, these new entrants tend to be run by entrepreneurs motivated by the hope of creating the next big thing, the desire to change the world or simply the joy of being their own boss. They are prepared to sacrifice immediate profitability to achieve their goals. They are also unencumbered by the bureaucracy and costly overhead of a large corporation.

Further, a new idea, well implemented and distributed on the web can impact any existing company. It's a mistake to categorise Web 2.0

as just another technology. Small start-ups can now succeed for longer on less than previously. Further, E-Novation can enable a start-up to achieve both the substance and the appearance of scale equivalent to a large corporation. At the same time, clever use of E-Novation enables large corporations to be as responsive as small enterprises, which can be a competitive advantage. As a result, failure to leverage E-Novation may be a competitive disadvantage. Thus for the unwary large corporation, E-Novation raises the threat of new entrants.

By contrast, E-Novation also reduces the threat of new entrants. The incumbents, who comprise the industry ecosystem, keep a close watch for new entrants, but not so they can retaliate against them. Incumbents, especially in growing industries like high-tech, have demonstrated a tendency to co-opt new entrants as additional contributors to their own industry ecosystem, rather than treat them as competitors. It has also become common in high tech industries for new entrants to deliberately position their products, and product architectures, to make themselves attractive acquisition targets for the stronger players in an industry ecosystem. New entrants are also likely to stimulate market growth – new offerings attract new spending – which benefits the entire industry. As a result, the ready availability of industry ecosystems makes them an attractive entry channel for new entrants. Thus E-Novation appears to promote new entrants, all the while offering the opportunity to turn the threats into opportunities.

How E-Novation Affects the Threat of Substitute Products

During the dot com boom, many pundits articulated the view that e-business increased the threat of substitute products by reducing transaction friction. In particular, the pundits stressed the way e-business facilitated product discovery, price comparison and click-through purchasing. By contrast, E-Novation appears to be reducing

the threat of substitute products. E-Novation enables the firm to validate every planned product or product release against demand from multiple customers in advance of the actual release. It also enables the firm to more deliberately filter new product ideas against the firms' differentiators and strengths across the entire value chain. Tibco's "active user experience™" is an example of how well this can work. And, as noted earlier, it has also become common in high tech industries for new entrants to deliberately position their products, and product architectures, to make themselves attractive acquisition targets for the stronger players in an industry ecosystem. A firm that aims to be acquired is hardly a threat. And finally, by harnessing E-Novation to give customers a voice, large corporations can improve their ability to customise their products to the wants needs and interests of individual customers, so-called mass customisation, thereby making those products more attractive and more distinctive. These factors combine to suggest that E-Novation can be harnessed to diminish the threat of substitute products.

Another advantage of E-Novation lies in customer engagement and the social networking phenomena. For example a bank might create a social networking portal for small and medium enterprise (SME) banking customers. This sort of E-Novation enables customers to connect directly to bank advisors, their SME peers, and their own potential customers especially in "long tail" businesses. Each E-Novation social network is noticeably different due to the difference in network members. Of course any particular network can parlay a modest advantage into long term dominance as can be seen in LinkedIn, EBAY and YouTube.

How E-Novation Affects Competitive Rivalry Within an Industry

E-Novation offers the firm an effective mechanism through to signal its intentions, as can be seen in the following example. Jonathan Schwartz's blog helps Sun's industry ecosystem follow the thinking and strategies of Sun's management. Similarly, Microsoft will provide strong commitments from leaders in terms of products and services directions. While at first glance this appears to make the firm more vulnerable, the opposite is actually true. This sort of signalling plays a key role in preventing costly confrontations in which the firm may have little choice but to engage in price wars and similar retaliatory measures. Effective signalling through E-Novation channels makes it easier for the firm to stake out a position of differentiation, thereby enabling other firms to seek clearly alternative positioning. The ability to avoid direct, point-for-point competition can thus reduces competitive rivalry within an industry, all the while offering customers a greater breadth of choice of suppliers, each with its own strategy for differentiation.

E-Novation communities take some time to establish and make productive. Note that the key word here is community, not technology. This learning curve creates something of a "first mover advantage", putting pressure on competitors to respond quickly and aggressively or fall behind. Once recognised, this dynamic increases competitive rivalry within the industry.

One important mechanism, for moderating competitive rivalry, is market signalling of corporate intent. One of the challenges of E-Novation is that the collaborative and, at least potentially, unrestrained flow of information can obscure the corporate voice. This is especially likely in firms just starting to experiment with E-Novation. It is necessary to create a shared sense of purpose between employer and employee, such that collaboration and networking improve productivity. Greater employee engagement, and greater commitment to the organisation as well as its goals and plans, provides for a self-governing approach that obviates the need for external controls over the technology. This is another learning curve that must be scaled in order to master E-Novation. Until it is scaled, there is significant potential for

a diminished "voice of the corporation" which in turn can diminish the chance for market signalling to moderate competitive intensity.

One of the subtlest and least discussed forms of competitive rivalry is the rivalry for the best employees. Even when there is no shortage of potential employees, the best employees are always in short supply. Although competition for the best employees is rarely a matter of direct rivalry, winning the competition is still a key to the long term success of the firm. E-Novation plays a role here too. In large corporations in the high tech industry, the workforce shows a broadly characteristic viewpoint that the latest technology is just a baseline expectation in the workplace. Many of the executives interviewed stated the view that their ability to offer the latest Web 2.0 technologies plays a key role in helping them attract the best employees. This will be increasingly true for the next generation of workers. They will have radically more aggressive expectations for enabling technologies. The generation of workers now entering the workforce have grown up with technology. They see technology as just another part of their everyday lives. It's nothing special or new. By contrast, they view the lack of the latest Web 2.0 technologies in the workplace as a real disappointment. If a corporation provides technology choices in the way people conduct work then the corporation has a better opportunity to attract future employees.

How the Pioneers Got Started on Their E-Novation Journey

The interviews asked executives in large, high tech organisations how they got started using E-Novation and Web 2.0 technologies. Was it a response to customer pressure? Was it a response to a response to partner or supplier requests? Was it a response to employee pressure? Was it a response to a leader's vision? Was it some mix of the above? Interestingly, every organisation gave a different answer. At first there appeared to be no broad pattern, but over time a pattern emerged. In each case the emergence of E-Novation was a direct reflection of the culture and climate of the corporation itself. In hindsight this was not such a surprise given the collaborative characteristics of E-Novation. Here are a few examples.

At Sun, E-Novation had two simultaneous sources. Sun's executives were early innovators and saw themselves as industry leaders providing the vision to the market at large. It was also a grassroots emergent behaviour, driven by the technical staff's requirements for communication and collaboration. The technical teams launched wikis for managed sharing of information internally three to four years ago, without the help of the IT department mind you, while at the same time Sun's leaders were blogging to customers. Results have been excellent in both areas. Nearly all employees utilise Web 2.0 technologies, quite matter-of-factly, during their work. Over 4500 staff actively write their own blogs. External blogs are available at www.blogs.sun.com and a significant numbers of blogs are only accessible from within Sun's own network (for more secure discussions). Executive blogs are a favoured form of announcements. Not surprisingly, ninety to one hundred percent of employees read blogs. All employees use email and most use calendaring. Sharepoint is widely used.

At Symantec, several initiatives signalled the foray into E-Novation – the Symantec Technology Network which is a direct channel and SymIQ which is an assisted channel. The Symantec Technology Network involves customers (it's a direct access channel). SymIQ supports an assisted channel - the more than 3000 sales engineers in the field. Before SymIQ, these field engineers were spending a significant percentage of their time looking for information. Without SymIQ, they found it difficult to judge how recent the information was, or what its quality was. SymIQ solved these problems, providing repository and search capabilities. Where there was once no community mechanism to support collaboration

between the field engineers, communities of interest are now being layering onto SymIQ. And of course, despite a strong focus on content and community, the technology savvy users of SymIQ are regularly pushing new technologies into use. Currently more than two thirds of employees are users of Web 2.0 technologies. For example the Vice President of Engineering in EMEA (Europe, Middle East and Africa) maintains a blog. And quite typically, while executives initially envisioned the E-Novation communities as hub-and-spoke models, the users turned them into peer-to-peer models by actively taking control for increased business impact. For example, a Latin American E-Novation community has started using the community tools for career planning and self-directed project management of virtual teams. They have also adopted the tools for self-designed status reporting to executives.

At Tibco, E-Novation is being harnessed to support the engineering community, the sales community, and the marketing community. Absolutely 100 percent of field (customer facing) staff, and more than 60 percent of all staff, are involved in E-Novation. Communities include Tibco.com/devnet for developers and power.tibco.com for customers. Both mashups and blogs are common.

At EDS All employees use email and calendaring. Sharepoint is very widely used, as is Microsoft Office Communicator. Video conferencing is widely used. "Folksonomies" and other tagging approaches have been in use for years. EDS has dozens of active communities and forums dedicated to technical and product related subject matter. Several wikis are in place, and in most instances the wikis were used to replace previous tool choices for longstanding E-Novation communities of interest. There is also a long standing open source community — EDSource — which applies Open Source best practices and tools within EDS. The EDS Source project represents a corporate vision for leveraging the concepts of the Open Source community development process to create a new way of developing internal EDS

Assets as well as influencing how the corporation delivers to customers. EDS Source provides an environment that channels the power of the EDS community to support and lead EDS through it's evolution into an Agile organization. By leveraging the Thought Leadership of a large and diverse community, EDS is demonstrating leadership in the adoption of Open Source principles to deliver value to the corporation and its customers. It is also demonstrating industry leadership in re-thinking the software delivery process.

As you can see from the previous examples, culture and climate are big issues in the success of E-Novation collaboration spaces. So where a Bank culture might be antithetical to open tools and collaboration, by contrast in a non-hierarchical, deliberately challenging culture where rank rarely plays and responsiveness is expected, like at Cisco, then collaboration spaces are more firmly embraced.

These examples of successful E-Novation pioneers provide important insights for organisations seeking to emulate that success. The next section examines the insights, beginning with the implications for the employee-employer relationship.

The Impact of E-Novation on Employees and, Especially, on the Employee-Employer Relationship

Enovation is having a road range of impacts on the employee-employer relationship. These sometimes conflicting impacts can be seen in:

- new demographics in the workforce
- new employee expectations of employers
- the reinforcement of corporate climate and culture
- new forms of contribution and value creation
- new and shifting, definitions of structural power and authority
- new challenges in training

New Demographics in the Workforce

The first, and perhaps most dramatic impact is in creating a workforce that is increasingly split, frequently on demographic terms, into two groups. (The following characterisations are only broadly representative of groups. Any given person must be treated as an individual.) The first group comprises those employees who use technology because the employer requires it for the job. The second group comprises those employees who default toward the use of technology in work and non-work situations and who, at least partially, evaluate an employer's attractiveness on the basis of the ready availability of technology tools. There is an inflection point, age wise, in the population as a whole. To oversimplify slightly, Gen Y (see box *Recognising Gen Y*) have grown up with the internet in the same manner as the older individuals grew up with the telephone. Call them Gen Y, echo baby boomers, Millenials, iGen, the internet generation, or what you like. They are different from the preceding demographic groups. Gen Y, expect, demand and use Web technologies more intensely - and expect the same of others. In all walks of life, Gen Y are in keen for always connected, always personal, mobile experiences. In the future it is likely that business leaders that cannot leverage Web 2.0 technologies will be viewed harshly by their younger staff, and eventually all staff.

Recognising Gen Y (Lancaster & Stillman, 2003)

- Group statistics
  - Born: 1980 – 2000
  - Age in 2009: 9 – 29 years old
  - Size: 76 million in US
- Characteristics
  - Realistic and upbeat
  - Confident and strong self-esteem
  - Impatient and eager to live life "now"
  - Not afraid to switch jobs
  - Pro-education and goal-oriented
  - Always-connected

- ○ Global social networks
- ○ Socially conscious and highly tolerant
- ○ Everything is interactive and games are everywhere
- ○ Family-centric

New Employee Expectations of Employers

E-Novation is changing the definition of what it means to be an employer-of-choice. Let's acknowledge that in most sectors, human capital is the key factor of productivity. No corporation can function without an adequate supply of knowledge workers. Even in an economic downturn when more workers are available, the top performing knowledge workers are in short supply even for a firm that is widely regarded as an employer-of-choice. E-Novation offers employers direct value in "the war for talent". People coming into the workforce now — your future recruits — have expectations that can't be satisfied without the latest technologies. The smarter and more talented they are, the higher their expectations are. Providing E-Novation tools makes it easier to attract and retain the best people. Thus E-Novation is redefining what it means to be an employer of choice.

The Reinforcement of Corporate Climate and Culture

E-Novation reinforces the corporate climate and culture thereby amplifying the employer-employee relationship for better or worse. Culture is a big issue in the success of collaboration spaces (which are more than just tools); a bank culture might be antithetical to open tools and open collaboration. This isn't surprising given how onerous regulatory requirements are. Contrast that with Cisco, a sales and advanced engineering firm, which has a non-hierarchical, deliberately challenging culture where rank rarely plays, and responsiveness is expected. The attitude is, do then seek approval. At Cisco collaboration spaces are firmly embraced.

As another example, Tibco is a traditional engineering-based technology culture. The corporation values merit above all else. With only 2000 people, Tibco gets work done with high performing teams, in a collegial, academic atmosphere. Collaboration is highly valued. E-Novation and Web 2.0 foster this culture of collaborative innovation, which makes tomorrow's leaders easier to find.

New Forms of Contribution and Value Creation

E-Novation is introducing two new significant, if informal, leadership roles to corporations. The first role is the "facilitator". Let me try to define the role of the facilitator by analogy. The publishing business requires both authors and editors. Authors produce value directly by writing articles, also know as editorial content. Editors produce a derivative form of value by combining editorial content and advertising content into a given issue of a magazine. A similar dynamic exists in the entertainment industry. Actors, writers and special effects professionals produce value directly. Directors and producers generate derivative forms of value comprising TV shows and movies. Returning to large, high tech corporations, engineers produce direct forms of value as in the example of application code. "Facilitators" generate derivative forms of value. For example a skilful architect may combine multiple components of application code into a new system or use one component to meet the needs of multiple projects. Another example is when a clever employee launches one or more new offerings based on that application code. As you can see from these examples, "facilitators" do not so much generate original content as merge it into new forms. Both roles are needed. So how does a manager measure and reward both? High tech corporations like EDS and Symantec have Distinguished Systems Engineering (DSE) programs which recognise and reward outstanding performance by engineers. These programs intentionally include direct creators of value and equally intentionally exclude creators of derivative forms of value. E-Novation pioneers are coming to the realisation that new approaches are needed because the value is not just in the creation of the original work. The derivative work of "facilitators" is where a lot of the value creation happens today. Management is just learning how to recognise and manage these contributions. Meanwhile the new tools make the role of the "facilitator" easier through networked communication and collaboration. The tools also make it easier for corporations to develop such roles in the first place., and easier to integrate such roles into organisational designs.

The second new E-Novation leadership role is the "connector". These are the people you go to because they'll have the goods — the information or contacts you need to get things done. Outside the corporation, stand-alone E-Novation communities like LinkedIn are built around a recognition of the value of "connectors". Inside the E-Novation pioneers, "connectors" are more likely to be an influencer, rather than a formal or positional business leader. They aren't in key positions in the org chart, nor do they manage large budgets. Nevertheless E-Novation pioneers highly value "connectors" for their contributions. Today's business leaders are learning how to use E-Novation to identify and collaborate with the "connectors" and "facilitators". As with the "facilitators", management are just learning how to recognise, manage and reward the contributions of "connectors". With E-Novation, it is now easier to identify the positions and make them more visible across the wider organisation.

Along with new forms of contribution and value creation, E-Novation brings a new form of a traditional challenge for managers. Recognising and rewarding individual's contributions is a bigger challenge with E-Novation than without. Even without E-Novation, in any large, high tech corporation a significant plurality of work is performed in extended processes that involve cross-functional teams working on projects. Either the entire process is functional or the entire process is non-functional. Either the entire team is productive or the entire team is un-productive. Either the entire project is successful or the entire project is unsuccessful. Isolating the contribution of any one person or element is a non-trivial challenge. Now add in the complexities of E-Novation communities using highly interactive Web 2.0 technologies producing large volumes of transient data. Given the highly collaborative nature of this work profile, and given the contributions of the "connectors and "facilitators", how can employers measure what any one employee actually accomplished? In any meritocracy, accomplishments drive reward decisions. Yet the effect of E-Novation can be to make it more difficult for a manager to separate the accomplishments of one individual from another. Poorly managed, this challenge strikes at the heart of a meritocracy.

New and Shifting Definitions of Structural Power and Authority

The last statement in the previous section comprises a little recognised but powerful revolution. E-Novation reinforces the long-standing trend away from hierarchy and toward a collaborative style of organisation by enabling all parties to go around the chain of command in all directions. That includes a new direction, from inside the corporation to outside the corporation, which is further redefining the nature of the larger employee-employer relationship by giving a much broader cross-section of employees the opportunity to directly interact with the market. This free flow of information in all directions is powerful. Communication through E-Novation, and more broadly through Web 2.0 technology, is instantaneous. Communication channels can be much more efficient, but also much less controlled. Fact spreads quickly, fiction spreads quicker. This can create a management challenge. When every employee's view can find public expression, every employee needs the ability, and good judgement, to identify suitable content to communicate. The ability to write succinctly and unambiguously becomes more important as well. When communication is instant (for example through blogs and podcasts), misunderstandings and errors are dispersed instantly to an enormous audience.

With or without Web 2.0 technologies, employees have to learn to police their own behaviour, and to limit it to business. This, along with the self-service, self-paced and collaborative aspects of E-Novation are pushing individuals to be their own managers and to reflect the organization's values. Once an employee just had to be good at their own job. With E-Novation they now have to be good at their manager's job too. When employees manage themselves, hierarchies become flatter and more permeable. Power flows downward.

E-Novation is thus creating a workforce that is increasingly independent, autonomous, and self-managing. For example, the culture of firms like Microsoft attracts the type of people who enjoy multi-processing; people who relish the challenge of hunting down lots of information and producing lots of information; people who are attracted to a collaborative working style emphasising teamwork; people who prefer a merit-driven, collegial and collaborative atmosphere. For instance, Microsoft's CODEPLEX – a collaborative environment to enable developer community to share and contribute development artefacts – is highly self-organised, similar to FaceBook. As one Microsoft executive put it, "It's the measures of performance that matter. We hire senior professionals who know how to do the job effectively in our culture. It's their job to manage themselves." Everyone at Microsoft twitters, IMs, blogs, and uses forums. The team is Web 2.0 savvy. Feedback in performance reviews reveals that staff feel empowered to execute, they also feel it's very cool to work at Microsoft, because they can choose their own tools, and project their own image in the communities. This is a primary reason they were attracted to working for Microsoft as an employer.

Executives at Sun see the morale and involvement of staff increased by the effective use of Web 2.0 technologies. Things like Instant Messenger (IM) allow more productive work through enabling people to interact in new ways with lesser interruption and disruption to their work process. For example while responding to my survey, one executive acknowledged engaging in a number of IM discussions on the side. Some were in-coming solicitations of information or help. Some were out-going solicitations seeking to confirm some opinions expressed in the survey response. In efficiency terms, probably 3-4 minutes of personal attention replaced roughly 30 minutes of phone calls.

There is some controversy about how much Web 2.0 technology is too much Web 2.0 technology. The survey explored the impact of the "electrical umbilical" — the increasing use of mobile phones, handheld devices, emails and instant messaging — on the quality of communications and decision making. Think of the blackberry; many people are now tethered to their job. Any global organisation operates 24 hours a day. E-Novation enables the creation of a larger community transcending location and time constraints thereby also improving quality of communications and decision making. Arguably the combination of 24 hours a day plus global diversity should equal higher quality decision making. On the other hand, many of the executives interviewed typically get 200-300 emails and messages a day. There is also a growing, and in some corporate cultures an explicit, expectation of expeditious response. This can easily lead to a self-imposed pressure to respond quickly. Which in turn can easily lead to a reduction in thoughtful, considered replies. Easy conclusions, about the net value of the technology, are proving elusive.

An executive at Microsoft articulated a positive view of the "electrical umbilical". Having a device that is always connected is not a disruption if you have the discipline to set bounds that separate work from family life. Instead it can improve the quality of life. For example an always connected device can provide closure on work assignments so attention can be turned to family life without lingering anxieties. And as a manager, it's a great source of information that enriches decision making by tapping into the reasons, reactions, and emotions in the team. The fact that communication is now instant, and instantaneously two way, can be used to improve the quality of communications. Similarly, the process of decision making can either improve through access to more opinions / feedback / information, or it can stall completely due to the flood of opinions / feedback / information and indecision.

The electrical umbilical can put us much more in touch with the pulse of the business, improving our situational awareness. Taken too far, it can create a little bit of attention deficit disorder, to the detriment of analysis and deep thinking. To the extent that E-Novation makes one more interrupt driven, which is good for responsiveness, it also tends to drive out structured time to think and analyse. The challenge is to drive a balance between the two, in order to get depth of thought. E-Novation can deliver vastly more information about competitors today compared to yesterday. But is more information the answer? Consider the example of the Cuban missile crisis. The poor quality of the photos was offset with excellent analysis. Today it's often reversed, and the same is true for business. Data is simply not a substitute for analysis. Hierarchical position has always been won by recognition of ones ideas and ability to think. If there is a difference under E-Novation, it is in how much easier it is for a web literate individual with good ideas to become more visible to a wider audience more quickly. The result may be that failure to properly harness E-Novation might prevent an individual, who might have succeeded in the past, from becoming a leader of tomorrow.

Here is one final thought on structural power in E-Novation. Decision making in E-Novation communities is really consensus building. This can lead to either helpful consensus or to narrow views. The opinion of peers is very important. People want to achieve the level of respect that comes with asking and achieving insightful questions. This dynamic can lead to group-think and peer pressure when the community has too strong a set of views or too narrow a set of perspectives. As with many things, a sense of balance and proportion is useful. A well managed firm will find ways leverage the E-Novation architecture of participation and democracy to increase the feeling of ownership by their staff.

New Challenges in Training

One additional consideration for future adopters of E-Novation is the potential need to teach people to effectively use the technologies. Remember the demographic forces mentioned earlier. The internet used today (especially the WWW browser interface) is really less than 15 years old. For much of the population, it is less than a decade old. With Web 2.0 technologies, the change employees are facing is momentous. One typical challenge is the growing need to multi-task. The effective use of these technologies sometimes requires you to be able to cope with writing a report or presentation while also surfing the web (sometimes related to the other task, sometimes not) while also participating in one or more IM sessions, etc, etc. This insight pre-dates Web 2.0. Very few people cope with the volumes of email they receive. Few are able to adequately use internet search engines. The shear volume of "content" that people have to deal with, whether push or pull, requires education to deal with it effectively. Otherwise the inability to cope is a drain on employee productivity or focus. Not every corporation adequately teaches people how to get the best from the web. This can cost a great deal in lost efficiency and effectiveness. To paraphrase Henry Ford: "If you need quality improvements and don't deploy them, you pay for them without getting them." (Kaplan & Norton, 2004). Even teaching people to use email properly has an ROI. As an employer, you cannot assume that effective use of Web 2.0 technology is an innate ability of staff, nor assume that all of your staff have the ability to effectively communicate with it. The opportunity that E-Novation opens for your business — whether it is in productivity and participation by your staff or in winning and holding your customers — does not come free of charge. Without support and training, E-Novation can estrange employees.

The Implications of E-Novation for Policies and Processes

The prior section explored the effect of E-Novation on the employee-employer relationship. Given the broad range of impacts, it is appropriate to explore how leaders should respond in terms of policy and processes. Where they exist, policies frequently lag the uptake of the technologies. The majority of the leaders surveyed downplayed the need for new policies to control E-Novation. As one observed, it's difficult to policies when lawyers and the law haven't addressed this space yet. Another leader suggested that instead of trying to control E-Novation, learn how to live with it and exploit it.

To this end, management faces at least three potential policy issues:

1. Maintaining credibility and consistency of information
2. Protecting sensitive information
3. Maintaining employees' focus on the company's business amid so many potential distractions

Maintaining the Credibility and Consistency of Information

One of the biggest challenges in the Web 2.0 era is determining the voices of authority from the opinion of individuals. One widespread problem is how to distinguish fact from fiction, information from noise. Judging from the experience of

E-Novation pioneers, credibility is most closely tied to the office and corporate station of the voice. For example, at Sun Jonathan Schwart's blog would have more authority than many others on general strategy and corporate messages, whilst someone like Brian Cantrel (one of the inventors of dTrace) would hold sway over that topic. Secondarily, credibility comes from the individual "voice" and its history of reliability. The tertiary factoring determining credibility is the control exercised (or freedom allowed) by the corporation over content. For example, Sun allows employees fairly free reign within the bounds of common sense, decency, strategic interests, and confidentiality.

Many early adopters have chosen to encourage personal freedom of expression. They also "walk the walk" with lots of formal and informal information sharing sessions aimed at enabling and encouraging E-Novation. Most E-Novation communities, in fact all in the sample examined, explicitly put their trust in the community to deliver quality. Particular attention is paid to facilitating the use of reputation and peer review — through approaches like rating systems — to drive quality and attribution for contributions. The communities tend to be highly self-organised, although it is not unusual to find a moderator function present. This moderator, a combination of "connector" and "Facilitator" is an informally recognised way to maintain focus on goals and outcomes.

Many early adopters, like Sun, have a number of internal policies that encourage employees to participate in E-Novation communities and use Web 2.0 technologies. These range from encouraging the authorship of Blogs to the group use of Wiki's like "a Wiki for all things related to Customer Engineering" as a means of consolidating and sharing the collective wisdom from the engineering community within Sun.

Protecting Sensitive Information

With all of the information being exchanged across organisational boundaries, there are bound to be some concerns about whether employees are exchanging appropriate information. Web 2.0 technologies make it easier for people to find the information even if they don't have the judgement to handle it properly. The technologies also make it easier to disseminate that information. With or without E-Novation, the vast majority of leakage is by mistake. Web 2.0 technology can help with that by prompting people with questions when they send or distribute things. It is also useful for corporations to set communication and collaboration protocols. Any collaborative community will benefit from sharing a set of standards. They also benefit from deliberate education and communication. Employee education has long been a preferred tactic in the effort to protect sensitive information.

There is a related risk of misinformation being disseminated when different community members submit content. The pioneers have built in governance to review content for accuracy, as well as brand-consistent look-and-feel. Risk cannot be eliminated, although it can be managed. Recognise that there is sufficient benefit in E-Novation to justify the managed risk.

Maintaining Employees' Focus on the Company's Business

In part, this concern is a generational issue, strongly correlated with the demographic split mentioned earlier. (As before, these characterisations are only broadly representative of groups. Any given person must be dealt with as an individual.) Leaders, frequently members of the older demographic group, are generally sceptical of technology. They were also educated and trained in a command-and-control mindset. Many of these leaders voiced the same concern with distractions when the World Wide Web emerged, with some justification as

it turned out. The novelty factor did lead some workers to waste time emailing jokes and cartoons. But the novelty factor has long worn off and there is little sign of it reappearing with Web 2.0 technologies. (Although to be fair I should acknowledge that as a Chief Technology Officer I get to experiment with a lot of new technology, so I may be a bit jaded. Others may find a great deal of novelty in Web 2.0 technologies.) The other half of employees were born after 1980. This is the digital generation. As stated earlier, these people come into the workforce with expectations of using the web 2.0 technologies. Most are self-motivated and highly driven. They take a job because they want that specific job, not just any job. Since they do what they like and they like what they do, they maintain their own focus on the company's business. What managers need to think about is how to recruit and train people who will behave properly with these tools and be productive. This is a better way to achieve an effective and efficient work place than to try control the technologies.

Ironically, it appears that the best way to suppress demand for E-Novation is to dictate the use of Web 2.0 technologies. Issuing a mandate to use LiveMeeting, while saying "we're getting rid of your travel budget", just turns people off. Establishing arbitrary performance measures, for the use of the tools, has a similar effect. So does requiring frequent and detailed reports. Otherwise, organisations are beyond the stage where they can completely control this technology. While the corporation can implement tools to limit access or make it awkward, many staff now expect to utilise Web 2.0 as a means of performing their jobs. For example, Sun employees use instant messaging (IM) more and more to enable impromptu as well as planned discussions in the daily job. Companies need to drive behaviour by setting clear expectations of acceptable behaviour, and then by training their staff in effective use of the tools. Like all technologies, Web 2.0 offers opportunities and risk. Both have to be managed.

The Role of the CIO in Realising the Promise of E-Novation

The last twenty years have revealed a, by now very predictable, pattern. At any one time, CIOs are dealing with the last wave of technologies. "Dealing with" comprises securing, hardening, scaling, and supporting the technologies. Meanwhile the business departments are busily experimenting with new technologies. Eventually the experiments amalgamate into a material portfolio of assets, or a material set of risks, or both. Compliance issues are also a frequent trigger for intervention by the CIO. At that point the corporation instructs the CIO to get the mess sorted out. At this moment, CIOs are busy securing, hardening, scaling, and supporting the Web 1.0, ERP, and CRM technologies. This is why a lot of Web 2.0 technology is adopted first in business departments. Interestingly, at least among the pioneers in my survey, the CIO and IT department were commonly seen as a leader in the adoption of E-Novation. This pattern was probably skewed by the preponderance of high-tech firms in the sample. Whatever the reason, this book's readers are the beneficiaries. Ultimately, so are the E-Novation communities. Sooner or later, probably sooner, they will want access to all that structured data sitting in the corporation's portfolio of legacy software assets. The CIO and IT department are not only the custodians of this portfolio, they are the only ones with the in-depth technical knowledge to make that happen.

Pioneering CIOS are making numerous contributions to E-Novation. They are providing the supporting infrastructure, and in many cases delivering the Web 2.0 technologies on teat infrastructure. They are leading by example, as visible users of the technology. They are running internal communication and education campaigns promoting both the Web 2.0 technologies and E-Novation communities. On which point, these pioneering CIOs acknowledge that the tools are just means to an end — E-Novation — and they put their focus on the end. They are taking on the critical challenges around confidentiality and privacy. That includes

- Getting information flow, storage and management under control.
- Establishing guidelines and protocols to protect sensitive information.
- Reinforcing the guidelines and protocols with education and communication.
- Supporting the education with appropriate technologies.

Mandates generally don't play a key role. Policies do. The key is to orient the policies to simultaneously enable use and prevent difficulties. On any given day, 99% of employees come to work to do a good job. They will do the right thing, provided they know what it is. Refer to the earlier citation of the attitude of SUN as "allow employees fairly free reign within the bounds of common sense, decency, strategic interests, and confidentiality". As others have commented before me, common sense isn't all that common. It never hurts for the corporation to reinforce a common definition of strategic interests and confidential information. Properly designed and communicated policies are part of the answer. With very little effort, existing policies — like policies for the appropriate use of email and for intellectual property protection — can be extended to cover most new technologies.

Overall, one can characterise the approach of pioneering CIOs as removing impedances and enabling progress. This compliments the strong tendency of end users to embrace E-Novation. As an example, at Tibco the internal IT department is seen as a leader in promoting E-Novation. At the same time the thrust of Tibco's product development is enabling the end-user to self-serve without placing demands on the IT department.

E-Novation is no longer just the CIO's responsibility, it's also the Chief Marketing Officer's responsibility. And the responsibility of every CxO. In some respects the CIO needs to act as the educator for the executive management, and the board of directors as they plan the future. Typically, company boards and senior management are older individuals, and their vision and ability to see the possibilities of the E-Novation should not be assumed. This is a role the CIO can and should fill.

SOLUTIONS AND RECOMMENDATIONS

The value proposition is real. Information becomes easier and cheaper to locate, generate or distribute. Collaboration and team work become faster, cheaper, and more convenient. Individual employees get information and tools that are customised to their work, without manual effort and lost productivity. Communities of interest get larger and stronger, improving their ability to deliver business results. It just makes good business sense.

Let's acknowledge that the CIO should be discussing E-Novation with other business leaders. If we've learned anything from the past 40 years IT has been around, it's that there is no such thing as an "IT project". There are only business projects that use IT enablers. The action is out in the business. That's where the end users are. That's where people are already experimenting with the new collaborative information platform. That's where the value gets created in the interaction between the organization and its customers. That's where the edge of the enterprise starts. That's where Porter's "Five Forces" are felt.

Now the opportunities — the new forms of value — are to be found in organising E-Novation communities and giving them the WEB 2.0 tools they need to harvest the intangible forms of value hidden within the unstructured, transient data. These intangible forms of value include:

- Brand promotion
- Market access
- Product promotion
- Compatibility
- Offline relationships
- Productivity
- Consumer loyalty
- Policy input
- Strategic insight
- Usage knowledge
- Preferential treatment
- Sense of community
- Flexible labour force access
- Legitimization of technology
- Recognition & visibility
- Enhanced sourcing flexibility
- Enhanced community relations
- Cooperation on rules & standards

New approaches will be needed to harness these forms of value. The key element is the community. IT, both in the sense of the department and the technology itself, is only a small part of the answer. The challenges are not trivial, but they are manageable.

Based on the experiences of the pioneers, some guidelines are available for the next wave of adopters:

- The tools are just means to an end, focus on the end.
- Lead the effort by addressing process and culture.
- Compliment process and culture with the tools.
- Play around with the technology. You can't understand its business value without using it.
- It helps when executives are visible users of the tools.
- Get information flow, storage and management under control early.
- Educate your people to use the technology.

Here is a short list of what to avoid:

- Avoid putting in a lot of rules. This will tend to drive the community to other tools.
- Avoid arbitrarily mandating a particular tool choice. People feel more empowered and more motivated when they are treated as part of the solution. That means asking staff for their opinions frequently, and acting on those opinions.
- Avoid the temptation to pick a tool first and go looking for an opportunity second. Always start with the need.
- Avoid arbitrary choices of performance metrics. The difficulty of identifying useful performance metrics is not unique to E-Novation. Web 2.0 technologies are subject to the same expectation as any other corporate spend: value for money.

People issues, especially the demographic divide, are likely to play a leading role in the success or failure of E-Novation. Well designed training programs will be vital. So will techniques for harnessing communities for mutual support and self-help.

FUTURE TRENDS

E-Novation is still an emerging trend. Based on the successes enjoyed by the pioneers, they will likely be followed by adopters in the mass market. As the long term trend plays out, the early techniques will evolve and mature. Tables 1 and 2 lay out some possible dynamics that may evolve.

The implications of these dynamics are not trivial. The digital economy is dependent on information capital. Information capital is increasingly crated by communities and individuals rather than institution like corporations. This trend could lead to a fundamental devolution of the corporation as we know it. The implications for business relationships could place intolerable overhead on industry ecosystems, brining them crashing down. Neither outcome is highly likely but, however improbable, they are possible outcomes. And therefore one can safely argue that

Table 1. Dynamics for people and employees

What's out?	What's in?	What's next?
Automation assisting Employees	Automation extending Employees	Automation anticipating employee's needs
Employees as Knowledge Managers	Employees as Knowledge Creators	Employees as knowledge collaborators
Command and Control	Command and Empowerment	Self-organised collaboration
Employees as objects of change	Employees as agents of change	Employees as free agents

Table 2. Dynamics for businesses and business relationships

What's out?	What's in?	What's next?
E-Commerce	E-World	E-Novation
Sense and Respond	Cause and Effect.	Anticipate and Create
Functional Visibility	Trans-Enterprise Visibility	Ecosystem Visibility, and Collaboration
Change at the speed of technology	Change at the speed of adoption	Change at the speed of partners
IT as a separate organization	IT integrated into business	IT invisible to the business

the long term success of E-Novation is by no means a sure thing.

There are some immediate challenges. The first is dealing with the immense increase in data, and sifting the useful information from that data which has a significant percentage of junk. Take email as a start. An organisation the size of Sun receives perhaps 20 million emails a day. Of these between 80 and 90% regularly turn out to be spam, and anything from 60-100,000 are virus laden. Multiply by the number of other Web 2.0 technologies, which also consume and produce data, especially at the edge of the organisation. Factor in the issue that much of the data is highly transient, in part due the immaturity of the technology and in part due to the highly iterative nature of the new collaborative knowledge cycle.

Before E-Novation, the knowledge cycle could be fairly described as having four sequential stages: generation, organisation, refinement, and distribution. Each stage was often performed by different parties. Web 2.0 technologies provide a venue for all parties to participate in all stages simultaneously. Take as an example the act of articulating a new concept during a virtual meeting in SecondLife. This one act encapsulates a mini

knowledge cycle. And before the virtual meeting is over the concept will have gone through any number of additional mini-cycles on its way to a mature idea. What if the concept is subject to compliance requirements? Do you capture some of the cycles or all of the cycles? Do you need attribution for every keystroke? Including backspaces? Do you need to capture the verbal interactions as well? How will you establish an audit trail? How will you establish non-repudiation of the identities of the people involved? Now you get a sense of the true scope and scale of the challenge. There are many new forms of data here [see Figure 2 adapted from Russom (2007)].

Let's also recognize that this unstructured, transient data is unfamiliar territory for the CIO, and most IT professionals. IT initially invested its funds in automating the control of goods, services and revenue. These are well understood and easily measured and monetised. Over time IT turned its attention to knowledge forms of value — from customer requirements to market intelligence to planning knowledge to specifications to technical knowledge.

E-Novation is not purely the domain of people. The explosion of the sheer number of devices at

Figure 2. The challenge of unstructured data (there's a deluge coming and we're not sure how to prepare for it)

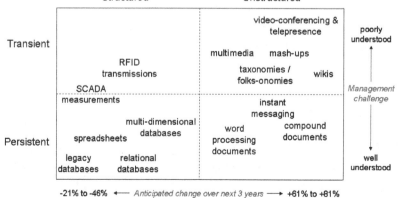

Source: Teradata Magazine and EDS

the edge of the enterprise is a major driving factor feeding E-Novation, and producing data overload within the firm. Mobile customers, mobile employees, mobile offices, and embedded technology like sensors and RFID are all flooding the enterprise with data. With digital content doubling every 12 months, individuals and companies are strained in acquiring, analysing, managing, and capitalizing on the explosion of data. This is exascale data. Enterprises are already experimenting with a number of ways to cope with the explosion. The irony is that making sense out of the content, i.e. a point-of-sale transaction, requires additional information about the context in which the transaction took place. So systems push still more information into the enterprise. And the enterprise is expected to respond ever faster. The speed of business may soon transcend the ability of humans to manage and operate the enterprise. How will people cope?

For one example, consider how the hypothetical scenario, that began this chapter, would play out in a firm where the CIO has acted on the solutions and recommendations presented above.

A product development team is in the final stages of preparing a product for launch. Some team members, who had been using Second Life at home, suggested it to their colleagues to consider it for team meetings at work. All special project teams are assigned a liaison from the IT department. This team is no exception. The IT liaison remembers reading on the CIO's blog that the firm had established a private virtual reality site. A quick Google Desktop search led the team not only to the virtual reality site, but also a Wiki and several other collaboration tools. The IT liaison helped the team provision it's own secured space in the tools. The liaison also helps the team organise its information and knowledge management schema. The shared spaces become the team's de facto collaboration tools because they compensated for the geographic dispersion of the team. The team use the tools extensively in their meetings to review product performance, efficacy and safety.

They supplement their own information with mash-ups of geospatial data sourced free online, combined with Census data (ditto), weather and climate data (ditto) and their own internal testing data from the field and labs. The results all show that a few worrisome incidents can be accounted for by environmental factors. After considerable analysis, the team decides to release the product, and target distribution for those geographic regions where there won't be any complications.

Throughout the project, the combination of employee education on data security, along with the policy-driven controls on the tools, keep all sensitive data inside the firm's firewalls. Both the internal and external data, as well as all of the analysis and calculations, are saved automatically along with an audit trail of who did what when. Later the data will be automatically archived according to requirements of industry regulators and company policy.

Meanwhile, a few months later...product liability claims begin to come in from the field. In preparation for meeting with the team, a staff attorney is granted authorisation to review the electronic files. Next the attorney meets with the team using the firm's private, virtual reality site. The team leads the attorney through the data they gathered and their analysis.

The team uploads and analyses electronic copies of the liability claims. Then the team gathers additional data from online sources. With guidance from the attorney, the team rapidly builds a factual case to show that the liability claims are resulting from factors beyond the firm's control. The IT liaison helps the attorney gather all of the electronic records in preparation for litigation. Here's how the meeting ends:

Attorney: That was a lot faster than I expected. These collaboration tools are really helpful.
Team: We couldn't work without them.
IT Liaison: It would be nice if someone gave the CIO a bit of positive feedback, he went out of his way to make the tools available.

Attorney: I can do that. I'll let you know if anything else comes up. Meanwhile, make sure nothing happens to any of our records.

IT Liaison: No worries. The archival system will not permit anyone to delete these records until 30 years from now.

Attorney: great. I'll twitter you if I need anything else. Bye for now.

CONCLUSION

For all its promise, Web 2.0 technology comes with its own set of challenges. One challenge with eAnything "2.0" is that it suggests a level of maturity, and a noticeable change in the Web from "1.0". In reality, there is a massive distance to go before maturity is reached. Moreover, the Web 2.0 technology is a subordinate element of E-Novation. The real focus of E-Novation is the simultaneous shift from more static content to dynamic content, and from one way communications to two-way participation by the end user in creating or changing content. This is less a revolutionary change than an evolutionary change. It's just that enough change has accumulated to be noticeable. The change to date may pale into insignificance in comparison to some of the unseen directions the Web may head. The web moves organically. Some might have predicted eBay, which is now passing more money than many countries' GDP, and pre-dates Web 2.0 formally. Some might have predicted Amazon, which now sells pretty much anything. But would anyone have predicted FaceBook and the ilk of social networking experiments? Could anyone foresee the millions of bedroom companies that are actually now making a living "doing something" on the web? Let's say someone comes up with a really cool idea that could creatively compete with an eBay. How much money and effort would it take to launch to the point it couldn't be stopped and may eventually threaten eBay? Considering two examples – how MP3 has changed the face of the music industry, and how YouTube is changing the face of the video industry – one could reasonably argue that a two man band could launch and sustain an "eBay buster" with a clever enough idea.

E-Novation is a demonstration that Web 2.0 technologies are creating entirely new ways of doing things. This is more than a replacement for simply walking down the hall or picking up the phone. The very definition of the corporation, or any institution, is being altered by the ready ability for employees to communicate with job-related subject matter experts and professional networks outside the organisation. Web 2.0 technologies broaden the definition of community and networking for employees. Increased access to professional communities outside of the employer, along with the enhanced ability to share information with colleagues, stimulates the employee's knowledge and interest in their job. This means improved employee engagement, improved performance, and improved retention, at least in the short term. In the longer term, being more involved in a new external community can distract the employee from the employer's priorities. Further, this appears to be moving us from an institution-based approach, and culture, to an approach based on industry ecosystems and, perhaps, ultimately to an approach based on the individual. As discussed earlier, this has significant implications for the relationship between employers and employees, not to mention the every nature of the corporation and similar institutions.

E-Novation is the latest evolution of a long-term trend: technology increasingly comprises every dimension of the corporation. To get the most out of E-Novation, future adopters will have to learn to trust the community.

REFERENCES

Cameron, B., Orlov, L. M., & Bright, S. (2006). *Digital business networks (Syndicated Report)*. Cambridge, MA: Forrester Research, Inc.

Friedman, T. L. (2005). *The world is flat 3.0: A brief history of the twenty-first century.* New York, NY: Picador.

Kaplan, R. S., & Norton, D. P. (2004). *Strategy maps.* Boston, MA: Harvard Business School Publishing Corporation.

Kurzweil, R. (2001). *The law of accelerating returns.* KurzweilAI.net. Retrieved February 11, 2009, from http://www.kurzweilai.net/articles/art0134.html?printable=1

Lancaster, L., & Stillman, D. (2003). *When generations collide.* New York, NY: HarperCollins Publishers, Inc.

Lowy, A., & Hood, P. (2004). *The power of the 2 x 2 matrix: Using 2x2 thinking to solve business problems and make better decisions.* San Francisco, CA: Jossey-Bass.

Porter, M. E. (1980). *Competitive strategy.* New York, NY: Free Press.

Russom, P. (2007). The shifting continuum: The increase in semi- and unstructured data means changes for your data warehouse. *Teradata Magazine,* December.

Tapscott, D. (2008). *Grown up digital: How the Net generation is changing your world.* New York, NY: McGraw-Hill.

Tapscott, D., Ticoll, D., & Lowy, A. (2000). *Digital capital: Harnessing the power of business webs.* Boston, MA: Harvard Business School Publishing Corporation.

Wikipedia. (2009). *Porter's five forces analysis.* Retrieved 11 February, 2009, from http://en.wikipedia.org/wiki/Porter%27s_5_Force_Model

Chapter 14
E–Novation Program Office and Roadmap:
Pathway to Achieving E-Novation in Government

Suresh Sood
University of Technology, Australia

Kevin Jin
QBE Insurance Group, Australia

ABSTRACT

This chapter introduces a new organizational entity for government organisations, the E-Novation Program Office (EPO). The basis for this structure is researcher experiences of the divide between organizational decision-making capability and the actual delivery of innovation using new technology initiatives within Australian organizations. Key EPO decision-making mechanisms include cognitive mapping, road maps, scenario planning, and complexity thinking. The proposed model of the EPO is informed through author experiences within a variety of Australian organisations and government enterprises focusing on technological innovation rather than other forms of innovation. The EPO serves to guide innovative actions, prioritization of effort, and better execution by acting as a counterbalance between technology, strategy, and delivery to ensure the successful introduction of innovation. The robustness, flexibility, and adaptability of the EPO arises from modeling processes arising from research in the governance of enterprise wide service oriented architectures for information systems. The EPO explicitly supports the central tenant of government organisations, the provision of service to citizens. Most importantly, service is taken to be the provision of knowledge and skills (Vargo & Lusch, 2004) for the benefit of citizens.

DOI: 10.4018/978-1-60566-394-4.ch014

INTRODUCTION

Based on first hand experience from eight cases comprising technology projects in a major Australian retailer, an investment bank, building society, semi-autonomous state government utility, government department, small software vendor, wine distributor and professional services organization the authors consistently witness dysfunctional behavior between "thinking" and "doing" amongst the 3 key areas of technology, business and delivery (project management) of new initiatives. Delivery relates to promoting, governing and managing innovations at a variety of levels through changes in process, product or service using project management techniques. An E-novation program office (EPO) provides the catalyst to ensure a smooth introduction of innovative technology driven ideas as well as the reuse of existing assets contributing to service (Vargo & Lusch, 2004).

Setting up an EPO assists by acting as a change agent mechanism to ensure harmony of business strategy, technology and project management through providing decision making tools and feedback to each impacted area, supporting well empowered cross functional teams, a knowledge base informing relevant stakeholders of best practice, success stories and the provision of further knowledge and specialized skills supporting related projects.

The objectives of this chapter are to:

1. Describe the research method underpinning the notion of the EPO
2. Share a vision of Government E-novation
3. Describe the EPO
4. Key steps to implementation
5. Conclusion and future opportunities

RESEARCH METHOD

Owing to the role of the researchers as consultants within existing workplace technology projects the overarching research method is ethnographic fieldwork. The ethnography is supported by triangulation of note taking, hand drawn maps of meeting interactions, digital photographs, analysis of existing documents and review of intranet sites. A special purpose instrument frequently used by project managers "the project post implementation review" (PIR) helps uncover key issues, lessons learnt and contributions from stakeholders with respect to the delivery of projects associated with innovation. Weekly debriefing meetings between researchers cover the sharing of stories on insights, emergent theories, relationships, hunches and potential implications of observations in shaping recommendations. An individual organization, although multiple site visits take place is treated as an individual case.

Each organization or case is found to exhibit idiosyncrasies with the common theme witnessed first hand by the researchers within cases and across cases when introducing new ideas is consistent no matter the industry. A lack of synchronicity amongst the 3 areas results in projects inevitably failing to meet business objectives and an inability to create cultural change to embrace innovation.

The key recommendation emergent from research insights is obtained through going backwards and forwards between the data collection, interpretation and researcher conjectures and insight. This method is best described as the informal execution of grounded theory. The actual recommendation flowing from the approach is the creation of a new organizational entity to reduce dissonance in strategy, design and operation of technological innovation.

Further, the research findings from the ethnographic interpretations and follow up storytelling by the researchers in the organisations under study informs the most efficient and effective introduction of an EPO to be in government organizations focusing on service.

The concept of the EPO and supporting processes emerging from the case study approach adopted is further tested in the context of e-government initiatives taking place globally.

THE ROLE OF E-GOVERNMENT IN THE 21ST CENTURY

The researchers find a high degree of uncertainty regarding the workplace emanating from employees within all but one of the study organisations. The most often cited comment amongst the case studies is "the business does not know where it's heading". The researchers firmly believe this to be endemic of the focus of businesses moving away from product to service. For example, in the software vendor this manifests as a shift from selling software for a major capital expenditure to a pay as you go model. Vargo and Lusch (2004) see this as a more profound change representing a tectonic shift not only in marketing but in macroeconomic theory from value derived from exchange of goods and services as espoused by Adam Smith in his seminal work "Wealth of Nations" in 1776 to value based on usage.

Only in the government department case study did the authors witness the notion of service. Vargo and Lusch (2004) distinguish between service and services. The latter (services) are intertwined with the old model of exchanging goods and regarded as an augmentation to a product or an intangible good while service is considered as skills and knowledge applied for the benefit of other government departments or citizens. During the exchange process, the dialogue (Lusch & Vargo, 2008) with the citizen creates value. True, the traditional transactions exist in key government organisations but the bulk are handled by a handful of Australian super sized government organisations including Centrelink providing in excess of 12 million transactions daily (Lazzari,

2004). The remainder of government excluding state utilities is not handling transactions per se but dialogues held with citizens or government personnel. In government, this is a continuum from a simple question to dialogue and diplomacy at higher levels. A focus on dialogue rather than transactions leads naturally to achieving innovation by sharing new knowledge within and outside government organisations. Here, the introduction of innovation is wholly dependent on creating new knowledge flows through updating or augmenting existing technology infrastructure with the collaboration tools of Web 2.0 (see next section). Examples include Patient Opinion (http://www.patientopinion.org.uk/) facilitating dialogue between patients in the United Kingdom and the National Health Service, MyBikeLane (http://nyc.mybikelane.com/) reporting bike lane violations in New York and Food Safety Offences (http://www.foodauthority.nsw.gov.au/aboutus/penalty-notices/) publishing breaches in food safety to the citizens of New South Wales in Australia.

GOVERNMENT 2.0

E-Novation in government underpins a transition to Government 2.0 from citizens merely searching for information to experiencing deep interactions through dialogue with relevant government departments. The enabler is the collaboration technology of Web 2.0 (Musser & O'Reilley, 2006) encompassing social networks, mapping, shared video, rich media and semantic search technology. The changing role of government underpinned by a move to a new service platform embracing Web 2.0 is supported not by technology for the sake of technology but a fundamental realization the actual business is service (Vargo & Lusch, 2004) provisioning the application of government competencies for the benefit of citizens. Today, the delivery of service faces challenges from changing socio-political factors including (but not limited to) aging population, archaic systems and new citizen demands. Thus, service is a co-creation of citizens, departmental resourcing (Lusch & Vargo,2008) and technology.

Service within government needs to ensure successful adoption of government service recommendations to citizens is based on citizens only needing to "tell once" (O'Brien & Hawkins, 2008). To achieve this, knowledge flows from skilled government personnel with access to knowledge repositories is a higher priority than efficiency of underlying technologies. Thus, the service shift is not about technology delivering benefits by trying to make services more like products but the whole transition to the service paradigm (Vargo and Lusch, 2004).

The 2006 Australian e-Government strategy is clear and concise, orientated to a citizen focus underpinned by the use of information technology to transform processes not just deliver services. The vision follows a timetable to achieve reality in 2010. By this time, citizens will possess personalized accounts for accessing government services. These citizens will come from today's millennial generation who are busily transforming social networking as a cornerstone of Web 2.0 technologies into a life and work phenomenon. Harnessing Web 2.0 to help citizens dialog via e-Government services is the key to the Australian Government's realization of the vision of a responsive government.

Responsive Government (AGIMO 2006) is defined as:

- Citizen-focused rather than customers getting the proverbial run-around from bureaucracy
- Co-ordination with disparate agencies operating in a collaborative manner
- Transformed rather than just automated around existing processes by ensuring "every door the right door when approaching government ".
- Offering value for money by effectively using online and voice services

Elsewhere, in a similar vein to Australia the Dutch Government is focusing on the 10 point e-Citizen Charter ((Polemans 2006) to transform systems and processes ensuring service delivery to citizens in the manner shown in Table 1.

SERVICE DELIVERY, SOA AND KNOWLEDGE

The key information technology to allow disparate Australian agency projects or Dutch agencies to join together and meet the overall design goal of a responsive government through connecting services is Service Orientated Architecture (SOA). The building blocks for SOA are the reusable business functions of a government organization reaching inwards or out to citizens. Today, No rules exist about the granularity of functions other than they should be implemented as a minimum as a fragment of a service capability (business process or function) rather than a technical capability. This direct linkage to SOA means governments are rapidly evolving to embrace shared services for cost reduction and improved service delivery. The service is not limited to being wholly technology based but includes low tech services inclusive of coffee making, dry cleaning and preparation of lunchtime sandwiches taking a handful of mundane examples. The usual suspects of traditional shared services are human resources, finance and accounting, procurement and information technology and telecommunications.

The shared services in turn facilitate the exchange of knowledge and skills resulting in service delivery to the citizen. Improvements in service delivery result from innovation in process and effectiveness of service delivery as well as meeting new service demands from citizens. Thus, the SOA based services and service are regarded to be interchangeable in the context of government departments serving citizens.

In order to ensure the strategy (planning and design of service) aligns with customer groupings

Table 1. Dutch Government e-citizen charter from http://www.burger.overheid.nl

e-Citizen Area of Charter	Citizen Choice & Focus
Channel of interaction	multi channel service delivery: counter, letter, phone, e-mail, internet.
Transparent Public Sector	one-stop-shop service delivery and act as one seamless entity with no wrong doors.
Rights and Duties	services and conditions rights and duties
Personalised Information	information complete, up to date and consistent and tailored to citizen needs.
Convenient Services	personal data required once only what records are kept about citizens and does not use data without citizen consent.
Comprehensive Procedures	know how government works and monitor progress. Government keeps citizens informed of procedures by tracking and tracing.
Trust and Reliability	electronically competent secure identity management and reliable storage of electronic documents.
Considerate Administration	ideas for improvement and lodge complaints. Government compensates for mistakes and uses feedback information to improve products and procedures.
Accountability and Benchmarking	Comparative analysis, check and measure government outcome. Government actively supplies benchmark information about its performance
Involvement and Empowerment	Participate in decision-making and citizen interests Support empowerment and ensures that the necessary information and forms are available.

and innovative government service, e.g., e-voting the EPO can help fill a gap to enable integration of advanced technology using a surface computing table (Romano, 2007) into citizen services. To achieve this, the researchers further reinforce the need for an organizational entity focusing on reusable services supporting the business of government, ensuring conformance to service (standards/policies) and services funding. The EPO facilitates the consolidation of services, collaboration between different but co-operative government departments ensuring seamless service delivery to citizens when a citizen enters through any "door".

THE E-NOVATION PROGRAM OFFICE

The E-Novation maturity model has been generated from a bricolage (Sood and Pattinson, 2006) of the case studies.

Historically, project management took place with little or no management. Many organizations particularly medium and large companies or government departments established project management offices out of necessity within the IT function. In fact, the researchers found in dealing with a medium sized wine distribution business whenever project management was required as in the instance of setting up franchise outlets at high volume customer locations the IT project capability was used even if technology played little or no part.

The next step in the evolution of managing innovation uses portfolio management as a managerial tool to monitor assets and project activities holistically. None of the organisations visited by the researchers use portfolio management as a useful business innovation capability but instead see benefits only for financial planning.

The traditional Enterprise Program Management Office (EPMO) maintains responsibility for enterprise projects crossing business divisions, which focus on business transformations via information technology initiatives. Frequently, the EPMO delivers silo-based projects for major organisational divisions accounting for a large proportion of the business or resources. These large divisional projects are multi-year and in effect programs (a logical multi-year grouping of projects) embraced by the entire organisation but can be at congruence with the organisation strategy. Against the background of ongoing "silo" projects how is an organisation to foster innovation remains a key question. Above all organisations are required to cope with the pace of technological and marketing change whilst simultaneously research, develop and market new products and services. These activities maintain resistance from the existing organisation and ecosystem but require cross-the-board resources and support. The transformation of the EPMO to an Enovation Program Office provides the catalyst to take new e-business initiatives from vision to reality in a collaborative manner with all stakeholders.

The EPO as organizational entity reduces friction to ensure synergy between marketing or business strategy, innovation and delivery of service. Hence, coupling the "thinking" with the actual "doing". (see Table 2)

DECISION MAKING TOOLS

A major issue continues to be the introduction of innovation in organisations studied including government. Too much emphasis is placed on delivery but limited attention given to thinking about the innovative practices introduced by the project. The EPO provides the opportunity to furnish members of projects teams and managers with new thinking using decision making tools and thinking not encountered on a daily basis. The tools assist with capturing the collective intelligence of people associated with the introduction of technological innovation into an organizational setting.

Sense-Making and Improvisation Framework

The work of Gary Klein (1999) provides a framework for the EPO decision-making capability.

Table 2. Enovation program office journey (Adapted from Craig-Jones, 2008)

Level	Organizational Entity	Description
1: Initial		• Organization runs project as business operation • Projects run informally with no standard process and tracking system.
2: Repeatable	Project Office	• Define, document and enforce a standard project management methodology • Consistency and co-ordination between projects • Project governance is focus on time, cost and quality
3: Defined	Program Office	• Project portfolio manages multiple project more efficiently especially resource allocation. • Project governance on project performance • Project portfolio is business unit based, without an enterprise view
4: Managed	Enterprise Program Mgmt Office	• Project portfolio management changes to find common themes, promote reuse and facilitate consolidation • Project governance focuses on synergy among projects within the whole enterprise
5: Optimized	Enovation Program Office	• Levels 1 to 4 focus on delivering the project portfolio and doing the right thing. • Level 5 is about establishing and maintaining a portfolio to meet government strategy. • Methodologies expand beyond project and portfolio management • Scenario planning, cognitive mapping, road-maps and complexity techniques applied for decision making • Paradigm shift for the program office from a change agent to an innovation agent. • SOA is used to deliver major technology initiatives • Web 2.0 pervades for service delivery to citizens

Klein's work validates people under pressure act based on experience and intuition using the "Recognition Primed" decision-making model (RPD). This model recognizes features analogous or different from previous experiences allowing the formation of accurate mental models against which an immediate course of action can be taken. The corollary is without experience one is apt to gather data and options and weigh them which cannot be fast enough under many circumstances resulting in cognitive overload or flooding from information paralyzing the decision-making unit.

Klein is valuable in informing how the EPO can help project team members to achieve expertise. Experts:

- Recognise patterns
- See the big picture
- Notice subtle differences
- Recognise leverage points
- Extract, codify and apply knowledge from storytelling, metaphors and analogues
- Take a "bricolage" approach (Sood and Pattinson, 2006) creating order out of whatever materials are at hand

The EPO utilizes case-based reasoning (CBR) to mimic an RPD environment for usage by stakeholders. Previous cases are held in a repository containing conceptual knowledge built on top of previous organizational cases associated with introducing innovation. "Infoshop" (Watson, 2001) represents an early implementation by the UK Government to use the approach discussed. The Infoshop project provides a "one stop shop" for front line staff to answer queries on any aspect of local government regulation. In this instance, the actual knowledge base comprises the full text making up the decision trees extracted from the policy and planning manual answering the most common questions e.g. Do I need planning permission for a satellite dish? Customer staff can search the full text of the knowledge base based on the query at hand.

Tools

The key tools and mechanisms for decision making complimenting the RPD framework and capturing knowledge include cognitive maps, roadmaps, scenario planning and complexity thinking.

Cognitive Maps

Cognitive maps prove to be an extremely useful tool when considering decisions regarding new innovations (Pattinson and Woodside, 2007). The maps represent the tacit knowledge about decisions on technology and organizational impact and can be extracted from PIRs using content analysis of text. The maps help minimize subjectivity in decision-making. Maps are often generated as cause effect relationships from an individual but in the context of the EPO maps representing the collective knowledge of stakeholders achieving successful technological innovation provides an opportunity to script (Schank and Abelson, 1977) the future delivery of innovation. Each PIR is ideally accompanied with a cognitive map to maintain memory for future stakeholders. The cognitive map (see Figure 1) is drawn to help focus on the connectivity between concepts (nodes) connected by outgoing or incoming links. A "minus" signed link indicates a negative relationship between concepts.

Roadmap

The roadmap (Whalen, 2007) embraces the business, information, applications, technologies and people of an organization providing the framework to monitor, initiate and chart overall changes across the organisation. The EPO works with a roadmap to co-ordinate activities across the entire organizational landscape. The focus on an information technology roadmap is no longer sufficient and as departments turn to increasingly rely upon information based products and services reusing the Web (e.g. social networking sites)

Figure 1. Sample cognitive map

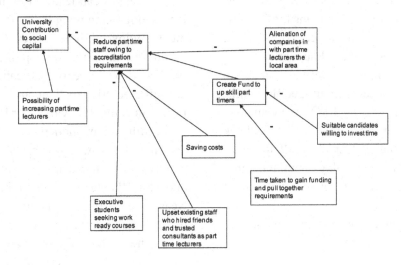

Figure 2. Actual roadmap

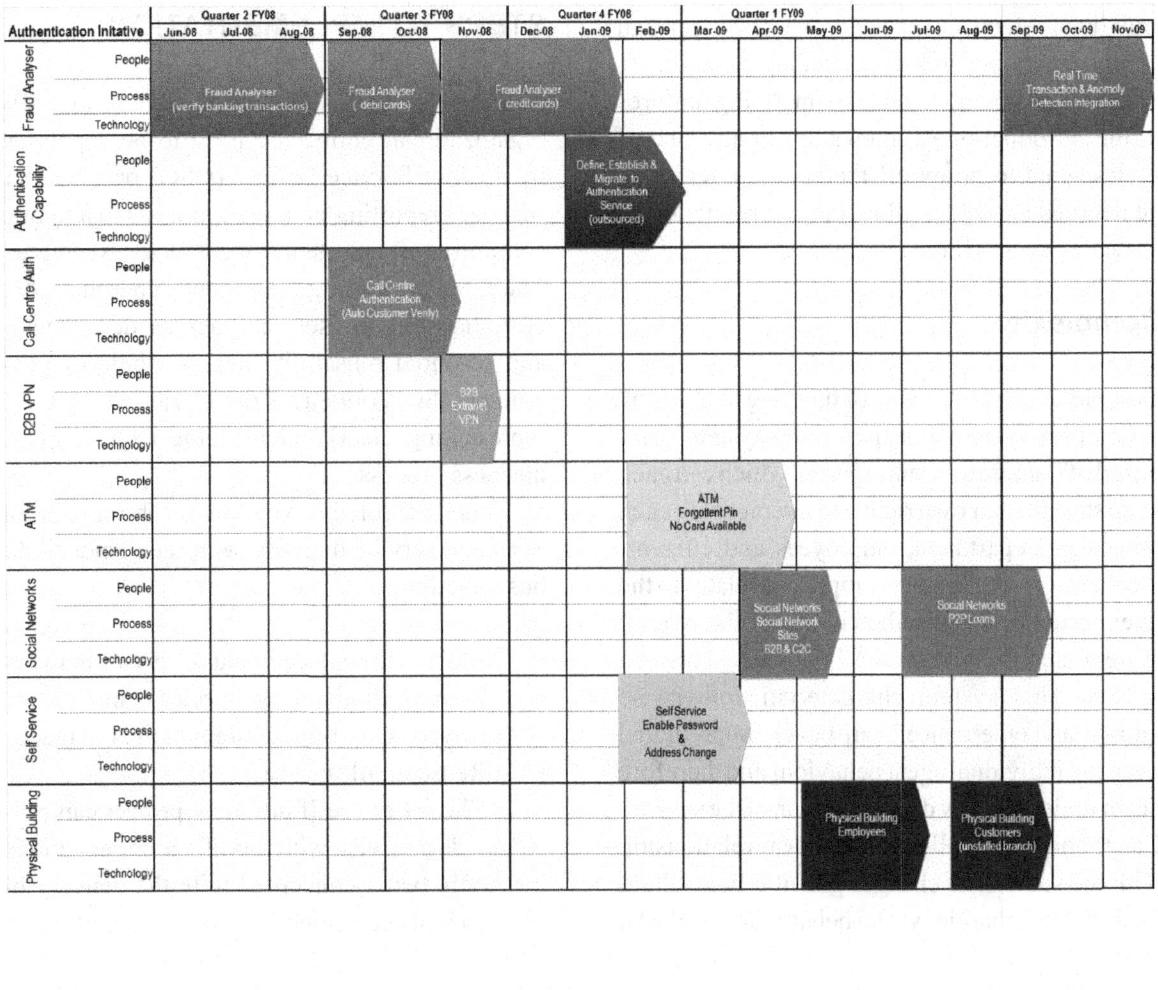

the roadmap (Figure 2) needs to embrace new products and technologies impacting the business processes and functions of the government as a whole in both physical and online worlds.

This versatile approach defines long-term direction without concerns about specific details. Roadmaps published by the EPO are a vehicle to publish information and thereby solicit feedback from a variety of stakeholders. Overall, the roadmap is expressed in a technology neutral manner and allows consideration of technology in a manner hitherto not previously considered. With a roadmap rapid changes in business vision and objectives can be achieved.

Scenario Planning

Scenario planning provides an opportunity to ensure that people are well experienced in extreme situations where unexpected events distort and confuse meaning and sense-making capabilities. Scenario planning includes simulating failures in the introduction of innovation in advance of such events to allow off the shelf strategies to be detailed as well as allow the determination of critical success factors.

Complexity

Complexity is more a way of thinking then a tool. A complex system constitutes any system composed of numerous agents (parts), which can each keep state in their own right and interact with each other e.g. department, employees and citizens. Furthermore, the system complexity relates to the unexpected or surprise behaviour of the overall system stemming from the interaction between agents. This system characteristic otherwise known as "emergence" can never be predicted from the individual agent behaviour and therefore never understood by decomposition of the system. Cause and effect follow a non-linear relationship with the subtlest of changes potentially resultant in producing chaotic system behaviour. Similarly,

major changes can lead to minimal impact. The key to embracing complexity is to have government employees share stories concerning counterintuitive thinking and capturing these as part of a knowledge base. If these campfire stories are not sufficient triggers than one need not look any further than the Paul Van Riper Red team victory of the millennium challenge of 2002. This was a testament to treating warfare as a complex system. His wisdom in using surprise outflanked his opposing Blue team who had the most costly of weapons and voluminous intelligence. Not only was this an important lesson in using complexity to one's advantage but Paul Van Riper had understood when experts make decisions they don't logically and systematically compare all options (Klein, 1999).

STEPS TO IMPLEMENTATION

The case research conducted signals the new organizational entity, the EPO to be supported by a Chief Service Officer (CSO) or a Service Manager reporting on a regular basis to a hybrid committee of business and technology executives. The CSO within a government department has custodianship for services across departments and potential reusability across whole of government. SOA organizes the world into services representing clearly identifiable and complete business processes.

This CSO role is a key role for the success of SOA and service delivery with the responsibilities including:

- "Teeth" for enforcement of service delivery
- Manage underlying services and ensure correct level of documentation is in place
- Reuse of all services
- Checks to see if any new project can provide a service with modification rather than only being concerned with the delivery of an isolated project.

The CSO works with business analysts to ensure that the new service requirements can be integrated within the existing SOA. The key responsibility of the business analyst is the translation of business requirements into services to support the delivery of service and the creation of a service contract. Other business analyst responsibilities include:

- Maintaining knowledge based view of the department
- Capturing business rules
- Creating and updating the service contract
- Assembly of atomic services into chains (processes)
- Creation of service artifacts for departmental and whole of government sharing

Technology needs not just to embrace SOA but must act in the context of a long-term service plan without tactical interruption. If government is to benefit and leverage from a shift to SOA as well as align with the service paradigm, the requirement is to execute a short to medium-term (18 to 36 month) roadmap comprising multiple projects which help build out services which are reusable across government. A by-product of the roadmap is the reduction in bureaucratic overhead by agreeing upfront the overall release plan and gaining pre-approvals for service delivery.

The initial implementation of the EPO is a service provider to key projects ensuring services are identified via the CSO. Once whole of department services are identified service contracts can be defined.

Services are reusable IT assets and as such within Australia attract a seven year depreciation schedule rather than the traditional five year depreciation on software. The key to providing value to government and citizens beyond financial savings is to release services on short release cycles of 30 to 90 days. With regard to SOA funding a move to embrace a utility model is paramount and becomes a matter of timing rather than debate.

Once business initiates a new project recognized to benefit from service, a service contract is initiated under the auspices of the EPO. Here, we assume the business analyst associated with an EPO has been upskilled or has access to a knowledge centric view. The service contract represents the commencement of a rigorous definition of the service at this stage in plain English terms including a variety of definitions e.g. service level arrangement as well as policies for usage. This contract is used to communicate service requirements to all stakeholders simultaneously inclusive of business and technical staff.

SERVICES (VERTICAL AND HORIZONTAL)

The primary focus is on the services or business functions reusable across government. These services are funded centrally (or shared) by prior negotiation with other government departments. Workgroup specific services within an individual government department and unlikely to be reused are funded by the department concerned. The most obvious way to partition services is as a set of clearly defined horizontal services reusable in a variety of situations. Vertical services are encouraged where possible to be moved from the vertical to the horizontal. This is the biggest mind set change in moving to SOA and therefore service delivery making the paradigm shift to service, the need to think about horizontal services rather than vertical applications with a set of clearly defined services reusable in a variety of ways. The challenge for the EPO is the specification of the overall service without being distracted by the underlying processes and services. Business analysts working within the EPO best handle the process centric view.

ROLE OF SERVICE CATALOG

Reusing services can save time but reuse can never be effective without a single, up-to-date catalogue.

Each service contained within the catalog has:

- A Service Contract
- Purpose and behavior (plain English)
- Interface definition(s)
- Quality of service commitments
- Provider (who is responsible)
- A list of consumers (citizen, business or government department)
- A list of other dependencies including knowledge and skills

A Services catalog provides for a universal naming of services and business process, skills and knowledge dependencies. Since the services are reusable knowledge assets the repository allows the creation of a service contract with a unique and consistent description for the entire department. For services the catalog is filled out to a level of service description anticipating project requests and giving the go ahead or "green lighting" such services in a proactive manner. However, situations exist where the service that a business analyst or user requests does not exist in the planned list of services and it becomes necessary to create the service and supporting artifacts. Only the CSO should be entitled to create new services. The services in the catalog are maintained and managed by the EPO team. This central control over services helps avoid the risk of having several services defined for tactical purposes but actually achieving the same purpose. Multiple services achieving the same objective significantly reduces the reuse of services and efficiencies. Example services managed centrally and providing significant value to stakeholders may well pertain to petitions, surveys, new planning regimes and rating of government services by citizens.

User Requests New Service

A user or business analyst can request new services only when no existing service can satisfactorily be applied to a required project. Once the business analyst and CSO identifies the new service or reuse of a service, the user should then:

1. Submit requests for new service to the CSO. The request should include:
   a. The requested service name e.g. "petition"
   b. A description of the service e.g. "individual groups or citizens can launch a petition and track the status"
   c. A description of the project to which the service will be applied e.g. "daylight saving"
2. User receives new services or suggested services to use from the CSO
   a. The user uses or modifies the service to fulfill citizen delivery e.g. "public shaming of businesses or citizens behaving antisocially."

The CSO decides whether or not a user request for a new service is valid. Further the CSO is responsible for maintaining the integrity of the catalog so that it does not get corrupted with ambiguous, and duplicate services in order to ensure maximum reusability.

The CSO needs to define an evaluation process to perform the following:

1. Ensure that the requested new service is valid and fits across the organization
   a. Service is unambiguous
   b. Service is not a duplicate
2. Suggest existing services (if applicable) to the user in place of the new service
3. Ensure new service name conforms to a service naming convention
4. Inform requestors of newly created service descriptions

Figure 3. Lifecycle of service request

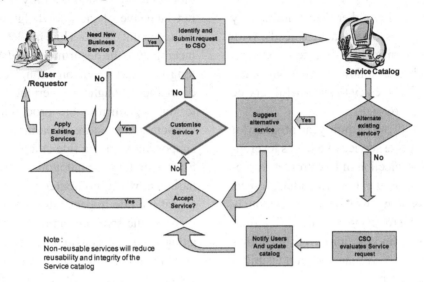

The overall process (Figure 3) creates clear expectations and saves time by eliminating confusion amongst existing and requested services. The consistency imposed by the process invoked by the CSO and participants saves time by eliminating unnecessary decisions.

PROJECT FUNDING AND PRIORITISATION

What the researchers witness across all the companies regarding project funding and priority is the norm, not the exception. Tactical needs always trump strategic direction resulting in an inflexible, static and brittle knowledge infrastructure difficult to change with ongoing citizen requirements. Thus, without Service pressure to overcome redirection

of development and project resources away from tactical IT projects an organization will be unable to shift into new and innovative service delivery.

Service enabling using the EPO is not a silver bullet but does help move strategy, technology and delivery into providing something more efficient and valuable to government departments than previous experience. A government department needs not just to embrace technology but must act in the context of a long-term strategic service plan without tactical interruption. Only then will a department be able to deliver on a citizen charter and thus find itself ahead of the game. If departments are to benefit and leverage from a shift to service, the requirement is to execute a short to medium-term (18 to 36 month) roadmap comprising multiple projects. The roadmap can move a government department toward a long-term

Figure 4. Project funding and prioritization via service roadmap

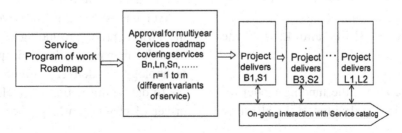

strategy via a program of work to build out desirable Service capability rather than continuously redirecting resources toward tactical needs. With a focus on long-term policy short term rewards will still nonetheless follow. Execution of the Service roadmap is the key to successful service delivery. (see Figure 4)

The roadmap drives a multiyear program of delivering high value service to citizens leveraging delivery of a selection of key projects represents the first stage or iteration with other projects e.g. decommissioning Not only as previously discussed does the roadmap provide clear strategic direction for technology initiatives but allows the ability to proactively plan and gain visibility of resource requirements.

A by-product of the roadmap is the reduction in overhead by agreeing upfront the overall release plan and gaining approvals. Of course, business priorities do change and this is accommodated in the short release cycles expected of delivering service. Taking this approach:

- Roadmap projects are centrally governed by the EPO to ensure conformance to service delivery objectives
- Individual projects helping to deliver the EPO service vision in part are "green lighted" based on the pre-approval of a release plan

SERVICE FUNDING MODEL

A service centric project investment comprises:

a. Cost of developing new service capability
b. Cost of reusing the pre-built service (behavior requiring encouragement)
c. Investment in skills and knowledge infrastructure

In light of the above, the funding model for service can be harmonized within an overall utility model encompassing not only the infrastructure but inclusive of the knowledge movement and management costs. This model helps provide incentives to the department whilst achieving the long-term service vision through distinct projects distributed throughout government. This approach to funding mirrors the procurement of assets impacting the entire department or enterprise supporting a "rising tide strategy" (Boar, 2001). Such a strategy is analogous to a rising tide in a harbor in which no matter the size or weight of a boat the tide impacts all boats equally raising them by the same amount. The power of leveraging a service is available to everyone within government and the service funding needs to be applied strategically. Whether this is imposed as a rent centrally still remains to be seen as real life examples of service funding are slow to become publicly available.

CONCLUSION AND FUTURE OPPORTUNITIES

This chapter shows that the EPO can assist in the delivery of technological innovation within government enterprises. The establishment of an EPO aims at ensuring centricity on service rather than individual projects. Complexity reminds us all projects are interrelated and should not be treated independent of one another. Projects are synchronized and aligned with a catalog of services underpinning service delivery to citizens. The EPO assists managers with the provisioning and application of decision-making tools to help think outside the box as well as longer term for ensuring the technological innovation of key service delivery initiatives.

At the most basic level a government department with appropriate funding and serving citizens needs to manage skills of people, knowledge, technology and delivery of innovation.

To date, information technology is the main driver of change but a plethora of other technology innovations built on bio, green & nano technology will increasingly bring about greater changes and stand to benefit from the concept of the EPO. In the meantime, the EPO has a remarkable future ahead smoothing delivery of citizen service for governments through harmonizing e-Government strategy, innovative technology and service delivery.

REFERENCES

AGIMO. (2006). *Responsive government – A new service agenda. March 2006*. Australian Government Department of Finance and Administration, Australian Government Information Management Office.

Allen, P. (Ed.). (2006). *Service orientation – Winning strategies and best practices*. Cambridge, UK: Cambridge University Press. doi:10.1017/CBO9780511541186

Arsanjani, A. (2004). Service-oriented modeling and architecture: How to identify, specify and realize your services. *IBM developerWorks*, November.

Bieberstein, N. (2006). *Service-oriented architecture compass – Business value, planning, and enterprise roadmap*. Armonk, NY: IBM Press.

Boar, B. (2001). *The art of strategic planning for Information Technology*. New York, NY: John Wiley and Sons.

Chappell, D. (2004). *Enterprise service bus*. Sebastopol, CA: O'Reilly Publishing.

Craig-Jones, C. (2008, January 30). Evolving the maturity level of your project management office. *CIO Update*. Retrieved 5 March, 2009, from http://www.cioupdate.com/trends/article.php/3724851/Evolving-the-Maturity-Level-of-Your-Project-Management-Office.htm

Klein, G. (1999). *Sources of power: How people make decisions*. Cambridge, MA: MIT Press.

Lusch, R. F., & Vargo, S. L. (2008). Toward a conceptual foundation for service science: Contributions from service-dominant logic. *IBM Systems Journal*, *47*(1). doi:10.1147/sj.471.0005

Marks, E., & Bell, M. (2006). *Service-oriented architecture – A planning and implementation guide for business and technology*. New York, NY: Wiley.

Musser, J., & O'Reilly, T. (2006). *Web 2.0 principles and best practices*. Sebastopol, CA: O'Reilly.

O'Brien, J., & Hawkins, J. (2008). *The future of shared services in the European public sector*. New York, NY: Ovum.

Pattinson, H., & Woodside, A. G. (2007). *Innovation and diffusion of software technology: Mapping strategies*. New York, NY: Elsevier Science.

Polemans, M. (2006). *Workbook e-citizen charter, version 2.2*.

Romano, B. (2007, June 28). Bringing something new to the table. *Seattle Times*.

Schank, R. C., & Abelson, R. P. (1977). *Scripts, plans, goals and understanding*. Hillsdale, NJ: Erlbaum.

Sood, S., & Pattinson, H. (2006). Urban renewal in Asia-Pacific: A comparative analysis of brainports for Sydney and Kuala Lumpur. *Journal of Business Research*, *59*(6). doi:10.1016/j.jbusres.2005.12.003

Vargo, S. L., & Lusch, R. F. (2004). Evolving a new dominant logic for marketing. *Journal of Marketing*, 68.

Watson, I. (2001). *INFOSHOP: A decision support tool for local government regulatory advice*. Advances in Artificial Intelligence. PRICAI 2000 Workshop Reader. Berlin, Germany: Springer.

Whalen, P. J. (2007). *Strategic and technology planning on a roadmapping foundation. Technology Management*. May-June.

Section 5
Emerging E–Novation, Platforms and Marketing

Chapter 15
Next Generation Collaborative Information Platforms

Hugh M. Pattinson
University of Western Sydney, Australia

David R. Low
University of Western Sydney, Australia

ABSTRACT

Current new and next generation e-novation collaborative platforms are explored through a "Day-In-The-Life-Of" scenario in 2020 based on key semantic concepts drawn from chapters within the E-Novation book. Key themes for an emerging e-novation collaborative platform include: triple convergence (before and after), Web 3.0/4.0 – the Web is a brain, redefined collaborative communication, virtual/augmented reality, service-dominant logic (SDL), marketing and innovation, open-source creation, development and distribution, digital branding, CRM redefined, complexity and SMEs, e-novation office, e-novation curriculum, social graphing e-novation, and sustainability platforms and innovation. These themes are discussed both in relation to the current new collaborative platform and how they may develop from 2010-2020. E-novation will be the innovation and marketing social and business service.

"A DAY IN THE LIFE OF E-NOVATION: 2020"

Alexander Drake, CEO of NetWear, stepped in his Executive Space. Today he is wearing a white shirt, charcoal-grey suit and shoes. The Office-Wear Suite (OWS) within his clothing has set his shirt at long-sleeve, but the suit to be light and

comfortable for an afternoon appointment at his favourite cafe outside on a typical humid February Sydney day.

OWS interacts with the Executive Space as he enters it, to set the walls and ambience with his preferred colours and sounds. His clothing is networked and contains most of the information he needs for his meetings and executive tasks. Alex can retrieve information from OWS to see through contact lenses or it projected wherever he

DOI: 10.4018/978-1-60566-394-4.ch015

wishes via the pocket button on his shirt. His suit and shirt are made up of nano-fibres that when networked, can store over 10TB of information, plus links to online productivity applications (there is a special emergency button though with selected applications that can be used when the OWS is offline).

Such a change from the old days when he had to carry round laptops, and documents and bags of various bits and pieces to meetings – *these days it's on me in my in clothes*.

Alex sits down and says "Travis Tyler 3H"; (Alex would rather see a full image of Travis rather than a flat panel 3D that was now technology from over five years ago, so he says "3H" rather than "3D"). 5 seconds later a holograph of Travis forms sitting about 2 metres from Alex. Alex asks "How's San Fran today Travis?" "Windy but warming up – should be nice and about 22 tomorrow", replied Travis, with his mid-length brown hair swishing around the breeze, and his nano-suit set in a sports-casual form. Alex: "Now tell me about your new SetSuit idea".

Travis outlined his concept for the SetSuit. As he starts talking, another holograph appears with a black bodysuit (smart-suit). Travis summarizes The SetSuit bodysuit:

- A One-piece suit made up of nano-fibres that can be programmed to change colours, adjust length, cut, flair and some styles.
- Built-in memory to enable carrying of all work and other data, projection, communication,
- There is a non-active Human Data Interface (HDI) that has the potential to link the smart-suit into the Human Network including the Brain. However, this version focuses on the "wearing the network" – rather than using a live human body network.
- Smart-suit is directly connected to the Web at Web 4.0 level standards. There is potential for the smart-suite to connect at emerg-

ing Web 5.0 specifications mimicking the human brain at global platform level
- The smart-suit may represent a powerful convergence of "networking using Nano-fibres + bio-networking + flexible and dynamic design
- However, there are significant political and social issues with linking nanotechnology with biotechnology and in particular with human beings.

Travis says to Alex: "So where do we go from here with this Innovation?". *A very good question* mused Alex, *and especially when you think of how where we've come from in the last 10 years*. He clicked a button and a comprehensive Social Graph of development from 2010 to 2020 appeared on a micro-lens across part of his right eye which Travis could not see. Let's recount Alex's journey from 2010 to 2020.

Alex Drake graduated in 2013 from the Google Innoversity Master of Innovation Management (GIMIM) course. For his capstone project he was required to produce new ideas in a Google Stream Package, after trawling information sources and communities. Using an early Version of the Google InnovOcean System, Alex was introduced to a diverse range of people, groups, organizations and information sources through and Using Google Stream. Common Interest Groups around the Group were forming into InnovOceans, Bays, Rivers and other pockets of communication linkage. Innoversity participants used Wave Communication principles to innovate collaboratively with relevant individuals, groups and organizations. E-Novation enabled "collabrapreneurship".

Alex focused the project on fibres developed using nanotechnology – fibres that could be used for clothing. He developed a Stream Discussion on the topic. Initially discussion was focussed on fibres adjusting for weather conditions, but changed direction when Jet Ling hatched the thought of fibres as a network. Zanda Dimitrovsky, based in St Petersburg rode the Stream by asking what could be stored and carried in such a network. Within 3 days, not only had the idea of a networked item of clothing been mused about, but several groups offered to develop and bring the idea to market.

In November 2013, the first fibre-network ET-Shirt was presented as a proof-of-concept through YOUVC. Alex Drake and Jet Ling registered as collabrapreneurs to start-up a new company – NetWear, seeking funding and "Collabs". Funding would be a mix of microfinancing contributions, corporate contributions, and funding from governments willing to invest beyond their own regions, states or nations. Collabs is a unit representing resources contributed through collaboration (usually programming, designing, engineering, testing, simulation and virtual readying of the good or service) – an exchange rate for Stream-like Web-based collaborative environments.

NetWear was able to deliver the ET-Shirt to market in time for Christmas 2014. In March 2015, Alicia Mendez joined NetWear via an E-Fashion design Stream, to develop a wider range of nano-networked clothing. Over the next five years, NetWear grew to be the largest supplier of a diverse range of nano-networked clothing.

Zanda Dimitrovosky was not impressed with NetWear's direction – she wanted to explore the full potential of networked clothing – and then some. In mid-2014 Zanda waged a well-publicized "Stream-dump" in mid–2014 pushing for linking networked clothing with human intelligence, and after much disruption, she set up the WearMeNet (WMN) Group in October 2014.

WMN worked with a global clothing company and Google to develop a smart casual business line of clothing that could store and share information and applications, and make minor user-driven adjustments to style and cut of the clothing. The WorkSmart clothing line was tested in Google's MarketWorld and launched in conjunction with the Andromedia Communications Device in November 2015.

Stacey Allen developed a children's clothing Wave in WMN and the ToddleNet range of clothing with nano-fabric to keep the toddler dry and to monitor location and wellbeing was launched in June 2016. WMN also tapped into a sustainability and social responsible consumption logic (SRCL) that emerging around 2010 to become a key business logic from early 2015. The idea of using less clothing more flexibly appealed strongly to SRCL and WMN focused on creating goods and services aimed toward SRCL collaborators and users.

NetWear responded by offering Service Packages for their nano-fibre clothing networks customized for various purposes. NetWear's OfficeNetWear (ONW) Range was launched as a general offering in June 2016, and by mid-2017, the ONW Range offered customised clothes and services for over 20 defined professions.

Zanda Dimitrovosky at WMN continued to pursue her vision to link the nano-clothing network into a human network and ultimately to the human brain. By mid-2015, networks using micro-electric currents throughout a human body had been identified and mapped, including into the brain. Experiments indicated that data could be fed through such a network - but enormous ethical and "nano-to-bio" issues remained to be addressed and resolved. During 2016, WMN invested heavily in development of a Human Data Interface (HDI) system. WMN almost collapsed in early 2017, facing financial, ethical and legal challenges claiming access to preliminary research to transmission and conversion of data into the brain.

In June 2017, NetWear "rescued" WMN through a strategic equity investment, gaining access to intellectual property, research, processes and new lines of clothing and service. However, there is a condition attached to the investment that NetWear spins out a substantial range of its own goods, services and research by the December 2020. NetWear is under pressure to take in what it needs from the WMN investment and to choose what will let go in within 30 months.

Meanwhile, Travis Tyler focused on his vision of one piece of clothing that could be configured for a diverse range of activities and conditions, and of course would be networkable. He set up the ThermalBay Stream Group – a global collaborative group named after thermals, foundation clothing used mainly in cold weather environments. ThermalBay discussed and pulled together a "proof-of-concept" suit in November 2016.

The concept was further developed and tested using the New Fashion World, coordinated development of a single nano-bodysuit. The SmartSuit was launched in May 2018 positioned as a suit for all occasions and sustainable through saving of materials for clothing, information management requirements and availability of resources for various tasks - and cost of ownership.

Tyler wanted to take the SmartSuit concept further, and worked with a collaborative cluster focused on reformable fabrics using the New-Wear World, he coordinated development of a single nano-bodysuit. Travis is now discussing this SetSuit idea with Alex Drake.

Tyler: "let's discuss this with the SetSuit team", four others appear sitting next to Tyler: Jet Ling (now chairman of NetWear), Stacey Allen, Alicia Me, and Zanda DI. The last two are actually avatar versions (or variations) of Alicia Mendez and Zanda Dimitrovsky.

Alicia Me manages NetWear's participation in the New Fashion World including design and operation directly within that world, and also moves into other Worlds relevant to development and testing of nano-networking fabrics. Alicia also enjoys changing her image in different worlds - *now that was so different to the real Alicia, mused Alexander Drake.*

Zanda offers advice on human interfaces and manages a mixed group of human and humatars (human avatars). Zanda has already developed software versions where nano-networked clothing is directly connected to humans – at she has in the form of several avatars operating in several worlds. *Zanda thinks that this project is already finished and she wants to move onto the next big human digital thing – Just like the real Zanda - Alex.*

Alicia speaks: "We need to go to market with SetSuit within 90 days. Fashion World is a green light for us".

Tyler: "What about the HDI? Can we ship with it activated?"

Jet: "We have already tried several times to have the HDI approved through the Human Authenticity Approval Agency, but they have consistently rejected us"

Zanda: "We can ship the SetSuit with the HDI disabled and leave it up to our human and humatar customers do what they want to do with it". "There is enough awareness of our HDI out there for users to work out how to enable it themselves"

Alex Drake: "It's not that simple, we have to be seen to be socially responsible and also to be innovative. We should launch the SetSuit with the HDI disabled"

Tyler: "We should consult further with our collaborators through the Nano-Wear Ocean, Let's see what they have to say about this idea"

Ten seconds later, thousands of waves of multidimensional and multi-media communications appeared as wisps in the Meeting Space merging into a changing block of red, green, orange and brown colours. On a separate wall a Social Graph is mapping as the wisps spread. What colour will the Ocean be, and what will that mean in terms of strategy and action for NetWear – and those in the Ocean?

DISCUSSION ON SCENARIO

The "Day in the life of E-Novation – 2019-20" scenario represents the use of storytelling methods to explore possible developments and options for an emerging set of technologies. Scenario development is based on a morphological approach where a range of issues are explored but the actual scenario is not pinned to a specific matrix-based map. The scenario is also focused toward Marketing Action in line with Pattinson & Sood's (2009) SPMA approach.

This particular scenario sets up a future scene but focuses on backcasting techniques to produce as stimulating narrative that deliberately includes several key concepts and issues drawn and developed further from contributions to this E-Novation Book. The variables within the E-Novation equation were also used as key concepts for scenario formulation (i.e. Collaborative Platforms, Innovation, and E-Marketing. (E-Novation equation is $(EN = CP(IN + EM))$.

An idea was developed incorporating sufficient uncertainty and capability to incorporate a large range of concepts and issues associated with E-Novation. The "Smart-Suit" idea was placed in "a-day-in-the-life-of" scenario framework, with commentary supported by a substantial search, and analysis and systematic conjecturalization of key E-Novation concepts and issues.

All chapters submitted for the E-Novation book project were run through a semantic search using Copernic Summarizer to reveal S-Nets (Semantic Nets based on minimum summaries of chapters) and key words from all the chapters. Figure 1 highlights key words.

These key words and concepts were incorporated in scenario development.

Although the scenario appears to be a single-shot sure-fire story, the main objective here is to stimulate the Reader to think about various possibilities for development of collaborative innovation – what we describe as next generation E-Novation.

The E-Novation system will continue to develop and emerge into something almost akin to a "global brain". While the E-Novation system is not likely to match a brain for reasoning and developing and exercising decision-making during the period from 2010 to 2020, it will attain low-level semantic and some simple reasoning capabilities. The E-Novation system will be-

come both sufficiently supportive and symbiotic to seamlessly co-create and co-produce various ideas into value-adding goods and services. The scenario provides some insight into how the E-Novation system helped Alex Drake conceive, create, develop, deliver and share networked nano-fibre clothing.

This chapter will discuss the current E-Novation system and then focus on next generation platforms addressing selected themes and issues contributing to next and emerging generation E-Novation.

CURRENT E-NOVATION PLATFORM.

In 2010, the global collaborative platform is very much a "Work-In-Progress". National E-Readiness indicators point toward economic development and value becoming more dependent on implementation and use by individuals, groups, businesses and governments of advanced high-speed broadband infrastructure enabled

Figure 1. Key words from e-novation chapters

Copernic S-Net Analysis – Key Concepts

- marketing
- customers
- business
- community
- Technology
- Collaborations
- e-novation
- Management
- Government
- Innovators
- internet
- Competitors
- Resources
- Networks
- online

by supporting political, economic and social environmental factors (Economist Intelligence Unit, 2009). The "infrastructure" defined by the Economist/IBM for E-Readiness assessment (and from 2010 Digital Economy Rankings - Economist Intelligence Unit, 2010), aligns reasonably with the platform developed out of Friedman's 10 Flatteners and expressed as his first of a triple convergence (Friedman, 2006). The technological convergence is at a level where it is more intelligent, interactive, and mobile than ever before.

The platform is enabling businesses to collaborate, create, design, share and deliver new goods and services. Moreover, as businesses learn to use the platform they will innovate both in ways that they develop and deliver new services and in the content that they develop amongst them (the second of the triple convergence). There is a reasonable case that collaboration and social networking has pushed the third convergence ahead of the second business convergence – and that is transforming both social and business collaboration.

From a Web 2.0 Perspective as based on a "Meme Map" by O'Reilly (2005), the Web 2.0 "Platform" is developing based on the following principles: (see Figure 2)

- The Web As A Platform
- Users Controlling Their Data
- Users Creating Content
- Collaboration and Participation
- Collective Development and Use (Co-Creation and Production; Open-Source)
- Network Effects – Applications and Services That Emerge and/or Improve As More Users "Use Them"
- Describing Activities In Terms of "Services"

User Creation and Control of content appears to enable or promote collaboration and participation leading to development and use – co-creation and production.

Network effects – where increasing numbers of individuals, groups and businesses interact with other online – are currently leading to creation and delivery of new content, applications and services. Symbiosis between the triple convergence factors, coupled with networking effects is pushing the platform and collaboration towards an emergent state.

Web 2.0 promotes a focus on development software presented as services rather than packages. This approach highlights development, delivery

Figure 2. Web 2.0 principles

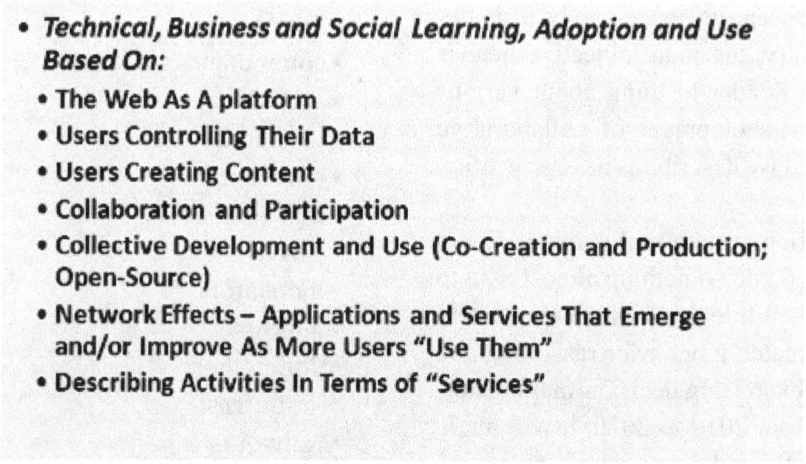

- **Technical, Business and Social Learning, Adoption and Use Based On:**
  - **The Web As A platform**
  - **Users Controlling Their Data**
  - **Users Creating Content**
  - **Collaboration and Participation**
  - **Collective Development and Use (Co-Creation and Production; Open-Source)**
  - **Network Effects – Applications and Services That Emerge and/or Improve As More Users "Use Them"**
  - **Describing Activities In Terms of "Services"**

Adapted from O'Reilly, 2005 http://www.flickr.com/photos/36521959321@N01/44349798

and use of technologies; applications and use, all using the Web as a platform. A Service-Dominant Logic (SDL) approach fits well with a Web 2.0 Service Orientation perspective. Additional supporting concepts such as Software As a Service (SaaS- running key business and other applications online) and Cloud Computing (run the whole business' application and systems online) are current enhancement of Web 2.0 development.

However, a strong case could be put that even the most advanced economies are still in the early stages of the first technological convergence, and there are significant gaps and challenges in terms of bandwidth access, web access and control, awareness and knowledge of online applications, and closed idea creation and sharing philosophies. Nevertheless through open-source, philanthropic and community initiatives, a base collaborative platform using low-cost laptop systems with open-source applications connected to increasingly Wi-Fi and mobile networks, is being deployed through emerging and developed countries. Such a base or entry-point platform will stimulate development of new business and social applications, goods and services.

So how do we shift from the E-Novation platform of 2010 and the next generation collaborative platforms of 2020?

This chapter will discuss several topics and issues that we believe will define next generation collaborative platforms and these are presented in Figure 3.

TRIPLE CONVERGENCE (BEFORE AND AFTER)

Friedman (2006) implies that there is a sequence associated with the technological, business and social convergences that collectively form a triple convergence. Convergence of the ten flatteners into a powerful platform (technological convergence) is well underway. There is substantial potential for development and incorporation of new technologies to develop a more powerful and intelligent platform that could support and be a part of future collaboration. Higher speed broadband in wired and wireless forms plus more sophisticated software applications (which can

Figure 3. Key themes for next generation e-novation

- **Triple Convergence (Before and After)**
- **Web 3.0/4.0 – The Web Is A Brain**
- **Redefined Collaborative Communication**
- **Virtual/Augmented Reality**
- **Service-Dominant Logic (SDL) Marketing and Innovation**
- **Open-Source Creation, Development and Distribution**
- **Digital Branding**
- **CRM Redefined**
- **Complexity and SME's**
- **E-Novation Office**
- **E-Novation Curriculum**
- **Social Graphing E-Novation**
- **Sustainability – Platforms and Innovation**

be seen as software technologies) will enable increased and new forms of collaboration.

Although there is an implied order to the Triple Convergence (Technological, Business, and Social), currently Social Convergence appears to be moving faster than Business Convergence. Individuals and Group through Social Media and other Web 2.0 applications are collaborating and developing new content and new communities and forms of collaboration. Some Social Media applications are being used in both business and social contexts, although there is substantial potential for new business applications, content and collaboration to be developed as these social media applications are translated into business – as variants of existing applications or as new applications and technologies. However, this is changing quickly as business, governments and educational institutions are learning to use the new platform and developing new goods and services that run on the platform.

Will technologies emerge that could be classified as additional flatteners? Friedman's views of 10 flatteners then converging to produce a new platform are reasonable, but could "freeze" perceptions of a "platform" in time. Or will emerging technologies developed from now on be classified as outcomes of the triple convergence? We think that if we fast-forward to 2020 and look back, a full triple convergence will have produced an emergent state to a platform with collaboration barely recognizable today.

WEB 3.0/4.0: THE WEB AS A BRAIN

Viewing the Web as evolving with discernable milestones helps to appreciate technological, business and social convergence – and collaborative activity. Tim O'Reilly's (2005) formulation of thinking around the Web as a platform (summarised in Figure 2) was heavily focussed on collaboration.

Since 2005, these themes have been applied to both developing the Web, to enhancing and developing new applications, and collaborating to create and share new things using this "platform". Network effects are reinforcing creating and sharing of new things - Web 2.0 is now moving toward a completed form.

Nova Spivack is the grandson of Peter Drucker. According to Spivack, "Drucker, who introduced the idea of decentralized organizations in the 1940s and viewed them as human communities, never really understood the Internet. But his ideas about organizations were timeless, Spivack felt, and he applied them to his own work." (Green 2007). Spivack is an entrepreneur who develops semantic applications focused on social connections. His latest applications are are Twine/T2 and LiveMatrix. Spivack has mapped out a timeline for development of the Web and associated social connection applications. This map (presented in Figure 4) highlights key collaborative applications for each "generation" of the Web.

According to Spivack's (2007) suggested timeline, Web 2.0 has fostered social networking, social media sharing and "lightweight collaboration". He sees Web 3.0 as a platform of intelligent systems with semantic capability, thus having some reasoning ability – and to be able to communicate and act on that capability. Web 4.0 sees the Web become one giant Operating System capable of creating and distributing human intelligence. Viewed from a different and updated angle by Novack (2010), (outlined in Figure 5) evolution of the Web can also be seen as:

- The Web *Connects Information*
- The Semantic Web *Connects Knowledge*
- Social Software *Connects People*
- The Metaweb *Connects Intelligence* (Spivack, 2010)

This conceptualisation of Web development presents a roadmap for combination of key elements of an E-Novation platform – social and

Figure 4. Web 2.0, 3.0, 4.0

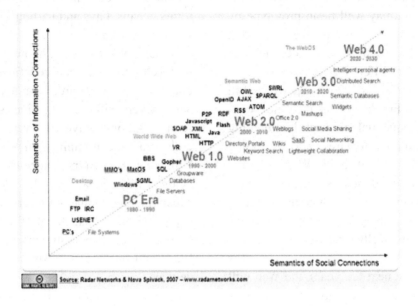

information connectivity – into an emergent meta-platform that can be viewed as about 1 to 2 generations from the current E-Novation platform.

Kevin Kelly's vision outlined in the next 5,000 Days of the Web (Kelly, 2007) sees the Web evolve into one "giant human brain" with strong parallels to synaptic and semantic capabilities of a biological human brain but expressed in a massive global system.

Kelly's vision can be linked to Bill Joy's (2000) views on links between humans and machines, published in Kelly's Wired Magazine – but they can also be traced further to Raymond Kurzweil's (1995) "Singularity" perspective where humans and machines merge. At the turn of the century such visions would have been viewed as Science Fiction, probably with a timeframe of 30-50 years from 2000. Not so 10 years on – foundations,

Figure 5. The future of the Web: Increasing information and social connectivity (source: Nova Spivack at www.mindingthe planet.net now www.novaspivack.com)

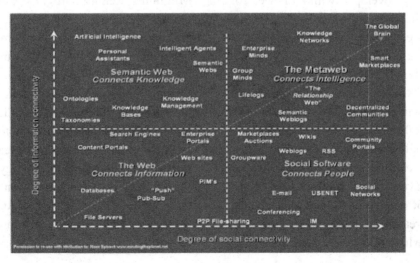

building blocks and indications are there to see that such a vision may well be in prototype by 2020 and reality in some form by 2030 – and that is why some of these elements have been included in the "Day-In-The-Life-Of-2020" Scenario.

Whether we look at Web 2.0 as a partial or full representation of Freidman's technological convergence, with sequential mileposts highlighting significant cumulative features of a developing environment (Web 2.0, Web 3.0, Web 4.0), or if we subscribe to Tim Berners-Lee's (1999) view of the Web passing through on ongoing evolution to semantic synchronisation betweens machines and humans, or the Kelly (and Kurzwell) vision of one integrated system and human brain - it is clear that over the next ten years, the Web will redefine communication, collaboration – and innovation. Just what will "Collective Intelligence" be in Web 4.0 or when the Web becomes a giant brain means that the Web and those connected to or in it, create and share ideas, goods and services together?

REDEFINED COLLABORATIVE COMMUNICATION

At the Developer Preview Session for Google Wave in May 2009, Lars Rasmussen highlighted that email communication technology was over 40 years old and developed without newer collaborative applications and technologies. Google Wave represented Google's response to the question, "What might email look if it was invented today?" (Google Inc., 2009). Google Wave pointed toward a new way of packaging and managing diverse communication application streams, using existing, web 2.0 and emerging semantic applications. The Google Wave project folded into other Google projects in June 2010. Our scenario takes the Google Wave idea and attempts to expand it into streams of communication associated with innovation. Streams link individuals, groups and communities which may be clustered in areas of

common interest – in "Stream talk" we used the terms oceans, bays and harbours in our scenario for these clusters.

Google Wave was one of the early approaches to developing a new and redefined collaborative communications environment. Other developers and thinkers will present visions similar and different to Google Wave and a version of redefined collaborative communication will likely emerge with some or even most attributes similar to the Google Wave idea. The idea of consolidating, packaging and managing information streams is apparent with management of mobile conversations and social media streams on Apple iPhones/IPads and on Google's Android driven mobile devices.

Experimentation will be required to see which combinations of "multi-communications", "multimedia" and multidimensional streams of information and application will be usable and will appeal to users. Such a redefined environment will be highly immersive and may demand a much higher user-involvement and participation than current online collaborative environments. This redefined environment may merge streams of communication into virtual and augmented worlds.

VIRTUAL/AUGMENTED REALITY

Milgram's Reality-Virtuality Continuum (Milgram & Kishino, 1994) outlines environments ranging from Purely Real to Purely Virtual. The Continuum is presented in Figure 6, with additional highlighting of "What Is Real In Collaborative Space"? Today's Virtual Worlds can be classed more toward the Purely Virtual Environment as representation is rendered animated such that it is an unconvincing expression of reality. However, platform and emerging technology developments should push environments toward the centre of the Continuum such that Mixed Reality is so close for Reality and Virtual to be non-differentiable.

Figure 6. Milgram's reality-virtuality continuum (Milgram & Kishino, 1994)

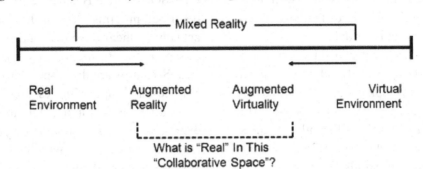

Over the last five years marketing practitioners and researchers have explored and experimented in generic virtual worlds such as Second Life. Marketers, advertisers and researchers have entered Second Life to experiment with marketing in forms such as avatars, squares, buildings or islands. Debate is intense with regard to sustained visitation in Second Life and generic virtual worlds. However, visitation and participation is strong and growing in specialised virtual worlds such as World of Warcraft (WOW). Shirky (2007) claimed that generic virtual worlds will not reach their very high expectations of participation, but specialised virtual worlds will continue to grow.

In 2010 virtual worlds such as Second Life exhibit animated graphics partly due bandwidth constraints and the applications used for development of these virtual worlds – not yet convincing as a "Mixed Reality" environment. Other virtual worlds such as massively multiplayer online role-playing games (MMORPGs) present higher resolution graphics, supporting a more immersive participatory experience – and perhaps a more convincing Mixed Reality environment.

Development of 3D technology is an area that is moving so fast that scenarios projected out to 2020 are now being rewritten for 2011-2015. In 2009-10 movies optimised for 3D viewing including *Avatar*, *Alice In Wonderland* and *Toy Story 3*, were released in cinemas and then for release on emerging 3D HDTV systems in 2010-2012. From 2007-2010, digital television manufacturers and broadcasters incorporated 3D into HD Digital TV Technology such that volume shipments of 3D HD TV's will be a reality in 2011-2012 (see Poor 2009).

While 3D HDTV systems may promote a more "immersive" entertainment experience, that will not be "interactive". Merging of online "immersive-interactivity" in 3D form may come through advanced MMORPGs, and in enhanced 3D Virtual Worlds from about 2012-2015.

In the 2020 scenario Travis Tyler is projected into the room as a hologram. Cisco demonstrated a mixed real and virtual business meeting in November 2007, where a real meeting was held in Santa Clara and holograms of Cisco managers in Virginia were beamed onto a stage at the real meeting. Cisco is working with Musion, to commercialise the holographic technology into a set of telepresence services (Cisco Inc. 2007). Holographic teleconferencing will be diffused as a collaborative business application over the next five years but should be embedded within real and augmented environments as a base technology within the Web within 10 years.

Such an environment in 2020 will enable people to literally walk into other peoples spaces, meeting places, with them, for them and even instead of them. At one extreme such an augmented space could be without any physical human presence, or it could be a mix of real and holographic presence. The possibilities are immense – as are new forms of collaboration, development and delivery of "things". Augmented Reality may seem to be real, but we may find it very difficult to discern what is real and what is virtual.

We might not have to wait that long to experience a 3D form of Augmented Reality. Augmented reality is also developing quickly particularly for mobile and gaming environments. By 2015, augmented reality will be sufficiently advanced and incorporated to make "worlds" almost indistinguishable from real-worlds. What implications are likely to emerge from a blurring of real, virtual and augmented worlds?

Augmented reality may offer an enhanced environment for conversation, collaboration and innovation where ideas and people may or may not be real – but collectively they will create new goods, services, and associated conversations. Augmented reality will be a key characteristic of emerging Research Development and Commercialization (RDC) environments where ideas, prototypes and early application will be able to be tested in specialised RDC "worlds". The scenario highlights testing of ideas and versions of clothing within such worlds.

SERVICE-DOMINANT LOGIC (SDL) MARKETING AND INNOVATION

A very strong case is presented in this book for a service-dominant approach to value creation, marketing and innovation. We believe that a Service Dominant Logic (SDL) approach will be essential for value creation within next generation innovation platforms.

A SDL approach focuses on innovation expressed through development of "appliances" containing knowledge and capabilities to be activated and used by the user - creating "value through use". SDL stretches beyond marketing to overall business strategy. Pattinson & Sood (2009) enhanced their Scenario Planning for Marketing Action (SPMA) method by developing Scenarios using SDL linked to Service-Oriented Architec-

ture (SOA) where Business Services are clearly described in terms of what they do when users actually use them. Resources and systems required to support the Business Services are also identified. Scenarios are developed for both Business Services, and supporting resources and systems.

"Collaboration" in an SDL approach can be expressed through co-creation, co-production and relationships – but how will that be expressed in development and delivery of innovation through next-generation collaborative platforms? SDL E-Novation will mean development of Business Services in conjunction with developing supporting platforms, resources and social networks – all by and for human and non-human "users". How such "Mixed Reality" development and use rolls out of the next 5-10 years will – or should be – a key focus of future innovation and marketing research and practice.

OPEN-SOURCE CREATION, DEVELOPMENT AND DISTRIBUTION

Almost inevitably, discussion on business models relevant for co-creation and co-production and collaboration, zooms in to Open-source approaches. Open-source development sets up principles permitting software developers to modify software application source code as part of revised or new software applications. Traditionally, software application users were only licensed to run software applications – not to modify them. Open-source software development offered an approach where developers – and users would collaborate to create and distribute software applications.

Initially open-source software development was focused on machine-level software, but gained notoriety in business thinking through development of the Linux operating system and IPO of Red Hat a developer and distributor of Linux for effectively zero product development costs (see McCormack & Herman 2000). At the same time, software application developers threw open applications for faster development and increased support and maintenance. Early examples included Mozilla, and at a level beyond machine software code, a range of CRM and ERP application providers.

Raymond offered justification and a simple framework for open-source development:

- a *Cathedral approach* where application development is heavily specified and managed with inputs from specific developers and experts.
- a *Bazaar approach* where anyone can contribute to application development usually through an online environment. A smaller coordinating group takes inputs and processes them into a revised or new version of the application

Goetz (2003) extended the Open-source approach beyond software applications to information products and services – a logical insight given that most information is expressed digitally as software files. Chesbrough (2006) also highlighted Innovation approaches using Open-Source.

Several Web 2.0 application developers and information services providers have elected to offer open-source access to their applications to speed up development and diffusion. Google and Apple have offered open-source development through Application Programming Interfaces (API's) to rapidly increase numbers of business and social apps and enhancements to their own applications. Google has offered open-source access to Google Wave to speed up development of features and functionality. Business and social apps effectively package and share information as "Business Services" – as vehicles for value creation under a Service-Dominant Logic (SDL) perspective.

Sood & Pattinson (2006) explored Open-source Marketing, developing an "Open Source Collaborative Creation Model (OCCM)" (see Figure 7) and discussed using Wiki's and other collaborative applications to support business-to-business creation of knowledge products and services

Low, Lee, Pattinson & Adam (2007) explored Web 2.0 applications for marketing which was further developed by Pattinson for an E-Marketing postgraduate teaching course in 2008, into "Marketing 2.0", with strong emphasis on Open-source creation, development and delivery – and an "Open-source" marketing concept.

Innovation and marketing using an Open-Source approach will continue to grow over the next five to ten years – but will be mixed with

Figure 7. Open source collaborative creation model (OCCM) (source: Sood & Pattinson, 2006)

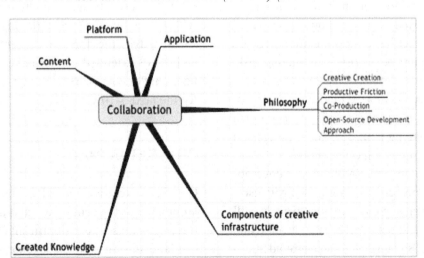

degrees of "closed-ness". Software and Information Services developers may for example select open-source applications to modify and then for a limited time offer their solution as closed-source to generate revenues, and then they may go for wider diffusion of their solution by offering it on open-source terms. Or in order to gain quick and early adoption, plus to gain further additions and enhancements, they may offer applications as open-source on release. Creative – and legal – tension related to creation and intellectual property rights will remain strong, although speed-to-market may favour Open-source research development and commercialization – or variations of it.

Whatever balance is struck, innovators and marketers will need to understand open-source implications associated with research, development and commercialisation of their idea – and how to address that to their – and their co-producers' advantage.

DIGITAL BRANDING

A Major challenge through the 2000s was for companies to translate their branding into online environments. For those who have successfully transitioned to digital branding (and for those who have not done so yet), new challenges face them as they learn about and work with social media and multiple communication "touchpoints".

Developing and implementing sophisticated Integrated Marketing Communications (IMC) plans continues to be a critical marketing task. Branding and brand management online is now the major pre-occupation of marketers. Expressing brand on a collaborative platform is much more than managing look, feel and messages on websites and through a mobile phone.

Interactive, immersive properties of developing virtual/augmented worlds, coupled with user-generated and managed conversational media will challenge how and who will create, develop and share branding. So far (that is since around 2005)

focus has been largely on attempting to control and maintain brand integrity and messages, but experimenting with viral sharing of messages and advertising campaigns to gain insights prior to large scaling launching of products, services and rebranding. Genuine development of branding directly with users combined with social conversation and testing has been limited – but is now becoming significant.

Kraft's attempts in 2009 to launch a differently formulated spread using the iconic Vegemite colours and image hit a wall when the company used a competition to select what appeared to be a cool Web 2.0 style name "I-Snack 2.0" for the new product. Social media conversation (and mainstream media) immediately condemned the new name and the way it was chosen. Kraft was forced to run a new competition conducted online and offline by Quantum Market Research, with over 30,000 people participating and 35% of participants voting for "Cheesybite" (Quirks.com, 2009). However, questions remain over the choice as over 10,000 participants did choose any of the six names offered for voting in the competition (mUmBREELA, 2009).

Another interesting issue that emerged from the Kraft I-Snack 2.0 campaign was a recognition that strong interaction through Social Media could produce several (possibly hundreds or thousands of) new ideas for a product or service – it could even conceivably add hundreds of marketers within social media to a marketing team. Understanding dynamics for development, coordination and life of extended social marketing teams will be a challenging marketing and branding focus for the next 5-10 years.

CRM REDEFINED

Customer Relationship Management emerged around the of the century as sales and marketing were key areas where significant costs, efficiencies and information management and sharing could be achieved through new and upgraded information systems. However, like development of Enterprise Resource Planning (ERP) systems in the late 1990s requiring philosophical, business and organizational consulting to develop and "Enterprise-Wide" focus, analysis and consulting was also required to define and develop "customer-focus". At the same time, the Web heralded an online revolution in Customer Activity and opportunities for tracking, managing and sharing customer information – eCRM.

By 2007, most medium to large companies had implemented CRM systems or CRM related modules of larger ERP systems. Several companies had also experienced disappointment over expected efficiencies and customer service management expected from their CRM implementation projects. Many companies refocused on defining the customer, how they engage with customers, and changing supporting CRM systems – often at great expense, but also claiming significant improvements in sales and marketing productivity.

Collaborative CRM (cCRM) emerged as a term around 2003 "an extended form of simple CRM that provides for the sharing of information among various departments of an organization" (Inside CRM, 2010). Greenberg (2004) extended cCRM to be viewed as "a distributed network of partners who are involved multiple networks themselves, where they are seen as part of an extended salesforce and technical community" (Greenberg, 2004).

However, Partner Relationship Management (PRM) emerged at about the same time as "a business strategy for improving communication between companies and their channel partners" (search CRM, 2010). In effect PRM is a substantial implementation of CRM systems extending out to other companies and channels partners. Development and delivery of PRM systems is now a key area of concern, discussion and analysis in B2B Marketing.

Since 2007, "Collaborative" CRM has taken on a new life as Web 2.0 and Social Media move toward centre-stage in a debate on the future of CRM. Terms such as CRM 2.0, Social CRM and sCRM are offered as descriptors for a new collaborative form of CRM ranging from relatively simple addition of selected Social Media applications to existing CRM systems through to new ecosystems, business social networks and customer conversation management. (See Social CRM debates at Greenberg, 2009; SocialCRMPioneers, 2010). Social CRM as defined by Greenberg is "a philosophy and a business strategy, supported by a technology platform, business rules, processes, and social characteristics, designed to engage the customer in a collaborative conversation in order to provide mutually beneficial value in a trusted and transparent business environment. It's the company's response to the customer's ownership of the conversation" (Greenberg 2010, 475)

Whichever new term is chosen an "E-Novation-based CRM" system will be a dynamically powerful platform capable of searching, mapping, networking and setting up business and group-based social networks central to supporting access, trust, immediacy and presence for innovation and marketing. Setting and managing secure, trusted and relevant information flows between co-creators and producers may require redefinition of how "open" CRM systems will need to be. Perhaps CRM should be redefined toward "Collaborative Relationship Management" to replace a Seller-focused CRM Perspective – more work is required to develop business and platform approaches.

COMPLEXITY AND SME'S

Sood's chapter in this book on SME's highlights that when start-up companies are viewed as complex systems, employees must be highly interconnected. High interconnectivity means using the advanced collaborative platform for developing and sharing ideas within and outside the start-up group. It also means that for future start-up companies they will be born in and will grow in the collaborative platform. The "start-up in a box" principle outlines a minimum requirement for start-up companies starting in 2010 - i.e. platform tools required for collaboration, and the ability to collaborate to produce surprise out of complexity.

Going forward over the next five years, for several types of innovations to be delivered in start-up company form, competencies and capabilities to imagine, discuss, develop, prototype, test and deliver ideas into Services must both be present at conception and birth of the company. Continual experimentation, and adaptation and agility will be essential. New capabilities will also be required as business and social developments through network effects converge with the continually advanced collaborative technology platform.

Of course, collaborators as small-groups will have to stake out at certain points what they intend to do in terms of freezing and delivering an idea good or service, and also when they may become a business (a start-up organization). We believe that creating and developing Startup companies and SMEs based on a complexity perspective court will lead to more finely tuned and timely innovation slashed the innovation than if a non complexity perspective was used.

E-NOVATION OFFICE

Transitioning an established organization toward a Service-Dominant Logic focused on innovation may require a focused initiative such as E-Novation Office, or Taskforce, Group.

Pattinson and Sood (2009) have outlined the Scenario Planning for Marketing Action (SPMA) approach for exploring developing ideas into innovative goods and services. An extension of SPMA in 2007 combines Service Dominant Logic with Service Oriented Architecture (SOA) to produce scenarios for Future Business Services

and future developments in supporting resources and systems, expressed through roadmaps. These tools can assist an E-Novation office to drive development of innovative goods and services.

An E-Novation office may also act as an agent to instil E-Novation throughout an organization. An interesting challenge may be whether to instil a larger, sustainable innovative organizational mindset, or to focus on a start-up, agile mindset addressing innovation collaboratively under conditions of complexity.

So far transitioning to or instilling E-Novation has been discussed in the form of E-Novation "Office". But what will constitute an "Office" in a environment when creators, users, developers, buyers and sellers are blurred in creation and sharing of goods and services? Following Raymond's (2001) archetypes for open-source development, will such an "Office" be characterised by firm moderation and driven specified collaborative direction ("Cathedral") or loose moderation to accept and integrate inputs from interested parties ("Bazaar"). Will such an Office require a mix real and virtual reality with human and dashboard systems to drive goods and services creation and development? Or will new forms and models for such an "Office" emerge over the next five years?

E-NOVATION CURRICULUM

E-Novation "Curriculum" in 2010 can be viewed from two key perspectives:

- Marketers engaging existing and potential customers through curricula on goods and services
- E-Learning and Knowledge Sharing Systems to teach and encourage creation and sharing of new and improvised knowledge and skills required to be incorporated into Service-Dominant-Logic devices (appliances) and users

Godin suggested that after consumers offer permission and attention, markers can offer a curriculum over time, teaching the consumer about their products and services. (Godin, 1999, 46). Extending interaction through curriculum may encourage marketers to further experiment with a range of Social Media and other Web 2.0 applications.

However, currently an "interaction paradox" seems to have emerged where marketers faced with choices to generate buzz, blitz and an immediate hit, or to patiently (but with great skill) build longer and deeper more insightful relationships – they have chosen the big adrenalin-driven viral hit. Much of social media and digital marketing experimentation over the last 5 years has been about reaching out to Generation Y and younger audiences – and not unreasonably, assumptions have been based on trying to break through ever-increasing noise and clutter of both mainstream and now social media itself. Undoubtedly such experimentation of "Web 2.0 on-steroids" will continue – but will it work? Can the "Buzz Hit" turn into meaningful conversations that build relationships and knowledge, and ultimately preferences, knowledge and skills to create or utilise value from the marketers' offerings?

Assuming that marketers turn to focus on engaging social media such that curricula can be presented as rich conversations through a dynamically developing platform, then how will idea generation and delivery develop over the next 5-10 years??

Curriculum in terms of E-Learning and Knowledge Sharing Systems points toward new expression of content and learning. In late 2009 as we prepared learning materials for new versions of our E-Marketing, E-Commerce and Innovation courses for 2010, due to management requirements of electronic publications we faced moving from printed and published books of readings and articles, to moving materials online. 5 years ago we would have seen PDF, HTML and other versions of Readings available online.

However, increasingly "links" to articles, papers or "stories" lead to a full online environment, in which the electronic document is part of a larger collection of materials including videos, related papers and publications, blogs, wikis., links to other related websites, connections to social media applications, alerts, podcasts, RSS feeds for synchronization, and even possibilities for further development and publishing of thoughts and conversations. The hardcopy and PDF Paper, and Readings died in 2010.

We have attempted to capture some key features and ideas in this revolution from paper to cloud in Figure 8. The platform to the right of Figure 8 is not exhaustive but a new Collaborative Learning Cloud is rapidly emerging and should be in place by 2013 with more advanced augmented aspects in place by 2015. Some key elements of this Collaborative Learning Cloud were utilised on the ongoing innovation activity outlined in the scenario.

The revolution from paper to Collaborative Learning Cloud presents major challenges for curriculum developers – whether they be marketers, educators or innovators. Innovation in terms of imagining, creating and delivering true interactive augmented learning expressed through new and next generation collaborative platforms. How these emerging curriculum delivery vehicles will be positioned with or instead of Face-to-Face or conventional online or blended learning environments will be key challenges over the next 5 years.

SOCIAL GRAPHING E-NOVATION

Sood & Pattinson (2010) have discussed multiple representations of networks related to conception and sharing of ideas for Business-to-Business Marketing activities online. Networks can be mapped linking:

- conversations on ideas, issues and actions
- online applications used for conversations

Figure 8. From paper to cloud: An emerging collaborative learning environment

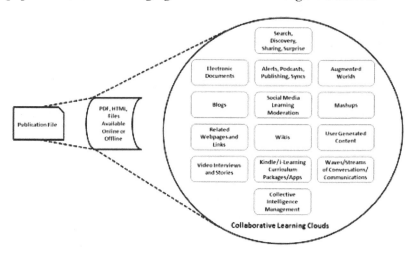

- the people actually conversing and watching these conversations

Such multi-layered Social Graphing will not only map disruptive changes in marketing, it will also redefine innovation. Such online conversations are already leading to new idea creation, debate, sharing and very quick conversion of ideas to real products and services. For example, online conversations on Social CRM lead to several major CRM Vendors releasing new Social CRM applications early in 2010 within 6 months of the idea of Social CRM being initially discussed online.

New Social Graph applications (Owyang 2007) are emerging to enable and map online conversations on innovation. Full release and enhancements to Google Wave and other similar environments will take these conversations to new levels of content, interaction and delivery over the next five years. E-Novation will be tracked through advancing Social Graphing.

SUSTAINABILITY: PLATFORMS AND INNOVATION

Sustainability is now a key theme for innovation both in terms of new products and services to be developed addressing sustainability, and how products and services are created and delivered. Sustainability principles will drive transition toward communication and sharing of ideas online using telepresence and advanced virtual/ augmented reality computer mediated environments. However, considerable debate rages about whether there may be less air travel and less face-to-face meetings – or whether air travel will become sufficiently "green" or sustainable to maintain substantial levels of physical business contact (see for example EU Transport Research "Towards Future Air Transport" – see European Commission Transport Research (2010)). How do face-to-face or geographically proximate or clustered elements contribute now and in the future to effective innovation?

More research, debate, development and experimentation of ideas on if innovation could become fully E-Novated (i.e. driven completely in computer mediated environments (CME's), or combinations of face-to-face/geographically-based communications with CME's) is required. Whichever combinations emerge, an advancing E-Novation platform will be a key enabler for all aspects of innovation now and in the foreseeable future.

E-NOVATION TODAY AND IN 2020: CLOSING COMMENTS

A new generation collaborative platform supporting E-Novation is now in place and will drive innovation over the next 2-5 years. The next generation of a collaborative E-Novation platform was explored through development and discussion of a scenario addressing a form of innovation out to 2020. Discussion was focused on revisiting themes from chapters within the E-Novation book and exploring possible future developments related to them.

Some aspects of the E-Novation platform will be logical progressions and upgrades from the current collaborative platform (such as increasing amounts of social media applications driving conversations on innovation, increased crowdsourcing producing new goods and services, the business part of the "triple convergence", and entities to encourage development and use of the platforms in firms and government, using selected technologies for communication and collaboration).

However, several features of the next generation platform will be emergent and although ideas were discussed using a scenario, new and different forms of idea generation, innovation and collaboration are likely. For example after the Triple Convergence has largely occurred, what will innovation and collaboration actually look like or be then? After Web 2.0, Social Media, and augmented reality has become commonplace (or "commonspace") what will then constitute effective E-Novation?

Innovators and marketers will need to be know and about and be active in the current new collaborative platform and then contribute to development of the next platform and goods and services associated with it.

E-Novation will be the Innovation and Marketing Social and Business Service.

REFERENCES

Berners-Lee, T., & Fischetti, M. (1999). *Weaving the Web: The past, present and future of the World Wide Web by its inventor*. London, UK: Orion Business.

Chesbrough, H. (2006). *Open innovation: The new imperative for creating and profiting from technology*. Boston, MA: Harvard Business School Press.

Cisco, Inc. (2007). *Cisco TelePresence - On-stage holographic video conferencing*. Retrieved 7 August, 2009, from http://www.musion.co.uk/Cisco_TelePresence.html

Copernic, Inc. (2010). *Copernic summarizer*. Retrieved 7 August, 2009, from http://www.copernic.com/en/products/summarizer/

Economist Intelligence Unit. (2009). *E-readiness rankings 2009: The usage imperative*. Armonkn, NY: EIU and The IBM Institute for Business Value. Retrieved August 7, 2009, from http://www-935.ibm.com/services/us/gbs/bus/pdf/e-readiness_rankings_june_2009_final_web.pdf

Economist Intelligence Unit. (2010), "Digital economy rankings 2010 Beyond e-readiness", EIU with The IBM Institute for Business Value, Retrieved 30 June 2010http://graphics.eiu.com/upload/EIU_Digital_economy_rankings_2010_FINAL_WEB.pdf.

European Commission Transport Research. (2010). Towards future air transport. Retrieved April 25, 2010, from http://ec.europa.eu/research/transport/transport_modes/aeronautics_en.cfm#

Friedman, T. L. (2006). Chapter three: The triple convergence. In T. L. Friedman (Ed.), *The world is flat* (updated and abridged). London, UK: Penguin.

Godin, S. (1999). *Permission marketing: Turning strangers into friends, and friends into customers*. New York, NY: Simon & Schuster.

Goetz, T. (2003). Open source everywhere. *Wired, 11*(11). Retrieved February 2010 from http://www.wired.com/wired/archive/11.11/opensource.html

Google Inc. (2009). *Google Wave developer preview at Google I/O 2009*. Lars Rasmussen. Retrieved May 29, 2009, from http://www.youtube.com/watch?v=v_UyVmITiYQ

Green, H. (2007, 9 July). A Web that thinks like you. *BusinessWeek.* Retrieved April 25, 2010, from http://www.businessweek.com/magazine/content/07_28/b4042066.htm?chan=search

Greenberg, P. (2009, 6 July). Time to put a stake in the ground on social CRM. *PGreenblog.* Retrieved 25 April, 2010, from http://the56group.typepad.com/pgreenblog/2009/07/time-to-put-a-stake-in-the-ground-on-social-crm.html

Greenberg, P. (2010). *CRM at the speed of light* (4th ed.). New York, NY: McGraw-Hill.

Joy, B. (2000). Why the future doesn't need us. *Wired, 8*(4). Retrieved August 7, 2009, from http://www.wired.com/wired/archive/8.04/joy_pr.html

Kelly, K. (2007). *The next 500 days of the Web.* TED Partner Series, EG Conference. Retrieved on March 1, 2010, from http://www.ted.com/index.php/talks/kevin_kelly_on_the_next_5_000_days_of_the_web.html

Kurzwell, R. (1995). *The singularity is near: When humans transcend biology.* New York, NY: Penguin Books.

Low, D. R., Lee, G., Pattinson, H. M., & Adam, S. (2007). *Web 2.0 effects on marketing management in the 21st century.* Special Session, ANZMAC 2007, Dunedin, New Zealand, 3-5 December.

MacCormack, A., & Herman, K. (2000). Red hat and the Linux revolution. *Harvard Business School, 9,* 600-009.

Milgram, P., & Fumio Kishino, A. (1994). Taxonomy of mixed reality visual displays. *IEICE Transactions on Information and Systems. E (Norwalk, Conn.), 77-D*(12), 1321–1329.

mUmBREELA. (2009, 7 October). *Vegemite 2.0: Now it's Cheesybite.* Retrieved April 23, 2010, from http://mumbrella.com.au/vegemite-2-0-now-its-cheesybite-10153

O'Reilly, T. (2005). *What is Web 2.0? Design patterns and business models for the next generation of software.* Figure 1. Retrieved August 7, 2009, from http://oreilly.com/web2/archive/what-is-web-20.html

Owyang, J. (2007). *Explaining what the social graph is to your executives (Web strategy).* Retrieved on January 16, 2010, from http://www.web-strategist.com/blog/2007/11/10/

Pattinson, H. M., & Sood, S. C. (2009). *Marketers expressing the future: Scenario planning for marketing action.* doi:10.1016/j.futures.2009.11.026

Poor, A. (2009). *3DTV: Making the transition from cinema to living room.* GigaOmPro Report, Giga Omni Media, October.

Quirks.com. (2009). i-Snack 2-point what? Vegemite reconsiders and renames product. *Quirk's Marketing Research Review,* October, (p. 6).

Raymond, E. S. (2001). *The cathedral & the bazaar: Musings on Linux and open source by an accidental revolutionary.* Sebastopol, CA: O'Reilly Media.

Shirky, C. (2007). Interview. *You Only Live Twice,* Four Corners Broadband edition, 19 March. http://www.abc.net.au/4corners/content/2007/s1873399.htm, Accessed 19 March 2007.

SocialCRMPioneers. (2010). Retrieved 25 April, 2010, from http://groups.google.com/group/social-crm-pioneers?pli=1

Sood, S. C., & Pattinson, H. M. (2006). The open source marketing experiment: Using Wikis to revolutionize marketing practice on the Web. In *Proceedings of the 22nd Industrial and Purchasing Group (IMP) Conference "Opening the Network: New Perspectives in Industrial Marketing and Purchasing."* IMP Group, Milan, Italy, 7-9 September 2006.

Sood, S. C., & Pattinson, H.M. (2010). *After the perfect storm: B2B sales and consulting representations in service-dominant markets.* Submission to IMP 2010.

Spivack, N. (2007). *Web 2.0, 3.0. 4.0.* [graphic]. Retrieved 10 April 2010 from www.radarnetworks.com, now www.novaspivack.com

Spivack, N. (2010). *Degrees of information and social connectivity,* [graphic]. Retrieved 10 April, 2010, www.novaspivack.com

Compilation of References

Aaker, D. A. (1991). *Managing brand equity.* New York, NY: The Free Press.

ADAge.com. (2004). *P&G marketing boss slams ad industry for foot-dragging.*

AGIMO. (2006). *Responsive government – A new service agenda. March 2006.* Australian Government Department of Finance and Administration, Australian Government Information Management Office.

Ahearne, M., Srinivasan, N., & Weinstein, L. (2004). Effect of technology on sales performance: Progressing from technology acceptance to technology usage and consequence. *Journal of Personal Selling & Sales Management, 24*(4), 297–310.

Ahmad, R., & Buttle, F. (2001). Customer retention: A potentially potent marketing management strategy. *Journal of Strategic Marketing, 9*(1), 29–45.

Ajzen, I. (1985). From intentions to actions: A theory of planned behavior. In Kuhl, J., & Beckmann, J. (Eds.), *Action control: From cognition to behaviour* (pp. 11–39). Heidelberg, Germany: Springer.

Allen, P. (Ed.). (2006). *Service orientation – Winning strategies and best practices.* Cambridge, UK: Cambridge University Press. doi:10.1017/CBO9780511541186

American Marketing Association. (1937). *American Marketing Association: An association for the advancement of science in marketing: Proposal for constitution and by-laws.* Chicago, IL: AMA.

American Marketing Association. (1985, March 1). The definition of marketing. *Marketing News, 2.*

American Marketing Association. (2004, September 15). Definition. *Marketing News.*

American Marketing Association. (2007). *Definition.* Retrieved from http://www.MarketingPower.com

Ang, L., & Buttle, F. (2006). Managing for successful customer acquisition: An exploration. *Journal of Marketing Management, 22,* 295–317. doi:10.1362/026725706776861217

Ang, L., & Buttle, F. (2006). Customer retention management processes: A quantitative study. *European Journal of Marketing, 40*(1/2), 83–99. doi:10.1108/03090560610637329

Archer, N., & Gebauer, J. (2000). Managing in the context of the new electronic marketplace. *Proceedings 1st World Congress on the Management of Electronic Commerce,* Hamilton, Ontario, Canada, January 19 – 21, 2000.

Armour, P. G. (2000). The case for a new business model – Is software a product or a medium? *Communications of the ACM, 43*(8), 19–22. doi:10.1145/345124.345131

Arnould, E. J. (2008). Service-dominant logic and resource theory. *Journal of the Academy of Marketing Science, 36,* 21–24. doi:10.1007/s11747-007-0072-y

Arsanjani, A. (2004). Service-oriented modeling and architecture: How to identify, specify and realize your services. *IBM developerWorks,* November.

Askarzay, W., & Unelkar, B. (2008). Strategic approach to globalization with mobile business. In Unelkar, B. (Ed.), *Handbook of research on mobile business: Technical, methodological and social perspectives.* Hershey, PA: IGI Global.

Atuahene-Gima, K. (1996). Market orientation and innovation. *Journal of Business Research, 35,* 93–103. doi:10.1016/0148-2963(95)00051-8

Baghai, M., Coley, S., & White, D. (2000). *The alchemy of growth*. New York, NY: Basic Books.

Bagozzi, R. P., & Dholakia, U. M. (2002). Intentional social action in virtual communities. *Journal of Interactive Marketing*, *16*(2), 2–21. doi:10.1002/dir.10006

Bagozzi, R. (1975). Marketing as exchange. *Journal of Marketing*, *39*(October), 32–39. doi:10.2307/1250593

Bailey, E. E., & White, L. J. (1974). Reversals in peak and offpeak prices. *The Bell Journal of Economics and Management Science*, *5*, 75–92. doi:10.2307/3003093

Baker, S. (2009, February 26). Mapping a new, mobile Internet. *BusinessWeek*.

Bakos, J. Y. (1991). A strategic analysis of electronic marketplaces. *Management Information Systems Quarterly*, *15*(3), 295–310. doi:10.2307/249641

Bakos, Y. (1998). The emerging role of electronic marketplaces on the Internet. *Communications of the ACM*, *41*(8), 35–42. doi:10.1145/280324.280330

Baldwin, C., & Clark, K. (1997). Managing in an age of modularity. *Harvard Business Review*, *75*(5), 84–93.

Bales, R. F. (1950). *Interaction process analysis*. Reading, MA: Addison Wesley.

Ballantyne, D., & Varey, R. (2006). Creating value-in-use through marketing interaction: The exchange logic of relating, communicating and knowing. *Marketing Theory*, *6*(3), 335–348. doi:10.1177/1470593106066795

Ballantyne, D., & Varey, R. (2008). The service-dominant logic and the future of marketing. *Journal of the Academy of Marketing Science*, *36*, 11–14. doi:10.1007/s11747-007-0075-8

Balmer, J. M. T. (2001). The three virtues and seven deadly sins of corporate brand management. *Journal of General Management*, *27*(1), 1–17.

Balmer, J. M. T., & Gray, E. R. (2003). Corporate brands: What are they? What of them? *European Journal of Marketing*, *37*(7/8), 20–33. doi:10.1108/03090560310477627

Banbury, C., & Mitchell, W. (1995). The effect of introducing important incremental innovations on market share and business survival. *Strategic Management Journal*, *16*, 161–182. doi:10.1002/smj.4250160922

Barley, N. (2002). Information Technology grows up-Five predictions for 2010. *Market Leader*, Spring. Retrieved from www.warc.com

Barnes, M., & Engle, R. (1995). Can sales force automation help you be a more effective manager? *Sales Process Engineering and Automation Review*, (September), 16-19.

Barratt, M., & Rosdahl, K. (2002). Exploring business-to-business market sites. *European Journal of Purchasing & Supply Chain Management*, *8*, 111–122. doi:10.1016/S0969-7012(01)00010-7

Bastiat, F. (1964). Selected essays on political economy. In de Huszar, G. B. (Ed.), *Seymour Cain reprint*. Princeton, NJ: D. Van Nordstrand.

Becker, J. U., Goetz, G., & Sönke, A. (2009). The impact of technological and organizational implementation of CRM on customer acquisition, maintenance, and retention. *International Journal of Research in Marketing*, *26*(3), 207–215. doi:10.1016/j.ijresmar.2009.03.006

Bell, T., Marrs, F., Solomon, I., & Thomas, H. (1997). *Auditing organizations through a strategic-systems lens: The KPMG business measurement process*. KPMG LLP.

Benkler, Y. (2006). *The wealth of networks: How social production transforms markets and freedom*. New Haven, CT: Yale University Press.

Bennett, R., McColl-Kennedy, J., & Coote, L. (2000). Trust, commitment and attitudinal brand loyalty: Key constructs in business-to-business relationships. *Proceedings of ANZMAC Conference: Visionary Marketing for the 21st Century: Facing the Challenge*.

Berger, C., & Piller, F. (2003). Customers as co-designers. *Manufacturing Engineering*, *82*(4), 42–45. doi:10.1049/me:20030407

Berglund, M. F. (1977). Institutional impediments to efficiency: The case of rail freight car supply. *Source: Land Economics*, *53*(2), 157–171. doi:10.2307/3145921

Berman, S., Abraham, S., Battino, B., Shipnuck, L., & Neus, A. (2007). New business models for the new media world. *Strategy and Leadership*, *35*(4), 23–30. doi:10.1108/10878570710761354

Berners-Lee, T., Hendler, J., & Lassila, O. (2001). The Semantic Web. *Scientific American, 284*(5), 34. doi:10.1038/scientificamerican0501-34

Berners-Lee, T., & Fischetti, M. (1999). *Weaving the Web: The past, present and future of the World Wide Web by its inventor.* London, UK: Orion Business.

Beyer, M. J., & Trice Harrison, M. (1978). *Implementing change: Alcoholism policies in work organizations.* New York, NY: Free Press.

Bieberstein, N. (2006). *Service-oriented architecture compass – Business value, planning, and enterprise roadmap.* Armonk, NY: IBM Press.

Blattberg, R. C., Getz, G., & Thomas, J. S. (2001). *Customer equity: Building and managing relationships as valuable assets.* Boston, MA: Harvard Business School Press.

Boar, B. (2001). *The art of strategic planning for Information Technology.* New York, NY: John Wiley and Sons.

Boehm, M. (2008). Determining the impact of Internet channel use on a customer's lifetime. *Journal of Interactive Marketing, 22*, 2–22. doi:10.1002/dir.20114

Boer, H., & During, W. (2001). Innovation, what innovation? A comparison between product, process and organisational innovation. *International Journal of Technology Management, 22*(1), 83–107. doi:10.1504/IJTM.2001.002956

Bolton, R. N. (1998). A dynamic model of the duration of the customer's relationship with a continuous service provider: The role of satisfaction. *Marketing Science, 7*(1), 45–65. doi:10.1287/mksc.17.1.45

Boujena, O., Johnston, W., & Merunka, D. (2009). The benefits of sales force automation: A customer's perspective. *Journal of Personal Selling & Sales Management, 29*(2), 137–150. doi:10.2753/PSS0885-3134290203

Boujena, O., Johnston, W., & Merunka, D. (2007). *Sales force automation benefits: A comparative study of sales managers and salespeople's perceptions.* Relationship Marketing Summit, Universidad Torcuato di Tella, Buenos Aires, December 13-15.

Boujena, O., Johnston, W., & Merunka, D. (2009). *The impact of sales force automation on customer-salesperson relationship quality: A conceptual model.* The 24th Annual National Conference in Sales Management, Norfolk, VA, 25-28th March, 2009.

Boujena, O., Merunka, D., & Johnston, W. (2009). *The impact of CRM on customer: Expected benefits and implementation issue.* The 8th International Congress Marketing Trends, ESCP-EAP, Paris, 16-17th January.

Bradley, D. B., & Peters, D. (1997). *Electronic marketplaces: Collaborate if you want to compete.* 42nd World Conference International Council for Small Business, San Francisco, June.

Brendel, J. (2008). *Information Technology the impact of virtual communities on marketing practices* [White paper].

Brown, J. S. a., & Duguid, P. (2000). Balancing act: How to capture knowledge without killing it. *Harvard Business Review, 78*(3), 73–80.

Brown, S. L., Tilton, A., & Woodside, D. M. (2002). The case for on-line communities. [from http://www.mckinseyquarterly.com]. *The McKinsey Quarterly, 1*, Retrieved 1 October, 2004.

Brown, J. J., & Reingen, P. H. (1987). Social ties and word-of-mouth referral behavior. *The Journal of Consumer Research, 14*(3), 350–362. doi:10.1086/209118

Buttle, F. (2004). *Customer relationship management: Concepts and tools.* Oxford, UK: Elsevier Butterworth Heinemann.

Buyukozkan, G., Baykasoglu, A., & Dereli, T. (2007). Integration of Internet and Web-based tools in new product development process. *Production Planning and Control, 18*(1), 44–53. doi:10.1080/09537280600940705

Büyüközkan, G. (2004). Multi-criteria decision making for e-marketplace selection. *Internet Research, 14*(2), 139–154. doi:10.1108/10662240410530853

Bygrave, W. (1989). The entrepreneurship paradigm (II): Chaos and catastrophes among quantum jumps? *Entrepreneurship Theory and Practice, 14*(2), 7–30.

Cameron, B., Orlov, L. M., & Bright, S. (2006). *Digital business networks (Syndicated Report).* Cambridge, MA: Forrester Research, Inc.

Campbell, J. (1968). *Hero with a thousand faces* (2nd ed.). Princeton, NJ: Princeton University Press.

Canton, J. (2007). *The top trends that will reshape the world in the next 20 years.* New York, NY: Plume Penguin Group.

Caruabna, A. (2002). Service loyalty. The effects of service quality and the mediating role of customer satisfaction. *European Journal of Marketing, 36*(7/8), 811–828. doi:10.1108/03090560210430818

Cassidy, R. J. (1967). *Auctions and auctioneering.* Berkeley & Los Angeles, CA: University of California Press.

Casti, J. (1994). *Complexification: Explaining a paradoxical world through the science of surprise.* New York, NY: Abacus.

Caves, R., & Ghemawat, P. (1992). Identifying mobility barriers. *Strategic Management Journal, 13*, 1–12. doi:10.1002/smj.4250130102

Chaffey, D. (2008). *What is online branding?* Retrieved from www.davechaffey.com/ E-marketing-Glossary

Chaharbaghi, K., Fendt, C., & Willis, R. (2003). Meaning, legitimacy and impact of business models in fast-moving environments. *Management Decision, 41*(4), 372–382. doi:10.1108/00251740310468013

Chang, W.-L. (2008). OnCob: An ontology-based knowledge system for supporting positions and classification of co-branding strategy. *Knowledge-Based Systems, 21*, 498–506. doi:10.1016/j.knosys.2008.03.007

Chapman, M. (2001). Branding.com: Building brand leadership in the new economy. *Corporate Reputation Review, 4*(3), 200–208. doi:10.1057/palgrave.crr.1540143

Chappell, D. (2004). *Enterprise service bus.* Sebastopol, CA: O'Reilly Publishing.

Chase, R., & Garvin, D. (1989). The service factory. *Harvard Business Review,* (July-August): 61–69.

Chavez, A., & Maes, P. (1996). Kasbah: An agent marketplace for buying and selling goods. In *Proceedings of the First International Conference on the Practical Application of Intelligent Agents and Multi-Agent Technology,* (pp. 75-90).

Chellappa, R. K., & Sin, R. G. (2005). Personalization versus privacy: An empirical examination of the online consumer's dilemma. *Information Technology Management, 6*, 181–202. doi:10.1007/s10799-005-5879-y

Chen, S. (2001). Assessing the impact of the Internet on brands. *Brand Management, 8*(4-5), 288–302. doi:10.1057/palgrave.bm.2540029

Cherkoff, J., & Moore, J. (2007). *Co-creation rules: The new realities of marketing in a networked world.* Market Research Society Annual Conference. Retrieved from www.mrs.org.uk

Chesbrough, H., & Rosenbloom, R. S. (2002). The role of the business model in capturing value from innovation: Evidence from Xerox Corporation's technology spin-off companies. *Industrial and Corporate Change, 11*(3). doi:10.1093/icc/11.3.529

Chesbrough, H. (2003). The era of open innovation. *MIT Sloan Management Review, 44*(4), 35–41.

Chesbrough, H. (2006). *Open business models: How to thrive in the new innovation landscape.* Boston, MA: Harvard Business School Press.

Chesbrough, H. (2006). *Open innovation: The new imperative for creating and profiting from technology.* Boston, MA: Harvard Business School Press.

Chicago Tribune. (2008, December 27). Stopping music piracy. *Chicago Tribune.* Retrieved from www.chicagotribune.com/ news/ opinion/ chi-1227 edit1dec 27,0,7536586.story

Choi, T. M., Li, D., & Yan, H. (2004). Optimal returns policy for supply chain with e-marketplace. *International Journal of Production Economics, 88*(2), 205–227. doi:10.1016/S0925-5273(03)00188-9

CHOICE. (2008). *Choice reply form.* Sydney, Australia: CHOICE.

Cisco, Inc. (2007). *Cisco TelePresence - On-stage holographic video conferencing.* Retrieved 7 August, 2009, from http://www.musion.co.uk/Cisco_TelePresence.html

Cognos. (2007). *What's your return on customer? An interview with Martha Rogers.* Retrieved April 1, 2008, from http://www.cognos.com/newsletter/business/ st_071017_01.html?mc=web_ns_rss

Constantin, J. A., & Lusch, R. F. (1994). *Understanding resource management*. Oxford, OH: The Planning Forum.

Cooke, M., & Buckley, N. (2008). Web 2.0, social networks and the future of market research. *International Journal of Market Research, 50*(2), 267–292.

Cooke, M., & MacFarlane, P. (2007). *Training the next generation: It's market research, but not as we know it*. Esomar Annual Congress, Berlin.

Cooper, R. G. (2001). *Winning at new products: Accelerating the process from idea to launch*. New York, NY: Perseus Books.

Copeland, M. (2006). How startups go global. *Business 2.0*, July, (pp. 107-112).

Copernic, Inc. (2010). *Copernic summarizer*. Retrieved 7 August, 2009, from http://www.copernic.com/en/products/summarizer/

Coppel, J. (2000). *E-commerce: Impacts and policy challenges*. OECD Economics Department Working Paper: 252.

Cova, B., & Cova, V. (2001). Tribal marketing: The tribalisation of society and its impact on the conduct of marketing. *European Journal of Marketing, 36*(5-6). Retrieved from http://visionarymarketing.com.

Craig-Jones, C. (2008, January 30). Evolving the maturity level of your project management office. *CIO Update*. Retrieved 5 March, 2009, from http://www.cioupdate.com/trends/article.php/3724851/Evolving-the-Maturity-Level-of-Your-Project-Management-Office.htm

Cringley, R. (1996). *Accidental empires*. New York, NY: HarperCollins Publishers.

Crosby, L. A. (2002). Exploding some myths about customer relationship management. *Managing Service Quality, 12*(5), 271–277. doi:10.1108/09604520210442056

Crosby, L. A., Evans, K. R., & Cowles, D. (1990). Relationship quality in services selling: An interpersonal influence perspective. *Journal of Marketing, 54*, 68–81. doi:10.2307/1251817

Dahan, E., & Hauser, J. R. (2002). The virtual customer. *Journal of Product Innovation Management, 19*(5), 332–353. doi:10.1016/S0737-6782(02)00151-0

Dahan, E., & Srinivasan, V. (2000). The predictive power of Internet-based product concept testing using visual depiction and animation. *Journal of Product Innovation Management, 17*(2), 99–109. doi:10.1016/S0737-6782(99)00029-6

Dai, Q., & Kauffman, R. J. (2002). Business models for Internet-based B2B electronic models. *International Journal of Electronic Commerce, 6*(4), 41–72.

Dai, Q., & Kauffman, R. J. (2003). *Understanding B2B e-market alliance strategies*. MISRC Working Papers 03-03. Carlson School of Management, The University of Minnesota. Minneapolis, MN.

Dai, Q., & Kauffman, R. J. (2000). *To be or not to B2B? An evaluative model for e-procurement channel adoption*. Working Paper, Carlson School of Management, University of Minnesota, Minneapolis, MN.

Damanpiur, F. (1991). Organisational innovation: A meta-analysis of effects of determinants and moderators. *Academy of Management Journal, 34*(3), 555–590. doi:10.2307/256406

Damanpour, F., & Fariborz, W. M. (1984). Organisational innovation and performance: The problem of organisational lag. *Administrative Science Quarterly, 29*(3), 392–411. doi:10.2307/2393031

Danaher, P. J., Wilson, I. W., & Davis, R. A. (2003). A comparison of online and offline consumer brand loyalty. *Marketing Science, 22*(4), 461–476. doi:10.1287/mksc.22.4.461.24907

Dann, S., & Dann, S. (2004). *Strategic Internet marketing 2.0*. Chichester, UK: Wiley.

Dans, E. (2002). Existing business models for auctions and their adaption to electronic markets. *Journal of Electronic Commerce Research, 3*(2).

Datta, P. R., Chowdhury, N., & Chakrabrty, B. R. (2005). Viral marketing: New form of word-of-mouth through Internet. *Business Review (Federal Reserve Bank of Philadelphia), 3*(2), 69–76.

Davis, F. D. (1989). Perceived usefulness, perceived ease of use, and user acceptance of Information Technology. *Management Information Systems Quarterly, 13*(3), 319–339. doi:10.2307/249008

Day, G. (1994). The capabilities of market-driven organization. *Journal of Marketing, 58*(October), 37–52. doi:10.2307/1251915

Dayal, S., Lanesberg, H., & Zeissberg, M. (2000). Building digital brands. *The McKinsey Quarterly, 2*, 42–51.

De Chernatony, L., & Christodoulides. (2004). Taking the brand promise online: Challenges and opportunities. *Interactive Marketing, 5*(3), 238–251. doi:10.1057/palgrave.im.4340241

De Chernatony, L., & McDonald, M. (1992). *Creating powerful brands*. Oxford, UK: Butterworth Heinemann.

Degeratu, A., Rangaswamy, A., & Wu, J. (2000). Consumer choice behavior in online and traditional supermarkets: The effects of brand name, price, and other search attributes. *International Journal of Research in Marketing, 17*(1), 55–78. doi:10.1016/S0167-8116(00)00005-7

Dellarocas, C. (2003). The digitization of word of mouth: Promise and challenges of online feedback mechanisms. *Management Science, 49*(10), 1407–1424. doi:10.1287/mnsc.49.10.1407.17308

Dholakia, U. M., Bagozzi, R., & Pearo, L. K. (2004). A social influence model of consumer participation in network- and small-group-based virtual communities. *International Journal of Research in Marketing, 21*(3), 241–263. doi:10.1016/j.ijresmar.2003.12.004

Dick, A., & Basu, K. (1994). Customer loyalty: Towards an integrated conceptual framework. *Journal of the Academy of Marketing Science, 22*(2), 99–113. doi:10.1177/0092070394222001

Dodgson, M., Gann, D., & Salter, A. (2006). The role of technology in the shift towards open innovation: The case of Procter & Gamble. *R & D Management, 36*(3), 333–346. doi:10.1111/j.1467-9310.2006.00429.x

Doherty, N. F., Ellis-Chadwick, F., & Hart, C. A. (1999). Cyber-retailing in the UK: The potential of the Internet as a retail channel. *International Journal of Retail and Distribution Management, 27*(1), 22–36. doi:10.1108/09590559910252685

Donthu, N., & Garcia, A. (1999). The Internet shopper. *Journal of Advertising Research, 39*(3), 52–58.

Doyle, P. (1998). *Marketing management and strategy* (2nd ed.). Harlow, UK: Prentice Hall.

Driedonks, C., Gregor, S., & Wassenaar, A. (2005). Economic and social analysis of the adoption of B2B electronic marketplaces: A case study in the Australian beef industry. *International Journal of Electronic Commerce, 9*, 49–72.

Driver, E., & Jackson, P. (2008). *Getting real work done in virtual worlds*. Cambridge, MA: Forrester Research.

Dweck, C. S. (2006). *Mindset*. New York, NY: Random House.

Economist Intelligence Unit. (2009). *E-readiness rankings 2009: The usage imperative*. Armonkn, NY: EIU and The IBM Institute for Business Value. Retrieved August 7, 2009, from http://www-935.ibm.com/services/us/gbs/bus/pdf/e-readiness_rankings_june_2009_final_web.pdf

Economist Intelligence Unit. (2010), "Digital economy rankings 2010 Beyond e-readiness", EIU with The IBM Institute for Business Value, Retrieved 30 June 2010http://graphics.eiu.com/upload/EIU_Digital_economy_rankings_2010_FINAL_WEB.pdf.

Edery, D. (2006). Reverse product placement in virtual worlds. *Harvard Business Review*, December.

Edmondson, A. (2008). The competitive imperative of learning. *Harvard Business Review*, (July-August): 60–67.

Ellison, N. B. (2007). Social network sites: Definition, history, and scholarship. *Journal of Computer-Mediated Communication, 13*(1).

Eng, T. Y. (2004). The role of e-marketplaces in supply chain management. *Industrial Marketing Management, 33*, 97–105. doi:10.1016/S0019-8501(03)00032-4

Erdil, S., Erdil, O., & Keskin, H. (2004). The relationships between market orientation, firm innovativeness and innovation performance. *Journal of Global Business and Technology, 1*(1).

Etzioni, A., & Etzioni, O. (1999). Face-to-face and computer-mediated communities: A comparative analysis. *The Information Society, 15*(4), 241–248. doi:10.1080/019722499128402

Eurodata, T. V. (2007). One television year in the world – 2008 edition. *Media Metrie*. Retrieved from http://www.mediametrie.com/ news.php? news_id=48

European Commission Transport Research. (2010). Towards future air transport. Retrieved April 25, 2010, from http://ec.europa.eu/research/transport/transport_modes/aeronautics_en.cfm# Friedman, T. L. (2006). Chapter three: The triple convergence. In T. L. Friedman (Ed.), *The world is flat* (updated and abridged). London, UK: Penguin.

Evans, P. B., & Wurster, T. S. (1997). Strategy and the new economics of information. *Harvard Business Review*, *75*(September-October), 71–82.

Evans, J. M., Trevino, L. K., & Weaver, G. R. (2006). Who's in the ethics driver's seat? Factors influencing ethics in the MBA curriculum. *Academy of Management Learning & Education*, *5*(3), 278–293. doi:10.5465/AMLE.2006.22697017

Ewing, J. (2007). Denmark's Masters of e-mail marketing. *Business Week Online*.

Fairchild, A. M., Ribbers, P. M. A., & Nooteboom, A. O. (2004). A success factor model for electronic markets: Defining outcomes based on stakeholder context and business process. *Business Process Management Journal*, *10*(1), 63–79. doi:10.1108/14637150410518338

Feller, J., Fitzgerald, B., Hissam, S. A., & Lakhani, K. (2005). *Perspectives on free and open source software*. Cambridge, MA: MIT Press.

Felton, J. R. (1970). *The problem of freight car supply*. Lincoln, NE: The Agricultural Experiment Station, University of Nebraska-Lincoln.

Felton, J. R. (1974). *The economics of freight car supply*. Report to the Association of American Railroads. Lincoln, Nebraska, Feb.

Fine, C. H. (1998). *Clockspeed, winning industry control in the age of temporary advantage*. New York, NY: Perseus Books.

Fortino, G., & Russo, W. (2004). A statecharts-based software development process for mobile agents. *Information and Software Technology*, *46*(13), 907–921. doi:10.1016/j.infsof.2004.04.005

Franz, R., & Wolkinger, T. (2003). Customer integration with virtual communities. Case study: The online community of the largest regional newspaper in Austria. In *Proceedings of the 36th Annual Hawaii International Conference on System Sciences,* (pp. 6-9).

Freiden, J., Goldsmith, R., Takacs, S., & Hofacker, C. (1998). Information as product: Not goods, not services. *Marketing Intelligence & Planning*, *16*(3), 210–220. doi:10.1108/02634509810217327

Friedkin, N. (1998). *A structural theory of social influence*. Cambridge, UK: Cambridge University Press. doi:10.1017/CBO9780511527524

Friedman, T. L. (2007). *The world is flat: The globalized world in the twenty-first century – Expanded and updated edition*. London, UK: Penguin Books.

Friedman, T. L. (2005). *The world is flat 3.0: A brief history of the twenty-first century*. New York, NY: Picador.

Friestad, M., & Wright, P. (1994). The persuasion knowledge model: How people cope with persuasion attempts. *The Journal of Consumer Research*, *21*(1), 1–31. doi:10.1086/209380

Fryer, B., & Stewart, T. (2008). The HBR interview: Cisco sees the future. *Harvard Business Review*, November.

Ganesan, S., Malter, A. J., & Rindfleisch, A. (2005). Does distance still matter? Geographic proximity and new product development. *Journal of Marketing*, *69*(October), 44–60. doi:10.1509/jmkg.2005.69.4.44

Gebauer, J. (1996). *Electronic market from an economic perspective*. 2nd International Workshop on Electronic Markets, University of St. Gallen, Ermatingen, Switzerland.

Gengatharen, D. E., & Standing, G. (2005). A framework to assess the factors affecting success or failure of the implementation of government-supported regional e-marketplaces for SMEs. *European Journal of Information Systems*, *14*, 417–433. doi:10.1057/palgrave.ejis.3000551

Ghenniwa, H., Huhns, M., & Shen, W. (2005). E-marketplaces for enterprise and cross enterprise integration. *Data & Knowledge Engineering*, *52*(1), 33–59. doi:10.1016/j.datak.2004.06.005

Gloor, P. (2006). *Swarm creativity: Competitive advantage through collaborative innovation networks*. New York, NY: Oxford University Press.

Glouberman, S., & Zimmerman, B. (2002). *Complicated and complex systems: What would successful reform of Medicare look like?* Institute of Health Services and Policy Research Discussion Paper, July, No. 8, (pp. 1-37).

Godin, S. (1999). *Permission marketing: Turning strangers into friends, and friends into customers*. New York, NY: Simon & Schuster.

Godson, M. (2009). *Relationship marketing*. Oxford, UK: Oxford University Press.

Goetz, T. (2003). Open source everywhere. *Wired, 11*(11). Retrieved February 2010 from http://www.wired.com/wired/archive/11.11/opensource.html

Google Inc. (2009). *Google Wave developer preview at Google I/O 2009*. Lars Rasmussen. Retrieved May 29, 2009, from http://www.youtube.com/watch?v=v_UyVmITiYQ

Google, Inc. (2010). *Google flu trends*. Retrieved 1 June, 2010, from http://www.google.org/flutrends/

Granovetter, M. (1983). The strength of weak ties: A network theory revisited. *Sociological Theory, 1*, 201–233. doi:10.2307/202051

Grant, R. M. (1997). The knowledge-based view of the firm: Implications for management practice. *Long Range Planning, 30*(3), 450–454. doi:10.1016/S0024-6301(97)00025-3

Green, H. (2007, 9 July). A Web that thinks like you. *BusinessWeek*. Retrieved April 25, 2010, from http://www.businessweek.com/magazine/content/07_28/b4042066.htm?chan=search

Greenberg, P. (2010). *CRM at the speed of light* (4th ed.). New York, NY: McGraw-Hill.

Greenberg, P. (2009, 6 July). Time to put a stake in the ground on social CRM. *PGreenblog*. Retrieved 25 April, 2010, from http://the56group.typepad.com/pgreenblog/2009/07/time-to-put-a-stake-in-the-ground-on-social-crm.html

Grieger, M. (2003). Electronic marketplaces: A literature review and a call for supply chain management research. *European Journal of Operational Research, 144*(2), 280–294. doi:10.1016/S0377-2217(02)00394-6

Grieger, M. (2004). An empirical study of business processes across Internet-based electronic marketplaces. A supply chain management perspective. *Business Process Management Journal, 10*(1), 80–100. doi:10.1108/14637150410518347

Griffiths, M. (2007). Oxygen: Social intranets, collective intelligence, and government practices. *The Electronic. Journal of E-Government, 5*(2), 177–190. Retrieved from www.ejeg.com.

Gronroos, C. (1994). From marketing mix to relationship marketing: Towards a paradigm shift in marketing. *Asia-Australia Marketing Journal, 2*(August), 9–29. doi:10.1016/S1320-1646(94)70275-6

Grönroos, C. (1990). Relationship approach to marketing in services contexts: The marketing and organizational interface. *Journal of Business Research, 20*(1), 3–11. doi:10.1016/0148-2963(90)90037-E

Grossman, R. P. (1997). Co-branding in advertising. *Journal of Product and Brand Management, 6*(3), 191–201. doi:10.1108/10610429710175709

Gummesson, E. (1999). *Total relationship marketing. Rethinking marketing management: From 4Ps to 30Rs*. Oxford, UK: Butterworth Heinemann.

Gummesson, E. (2008). Extending the new dominant logic: From customer centricity to balanced centricity. *Journal of the Academy of Marketing Science, 36*(1), 15–17. doi:10.1007/s11747-007-0065-x

Gummesson, E. (1995). Relationship marketing: Its role in the service economy. In Glynn, W. J., & Barnes, J. G. (Eds.), *Understanding service management*. New York, NY: John Wiley and Sons.

Gummesson, E. (2006). Many-to-many marketing as grand theory: A Nordic school contribution. In Lusch, R. F., & Vargo, S. L. (Eds.), *The service-dominant logic of marketing: Dialog, debate, and directions* (pp. 339–353). Armonk, NY: M.E. Sharpe.

Gummesson, E. (2004). From one to one to many to many. In B. Edvardsson, et al (Eds.), *Marketing service excellence in management: Interdisciplinary Contributions, Proceedings from QUIS 9 Symposium,* (pp. 16-25). Sweden: Karlstad University.

Gundlach, G. T. (2007). The American Marketing Association's 2004 definition of marketing: Perspectives on its implications for scholarship and the role and responsibility of marketing in society. *Journal of Public Policy & Marketing, 26*(2), 243–250. doi:10.1509/jppm.26.2.243

Hadaya, P. (2004). Determinants of the future level of use of electronic marketplaces among Canadian firms. *Proceedings of the 37th Hawaii International Conference on System Sciences,* 2004.

Haeckel, S. (1999). *Adaptive enterprise: Creating and leading sense-and-respond organizations.* Boston, MA: Harvard School of Business.

Hagel, J., & Armstrong, A. (1997). *Net gain: Expanding markets through virtual communities.* Boston, MA: Harvard Business School Press.

Hamel, G. (2000). *Leading the revolution.* Boston, MA: Harvard Business School Press.

Han, J. K., Kim, N., & Srivastava, R. K. (1998). Market orientation and organisational performance: Is innovation a missing link? *Journal of Marketing, 62*(October), 30–45. doi:10.2307/1252285

Hanson, W. (2000). *Principles of Internet marketing.* Cincinnati, OH: South Western College Publishing.

Harris, L. C., & Goode, M. M. H. (2004). The four levels of loyalty and the pivotal role of trust: A study of online service dynamics. *Journal of Retailing, 80*(2), 139–158. doi:10.1016/j.jretai.2004.04.002

Hashim, N. H., & Murphy, J. (2007). Branding on the Web: Evolving domain name usage among Malaysian hotels. *Tourism Management, 28*(2), 621–624. doi:10.1016/j.tourman.2006.09.013

Hawkins, R. (2001). *The business model as a research problem in electronic commerce. STAR (Socio-economic Trends Assessment for the digital Revolution) IST Project, Issue Report, 4, July 2001.* Brighton, UK: SPRU – Science and Technology Policy Research.

Hedman, J., & Kalling, T. (2001). *The business model: A mean to understand the business context of information and communication technology.* Working paper 2001/9, Institute of Economic Research, School of Economics and Management, Lund Universitet, Lund Sweden.

Henderson, D. R. (1984). Electronic marketing in principle and practice. *American Journal of Agricultural Economics, 66*(5). doi:10.2307/1241012

Hills, G. E., & Shrader, R. C. (1998). *Successful entrepreneurs' insights into opportunity recognition. Frontiers of Entrepreneurship Research.* Wellesley, MA: Babson College.

Hoffman, D. L., & Novak, T. P. (2009). Flow online: Lessons learned and future prospects. *Journal of Interactive Marketing, 23,* 23–34. doi:10.1016/j.intmar.2008.10.003

Hoffmann, D. L., & Novak, T. P. (1996). Marketing hypermedia computer mediated environments: Conceptual foundations. *Journal of Marketing, 60,* 50–68. doi:10.2307/1251841

Holbrook, M. (2005). Marketing miseducation and the MBA mind: B******t happens. *Marketing Education Review, 15.*

Holmquist, L. E. (2007). *2.0. Interaction.* Mobile: March-April.

Homburg, C., & Rudolph, B. (2001). Customer satisfaction in industrial markets: Dimension and multiple role issues. *Journal of Business Research, 52,* 15–33. doi:10.1016/S0148-2963(99)00101-0

Huang, C. Y., Shen, Y.-Z., Lin, H.-X., & Chang, S.-S. (2007). Bloggers' motivations and behaviors: A model. *Journal of Advertising Research, 47*(4). doi:10.2501/S0021849907070493

Huisman, D. (1997). *Information Technology brings us back to the basics.* Esomar Information Technology.

Hunter, G. K., & Perreault, W. D. Jr. (2007). Making sales technology effective. *Journal of Marketing, 71*(1), 16–34. doi:10.1509/jmkg.71.1.16

Huston, L., & Sakkab, N. (2006). Connect and develop: Inside Procter & Gamble's new model for innovation. *Harvard Business Review,* March.

Iansiti, M., & Levien, R. (2004). Strategy as ecology. *Harvard Business Review, 82*(3), 68–78.

Iansiti, M. (1998). *Technology integration: Making critical choices in a dynamic world.* Boston, MA: Harvard Business School Press.

Ibeh, K. I. N., Luo, Y., & Dinnie, K. (2005). E-branding strategies of Internet companies: Some preliminary insights from the UK. *Journal of Brand Management, 12*(5), 355–373. doi:10.1057/palgrave.bm.2540231

IBM. i2, & Ariba, A. M. (2000). *E-marketplaces changing the way we do business.* Ariba whitepaper. Retrieved from www.ibm-i2-ariba.com

Ilfield, J. S., & Winter, R. S. (2000). Generating website traffic. *Journal of Advertising Research, 42*(5), 49–61.

Interbrand. (2004). *Integrated brand communications.* Toronto, Canada: Interbrand Canada.

InvestorWords.com. (2006). *Business model definition.* Retrieved 21 April, 2006, from http://www.investorwords.com/629/business_model.html

iTunes. (n.d.). *iTunes.* Retrieved from www.apple.com/itunes

Jaffe, D. (2007). *Do not disturb.* The Advertiser.

Jain, D., & Singh, S. S. (2002). Customer lifetime value research in marketing: A review and future directions. *Journal of Interactive Marketing, 16*(2), 34–46. doi:10.1002/dir.10032

Jelinek, R., Ahearne, M., Mathieu, J., & Schillewaert, N. (2006). A longitudinal examination of individual, organizational and contextual factors on sales technology and adoption and job performance. *Journal of Marketing Theory and Practice, 14*(Winter), 7–23. doi:10.2753/MTP1069-6679140101

Jiang, P. (2004). The role of brand name in customization decisions: A search vs. experience perspective. *Journal of Product and Brand Management, 13*(2), 73–83. doi:10.1108/10610420410529708

Johnson, M. (1995). *Managing in the new millennium.* New York, NY: Butterworth Heinemann and Management Centre Europe.

Johnson, C. (2008, May 20). In praise of silence. *Sydney Morning Herald.* Retrieved 23rd May, 2008, from www.smh.com.au/news/technology/in-praise-of-silence/2008/05/20/1211182807058.html

Johnston, R., & Clark, G. (2005). *Service operations management: Improving service delivery.* Harlow, UK: Financial Times/ Prentice Hall.

Johnston, W. J., & Hite, R. (1997). *Managing salespeople: A relationship approach.* Cincinnati, OH: Southwestern Publishing Co.

Johnston, W. J., Zablah, A. R., & Bellenger, D. N. (2003). *Understanding user acceptance of CRM technology.* In 12th International Purchasing and Supply Education Research Association Conference.

Johnston, W. J., Zablah, A. R., & Bellenger, D. N. (2005). *Organizational innovation and change dissonance: Understanding user acceptance of CRM technology.* (Working paper series, Centre de Recherche de Bordeaux Ecole de Management, 73-04).

Jones, E., Sundaram, S., & Chin, W. (2002). Factors leading to salesforce automation use: A longitudinal analysis. *Journal of Personal Selling & Sales Management, 22*(3), 145–156.

Joy, B. (2000). Why the future doesn't need us. *Wired, 8*(4). Retrieved August 7, 2009, from http://www.wired.com/wired/archive/8.04/joy_pr.html

Kambil, A., & Heck, E. V. (2002). *Making markets: How firms can design and profit from online auctions and exchanges.* Boston, MA: Harvard Business School Press.

Kapferer, J.-N. (2004). *The new strategic brand management: Creating and sustaining brand equity long term.* Boston, MA: Kogan Page.

Kaplan, R. S., & Sawhney, M. (2000). B-to-B e-commerce hubs: Towards a taxonomy of business models. *Harvard Business Review, 79*(1), 97–100.

Kaplan, R. S., & Norton, D. P. (2004). *Strategy maps: Converting intangible assets in to tangible outcomes.* Boston, MA: Harvard Business School Press.

Kaplow, D., & Pelaez, J. (2002). *Understanding the economic value and business impact of B2B portals.* FactPoint Group White Paper.

Keaveney, S. M. (1995). Customer switching behavior in service industries: An exploratory study. *Journal of Marketing, 59*(April), 71–82. doi:10.2307/1252074

Keefe, L. M. (2004, September 15). What is the meaning of marketing? *Marketing News.*

Keefe, L. M. (2008, January 15). Marketing defined. *Marketing News*, (pp. 28-29).

Kelly, K. (2007). *The next 500 days of the Web*. TED Partner Series, EG Conference. Retrieved on March 1, 2010, from http://www.ted.com/index.php/talks/kevin_kelly_on_the_next_5_000_days_of_the_web.html

Kelly, S. (2008). *Identity "at risk" on Facebook.* Retrieved May 14, 2008, from http://news.bbc.co.uk/2/hi/programmes/click_online/7375772.stm

Kinney, S. (2000, April). R.I.P. fixed pricing: The Internet is on its way to "marketizing" everything. *Business Economics (Cleveland, Ohio)*, 39–44.

Klein, G. (1999). *Sources of power: How people make decisions*. Cambridge, MA: MIT Press.

Klein, G. (1999). *Sources of power: How people make decisions*. Cambridge, MA: MIT Press.

Kock, N. (2008). E-collaboration and e-commerce in virtual worlds: The potential of Second Life and World of Warcraft. *International Journal of e-Collaboration, 4*(3), 1–13. doi:10.4018/jec.2008070101

Kohler, T., Matzler, K., & Füller, J. (2008). *Avatar-based innovation: Using virtual worlds for real world innovation.* In 15th International Product Development Management Conference. Hamburg: EIASM (European Institute for Advanced Studies in Management).

Kohli, A. K., & Jaworski, B. J. (1990). Market orientation: The construct, research propositions, and managerial implications. *Journal of Marketing, 54*(2), 1–18. doi:10.2307/1251866

Koplowitz, R., & Driver, E. (2008). *Walking the fine line between chaos and control in the world of enterprise Web 2.0*. Cambridge, MA: Forrester Research.

Kozinets, R. V., De Valck, K., Wojnicki, A., & Wilner, S. (2010). Networked narratives: Understanding word-of-mouth marketing in online communities. *Journal of Marketing, 74*, 71–89. doi:10.1509/jmkg.74.2.71

Krantz, M. (1999, July 12). The next e-volution. *Time, 47*, 1999.

Krishnan, V., & Ulrich, K. T. (2001). Product development decisions: A review of the literature. *Management Science, 47*(1), 1–21. doi:10.1287/mnsc.47.1.1.10668

Kucuk, S. U. (2008). Negative double jeopardy: The role of anti-brand sites on the Internet. *Journal of Brand Management, 15*(3), 209–222. doi:10.1057/palgrave.bm.2550100

Kumar, V., & Werner, R. (2005). *Customer relationship management: A data-based approach*. Chichester, UK: John Wiley & Sons, Inc.

Kuppler, F., Mertens, M., Skiba, A., & Linnow, J. (2008). *Customer@Company.net: Competitive advantage through Web-based interaction with customers in innovation and production*. Detecon International. Retrieved from http://www.detecon.com

Kurzweil, R. (2001). *The law of accelerating returns*. KurzweilAI.net. Retrieved February 11, 2009, from http://www.kurzweilai.net/articles/art0134.html?printable=1

Kurzwell, R. (1995). *The singularity is near: When humans transcend biology*. New York, NY: Penguin Books.

Kwon, S. D., Yang, H. D., & Rowley, C. (2009). The purchasing performance of organizations using e-marketplaces. *British Journal of Management, 20*(1), 106–124. doi:10.1111/j.1467-8551.2007.00555.x

Lancaster, L., & Stillman, D. (2003). *When generations collide*. New York, NY: HarperCollins Publishers, Inc.

Laseter, T., Long, B., & Caper, C. (2001). B2B benchmark: The state of electronic exchanges. *Strategy+Business, 25*, 33–42.

Latane, B. (1981). The psychology of social impact. *The American Psychologist, 36*, 343–356. doi:10.1037/0003-066X.36.4.343

Lau, R. Y. K. (2007). Towards a Web services and intelligent agents-based negotiation system for B2B e-commerce. *Electronic Commerce Research and Applications*, *6*(3), 260–273. doi:10.1016/j.elerap.2006.06.007

Lau, R. Y. K., Li, Y., Song, D., & Kwok, R. C. W. (2008). Knowledge discovery for adaptive negotiation agents in e-marketplaces. *Decision Support Systems*, *42*(2), 310–323. doi:10.1016/j.dss.2007.12.018

Lavassani, K., Movahedi, B., & Kumar, V. (2008). Transition to B2B e-marketplace enabled supply chain: Readiness assessment and success factors. *Proceedings of 2008 International Conference on Information Resources Management (Conf-IRM 2008)*, Ontario, Canada.

Lazar, J. R., Tsao, R., & Preece, J. (1999). One foot in cyberspace and the other on the ground: A case study of analysis and design issues in a hybrid virtual and physical community. *Web Net Journal: Internet Technologies. Applications and Issues*, *1*(3), 49–57.

Ldraw. (n.d.). *Home page*. Retrieved from www.ldraw.org

Leader, S. (2007). Send marketing emails that boost responses. *Sales Leader*, *12*(24), 1.

Lee, M. R., & Lan, Y. (2007). From Web 2.0 to conversational knowledge management: Towards collaborative intelligence. *Journal of Entrepreneurship Research*, *2*(2), 47–62.

Lei, J., Dawar, N., & Lemmink, J. (2008). Negative spillover in brand portfolios: Exploring the antecedents of asymmetric affects. *Journal of Marketing*, *72*(May), 111–123. doi:10.1509/jmkg.72.3.111

Leong, E., Huang, X., & Stannersa, P.-J. (1998). Comparing the effectiveness of the website with traditional media. *Journal of Advertising Research*, *38*(5), 44–49.

Lewicki, R. J., McAllister, D. J., & Bies, R. J. (1998). Trust and distrust: New relationships and realities. *Academy of Management Review*, *23*, 438–458.

Lewis, M. (2006). Customer acquisition promotions and customer asset value. *JMR, Journal of Marketing Research*, *43*(May), 195–203. doi:10.1509/jmkr.43.2.195

Li, H., Cao, J., Castro-Lacouture, D., & Skibniewski, M. (2002). A framework for developing a unified B2B e-trading construction marketplace. *Automation in Construction*, *12*, 201–211. doi:10.1016/S0926-5805(02)00076-6

Libert, B., & Spector, J. (2008). *We are smarter than me*. Upper Saddle River, NJ: Wharton School Publishing.

Lipis, L. J., Villars, R., Byron, D., & Turner, V. (2000). *Putting markets into place: An e-marketplace definition and forecast*. Retrieved from http://www.idc.com

Livejournal. (n.d.). *Home page*. Retrieved from www.livejournal.com

Louta, M., Roussaki, I., & Pechlivanos, L. (2008). An intelligent agent negotiation strategy in the electronic marketplace environment. *European Journal of Operational Research*, *187*(3), 1327–1345. doi:10.1016/j.ejor.2006.09.016

Low, D. R., Lee, G., Pattinson, H. M., & Adam, S. (2007). *Web 2.0 effects on marketing management in the 21st century*. Special Session, ANZMAC 2007, Dunedin, New Zealand, December 3-5.

Lowy, A., & Hood, P. (2004). *The power of the 2 x 2 matrix: Using 2x2 thinking to solve business problems and make better decisions*. San Francisco, CA: Jossey-Bass.

Luczkiw, G. (2005). *Jazzin' in the vineyard –Entrepreneurial education in an age of chaos, complexity and disruptive change*. OECD's International Conference Fostering Entrepreneurship: The Role of Higher Education, June 23.

Lusch, R. F., Brown, S. W., & Brunswick, G. J. (1992). A general framework for explaining internal vs. external exchange. *Journal of the Academy of Marketing Science*, *20*(Spring), 119–134. doi:10.1007/BF02723452

Lusch, R. F., Brown, S. W., & Malter, A. (2006). Marketing as service-exchange: Taking a leadership role in global marketing management. *Organizational Dynamics*, *35*(3), 264–278. doi:10.1016/j.orgdyn.2006.05.008

Lusch, R. F., Brown, S. W., & O'Brien, M. (2007). Competing through service: Insights from service-dominant logic. *Journal of Retailing*, *83*(1), 5–18. doi:10.1016/j.jretai.2006.10.002

Lusch, R. F., Brown, S. W., & Tanniru, M. (forthcoming). Service, value networks and learning. *Journal of the Academy of Marketing Science.*

Lusch, R. F., & Vargo, S. L. (2008). Toward a conceptual foundation for service science: Contributions from service-dominant logic. *IBM Systems Journal, 47*(1). doi:10.1147/sj.471.0005

Lynch, P., & Beck, J. (2001). Profiles of Internet buyers in 20 countries: Evidence of region specific strategies. *Journal of International Business Studies, 32*(4), 725–748. doi:10.1057/palgrave.jibs.8490992

MacCormack, A., & Herman, K. (2000). Red hat and the Linux revolution. *Harvard Business School, 9,* 600-009.

Mack, J. (2005). Tribal Marketing. *Pharma Marketing News, 4.* Retrieved January 14, 2008, from www.news.pharma-mkting.com/pmn411-oped.html

Mackay, H. (2007). *Advance Australia... where? How we've changed, why we've changed, and what will happen next?* Sydney, Australia: Hachette Livre.

Madanmohan, T. R., Kumar, V., & Kumar, U. (2005). Success or failure of e-marketplaces. *Proceedings of Administrative Sciences Association of Canada.* Technology and Innovation Management Division. Toronto, Canada, May 2005.

Madhavaram, S., & Hunt, S. D. (2008). The service-dominant logic and a hierarchy of operant resources: Developing masterful operant resources and implications for marketing strategy. *Journal of the Academy of Marketing Science, 36*(Spring), 67–82. doi:10.1007/s11747-007-0063-z

Maes, P., Guttman, R., & Moukas, A. (1999). Agents that buy and sell. *Communications of the ACM, 42*(3), 81–91. doi:10.1145/295685.295716

Mahoney, J. (2008, December 26). The 10 best Android apps of 2008. *Gizmodo.*

Malone, T., Yates, J., & Benjamin, R. (1994). Electronic markets and electronic hierarchies. In Malone, T., & Morton, M. S. (Eds.), *Information Technology and the corporation of the 1990s* (pp. 61–83). New York, NY: Oxford University Press.

Malthus, T. (1798). *An essay on the principle of population.* London, UK: J. Johnson, St. Paul's Church-Yard.

Market Sentinel. (2007). *Online brand building – A case study from Avis Europe.* Retrieved from www.market-sentinel.com

Marketing, P. (2005). Tribal marketing. *Pharma Marketing News, 4,* 1-2. Retrieved January 14, 2008, from www.news.pharma-mkting.com/pmn411-oped.html

Marks, E., & Bell, M. (2006). *Service-oriented architecture – A planning and implementation guide for business and technology.* New York, NY: Wiley.

Martina, G., & Kia, J. (2007). E-business standardization in the automotive sector: Role and situation of SEMs. In MacGregor, R. C., & Hodgkinson, A. (Eds.), *Small business clustering technologies.* Hershey, PA: Idea Group Inc.

Mason, P., & Davis, B. H. (2007). More than the words: Using stance-shift analysis to identify crucial opinions and attitudes in online focus groups. *Journal of Advertising Research, 47*(4). doi:10.2501/S0021849907070511

Mathwick, C. (2002). Understanding the online consumer: A typology of online relational norms and behavior. *Journal of Interactive Marketing, 16*(1), 40–55. doi:10.1002/dir.10003

McCoy, J. H., & Sarhan, M. E. (1988). *Livestock and meat marketing.* New York, NY: Van Nostrand Reinhold.

McDonald, M. (2008). Viewpoint-After 50 years of IJMR, the state of marketing. *International Journal of Market Research, 50.* Retrieved from www.ijmr.com

McGirt, E. (2008). *How Cisco's CEO John Chambers is turning the tech giant socialist.* Retrieved March 2, 2009, from http://www.fastcompany.com/magazine/131/revolution- in- san- jose.html

McKay, L. (2008). *A startup feeds off feedback.* Retrieved on March 1, 2009, from http://www.destinationcrm.com/Articles/Columns-Departments/Secret-of-My-Success/A- Startup- Feeds- Off- Feedback- 51751.aspx

Mckelvey, B. (2004). Toward a complexity science of entrepreneurship. *Journal of Business Venturing, 19*(3). doi:10.1016/S0883-9026(03)00034-X

McNealy, S. (2001). Welcome to the bazaar. *Harvard Business Review, 79*(3), 18–19.

McNichols, T. J., & Brennan, L. (2006). Evaluating partner suitability for collaborative supply networks. *International Journal of Networking and Virtual Organizations, 3*(2), 220–237.

Meraki. (n.d.). *Home page*. Retrieved from www.meraki.com

Merisavo, M., & Raulas, M. (2004). The impact of email marketing on brand loyalty. *Journal of Product and Brand Management, 13*(7), 498–505. doi:10.1108/10610420410568435

Meuter, M. L., Ostrom, A. L., Rountree, R. I., & Bitner, M. J. (2000). Self-service technologies: Understanding customer satisfaction with technology-based service encounters. *Journal of Marketing, 64*(3), 50–64. doi:10.1509/jmkg.64.3.50.18024

Meyers, H., & Gerstman, R. (2001). *Branding at the digital age*. Toronto, Canada: Interbrand. doi:10.1057/9781403905468

Microsoft. (2008). *Most valuable professional program*. Retrieved June 17, 2008, from http://mvp.support.microsoft.com/gp/mvpawardintro

Milgram, P., & Fumio Kishino, A. (1994). Taxonomy of mixed reality visual displays. *IEICE Transactions on Information and Systems. E (Norwalk, Conn.), 77-D*(12), 1321–1329.

Minniti, M., & Bygrave, W. (2001). A dynamic model of entrepreneurial learning. *Entrepreneurship: Theory and Practice*, Spring.

Mintzberg, H. (1983). *Structure in fives: Designing effective organizations*. Englewood Cliffs, NJ: Prentice Hall.

Mokyr, J. (2002). *The gifts of Athena: Historical origins of the knowledge economy*. Princeton, NJ: Princeton University Press.

Moon, J. Y., & Sproull, L. (2001). *Turning love into money: How some firms may profit from voluntary electronic customer communities*. Unpublished manuscript

Moore, A. (2005). Simple ideas lightly held. In Sattersten, T. (Ed.), *More space: Nine antidotes to complacency in business, astronaut projects*.

Morali, A., Varela, L., & Varela, C. (2005). *An electronic marketplace: Agent-based coordination models for online auctions*. In XXXI Conferencia Latinoamericana de Informática, Cali, Colombia, October 2005.

Morgan, R. M., & Hunt, S. D. (1994). The commitment-trust theory of relationship marketing. *Journal of Marketing, 58*, 20–38. doi:10.2307/1252308

Morris, M., Schindehutte, M., & Allen, J. (2005). The entrepreneur's business model: Toward a unified perspective. *Journal of Business Research, 58*(6), 726–735. doi:10.1016/j.jbusres.2003.11.001

Motion, J., Leitch, S., & Brodie, R. J. (2003). Equity in corporate co-branding: The case of Adidas and the All Blacks. *European Journal of Marketing, 37*(7/8), 1080–1094. doi:10.1108/03090560310477672

Mueller, R. A. E. (2000). Emergent e-commerce in agriculture. Agriculture Issues Center. *AIC Issues Brief, 14*, December.

mUmBREELA. (2009, 7 October). *Vegemite 2.0: Now it's Cheesybite*. Retrieved April 23, 2010, from http://mumbrella.com.au/vegemite-2-0-now-its-cheesybite-10153

Murphy, J., Rafa, L., & Mizerski, R. (2003). The use of domain names in e-branding by the world's top brands. *Electronic Markets, 13*(3), 222–232. doi:10.1080/1019678032000108310

Murphy, J., & Scharl, A. (2007). An investigation of global versus local online branding. *International Marketing Review, 24*(3), 297–312. doi:10.1108/02651330710755302

Murtaza, M. B., Gupta, V., & Carroll, R. C. (2004). E-marketplaces and the future of supply chain management: Opportunities and challenges. *Business Process Management Journal, 10*(3), 325–335. doi:10.1108/14637150410539722

Musser, J., & O'Reilly, T. (2006). *Web 2.0 principles and best practices*. Sebastopol, CA: O'Reilly.

Muylle, S., & Basu, A. (2008). Online support for business processes by electronic intermediaries. *Decision Support Systems, 45*(4)..doi:10.1016/j.dss.2008.02.005

Nambisan, S. (2002). Designing virtual customer environments for new product development: Toward a theory. *Academy of Management Review, 27*(3), 392–413.

Nambisan, S., & Sawhney, M. (2008). *The global brain.* Upper Saddle River, NJ: Wharton School Publishing.

Naumann, E. (1995). *Creating customer value: The path to sustainable competitive advantage.* Cincinnati, OH: Thomson Executive Press.

NetBeans. (2008). *IDE 6.9 features.* Retrieved June 17, 2008, from http://www.netbeans.org/features/index.html

Nine, M. S. N. (2008). *DJ jailed for luring teenager for sex.* Retrieved May 26, 2008, from http://news.ninemsn.com.au/article.aspx?id=569408

Nonis, S. A., Philhours, M., Syamil, A., & Hudson, G. I. (2005). The impact of non-intellectual variables on the academic success of business students. *Marketing Education Review, 15*(3).

Nord, R. W., & Tucker, S. (1987). *Implementing routine and radical innovations.* Washington, DC.

Normann, R., & Ramirez, R. (1993). From value chain to value constellation: Designing interactive strategy. *Harvard Business Review,* (Jul/Aug): 65–77.

Normann, R. (2001). *Reframing business: When the map changes the landscape.* Chichester, UK: John Wiley & Sons, Ltd.

Nyliasy, G., & Reid, L. N. (2007). The academician-practitioner gap in advertising. *International Journal of Advertising, 26,* Retrieved from www.warc.com.

Nysveen, H., Pedersen, P. E., Thorbjornsen, H., & Berthon, P. (2005). Mobilizing the brand: The effects of mobile services on brand relationships and main channel use. *Journal of Service Research, 7*(3), 257–276. doi:10.1177/1094670504271151

O'Brien, J., & Hawkins, J. (2008). *The future of shared services in the European public sector.* New York, NY: Ovum.

O'Reilly, T. (2005). *What is Web 2.0? Design patterns and business models for the next generation of software.* Figure 1. Retrieved August 7, 2009, from http://oreilly.com/web2/archive/what-is-web-20.html

O'Reilly. (2006). *Web 2.0 compact definition: Trying again.* Retrieved July 6, 2008, from http://radar.oreilly.com/archives/2006/12/web_20_compact.htm/Pattinson, H. M., & Woodside, A. G. (2007). *Innovation and diffusion of software technology: Mapping strategies.* Oxford, UK: Elsevier.

Oliver Young, G. (2008). *Top enterprise Web 2.0 predictions for 2008.* Cambridge, MA: Forrester Research.

Oliver Young, G., Brown, E. G., Keitt, T., Owyang, J. K., Koplowitz, R., & Lo, H. (2008). *Global enterprise Web 2.0 market forecast: 2007 to 2013.* Cambridge, MA: Forrester Research.

OpenSolaris Governing Board. (2007). *OpenSolaris constitution – Current version.*

OpenSolaris Governing Board. (2008). *Statement of the OGB class of 2008's "can-do" attitude and approach to governance.* Retrieved June 17, 2008, from http://www.genunix.org/wiki/index.php/OGB_2008/001

Opoku, R., & Hinson, R. (2006). Online brand personalities: An exploratory analysis of selected African countries. *Place Branding, 2*(2), 118–129. doi:10.1057/palgrave.pb.5990050

Oracle. (2008). *Sun sponsors open source community $1M innovation award.* Retrieved from http://www.sun.com/software/opensource/awards/index.jsp

Owyang, J. (2007). *Explaining what the social graph is to your executives (Web strategy).* Retrieved on January 16, 2010, from http://www.web-strategist.com/blog/2007/11/10/

Park, J. S. (2005). Opportunity recognition and product innovation in entrepreneurial hi-tech start-ups: A new perspective and supporting case study. *Technovation, 25,* 739–752. doi:10.1016/j.technovation.2004.01.006

Parthasarathy, M., & Sohi, R. S. (1997). Sales force automation and the adoption of technological innovations by salespeople: Theory and implications. *Journal of Business and Industrial Marketing, 12*(3), 196–201. doi:10.1108/08858629710188036

Pattinson, H., & Woodside, A. G. (2007). *Innovation and diffusion of software technology: Mapping strategies.* New York, NY: Elsevier Science.

Pattinson, H. M., & Low, D. R. (2008). *E-novation: An offbeat view of innovation, e-marketing and a new collaborative information platform.*

Pattinson, H. M., & Sood, S. C. (2009). *Marketers expressing the future: Scenario planning for marketing action.* doi:10.1016/j.futures.2009.11.026

Paustian, C. (2001). Better products through virtual customers. *MIT Sloan Management Review*, Spring.

Payne, A., & Frow, P. (2004). The role of multichannel integration in customer relationship management. *Industrial Marketing Management, 33*(6), 527–538. doi:10.1016/j.indmarman.2004.02.002

Peer, D. (1976). *Pricing systems for hogs in Ontario.* Lecture, Agr. Econ. and Extens. Educ., University of Guelph, 22 Oct. 1976.

Peikin, D. (2003). Data quality: The foundation for effective CRM. *Target Marketing, 26*(2), 49–50.

Peppers, D., & Rogers, M. (2004). *Managing customer relationship: A strategic framework.* Chichester, UK: John Wiley & Sons Inc.

Petersen, K. J., Ogden, J. A., & Carter, P. L. (2007). B2B e-marketplaces: A typology by functionality. *International Journal of Physical Distribution & Logistics Management, 37*(1), 4–18. doi:10.1108/09600030710723291

Peterson, R. A. (Ed.). (1997). *Electronic marketing and the consumer.* Thousand Oaks, CA: Sage.

Pine, B. J., & Gilmore, J. H. (1999). *The experience economy: Work is theater & every business a stage.* Cambridge, MA: Harvard Business School Press.

Polemans, M. (2006). *Workbook e-citizen charter,* version 2.2.

Poor, A. (2009). *3DTV: Making the transition from cinema to living room.* GigaOmPro Report, Giga Omni Media, October.

Porter, M. E. (1980). *Competitive strategy.* New York, NY: Free Press.

Poslad, R. (2009). *Ubiquitous computing: Smart devices, environment and interactions.* Chichester, UK: Wiley.

Prahalad, C. K., & Ramaswamy, V. (2004). Co-creation experiences: The next practice in value creation. *Journal of Interactive Marketing, 18*(3), 5–14. doi:10.1002/dir.20015

Prahalad, C. K., & Hamel, G. (1990). The core competence of the corporation. *Harvard Business Review, 68*(May-June), 79–91.

Prahalad, C. K., & Ramaswamy, V. (2000). Co-opting customer competence. *Harvard Business Review, 78*(January-February), 79–87.

Prahalad, C. K., & Krishnan, M. S. (2008). *The new age of innovation: Driving co-created value through global networks.* New York, NY: McGraw-Hill Professional.

Prahalad, C. K. (2008). *Inaugural address.* Special Conference of the Strategic Management Society, December 12-14, Hyderabad, India.

Prandelli, E., Verona, G., & Raccagni, D. (2006). Diffusion of Web-based product innovation. *California Management Review, 48*(4), 109–135.

Productions, I. T. V. (2007). *Trinny and Susannah undress the nation.* United Kingdom.

Pura, M. (2003). Case study: The role of mobile advertising in building a brand. In Mennecke, B. E., & Strader, T. J. (Eds.), *Mobile commerce: Technology, theory and applications* (pp. 291–309). Hershey, PA: Idea Group Publishing. doi:10.4018/9781591400448.ch017

Purewal, S. (2001, June 27). This entrepreneur makes you laugh. *The Tribune India.* Retrieved December 27, 2008, from http://www.tribuneindia.com/ 2001/ 20010627/ biz.htm

Quirks.com. (2009). i-Snack 2-point what? Vegemite reconsiders and renames product. *Quirk's Marketing Research Review,* October, (p. 6).

Rafiq, M., & Fulford, H. (2005). Loyalty transfers from offline to online stores in the UK grocery industry. *International Journal of Retail & Distribution Management, 33*(6), 444–460. doi:10.1108/09590550510600861

Ragone, A., Straccia, U., Noia, T. D., Sciascio, E. D., & Donini, F. M. (2009). Fuzzy match making in e-marketplaces of peer entities using Datalog. *Fuzzy Sets and Systems, 160*, 251–268. doi:10.1016/j.fss.2008.07.002

Ramocki, S. (2007). A critical challenge awaiting marketing education. *Marketing Education Review*, 17.

Rangarajan, D., Jones, E., & Chin, W. (2005). Impact of sales force automation on technology-related stress, effort, and technology usage among salespeople. *Industrial Marketing Management*, 34(4), 345–354. doi:10.1016/j.indmarman.2004.09.015

Rasmusen, E. (2001). *Games and information: An introduction to game theory*. London, UK: Blackwell Publishing.

Rasmusen, E. (2001). *Strategic implications of uncertainty over one's own private value in auctions*. Working Papers-2001, Indiana University, Kelley School of Business, Department of Business Economics and Public Policy.

Rasmusen, E. (2007). *Getting carried away in auctions as imperfect value discovery*. Working Papers 2007-05, Indiana University, Kelley School of Business, Department of Business Economics and Public Policy.

Ratnasingham, P. (1998). The importance of trust in electronic commerce. *Internet Research*, 8(4), 313–321. doi:10.1108/10662249810231050

Raymond, E. S. (2001). *The cathedral & the bazaar-Musings on Linux and open source by an accidental revolutionary*. Sebastopol, CA: O'Reilly Media Inc.

Rayport, J. F., & Sviokla, J. J. (1994). Managing in the marketspace. *Harvard Business Review*, 72(6), 141–150.

Reedy, J., & Schullo, S. (2004). *Electronic marketing*. Mason, OH: Mason Publishing.

Reichheld, F., & Sasser, W. (1990). Zero defects: Quality comes to services. *Harvard Business Review*, (September-October): 105–111.

Reinartz, W., Thomas, J. S., & Kumar, V. (2005). Balancing acquisition and retention resources to maximize customer profitability. *Journal of Marketing*, 69(January), 63–79. doi:10.1509/jmkg.69.1.63.55511

Reinhold, N., & Bhutiaia, K. L. (2007). *The virtual home visit: identifying people insights in the virtual world*. Esomar Qualitative Research Paris. Retrieved from www.esomar.org

Report, W. (2006). *Surveillance company implants workers with RFID chips*. Retrieved August 1, 2008, from http://www.thewirelessreport.com/2006/02/13/surveillance-company-implants-workers-with-rfid-chips/

Ridings, C. M., Gefen, D., & Arinze, B. (2002). Some antecedents and effects of trust in virtual communities. *The Journal of Strategic Information Systems*, 11, 271–295. doi:10.1016/S0963-8687(02)00021-5

Riegner, C. (2007). Word of mouth on the Web: The impact of Web 2.0 on consumer purchase decisions. *Journal of Advertising Research*, 47(4), 436–447. doi:10.2501/S0021849907070456

Ries, A., & Ries, L. (2000). *The 11 immutable laws of Internet branding*. London, MA: Harper Collins.

Rodgers, C. (2006). *Informal coalitions: Mastering the hidden dynamics of organizational change*. New York, NY: Palgrave Macmillan.

Rogers, M. R. (1995). *Diffusion of innovations* (2nd ed.). London, UK: MacMillian.

Romano, B. (2007, June 28). Bringing something new to the table. *Seattle Times*.

Romm, C., Pliskin, N., & Clarke, R. (1997). Virtual communities and society: Toward an integrative three phase model. *International Journal of Information Management*, 17(4), 261–270. doi:10.1016/S0268-4012(97)00004-2

Rosson, P. (2000). Electronic trading hubs: Review and research questions. *Proceedings, 16th. IMP Conference*, Bath, UK.

Rousseau, D. M., Sitkin, S. B., Burt, R. S., & Camerer, C. (1998). Not so different after all: A cross-discipline view of trust. *Academy of Management Review*, 23, 393–404. doi:10.5465/AMR.1998.926617

Rowley, J. (2004). Online branding. *Online Information Review*, 28(2), 131–138. doi:10.1108/14684520410531637

Rowley, J. (2004b). Online branding: The case of McDonald's. *British Food Journal*, 106(3), 228–237. doi:10.1108/00070700410528808

Rowley, J. (2008). Online branding strategies of UK fashion retailers. *Internet Research*, 19(3).

Rowley, J., Kupiec-Teahan, B., & Leeming, E. (2007). Customer community and co-creation: A case study. *Marketing Intelligence & Planning, 25*(2), 136–146. doi:10.1108/02634500710737924

Rubenstein, H. (2002). Branding on the Internet – Moving from a communication to a relationship approach to branding. *Interactive Marketing, 4*(1), 33–40. doi:10.1057/palgrave.im.4340161

Rubenstein, H., & Griffiths, C. (2001). Branding matters more on the Internet. *Brand Management, 8*(6), 394–404. doi:10.1057/palgrave.bm.2540039

Russom, P. (2007). The shifting continuum: The increase in semi- and unstructured data means changes for your data warehouse. *Teradata Magazine,* December.

Saifar, D. (2008). *Community statement of intent.* Retrieved June 16, 2008, from http://www.australiadotnet.com.au/

Sandberg, K. D. (2002). Is it time to trade in your business model? *Harvard Management Update,* (January), 3-5.

Sawy, O., Eriksonnon, I., Raven, A., & Carlsson, S. (2001). Understanding shared knowledge creation spaces around business processes: Precursors to process innovation implementation. *International Journal of Technology Management, 22*(1), 149–173. doi:10.1504/IJTM.2001.002959

Schank, R. C., & Abelson, R. P. (1977). *Scripts, plans, goals and understanding.* Hillsdale, NJ: Erlbaum.

Schaper, M., & Colery, T. (2003). *Entrepreneurship and small business: A Pacific Rim perspective.* Brisbane, Australia: John Wiley.

Schillewaert, N., Ahearne, M., Frambach, R. T., & Moenaert, R. K. (2005). The adoption of Information Technology in the sales force. *Industrial Marketing Management, 34,* 323–336. doi:10.1016/j.indmarman.2004.09.013

Schmid, B. F. (1999). Elektronische Maerkte - Merkmale, Organisation und Potentiale. In Sauter, M., & Hermanns, A. (Eds.), *Handbuch Electronic Commerce* (pp. 29–48). Munich.

Schmid, B. F., & Lindemann, M. A. (1998). *Elements of a reference model for electronic markets.* 31st Hawaii International Conference on System Sciences, IEEE Computer Society Press, (pp. 193-201) Los Alamitos, CA.

Schrader, L. F., Heifner, R. G., & Larzelere, H. E. (1968). *The electronic egg exchange, an alternative system for trading shell eggs.* Michigan State University. Agr. Econ. Rep. No. 119, Dec. 1968.

Segev, A., Gebauer, J., & Farver, F. (1999). Internet based electronic markets. *Electronic Markets, 9*(3), 138–146. doi:10.1080/101967899359021

Serjeant, J. (2008, May 20). Why the switched on are switching off. *Sydney Morning Herald.* Retrieved 22nd May, 2008, from www.smh.com.au/news/technology/why-the switched-on-are-switching-off/2008/05/20/121118

Shankar, V., Urban, G. L., & Sultan, F. (2002). Online trust: A stakeholder perspective, concepts, implications, and future directions. *The Journal of Strategic Information Systems, 11*(3/4), 325–344. doi:10.1016/S0963-8687(02)00022-7

Shapiro, B. P. (1988). What the hell is market orientated? *Harvard Business Review, 66,* 119–125.

Shen, Z., & Su, X. (2007). Customer behavior modeling in revenue management and auctions-A review and new research opportunities. *Production and Operations Management, 16*(6), 713–728. doi:10.1111/j.1937-5956.2007.tb00291.x

Shirky, C. (2007). Interview. *You Only Live Twice,* Four Corners Broadband edition, 19 March. http://www.abc.net.au/4corners/content/2007/s1873399.htm, Accessed 19 March 2007.

Shuen, A. (2008). *Web 2.0: A strategy guide.* Sebastopol, CA: O'Reilly Media, Inc.

Simmons, G. J. (2007). "I-branding": Developing the Internet as a branding tool. *Marketing Intelligence & Planning, 25*(6), 544–562. doi:10.1108/02634500710819932

Singh, M., & Waddell, D. (2003). *E-business innovation and change management.* Hershey, PA: IGI Global.

Skjøtt-Larsen, T., Kotzab, H., & Grieger, M. (2003). Electronic marketplaces and supply chain relationships. *Industrial Marketing Management, 32*, 199–210. doi:10.1016/S0019-8501(02)00263-8

Slywotzky, A. J. (1996). *Value migration: How to think several moves ahead of the competition.* Boston, MA: Harvard Business School Press.

Smeltzer, L., & Carr, A. (2003). Electronic reverse auctions: Promises, risks, and conditions for success. *Industrial Marketing Management, 32*(6), 481–488. doi:10.1016/S0019-8501(02)00257-2

Smith, A. (2000). *The nature and causes of the wealth of nations.* New York, NY: The Modern Library.

Smith, A. (1904). *An inquiry into the nature and causes of the wealth of nations* (5th ed. by Edwin Cannan). London, UK: Methuen and Co., Ltd.

SocialCRMPioneers. (2010). Retrieved 25 April, 2010, from http://groups.google.com/group/social-crm-pioneers?pli=1

Sood, S., & Pattinson, H. (2006). Urban renewal in Asia-Pacific: A comparative analysis of brainports for Sydney and Kuala Lumpur. *Journal of Business Research, 59*(6). doi:10.1016/j.jbusres.2005.12.003

Sood, S. C., & Pattinson, H. M. (2005). *Semantics in marketspace: Emerging semantic marketing computer-mediated environments.* Presented at The Annual Meeting Of The Society For Marketing Advances, San Antonio, Texas – November 2-5, 2005.

Sood, S. C., & Pattinson, H. M. (2006). The open source marketing experiment: Using Wikis to revolutionize marketing practice on the Web. In *Proceedings of the 22nd Industrial and Purchasing Group (IMP) Conference "Opening the Network: New Perspectives in Industrial Marketing and Purchasing,"* IMP Group, Milan, Italy, 7-9 September 2006.

Sood, S. C., & Pattinson, H.M. (2010). *After the perfect storm: B2B sales and consulting representations in service-dominant markets.* Submission to IMP 2010.

Speier, C., & Venkatesh, V. (2002). The hidden minefields in the adoption of sales force automation technologies. *Journal of Marketing, 66*(3), 98–112. doi:10.1509/jmkg.66.3.98.18510

Spivack, N. (2007). *Web 2.0, 3.0. 4.0.* [graphic]. Retrieved 10 April 2010 from www.radarnetworks.com, now www.novaspivack.com

Spivack, N. (2010). *Degrees of information and social connectivity,* [graphic]. Retrieved 10 April, 2010, www.novaspivack.com

Stabell, C. B., & Fjeldstad, D. (1998). Configuring value for competitive advantage: On chains, shops and networks. *Strategic Management Journal, 19*, 413–437. doi:10.1002/(SICI)1097-0266(199805)19:5<413::AID-SMJ946>3.0.CO;2-C

Stacey, R. (1996). *Complexity and creativity in organisations.* San Francisco, CA: Berrett Koehler.

Standing, C., Love, P. E. D., Stockdale, R., & Gengatharen, D. (2006). Examining the relationship between electronic marketplace strategy and structure. *IEEE Transactions on Engineering Management, 53*(2), 297–311. doi:10.1109/TEM.2005.861801

Steampowered. (n.d.). *Home page.* Retrieved from www.steampowered.com

Steamworks. (n.d.). *Home page.* Retrieved from www.steamworks.com

Step Two Designs. (2008). *Intranet innovations 2008.* Retrieved March 1, 2009, from http://www.steptwo.com.au/ products/iia2008

Strauss, J., El-Ansary, A., & Frost, R. (2003). *E-marketing.* Upper Saddle River, NJ: Prentice Hall.

Strebinger, A., & Treiblmaier, H. (2004). E-adequate branding: Building offline and online brand structure within a polygon of interdependent forces. *Electronic Markets, 14*(2), 153–164. doi:10.1080/101967804100 01675095

Stuart, H., & Jones, C. (2004). Corporate branding in marketspace. *Corporate Reputation Review, 7*(1), 84–93. doi:10.1057/palgrave.crr.1540213

Subramaniam, C., Shaw, M. J., & Gardner, D. M. (2000). Product marketing and channel management in electronic commerce. *Information Systems Frontiers, 1*(4), 363–378. doi:10.1023/A:1010061924822

Sundaram, S., Schwarz, A., Jones, E., & Chin, W. (2007). Technology use on the front line: How Information Technology enhances individual performance. *Journal of the Academy of Marketing Science, 35*(March), 101–112. doi:10.1007/s11747-006-0010-4

Sundia Corp. (2009). *Sundia true fruit website.* Retrieved March 3, 2009, from http://www.sundiafruit.com

Sweet, P. (2001). Strategic value configuration logics and the "new" economy: A service economy revolution? *International Journal of Service Industry Management, 12*(1), 70–83. doi:10.1108/09564230110382781

Sweney, M. (2007, 16 July). Top 10 online brand campaigns named. *The Guardian.* Retrieved from www.guardian.co.uk/ media

Sydney Morning Herald. (2008). *Facebook unveils more minimalist look.* Retrieved May 22, 2008, from www.smh.com.au/news/web/facebook-unveils-more-minimalist-look/2008/05/22/121118296460

Tapscott, D., Ticoll, D., & Lowy, A. (2000). *Digital capital: Harnessing the power of business Webs.* Boston, MA: Harvard Business School Publishing Corporation.

Tapscott, D. (2008). *Grown up digital: How the Net generation is changing your world.* New York, NY: McGraw-Hill.

Tapscott, D., Ticoll, D., & Lowy, A. (2000). *Digital capital: Harnessing the power of business webs.* Boston, MA: Harvard Business School Publishing Corporation.

Teece, D. J. (2002). *Managing intellectual capital.* Oxford, UK: Oxford University Press. doi:10.1093/0198295421.001.0001

Terdiman, D. (2007). *The entrepreneur's guide to Second Life: Making money in the metaverse.* Indianapolis, IN: Sybex.

Terziyan, V. (2005). Semantic Web services for smart devices based on mobile agents. *International Journal of Intelligent Information Technologies, 1*(2), 43–55. doi:10.4018/jiit.2005040104

Thomas, J. S., & Sullivan, U. Y. (2005). Managing marketing communications with multichannel customers. *Journal of Marketing, 69,* 239–251. doi:10.1509/jmkg.2005.69.4.239

Tibco. (2008). *Tibco culture.* Retrieved December 27, 2008, from http://www.tibco.com/ company/ recruiting/ tibco_culture.jsp

Timmers, P. (1998). Business model for electronic markets. *Electronic Markets, 8,* 3–8. doi:10.1080/10196789800000016

Toffler, A. (1980). *The third wave.* New York, NY: Bantam Books.

Tormabene, C. A., & Wiederhold, G. (1998). Software component licensing: A primer. *IEEE Software, 15*(5), 47–53. doi:10.1109/52.714771

Tornatzky, L. G., Eveland, J. D., & Fleischer, M. (1990). Technological innovation as a process. In Tornatzky, L. G., & Fleischer, M. (Eds.), *The processes of technological innovation* (pp. 27–50). Lexington, MA: Lexington Books.

Torvalds, L., & Diamond, D. (2001). *Just for fun: The story of an accidental revolutionary.* New York, NY: Texere.

Turban, E., King, D., Lee, J., Warkentin, M., & Chung, H. M. (2002). *Electronic commerce.* Upper Saddle River, NJ: Prentice-Hall.

Ulrich, K., & Eppinger, S. (2004). *Product design and development.* New York, NY: McGraw-Hill/Irwin.

Uncles, M., Dowling, G., & Hammond, K. (2003). Customer loyalty and customer loyalty programs. *Journal of Consumer Marketing, 20*(4). doi:10.1108/07363760310483676

Urban, G. L., & Hauser, J. R. (1993). *Design and marketing of new product.* Englewood Cliffs, NJ: Prentice-Hall.

Vakrat, Y., & Seidmann, A. (1999). *Optimal design of online auction.* William E. Simon Graduate School of Business Administration, University of Rochester, Rochester, NY. Working Paper, November, 1999.

Valve Software. (n.d.). *Home page.* Retrieved from www.valvesoftware.com

Varadarajan, R. P., & Yadav, M. S. (2002). Marketing strategy and the Internet: An organizing framework. *Journal of the Academy of Marketing Science, 30*(4), 296–312. doi:10.1177/009207002236907

Vargo, S. L. (2008). Customer integration and value creation: Paradigmatic traps and perspectives. *Journal of Service Research, 11*, 211–215. doi:10.1177/1094670508324260

Vargo, S. L., & Lusch, R. F. (2004). Evolving to a new dominant logic for marketing. *Journal of Marketing, 68*, 1–17. doi:10.1509/jmkg.68.1.1.24036

Vargo, S. L., & Lusch, R. F. (2008). Service-dominant logic: Continuing the evolution. *Journal of the Academy of Marketing Science, 36*(1), 1–10. doi:10.1007/s11747-007-0069-6

Vargo, S. L., & Morgan, F. W. (2005). Services in society and academic thought: A historical analysis. *Journal of Macromarketing, 25*(1), 42–53. doi:10.1177/0276146705275294

Vargo, S. L., & Lusche, R. F. (2006). Service-dominant logic: What it is, what it is not, what it might be. In Lusch, R. F., & Vargo, S. L. (Eds.), *The service-dominant logic of marketing: Dialog, debate and directions* (pp. 43–56). Armonk, NY: M.E. Sharpe, Inc.

Vargom, S., & Lusch, R. (2004). Evolving to a new dominant logic for marketing. *Journal of Marketing, 68*, 1–17. doi:10.1509/jmkg.68.1.1.24036

Vascellaro, J. E. (2007). Social networking goes professional. *Wall Street Journal.* Retrieved from http://online.wsj.com/article/SB118825239984310205.html

Venkatesh, V., & Davis, F. D. (1996). A model of the antecedents of perceived ease of use: Development and test. *Decision Sciences, 27*(3), 451–481. doi:10.1111/j.1540-5915.1996.tb01822.x

Venkatraman, N. V. (2008). From the industrial age to the network age. *Market Leader*, Spring. Retrieved from www.warc.com

Vickrey, W. (1961). Counterspeculation, auctions, and competitive sealed tenders. *The Journal of Finance*, 16.

Villanueva, J., Yoo, S., & Hanssens, D. M. (2008). The impact of marketing-induced vs. word-of-mouth customer acquisition on customer equity. *JMR, Journal of Marketing Research, 45*, 48–59. doi:10.1509/jmkr.45.1.48

Von Hippel, E. (2005). *Democratizing innovation.* Cambridge, MA: MIT Press.

Waldrop, M. (1992). *Complexity: The emerging science at the edge of order and chaos.* New York, NY: Simon & Schuster.

Wang, Y. D., & Emurian, H. H. (2005). An overview of online trust: Concepts, elements, and implications. *Computers in Human Behavior, 21*(1), 105–125. doi:10.1016/j.chb.2003.11.008

Ward, M., & Lee, M. (2000). Internet shopping, consumer search and product branding. *Journal of Product and Brand Management, 9*(1), 6–20. doi:10.1108/10610420010316302

Watson, I. (2001). *INFOSHOP: A decision support tool for local government regulatory advice.* Advances in Artificial Intelligence. PRICAI 2000 Workshop Reader. Berlin, Germany: Springer.

Wei, T., Kan, J., & Zi-Gang, Z. (2007). *Supply chain coordination study based on retailers' inventory transshipment via e-marketplace.* International Conference on Management Science and Engineering, China, (pp. 1019-1024).

Weller, T. C. (2000). *B2B e-commerce: The rise of e-marketplaces. Research report.* Reston, VA: Legg Mason Wood Walker, Inc.

Wells, R. (2007). Outstanding customer satisfaction: The key to a talented workforce? *The Academy of Management Perspectives*, 87–89. doi:10.5465/AMP.2007.26421243

Whalen, P. J. (2007). *Strategic and technology planning on a roadmapping foundation. Technology Management.* May-June.

Wheelwright, S., & Clark, K. (1992). *Revolutionizing product development: Quantum leaps in speed, efficiency, and quality.* Florence, MA: Free Press.

White, A., Daniel, E., Ward, J., & Wilson, H. (2007). The adoption of consortium B2B e-marketplaces: An exploratory study. *The Journal of Strategic Information Systems, 16*, 71–103. doi:10.1016/j.jsis.2007.01.004

White, A. D., & Mohdzain, M. B. (2009). An innovative model of supply chain management: A single case study in the electronic sector. *International Journal of Information Technology and Management, 8*(1), 69–84. doi:10.1504/IJITM.2009.022271

Wikipedia. (2009). *Porter's five forces analysis*. Retrieved 11 February, 2009, from http://en.wikipedia.org/wiki/Porter%27s_5_Force_Model

Willcocks, L., Petherbridge, P., & Olson, N. (2002). *Making IT count: Strategy, delivery, infrastructure.* Butterworth-Heinemann.

Wilson, S., & Abel, I. (2002). So you want to get involved in e-commerce. *Industrial Marketing Management, 31*(2), 85–94. doi:10.1016/S0019-8501(01)00188-2

Wilson, N. (2009). *Virtual qorlds for business.* Clever Zebra, Q2.1.

Woodman, R. W., Sawyer, J. E., & Griffin, R. W. (1993). Toward a theory of organizational creativity. *Academy of Management Review, 18*(2), 293–321.

Xie, H., & Boggs, D. (2006). Corporate branding versus product branding in emerging markets: A conceptual framework. *Marketing Intelligence & Planning, 24*(4), 347–364. doi:10.1108/02634500610672099

Yamin, S., Gunasekaran, A., & Mavondo, F. (1999). Innovation index and its implications on organisational performance: A study of Australian manufacturing companies. *International Journal of Technology Management, 17*, 495–503. doi:10.1504/IJTM.1999.002733

Yan, J. (2001, March 17). Online branding: An Antipodean experience. *CAP Online*. Retrieved from www.jyanet.com

Yen, H. R. (2005). An attribute-based model of quality satisfaction for Internet self-service technology. *The Service Industries Journal, 25*(5), 641–659. doi:10.1080/02642060500100833

Yu, C. S., & Tao, Y. H. (2007). Enterprise e-marketplace adoption: From the perspectives of technology acceptance model, network externalities, and transition costs. *Journal of International Management, 14*(4), 231–265.

Zablah, A. R., Bellenger, D. N., & Johnston, W. J. (2004). Customer relationship management implementation gaps. *Journal of Personal Selling & Sales Management, 24*(Fall), 279–295.

Zahra, S. A., & Covin, J. G. (1993). Business strategy, technology policy and firm performance. *Strategic Management Journal, 14*, 451–478. doi:10.1002/smj.4250140605

Zaltman, G., Duncan, R., & Holbek, J. (1973). *Innovations and organisations.* New York, NY: Wiley.

Zappala, S., & Gray, C. (2006). *Impact of e-commerce on consumers and small firms.* Surrey, UK: Ashgate Publishing, Ltd.

Zappos. (2007). *Zappos 07 culture.* Retrieved December 27, 2008, from http://zapp.me/z7427746

Zappos. (2008, December 5). *Inside Zappos culture class.* Retrieved December 27, 2008, from http://au.youtube.com/ watch?v=vq2VZH3jZ7U

Zeithaml, V. A., Parasuraman, A., & Berry, L. L. (1985). Problems and strategies in services marketing. *Journal of Marketing, 49*(Spring), 33–46. doi:10.2307/1251563

Zhang, X., & Prybutok, V. R. (2005). A consumer perspective of e-service quality. *IEEE Transactions on Engineering Management, 52*(4), 461–477. doi:10.1109/TEM.2005.856568

Zhu, F. X., Wymer, W., & Chen, I. (2002). IT-based services and service quality in consumer banking. *International Journal of Service Industry Management, 13*(1), 69–91. doi:10.1108/09564230210421164

Zimmerman, E. (1951). *World resources and industries.* New York, NY: Harper and Row.

About the Contributors

Hugh M. Pattinson is Senior Lecturer in the School of Marketing at the University of Western Sydney. He recently completed a PhD on applying storytelling and decision systems analysis to new Internet-based software application development and delivery. Other areas for research focus include scenario planning and its application in marketing, scenario planning of new and emerging e-business technologies, negotiation research from a complex systems perspective, and new methodologies for analysis and visualisation of unstructured information. He also maintains a strong research interest in strategic alliances and Internet marketing. Pattinson has a substantial record of curriculum development particularly in the area of e-marketing and e-business and was the Director of E-Business Marketing Programs in the Faculty of Business at UTS. He has developed several courses and subjects from pre-university level through to MBA and Executive MBA courses. Prior to joining UTS, he spent over 12 years in various marketing roles within the information technology industry including Channels Marketing Manager, Competitive Intelligence Manager, Marketing Business Analyst, and Market Research Consultant.

David R. Low is Head of the School of Marketing at the University of Western Sydney. Since his appointment to UWS he has written and implemented a program of studies in E-Marketing at both the undergraduate and postgraduate levels. Prior to joining UWS he was a lecturer in E-Marketing at the University of Technology, Sydney. His research interests include cross cultural issues; country of origin studies, ethnicity, market orientation, firm performance, e-marketing, innovation, SMEs, and the use of technology in business value chains. His research has appeared in many industry publications as well as the *International Journal of Cross Cultural Management, International Journal of Employment Studies,* and the *Employment Relations Record.* Low has been involved in a number of successful competitive grants involving projects investigating the role of ICT in manufacturing firms. Low is a member of the ***Australian Market and Social Research Society as*** well as a graduate member of the Australian Institute of Company Directors and a member of the Australia-New Zealand Marketing Academy (ANZMAC). He is currently a Director of the Western Sydney Business Connection, a networking based organisation in the same regional area as the University of Western Sydney, and he is Chair of the Riverside Theatres Advisory Board. Prior to becoming an academic, Low gained extensive experience in industries as diverse as Manufacturing, Retail, Professional Services, Entertainment, Construction, and IT. Positions held included roles such as CFO, Channel/Product Manager, and GM Service.

* * *

Melissa Archpru Akaka is a doctoral student in marketing at the Shidler College of Business at the University of Hawaii at Manoa. Her research interests include value and value co-creation, service-dominant logic, social networks, and cross-cultural issues. Prior to her graduate and doctoral studies, Akaka worked in the travel industry and the not-for-profit sector. She has an MBA and a BBA in marketing, both from the University of Hawaii at Manoa.

David Bird, having taught in Web Design and E-Learning at Salford in the mid 90s, joined Academee as a Chief Learning Architect for 2 years before a brief spell at Sheffield Hallam. In 2004, he joined MMU Business School as a lecturer in digital marketing. He now runs both the internationally renowned E-consultancy MSc in Digital Marketing Communications and the E-consultancy MSc in Internet Retailing. David has also run several small businesses in the digital media sector and held a number of non-executive roles in digital creative firms. He is also a Council Member at Manchester Digital, the trade association for firms in the digital sector.

Othman Boujena is an Associate Professor of Marketing at Rouen Business School (France) and Director of the Center for Customer, Retail, and Supply Chain. He is also responsible for the Major in Marketing of the Master's Program. He holds a Research Master's of Science in Management with a specialization in Marketing and Information Systems and his PhD from Paul Cézanne University Aix-Marseilles III. He is also an associate research fellow of the Center of Studies and Research on Management at the Graduate School of Management in Aix-en-Provence. He teaches consumer behavior, relationship marketing, marketing strategy, and CRM. He developed or contributed to many marketing pedagogical projects. His research interests focus on relationship marketing, customer relationship management, and sales force automation. He has been a visiting research fellow at Georgia State University. He is affiliated to the IMP Group and French Marketing Association and member of the scientific committee of different international conferences on marketing. He is author/coauthor of several papers in international conferences (NCSM, MSI, GSSI, etc.) and has been recently a coauthor of a paper on sales technologies published in JPSSM.

Michael Conlin is the Chief Technology Officer for HP Enterprise Services Asia. In this capacity he sets the technology direction for an organisational unit that spends over two billion US dollars per year on IT and for clients spending a combined more than 50 billion per year on IT. Widely recognised for his consulting work, he advises business executives on IT strategy and IT executives on business strategy. He is particularly well known for his ability to help clients turn insight into impact at pace. With over 30 years of experience in IT, Michael is well versed in setting technical direction and strategy. Conlin has served a wide range of organizations, from the Fortune 1 firm to start-ups, and from commercial enterprises to governments. He has hands-on experience in every aspect of the IT business. He has done business in more than 20 countries and in all industry sectors. He currently lives in Singapore with his wife and children. When he is not helping clients with the esoterica of strategy, he pursues his passions in glass blowing, black smithing, gold smithing, lapidary carving, and wood butchery.

Alessia D'Andrea received her degree in Communication Science at the University of Rome La Sapienza. She is a PhD student in Multimedia Communication at the University of Udine sponsored by the IRPPS of the National Research Council of Italy. She is mainly interested in communication science, social science, risk management, virtual communities, mobile technologies, and health studies.

Stephen Dann is Senior Lecturer in the School of Management, Marketing, and International Business, College of Business and Economics at the Australian National University. His research has been published in *Social Marketing Quarterly, The Monash Business Review, Quality Assurance in Education,* and the *Journal of Public Affairs.* He has published a range of marketing text books including *Strategic Internet Marketing, Competitive Marketing Strategy,* and is a regular contributor to the *Australian and New Zealand Marketing Academy Conference.* His research interests include political marketing, consumer behaviour, Internet marketing, marketing strategy, and innovation adoption.

Ehsan Ehsani is a researcher and consultant in the area of innovation and product development. Ehsan is currently working with Accenture Product Innovation and PLM practice in New York City Office and has consulted and worked with a variety of firms including ExxonMobil, Diageo, Sara Lee, Henkel, Unilever, UPM-Kymmene, Ericsson, SKF, Telefonica, Repsol, SAB Miller, Abertis Telecom, and Lego. Ehsan has a Bachelor's in Chemical Engineering, a Master's in Production and Operations Management from Chalmers University in Sweden, and a Master's in Supply Chain Management from MIT-Zaragoza International Logistics Program.

Fernando Ferri received degrees in Electronic Engineering in 1990 and PhD in Medical Informatics at the University of Rome "La Sapienza" in 1993. He is senior researcher of the National Research Council of Italy. He has been contract Professor from 1993 to 2000 of "Sistemi di Elaborazione" at the University of Macerata. He is the author of more than 140 papers on international journal, books, and conferences. His main research areas of interest are: Geographic Information Systems, data and knowledge bases, human-computer interaction, user modelling, visual interfaces, sketch based interfaces, risk management, and medical informatics. He has coordinated two European research project: MIDIR (FP6, Contract number: 036708) and INCA (FP7, Contract number 070401/2008/507855), as well as various national projects.

Daphne Freeder is the Manager of CMOS (Centre for Management and Organisations), a key research centre in the Faculty of Business at the University of Technology, Sydney Australia (UTS). Freeder has extensive academic teaching experience in the disciplines of e-business marketing, management, and Information Sciences conducting undergraduate, postgraduate, and executive level training. She has professional expertise in the public, private, and volunteer sectors working in the fields of radio, public relations, and knowledge management. Freeder is currently undertaking PhD research concerning leadership and social intelligence. She is also a small business owner following on from the traditions and inspiration of her family. At present she is also President of the University of Technology, Sydney Branch of the National Tertiary Education Union, and National Councillor.

Patrizia Grifoni received the degree in Electronic Engineering at the University of Rome "La Sapienza." She is researcher of the National Research Council of Italy. From 1994 to 1999, she was contract Professor of "Elaborazione digitale delle immagini" at the University of Macerata. She is the author of more than 90 papers on journal, books, and conferences. Her main research interests are in human computer interaction, visual interfaces, sketch based interfaces, accessing Web information, and Geographic Information Systems.

Kevin Jin received his Master's degree in Information Systems from University of New South Wales, Australia. He also holds a Post-graduate Diploma in Business and Administration from Massey University, New Zealand, and a Bachelor of Economics degree from Shandong Economics Institute in China. During his study, he co-authored "Business-Oriented Development Methodology for IT Service Management" for Hawaii International Conference on System Science (HICSS) in 2008. With a career in IT industry spanning nearly 20 years, Jin has been working in Strategy and Enterprise Architecture field for over a decade in both large corporation and consulting firms. Regarded as a Business Technology Visionary with executive and hands-on experience gained from software vendor, corporate enterprise, and strategy consultancy, Jin has great success in creating robust IT strategy and architecture, and has been involved in large IT-enabled innovation and business transformation programs. In addition to big transformation initiatives, Kevin is also interested in business and IT process improvement and optimization. He has worked in IT governance, SDLC methodology, portfolio management, and risk management. He has led in many projects to build and enhance IT service delivery. Jin is an ISACA Certified Information System Auditor (CISA).

Wesley J. Johnston is the CBIM RoundTable Professor of Marketing and Director of the Center for Business and Industrial Marketing in the Robinson College of Business at the Georgia State University. In addition, he is currently the editor of the *Journal of Business and Industrial Marketing.* He received his BA in Economics from the University of Pittsburgh, an MA in Psychology from Ball State University, and an MBA and Ph.D. in Marketing from the University of Pittsburgh. Professor Johnston's research interests include application of the behavioral sciences to marketing in the areas of business-to-business marketing and customer relationship management. His research has been published in the *Journal of Marketing*, the *Journal of Consumer Research, Information Systems Research,* and numerous other publications. He was selected as one of the best researchers in marketing by a recent poll of marketing department chairman in U.S. universities. His number of publications places him in the top three researchers in business-to-business marketing in the world. He has authored or co-authored six books with Managing Salespeople: A Relationship Approach being the most recent. Professor Johnston was a Summer Fellow at the Center for Creative Leadership and a Presidential Fellow at the American Graduate School for International Management.

Vinod Kumar, a graduate of the University of California, Berkeley, is a Professor of Technology and Operations Management of the Sprott School of Business (Director of School, 1995-2005), Carleton University. Kumar has published over 300 articles in refereed journals and proceedings. He has won several Best Paper Awards in prestigious conferences, Scholarly Achievement Award of Carleton University for the academic years 1985-86 and 1987-88, and Research Achievement Award for the years 1993, 2001, and 2007. He is on the editorial board of two international journals. In addition, Kumar has also served for several years on the Board of Governors and the Senate for Carleton University and on the Board of the Ontario Network of e-Commerce.

Robert Lusch is the Executive Director of the McGuire Center for Entrepreneurship and the James and Pamela Muzzy Chair in Entrepreneurship in the Eller College of Management at the University of Arizona. He holds a Ph.D. in Business Administration from the University of Wisconsin, Madison. Previously he has served as Dean of the Michael F. Price College of Business at the University of Oklahoma and the Dean of the Neeley School of Business at Texas Christian University. He is the author of over

150 articles and 18 books on the topics of marketing strategy, retailing, planning and control systems, and service-dominant logic. He is a past editor of the Journal of Marketing and past chairperson of the American Marketing Association. He is a two time recipient of the Maynard/AMA award for outstanding theoretical contributions in marketing.

Kayvan Miri-Lavassani is a Postdoctoral fellow at Carleton University's Research Center for Technology Management. He has worked as a manager, entrepreneur, and analyst with manufacturing, high-tech, and consulting firms in Canada and internationally. He is the President of La SIG Inc research & consulting, and has published over 50 academic papers in refereed publications.

Bahar Movahedi is a Postdoctoral fellow at Carleton University's Research Center for Technology Management. She earned her PhD from Carleton University's Sprott School of Business. In the past few years, she has published over 50 papers in refereed journals, book chapters, and proceedings, and has won several awards for her academic achievements in Canada and the US.

Jennifer Rowley is Professor in Information and Communications at Manchester Metropolitan University. She has over 30 years experience in higher education, as a researcher, manager, teacher, and author. Her reputation is founded on work in marketing, e-business, information and knowledge management, quality in higher education, and related disciplines. Within marketing, in recent years she has contributions in digital branding, e-service, convenience, entrepreneurial marketing, and branding. She has published over 150 refereed journal articles, and numerous books, and regularly presents conference papers at UK and international conferences. Recently published articles have included articles in the *Journal of Marketing Management, Internet Research, Qualitative Marketing, Marketing Theory*, and the *Journal of the American Society for Information Science and Technology*.

Suresh Sood is a key instigator leading the embracement of e-commerce and social media technologies in curriculum development, executive education, and research at the University of Technology in Sydney (UTS) since 1995. He now runs the popular social media executive education and advanced concepts workshops. As a Senior Vice President with Reuters/TIBCO Finance, he was instrumental in creating new and innovative B2B online communities across Asia including Australia, China, India, Singapore, and Thailand. Currently, Sood is advisor to Mighty Media Group (an early stage digital agency), focusing on community and content using Twitter, Facebook, and elgg/Ning platforms. Sood writes numerous thought leadership articles and presents at a variety of global conferences to help shape opportunities associated with his interest in social media marketing practice. Initially graduating in Physics from London University, he holds a MBA from UTS. He is a past visiting fellow, Faculty of Business, UTS, part time lecturer, and Co-director/founder of the Complex Systems Research Centre (CSRC). Sood has taught doctoral and undergraduate students at both the University of Technology Sydney and University of Western Sydney on conducting social media experiments. His current research interest converges storytelling, linguistic analysis, and social media to achieve iconic branding.

Stephen L. Vargo is a Shidler Distinguished Professor and Professor of Marketing at the University of Hawai'i at Manoa. His primary research areas are marketing theory and thought and consumers' evaluative reference scales. He has had articles published in the *Journal of Marketing*, the *Journal of the Academy of Marketing Science*, the *Journal of Service Research*, and other major marketing journals and serves on six editorial review boards, including the *Journal of Marketing, Journal of the Academy of Marketing Science,* and the *Journal of Service Research.* Professor Vargo has been awarded the *Best Article of the Year Award* by the Australia and New Zealand Marketing Academy and the *Harold H. Maynard Award* by the American Marketing Association for "significant contribution to marketing theory and thought." His 2004 article with Robert Lusch in the *Journal of Marketing,* "Evolving to a New Dominant Logic for Marketing," is the most-cited marketing article published in the last 10 years.

Index